MAGILL'S LITERARY ANNUAL

2016

Essay-Reviews of 150 Outstanding Books
Published in the United States During 2015

With an Annotated List of Titles

Volume One
A-K

Edited by
Matthew Akre
Kendal Spires
Gabriela Toth

SALEM PRESS
A Division of EBSCO Information Services, Inc.
Ipswich, Massachusetts

GREY HOUSE PUBLISHING

Cover photo: Photograph of Ta-Nehisi Coates. John D. & Catherine T. MacArthur Foundation/CC BY 4.0/Wikimedia Commons

Magill's Literary Annual, 2016, published by Grey House Publishing, Inc., Amenia, NY, under exclusive license from EBSCO Information Services, Inc.

∞ The paper used in these volumes conforms to the American National Standard for Permanence of Paper for Printed Library Materials, Z39.48-1992 (R2009).

Publisher's Cataloging-In-Publication Data
(Prepared by The Donohue Group, Inc.)

Names: Magill, Frank N. (Frank Northen), 1907-1997, editor. | Wilson, John D., editor. | Kellman, Steven G., 1947- editor. | Goodhue, Emily, editor. | Poranski, Colin D., editor. | Akre, Matthew, editor. | Spires, Kendal, editor. | Toth, Gabriela, editor.
Title: Magill's literary annual.
Description: <1977->: [Pasadena, Calif.] : Salem Press | <2015->: Ipswich, Massachusetts : Salem Press, a division of EBSCO Information Services, Inc. ; Amenia, NY : Grey House Publishing | Essay-reviews of ... outstanding books published in the United States during the previous year. | "With an annotated list of titles." | Editor: 1977- , F.N. Magill; <2010-2014>, John D. Wilson and Steven G. Kellman; <2015>, Emily Goodhue and Colin D. Poranski; <2016->, Matthew Akre, Kendal Spires, and Gabriela Toth. | Includes bibliographical references and index.
Identifiers: ISBN 978-1-61925-880-8 (2016 edition : set) |
   ISBN 978-1-61925-882-2 (2016 edition : vol. 1) | ISBN 978-1-61925-883-9 (2016 edition : vol. 2) | ISSN: 0163-3058
Subjects: LCSH: Books--Reviews--Periodicals. | United States--Imprints--Book reviews--Periodicals. | Literature, Modern--21st century--History and criticism--Periodicals. | Literature, Modern--20th century--History and criticism--Periodicals.
Classification: LCC PN44 .M333 | DDC 028.1--dc23

CONTENTS

CONTENTS

PUBLISHER'S NOTE

Magill's Literary Annual, 2016 follows a long tradition, beginning in 1954, of offering readers incisive reviews of the major literature published during the previous calendar year. The *Magill's Literary Annual* series seeks to critically evaluate 150 major examples of serious literature, both fiction and nonfiction, published in English, from writers in the United States and around the world. The philosophy behind our selection process is to cover works that are likely to be of interest to general readers that reflect publishing trends, that add to the careers of authors being taught and researched in literature programs, and that will stand the test of time. By filtering the thousands of books published every year down to notable titles, the editors have provided librarians with an excellent reader's advisory tool and patrons with fodder for book discussion groups and a guide for choosing worthwhile reading material. The essay-reviews in the *Annual* provide a more academic "reference" review of a work than is typically found in newspapers and other periodical sources.

The reviews in the two-volume *Magill's Literary Annual, 2016* are arranged alphabetically by title. At the beginning of each volume is a complete alphabetical list of all covered books that provides readers with the title and author. In addition, readers will benefit from a brief description of each work in the volume. Every essay is approximately four pages in length. Each one begins with a block of reference information in a standard order:

- Full Book Title, including any subtitle
- *Author:* Name, with birth year, and death year when applicable
- *First published:* Original foreign-language title, with year and country, when pertinent
- Original language and translator name, when pertinent
- Introduction, Foreword, etc., with writer's name, when pertinent
- *Publisher:* Company name and city, and the number of pages
- *Type of work* (chosen from standard categories):

Anthropology	Fine arts
Archaeology	History
Autobiography	History of science
Biography	Language
Current affairs	Law
Diary	Letters
Drama	Literary biography
Economics	Literary criticism
Education	Literary history
Environment	Literary theory
Essays	Media
Ethics	Medicine
Film	Memoir

Miscellaneous	Psychology
Music	Religion
Natural history	Science
Nature	Short fiction
Novel	Sociology
Novella	Technology
Philosophy	Travel
Poetry	Women's issues

- *Time:* Period represented, when pertinent
- *Locale:* Location represented, when pertinent
- Capsule description of the work
- *Principal characters* (for novels, short fiction) or *Principal personages* (for bibliographies, history): List of people, with bried descriptions, when pertinent

The text of each essay-review analyzes and presents the focus, intent, and relative success of the author, as well as the makeup and point of view of the work under discussion. To assist readers further, essays are supplemented by a list of additional "Review Sources" for further study in a bibliographic format. Every essay includes a sidebar offering a brief biography of the author or authors. Thumbnail photographs of book covers and authors are included as available.

Three indexes can be found at the end of volume 2:

- Category Index: Groups all titles into subject areas such as current affairs and social issues, ethics and law, history, literary biography, philosophy and religion, psychology, and women's issues.
- Title Index: Lists all works reviewed in alphabetical order, with any relevant cross references.
- Author Index: Lists books covered in the Annual by each author's name.

A searchable cumulative index, listing all books reviewed in *Magill's Literary Annual* between 1977 and 2016, as well as in *Magill's History Annual* (1983) and *Magill's Literary Annual, History and Biography* (1984 and 1985), can be found at www.online.salempress.com.

Our special thanks go to the outstanding writers who lend their time and knowledge to this project every year. The names of all contributing reviewers are listed in the beginning of Volume 1, as well as at the end of their individual reviews.

COMPLETE ANNOTATED LIST OF TITLES

VOLUME 1

The story of a woman who grows up among a large family in rural Ireland but spends most of her life isolated in the most populous city of the United States, Academy Street *packs more than fifty years of heartbreak, disappointment, disillusion, and indecision into a small volume.*

In his first novel, Ben Metcalf writes about childhood life in rural Goochland County, Virginia, in a deliberately disjointed and nonlinear fashion, portraying country life in a hostile light.

Olen Steinhauer adds a new twist to the spy genre with this intelligent and intriguing tale about two former lovers and CIA colleagues who reunite for dinner six years after experiencing a horrific terrorist incident together in Vienna, Austria.

Among the Ten Thousand Things, *Julia Pierpont's debut novel, is a nuanced exploration of the effect of infidelity on a family. Pierpont's narrative traces the emotional ebb and flow of the various members as they grapple with what has happened and its aftermath.*

Ancillary Mercy *is the final book in the Imperial Radch space opera trilogy by American author Ann Leckie.*

A graphic memoir written by cartoonist and filmmaker Riad Sattouf, The Arab of the Future *chronicles the author's varied childhood experiences growing up in Libya, Syria, and France.*

Aurora *is the story of a generational starship and the people aboard. The novel explores the practicality of space expeditions and colonization, as well as who bears the responsibilities and consequences of the success or failure of such a voyage.*

John Irving returns to form with Avenue of Mysteries, *a complex, multifaceted novel about a Mexican American writer who, after falling into a drug-induced dream state during a trip to the Philippines, accesses his most beloved childhood memories in 1970s Mexico.*

A collection of ten short stories about millennial characters who are struggling with life, sex, and family issues.

In Barbarian Days, *journalist William Finnegan recalls how surfing has shaped his life. From his formative years in Hawaii in the 1960s and his youthful search for the perfect wave to his journalistic travels and his present home in New York City, the surfing life has beckoned Finnegan from every corner of the globe.*

The Beauty *is the latest collection of verse by acclaimed poet Jane Hirshfield. It deals in simple, accessible, but often very subtle phrasing and forms and addresses a wide variety of topics, showing the poet's familiarity with both everyday life and scientific facts.*

Beauty Is a Wound *is a sprawling novel that explores Indonesian society, culture, traditions, customs, and beliefs through the exploits and relationships of several generations. One family endures the turbulence of the country's social and political upheavals during the twentieth century, through Dutch colonization, Japanese occupation, and independence.*

Narrated by a middle-aged autistic man, Best Boy *vividly illustrates many of the difficulties of diagnosing, managing, and treating mental conditions in general and developmental disorders in particular.*

Inspired by James Baldwin's classic 1963 book The Fire Next Time, *journalist Ta-Nehisi Coates began a letter to his teenage son that became a book-length essay and memoir about his intellectual coming-of-age.*

Binary Star, *a short novel told from the perspective of a young woman struggling with eating disorders, is an exploration of codependence and self-destruction.*

COMPLETE LIST OF ANNOTATED TITLES

Laura Ruby's new novel Bone Gap *combines ancient myth, fairy tale, and midwestern realism to produce a story about friendship, betrayal, and learning to love someone for who they are.* Bone Gap *was a finalist for the National Book Award for Young People's Literature in 2015.*

Bonita Avenue *is a generation's spanning novel about the Sigerius family and son-in-law Aaron Bever. Told from the perspectives of four characters, the novel explores the dark side and frailties of human nature in a digital age. The story is told in a fast-paced style that finds each chapter jumping between time periods in the narrative.*

The Book of Aron *explores the Holocaust and one of its heroes, Polish doctor and writer Janusz Korczak, from the perspective of an ordinary child. Aron, a young boy growing up in Warsaw's Jewish ghetto, learns to survive in desperate times by stealing, smuggling, and even becoming an informer for local police. When Aron loses everything, he is taken in by Korczak, who runs an orphanage and offers hope and kindness to children trapped in the bleakest of circumstances.*

Book of Numbers *is an exploration of the modern age of technology. This novel engages the reader in an examination of what it means to be truly transparent on both sides of any interaction in the Internet age.*

Carly Simon shares personal stories about her family, her music, and her relationships ranging from her childhood through the end of her marriage to James Taylor.

Bright Dead Things *is the latest collection of verse by the prize-winning poet Ada Limón, author of three earlier volumes of poetry. Her latest poems are often set in Kentucky and deal with such topics as love, death, and familial relationships.*

In his seventh novel—his first in ten years—Kazuo Ishiguro takes readers on an allegorical journey through medieval England during the dark period after both the Romans and King Arthur had departed.

Don Winslow describes in graphic detail the workings of the Mexican drug trade and the savagery associated with the struggle for dominance among the country's drug cartels, and he dramatizes the personal tragedies of innocent victims caught up in the violence.

Challenger Deep *describes a boy's struggles after he begins to experience symptoms of schizophrenia. Shusterman wrote the novel to help open a dialogue about mental illness and reduce its stigma. The illustrations are by his son, Brendan, who was diagnosed with schizoaffective disorder as a teenager.*

Ann Packer's The Children's Crusade *offers a stirring examination of family reality and dysfunction in a California home where four children grow to adulthood in the shadow of their benevolent father and distant mother.*

The sequel to the best-selling Crazy Rich Asians *(2013) and the second entry in a planned trilogy,* China Rich Girlfriend *continues the chronicle of relationships, activities, and aspirations of a group of fabulously and ostentatiously wealthy Asians as they maneuver to compete in status and influence.*

This historical novel reimagines the early life of Beryl Markham, who was raised in Africa. It closes with her famous flight west across the Atlantic Ocean; Markham was the first person to make this flight successfully.

City on Fire *is a sprawling tale of New York City in the 1970s. Told from multiple points of view, this novel paints a gripping picture of a troubled time, intertwining a mystery in the process.*

In Counternarratives, *a collection of thirteen short stories and novellas, John Keene reimagines black history through revised accounts of colonization, slavery, war, and black resistance from the seventeenth century to the present. Both employing and subverting forms and genres including historical documents, textbooks, slave narratives, diaries, and gothic fiction, Keene suggests that black resistance to white supremacy has long pulsed just below the surface of the historical register.*

COMPLETE LIST OF ANNOTATED TITLES

In his latest collection, author Thomas McGuane presents seventeen new, mostly comic stories about the misadventures of Montana men.

A Cure for Suicide is Jesse Ball's fifth novel. In this dystopian work, Ball explores the nature of identity, memory, the ability to re-create oneself, and the consequences of well-intentioned actions.

Dead Wake: The Last Crossing of the Lusitania details the final days of the luxurious British ocean liner, one of the world's largest ships, prior to its sinking on May 6, 1915, off the coast of Ireland after being hit by a torpedo fired from a German U-boat. Among the drowned passengers were a significant number of Americans, and the incident helped propel the previously neutral United States into participation in World War I.

Death and Mr. Pickwick follows the investigative work of two literary sleuths as they uncover information supporting their claim that Charles Dickens stole credit for creating The Pickwick Papers from the book's original illustrator, Robert Seymour.

James Hannham's second novel, Delicious Foods, *takes its title from a fictitious farm that exploits down-on-their-luck workers. The story focuses on Eddie and his crack-addicted mother, Darlene, who work for the farm and try desperately to escape their plantation-like surroundings.*

June Reid lives a quiet life in Litchfield, Connecticut, with her boyfriend, Luke. But on the morning of her daughter's wedding day, a gas explosion kills June's entire family and changes her life forever. Did You Ever Have a Family *follows June in the months after her family tragedy as she seeks answers, grieves, and begins to imagine how she might move on.*

The debut novel of author Sarai Walker, Dietland explores the effects of the beauty industry and gender inequality on American women.

Ottessa Moshfegh burnishes her reputation as one of the literary world's brightest new voices with Eileen, an unsettling coming-of-age noir about a lonely young Massachusetts woman whose life is forever changed when she becomes drawn into a bizarre crime.

COMPLETE LIST OF ANNOTATED TITLES

Go Set a Watchman *is a novel told from the perspective of Jean Louise Finch, a southern liberal living in New York, who is shocked and disappointed when, during a visit home to Alabama, she discovers that her beloved father, Atticus, seems to be an opponent of integration.*

God Help the Child, *a short novel written from multiple points of view, explores perceptions of race and self-worth through the story of a young black woman rejected by her light-skinned mother and her desperate attempt to win her mother's love.*

A God in Ruins *details generational changes in lifestyle and attitude since 1925 as represented through the personal observations and experiences of a British man, Teddy Todd, and his extended family before and after his service in World War II.*

Inspired by the global climate change that has caused drought conditions in California, Gold Fame Citrus *posits a bleak, dried-out twenty-first century Western landscape dominated by a gigantic sand dune where stubborn individuals from diverse backgrounds band together in a desperate attempt to survive the implacable forces of nature.*

Golden Age *is the final book in Jane Smiley's Last Hundred Years trilogy, which began with* Some Luck *(2014) and continued with* Early Warning *(2015). In this final installation of the series, Jane Smiley takes the extended Langdon family from 1987 through 2019.*

Anne Enright's latest novel, long-listed for the Man Booker Prize, chronicles the breakdown and attempted reunion of an Irish family from 1980 to the early 2000s. Dominated by the family's troubled matriarch, the four Madigan children struggle for decades to connect with their mother, each other, and themselves before finally being reunited when their mother considers selling the family home.

After Helen Macdonald's father died unexpectedly, she turned to her childhood love of falconry to assuage her grief. H Is for Hawk *explores what birds of prey mean to Macdonald—and to the tortured author of* The Sword in the Stone, *T. H. White—but is also about confronting death through a wilderness you can tame.*

COMPLETE LIST OF ANNOTATED TITLES

Inspired by real-life events, this darkly absorbing novel centers on three pro-tagonists who are forced to confront the consequences wrought by their violent and rebellious actions.

Anna Benz lives an ideal life as the wife of a successful banker and mother in a small town near Zurich, Switzerland. But when Anna starts having illicit affairs with other men, her life spirals out of control, and she must learn some of the most dif-ficult lessons of all.

Phillips's poems are eclectic and sophisticated, often dealing with the topic of poetry itself and featuring allusions to various other texts in a style full of rich sound effects.

A History of Loneliness chronicles societal changes since the 1960s and their ef-fects on Ireland—especially the evolving attitudes toward the dominance, power, and reputation of the Irish Catholic Church—as observed and experienced by a disillu-sioned priest who has remained isolated and uninvolved throughout his professional career.

Hold Still offers thoughtful reflections on the photographer's art, exploring Sally Mann's work from her earliest photographs through her current oeuvre. At the same time, the book excavates the history of Mann's family across several generations by tracing the complex confluence of personalities that flow into a single individual.

Honeydew collects twenty of author Edith Pearlman's short stories, which tend to focus on small-town life but often veer into the realm of fable and fairy tale.

How to Be Drawn, a finalist for the National Book Award, is the latest collection of verse by the Pushcart Prize–winning poet Terrance Hayes, author of three earlier volumes of poetry.

Written by best-selling novelist Lisa Lutz, How to Start a Fire *chronicles the lives and friendships of three women over the course of twenty years.*

Hunger Makes Me a Modern Girl *chronicles the youth, musical development, and personal evolution of rock star and actor Carrie Brownstein, both onstage and off.*

Author Reif Larsen's second novel consists of several, almost freestanding, narratives that are gradually woven into the central narrative focusing on the life of the protagonist, Radar Radmanovic. The author eventually peels back the layers of the past to tie together the disparate elements into a main thread, and in so doing, explores the psychology behind being "the other" who deviates from the conventional.

Mia Alvar shares nine stories of the Filipino diaspora. The characters, who range in class status, live and work in the Philippines, Bahrain, and the United States.

In the Unlikely Event, *based on events during her own eighth-grade year, is Blume's fourth novel for adult readers.*

Susan Barker's sprawling historical novel The Incarnations *recounts the past lives of a Beijing cab driver and his mystery soul mate.*

The Invention of Nature *is a sweeping biography that narrates and champions the life of Prussian scientist and explorer Alexander von Humboldt. The book follows Humboldt on his travels while also introducing the reader to his intellectual journeys and his spheres of acquaintance and influence.*

Isabel Allende's Japanese Lover, *like much of her earlier fiction, bridges cultures and generations in a multi-stranded narrative of love and war. The novel was one of* Publishers Weekly's *top ten works of literary fiction for 2015.*

Killing and Dying *is the latest collection of Adrian Tomine's enigmatic comics, featuring men and women searching for love, security, and meaning in their lives in a stark suburban landscape.*

J. Ryan Stradal's debut novel, Kitchens of the Great Midwest, *chronicles Eva Thorvald's growth from a misfit child to a sought-after but elusive celebrity chef.*

VOLUME 2

In her very accessible account of the later years of the American Revolution, Sarah Vowell examines the role that the Marquis de Lafayette, a French aristocrat and army officer, played in the war and the phenomenon of his continued popularity in the United States long after the war with Britain was over.

Through the vehicle of a coming-of-age novel, an odyssey, and a picaresque hero, Last Bus to Wisdom *chronicles the journey of an eleven-year-old orphan during the summer of 1951, recalling an era when children traveled in a more innocent atmosphere. Ivan Doig uses a series of vignettes and portraits to weave the tale, with the last stop symbolizing the lessons the boy learns through his adventures.*

A Little Life *is the story of the lifelong friendship between four men who meet in college. The second novel by Hanya Yanagihara,* A Little Life *was a 2015 National Book Award finalist, short-listed for the 2015 Man Booker Prize, and a finalist for the 2015 Kirkus Prize for fiction.*

Part journal, part travelogue, part rumination on the process of writing, M Train *is a memoir by poet and rock singer Patti Smith that evades easy categorization. Critics have lauded Smith's book for its lyricism and treatment of memory and loss.*

The debut novel of Jennine Capó Crucet, Make Your Home among Strangers *is a coming-of-age story for first-generation Americans.*

A Manual for Cleaning Women *is a posthumous collection of Lucia Berlin's previously published stories about the varied lives of strong-minded women.*

A moving visual and verbal account, March: Book Two *continues the story of the American civil rights movement of the 1960s from the perspective of a key participant: activist, nonviolence advocate, demonstration organizer, and eventual congressman John Lewis.*

The Mare *tells the story of an affluent, insecure white woman and the deep, unexpected bond she forms with a Latina girl from the Fresh Air Fund. Their connection is emboldened by the talented young girl's introduction to the world of horses and equestrian competition.*

Mrs. Engels, *the first novel from the Irish writer Gavin McCrea, brings to vivid life Lizzie Burns, the illiterate, working-class companion of Friedrich Engels, co-author—with Karl Marx—of The Communist Manifesto. From Lizzie's perspective, readers experience Marx and Engels wrestling with domestic complications while they strive to inspire a revolution.*

Longtime feminist activist and author Gloria Steinem writes about how her unusual upbringing and years of travel have shaped her world view in her memoir My Life on the Road.

Part autobiography, part confession, part fiction, My Struggle: Book 4 *is the fourth installment of an epic six-volume, 3,500-page work to be translated from Norwegian into English. In this entry, recent high school graduate and protagonist Karl Ove Knausgaard is hired to teach at a school in the far north of Norway.*

A man who grew up in Baton Rouge, Louisiana, delivers a confessional narrative of his teenage years to come to grips with the guilt he feels for exposing information about the rape of a young girl on whom he had a crush some twenty years earlier.

The novel Mycroft Holmes *presents a suspenseful Victorian-era transatlantic adventure, featuring the titular hero, the elder brother of Sherlock Holmes, in a mysterious case that seems to have supernatural overtones.*

Armand Gamache becomes involved in a murder investigation that turns out to have national significance and connections to a previous case.

Pulitzer Prize–winning critic Margo Jefferson recalls her childhood among the African American elite in her memoir Negroland. *The title, a word of her own devising, refers to the rarified world of black privilege in 1950s Chicago.*

The Nightingale *is a story of war and family. It follows a pair of sisters through the tragedies, violence, and heroism of life in France during World War II. Amid such significant events, it calls readers to focus on the meaning of family bonds.*

COMPLETE ANNOTATED LIST OF TITLES

Rachel Cusk blurs memoir and fiction in her new novel Outline, *about an author teaching a writing workshop in Athens, Greece.*

Jonathan Franzen's fifth novel, Purity, *combines intimate tales of mothers and marriages with political intrigue.*

The thirteen stories in Karen E. Bender's first story collection, Refund *center on modern Americans suffering the fallout from the 2009 recession.*

In Satin Island, *renowned writer and avant-garde thinker Tom McCarthy explores the problem of creating genuine intellectual and social meaning, as well as relationships, in the context of a society defined and governed by a corporate monoculture.*

Scattered at Sea *is a collection of poetry by the award-winning writer Amy Gerstler. The poems in this collection are often light, witty, and humorous, but some are on serious subjects and are frequently somber and thoughtful in tone.*

The Sculptor, *a graphic novel that follows the last days of a struggling artist, is an exploration of the meaning of art and life by one of America's best-known comics theorists.*

Pulitzer Prize–winning author Geraldine Brooks's novel The Secret Chord is historical fiction based on the Bible. It tells the story of David, king of Israel, through the eyes of the prophet Natan.

Paul Beatty's new novel, The Sellout, *is a caustic, absurdist take on race and cultural identity in America as told through the eyes of a man who brings back slavery and segregation in an effort to save his town.*

Seveneves *chronicles the blowing up of the moon and then the inevitable destruction of Earth. The book follows the human race's painstaking, clinical decisions on how to preserve life in an outer-space setting, detailing who would be chosen to live aboard the space station and why.*

The Story of My Teeth *is an experimental novel about Gustavo "Highway" Sánchez, a legendary auctioneer who excels at storytelling. Told in six parts, with a seventh part added for the English edition, the narrative uses unconventional methods, like assigning allegories to teeth on an auction block, to tell the story.*

The Story of the Lost Child *is the fourth and final installment of the Neapolitan novels, an internationally successful series published by Elena Ferrante. The final book continues the story of lifelong friends Elena Greco and Raffaella Cerullo.*

The ninth novel by Nobel Prize–winning author Orhan Pamuk, A Strangeness in My Mind *is a love story that unfolds over the course of decades. As in Pamuk's other works, this novel centers on life in Istanbul.*

A Stranger's Mirror *offers twenty-five new poems by the distinguished poet Marilyn Hacker, plus a generous selection of previous works. It illustrates Hacker's command of varied subjects, styles, and forms.*

A dystopian satire of the future of France, Submission *is the sixth novel by the controversial French author Michel Houellebecq.*

Surrounded by Friends *is the newest book of poems by Matthew Rohrer, author of numerous previous volumes. This book is understated in tone and phrasing, modest in ambition and topics, and appealing in its accessibility, its lightheartedness, and its emphasis on connections with others, including various poets of the past.*

The Sympathizer *is an ingenious and powerful spy novel that focuses on a Communist sleeper agent who has been ordered to spy on South Vietnamese émigrés in Southern California who are working to spark a counterrevolution in their homeland.*

The Thing about Jellyfish *is Ali Benjamin's critically acclaimed first novel. A New York Times best seller and a 2015 finalist for the National Book Award in young people's literature, it tells the story of a young girl's difficult adjustment to the death of her best friend.*

COMPLETE ANNOTATED LIST OF TITLES

War of the Foxes *is the second collection of poetry by Richard Siken, whose previous volume,* Crush, *won the Yale Series of Younger Poets prize. The book returns repeatedly to issues of artistic representation in general and painting in particular, giving the book a kind of developing coherence rare in volumes of collected lyric poems.*

In her debut novel, Natasha Pulley blends historical fiction, science fiction, and fantasy to tell the story of a young man in an alternate Victorian Britain whose life is changed through his acquaintance with a mysterious watchmaker.

The Water Knife *is a hard-boiled thriller set in a dystopian near future where catastrophic climate change has forced states in the arid American Southwest to compete, sometimes violently, for rapidly diminishing water resources.*

Welcome to Braggsville *is a satirical novel about the state of race relations in the United States. Four college students set out to draw attention to racial injustice in a small Georgia town, in the process bringing both small-town southern life and American academia under the author's microscope.*

Award-winning novelist Richard Price, publishing under the name Harry Brandt, writes about justice and revenge in his new crime novel The Whites.

Michael Cunningham's short-story collection A Wild Swan *pairs contemporary concerns with the timeless motifs of fairy tales to create fresh interpretations for twenty-first-century adults.*

World Gone By *is a novel by Dennis Lehane set in the criminal underworld of 1940s Florida that follows retired gangster Joe Coughlin as he confronts the wrongdoings of his past.*

Two-time Pulitzer Prize–winning author David McCullough presents a meticulously researched chronicle of Wilbur and Orville Wright's pioneering efforts to build and fly the first airplane—an invention that would ultimately lead to modern commercial air and space travel.

X *chronicles the formative years of Malcolm Little, the young boy who grew up to become civil rights leader Malcolm X. The story is presented as historical fiction, and it traces his life story from the age of five to his imprisonment at age twenty and concludes with his conversion and acceptance of Islam during his incarceration.*

CONTRIBUTING REVIEWERS

Pegge Bochynski

Chris Cullen

Leah Easley

Robert C. Evans

Jack Ewing

Keith M. Finley

Stephanie Finnegan

Melynda Fuller

Molly Hagan

Gina Hagler

Raymond Pierre Hylton

Ashleigh Imus

Judy A. Johnson

Mark S. Joy

Kathyrn Kulpa

Richard Ladd

A. Lewandowski

Charles E. May

Laurence W. Mazzeno, PhD

Daniel P. Murphy

Marybeth Rua-Larsen

Julia A. Sienkewicz

Amy Sisson

Theresa L. Stowell

Emily Turner

Kenrick Vezina

Thomas Willard, PhD

Academy Street

Author: Mary Costello
First published: 2014, in the United King-
dom
Publisher: Farrar, Straus and Giroux (New
York). 160 pp.
Type of work: Novel
Time: Mid-1940s–early 2000s
Locales: Ireland; New York City, New York

The story of a woman who grows up among a
large family in rural Ireland but spends most
of her life isolated in the most populous city
of the United States, Academy Street *packs*
more than fifty years of heartbreak, disap-
pointment, disillusion, and indecision into a
small volume.

(Courtesy of Farrar Straus & Giroux)

Principal characters:
TERESA "TESS" LOHAN, a woman born to a large family in Ireland who eventually
     moves to New York City
EVELYN LOHAN, her older sister
CLAIRE LOHAN, her older sister
MAEVE LOHAN, her older sister
DENIS LOHAN, her older brother
OLIVER LOHAN, her younger brother, who grows up wild
MOLLY, her aunt, who lives in the United States and works at Bell Telephone
THEO, her child, born out of wedlock
WILLA, one of her neighbors in New York City
MICHAEL JOSEPH "MIKE" CONNOLLY, a kindly workman on the Lohan farm
ANNE BECKETT, an Irish nurse in New York City
DAVID O'HARA, Anne's cousin from Dublin, a lawyer

Academy Street (2015) begins with a tragedy that forever afterward defines the sense
of loss and longing that marks the life of protagonist Teresa "Tess" Lohan. It is the
mid-1940s, and the opening scene is a rural farm in the west of Ireland near Galway,
where cattle, sheep, pigs, and chickens are raised. In the large, ancient farmhouse
called Easterfield, seven-year-old Tess is dressed in her best clothes. The rest of the
family—Tess's four older siblings and one infant brother, plus various aunts, uncles,
and local acquaintances—are gathered for a solemn occasion. Tess's mother, just forty
years old, has died of tuberculosis, and her coffin is being hauled downstairs to be
placed in a hearse for the trip to the cemetery. Tess, her sister Maeve, and her baby
brother Oliver are considered too young to attend the funeral, so they are left behind

in the care of Mike Connolly, the competent longtime farmhand. Her mother's death is just the first in a string of small and large tragedies that deeply affect Tess.

In the absence of the influence of a woman, the formerly carefree, loving environment of the farm drastically changes. Tess's father becomes morose, the children fall silent to avoid incurring his ire, and gloom descends. A portent of what is to come occurs just days after the funeral. A tinker and his family stop by the farmhouse to beg. The tinker's daughter, Tess's age, sticks out her tongue at Tess, which Tess feels is like a curse. At school, other children, who know about her mother's death, torment her with stories of grave robbers. Walking home from school, Tess passes the tinker family camp, and she sticks out her tongue at the tinker's daughter, who mysteriously sickens and dies days later. Stunned by what she thinks she has done, Tess stops talking. Neither doctors nor teachers nor family members can make her utter a word until she is ready to do so on her own.

A few years later, Tess and her sister Maeve board at a convent school. Latin teacher Mr. Clarke, who was born at the Lohan house when it was under different ownership, tells her the history of her home, built in the seventeenth century. During the mid-nineteenth century, Easterfield was a hospital for victims of the Irish potato famine, and hundreds of patients who died of sickness and starvation were buried on the farm. Death was planted long before the Lohans arrived, and death from starvation of the spirit is to be the family's destiny.

The Lohan fortunes indeed change for the worse. Because of financial strain, at age thirteen Tess has to drop out of school to assist her sister Evelyn, now married and the mother of three children. Tess returns home in her late teens to find things greatly changed. Her sister Claire has immigrated to the United States and is working at Bell Telephone alongside their aunt Molly; Mike Connolly has retired; and her younger brother, Oliver, is growing up wild. With nothing left for her at home, Tess applies to become and is accepted as a nursing trainee in Dublin, following her late mother's former profession.

In 1962, Tess, in her early twenties, moves to New York City to be near Claire, now married and the mother of a small child, and lands a job as a nurse at a medical center. Almost immediately, Claire moves with her husband to San Francisco, California, and Tess is on her own again. She befriends Anne Beckett, a fellow nurse also from Ireland who is engaged to be married, and the two women share an apartment for a time. Tess meets Anne's cousin from Ireland, David O'Hara, a tall, blond lawyer, and is drawn to him. After encouragement from Tess, Oliver moves to New York as well, working in construction and occasionally visiting with his sister and Anne on weekends; however, their relationship ultimately faces hardship as well.

Tess and David keep running into one another at various social functions. Just before David leaves to join the Air Force, he seduces Tess, who becomes pregnant around the time of a national tragedy: the assassination of John F. Kennedy. Tess attempts to contact David, but receives no reply, so she buys a cheap wedding band to pretend she is married. She informs Claire of her situation. Claire would gladly fly out to help Tess, except she has small children who need her care, and is ill herself.

Eventually, Tess gives birth to a son she names Theo. Though initially she thinks of putting him up for adoption, she decides to raise him on her own. In a new apartment on Academy Street, she becomes friends with her downstairs neighbor, Willa, a down-to-earth married mother of several children who gives Tess practical advice about raising her son. Tess writes her siblings in Ireland and sends them photos of little Theo, but their re-

Mary Costello first began publishing short stories in 1989, and her first collection of short fiction, The China Factory, was nominated for the Guardian First Book Award and other honors. Her debut novel, Academy Street, won the Eason Novel of the Year award at the 2014 Irish Book Awards.

sponses are lukewarm; it is apparent that they, good Catholics, disapprove of what they perceive as her wanton, nontraditional lifestyle. Nothing, however, could be farther from the truth. Tess is more alone than ever. She craves a man, and desperately wishes for some passion in her life. Since she is shy and awkward around other people, and she tends to compare each of the few men she steps out with to her single romantic experience, nothing ever comes from such dates.

Theo grows up as a solitary child who enjoys reading, like his mother. At age fourteen he begins to ask about his father. When he is a little older, Tess shows him a newspaper clipping announcing the wedding of David O'Hara to a Peruvian flight attendant and talks about the culmination of her brief fling. Needing a father figure, Theo begins to grow distant from his mother. In his late teens he moves out to attend college while rooming with friends. Theo and Tess remain in sporadic communication, with long periods of silence between infrequent meetings. At twenty-eight, having become a commodity trader, Theo marries a Jewish lawyer, Jennifer, and fathers two children. Tess, having retired from the hospital, reestablishes contact with Theo and his new family. They all get together regularly for holidays, birthdays, and other occasions, until the horror of September 11, 2001, disrupts their lives.

A final tragedy unfolds that requires Tess's return to Ireland for the first time in many years. Nothing is as she remembered or imagined, prompting a direct comparison of her life in the United States with the world that she left behind in Ireland.

Academy Street is the debut novel from Mary Costello, following her well-received story collection *The China Factory* (2012). Downbeat and atmospheric, the story accomplishes much in just over 150 pages. Critics praised Costello's ability to portray such a complicated story in her distinct style, with Maria Crawford writing in a review for the *Financial Times*, "She has a gift for relating even life's most calamitous events in matter-of-fact prose, and in doing so laying bare their true devastation."

Essentially the portrait of a woman who internalizes the effects of traumatic external events over which she has no control, the novel spans more than fifty years, from childhood to senior-citizen status, in the existence of a unique individual. Tess lives a life of quiet desperation, unwilling or unable to take the initiative necessary to better herself or improve her situation, a prisoner who cannot shake off the iron grip of inertia. Physical descriptions of characters are scarce, so readers learn about aspects of their personalities solely through their actions—or in the case of Tess, caught between the old world of her youth and the new world of her mature years, by her failure to take action. Inwardly, her heart and soul are in constant turmoil; however, outwardly she remains placid. As Sinéad Gleeson notes in a review of the book for the *Guardian*, Tess's subdued lifestyle still speaks volumes: "Hers is a quiet life, but one with an enormous impact on the reader."

The novel is divided into three parts. Part one, told in present tense, details Tess's time in Ireland, the emotional highlight of her life. Part two, in past tense, concerns her time in New York. Part three, also in past tense, sets up the final tragedies that propel her back to Ireland. The story is presented entirely from the third-person limited point of view, which allows inklings of Tess's thoughts and feelings, but with a lesser degree of intimacy than first-person voice would provide.

The strong connections between Ireland and the United States hold the sections together as the story completes a cycle, beginning and ending in personal tragedy. As a young woman in Ireland, Tess dreams of escaping from the predictable future role of wife and mother; in the United States, as a reluctant single mother, she dreams fondly of her youth in Ireland. Neither dream is realistic. Further enhancing the theme, Tess's childhood home was once a haven for victims of the Irish famine, the event that drove many Irish to the United States. Similar to Irish immigrants before her, Tess comes to the United States following in the footsteps of an older sister, and draws her younger brother west after her—and the country destroys them all, in different ways. Tess's hopes for a wonderful new life are dashed by David, yet another Irish immigrant, condemning her to an existence from which, because of her submissive, introspective nature, she does not have the inner strength to escape.

Jack Ewing

Review Sources

Rev. of *Academy Street*, by Mary Costello. *Publishers Weekly* 9 Feb. 2015: 44. Print.

Crawford, Maria. Rev. of *Academy Street*, by Mary Costello. *Financial Times*. Financial Times, 16 Jan. 2015. Web. 22 Dec. 2015.

Gleeson, Sinéad. "*Academy Street* by Mary Costello Review—Woman on the Sidelines." *Guardian*. Guardian News and Media, 25 Oct. 2014. Web. 22 Dec. 2015.

McKeon, Belinda. Rev. of *Academy Street*, by Mary Costello. *New York Times*. New York Times, 1 May 2015. Web. 22 Dec. 2015.

Against the Country

Author: Ben Metcalf (b. 1966)
Publisher: Random House (New York). 336 pp.
Type of work: Novel
Time: 1970s and early 1980s
Locale: near Fife, Goochland County,
Virginia

In his first novel, Ben Metcalf writes about child-
hood life in rural Goochland County, Virginia, in
a deliberately disjointed and nonlinear fashion,
portraying country life in a hostile light.

Principal personages:

(Courtesy of Random House)

THE NARRATOR, originally from southern Illinois
but reared in Goochland County
FRANK, his father, also from Southern Illinois, who migrated to Virginia to attempt
small-scale farming
HIS MOTHER, who supplements her work as a farmer's wife as a county social-services worker
HIS OLDER BROTHER, who is physically strong but has a speech impediment and limited attention span
HIS SISTER, who rebels against her upbringing and comes into sharp conflict with her
mother

In *Against the Country*, Columbia University professor Ben Metcalf's first novel, the
narrator leads readers through a maddening, difficult-to-ascertain, but nonetheless intriguing condemnation of the American agrarian ideal. The novel is divided into seven
"books," which, in turn, are subdivided into reasonably short (sometimes very short)
"chapters." The chapter divisions seem to depend more upon changes of subject than
time progression. The narrator challenges William Wordsworth's vision of a "vernal"
impulse serving as a better moral instructor than "all the sages." He implies just the
opposite: that rural living tends to render one more callous toward others and therefore
less moral.

As befits the title, the novel is a rejection of the long-held, ingrained notion of
country dwelling being more "pure" and "American" than urban life. The lasting myth
of the sturdy, incorruptible, clean-living yeoman farmer is one that predates colonial
America. However, it gained added currency and impetus among European immigrants to the New World. Coming in for heavy condemnation from the narrator as
he attempts to explode this myth are such iconic, if divergent, personages as Thomas
Jefferson, Horace Greeley, Daniel Boone, John C. Calhoun, John Muir, E. B. White,
Louisa May Alcott, Ralph Waldo Emerson, Henry David Thoreau, James Fennimore
Cooper, Walt Whitman, and Joel Chandler Harris.

The narrator is one of three siblings: he has an older brother and a younger sister. Initially, they live in an unspecified southern Illinois "town." As with many aspects of the story, the narrator's gives only the bare minimum of background information, so readers are left to conjecture about the specific place from which the family comes. Apparently acting on the assumption that rural life is morally and physically superior to town life, and therefore more conducive to rearing a family, the narrator's parents pack up and drive to Richmond, Virginia, and then west into the countryside to Goochland County, where they lease land and a house in a nondescript country bailiwick dubbed "Fife."

In often flowery and verbose language, the narrator describes the family's dysfunction, particular emphasizing the negative relationship between him and his father, Frank, the only human character actually named. The narrator depicts Frank as patriarchal but extremely lazy (the laziness sometimes moderating the tyranny he exercises over his children); incompetent as a farmer; self-hating and even self-destructive (as a voracious consumer of cigarettes); and unconcerned with hygiene and sanitation. Frank's use of corporal punishment is the norm rather than the exception, and the chief method by which he demonstrates his authority. The narrator goes to some length to describe the different types of switches his father uses to punish the children, noting the types of trees (birch, magnolia, maple) they are cut from and their comparative effectiveness, as far as raising welts is concerned. Frank's work ethic is questioned and often involved foisting wood chopping, egg collecting, fence repair, garbage dumping, and other chores on his children. Nonetheless, at times, the narrator grants the reader the insight that his sire is not completely intellectually deficient, noting his ability to write coherent college-level essays. Later in the book, the narrator mentions having beaten his father in a fistfight and hints at a slight amelioration of relations, after the son has struck out on his own. The narrator alludes to a partial reconciliation with his father, during the latter's struggle with cancer, but references to a renewal in the father-and-son relationship seem like obligatory add-ons rather than a filially inspired change of heart.

The narrator sketches his other family members incompletely. His intellectually bright mother survives her environment (and perhaps preserves her marriage) by a self-deceptively optimistic faith in the virtues of rural living, denying all evidence to the contrary, and securing a position in the Goochland County social-services sector. The older brother is taciturn, slow-witted, standoffish, and more absorbed in television than in whatever unfolding traumatic event might be taking place around him. The sister seems to be solely interested in escaping the confines of the family's rural life and, when she succeeds, her mother questions her daughter's sanity. The family is alienated from the outside community, which figures infrequently and is most notably manifested in the Jehovah's Witnesses who occasionally make their rounds. The family members are grouped among "the others" because

Ben Metcalf has served as the literary editor for Harper's Magazine, *an associate professor of writing at Columbia University, and an essayist. His essays have appeared in* Harper's Magazine *and the* Baffler. *Against the Country is his first novel.*

of their isolation, poverty, and religious affiliation. They are Roman Catholics in an overwhelmingly Protestant area.

The narrator's most vivid recollections, apart from the paternal canings and brow-beating, revolve around the school bus as well as the farm animals (dogs, cats, chickens) and pests (snakes, rats, ticks) with which he interacts. As is often the case in literary works, the animals are accorded a greater degree of identity, and even humanity, than the people. In contrast to the narrator's human family, six of the farm animals are named and are even honored with short biographies in the final chapter, "A note on the dogs" (which the narrator expands to include one cat and one rooster). These biographies are among the most interesting and witty portions of the book; the narrator seems most at home with these descriptions and most sympathetic toward these creatures.

Against the Country is so strident, and the narrator's commentary is so consistently negative on every point, that it is often difficult to discern bitterness from humor. One the narrator's survival mechanisms is to turn whatever mundane and irritating task might be at hand (such as raising chickens) into a game or an "experiment." In the rustic antiparadise evoked by the narrator, everything takes on a sinister connotation. Rather than sheltering, the trees become menacing; even blackberries become objects of loathing. However, the school bus receives the greatest opprobrium. It serves as the site for bullying, humiliation, and the one instance of self-assertion on the narrator's part. Infuriated by the theft of his textbooks on the bus, he takes what is variously described as a shotgun or rifle and stations himself at the bus stop to menace the driver and students until the books are returned. Subsequently, he fears police or legal repercussions—but the incident is instead "passed over."

This is not a book from which one can derive much faith in the human condition, and the ethos of failure and futility pervades much of it. The author's considerable skill as a wordsmith, and his deft use of irony, though, prevent the reader from sinking into depression, enabling one to ferret out the elements of humor from the otherwise grim reality. The danger here (and the trap into which the author may have fallen) is that when a long-standing shibboleth, such as simple rural life being better than life in the city, is being demolished, those who conduct the demolition process tend, in their zeal to finally unearth the truth, to charge too far into the opposite direction. *Against the Country* has not received glowing reviews, mostly because of the negative tone and verbose use of language Metcalf employs, though critics have noted his strength as a writer. As Ron Charles for the *Washington Post* notes, "For a reader, the question quickly becomes: How long can I listen to this clever crank who claims that 'pain and pretense and foolishness [are] the only themes still available to the honest American writer,'" yet he also calls the opening section "joltingly brilliant." Thad Ziolkowski for the *New York Times*, in his review of the book, says a "clause-piling, recursive mode is the book's dominant one . . . and its flaws—sermonic windiness, hyperbole, a straining after wordplay and wit—can be wearisome," but that his unique style translates into a novel that "pursue[s] neither realist illusion nor factuality but a species of truth," a boon for readers able to endure Metcalf's negativity and parse his rambling syntax.

Raymond Pierre Hylton

Review Sources

Brady, Michael Patrick. Rev. of *Against the Country*, by Ben Metcalf. *Boston Globe*. Boston Globe Media Partners, 6 Jan. 2015. Web. 5 Jan. 2016.

Charles, Ron. Rev. of *Against the Country*, by Ben Metcalf. *Washington Post*. Washington Post, 30 Dec. 2014. Web. 5 Jan. 2016.

Rosen, Adam. "Adam Rosen on 'Against the Country': When Going Back to the Land Goes Wrong." Rev. of *Against the Country*, by Ben Metcalf. *Los Angeles Review of Books*. Los Angeles Review of Books, 15 Jan. 2015. Web. 5 Jan. 2016.

Zlokowski, Thad. "Southern Grotesque." Rev. of *Against the Country*, by Ben Metcalf. *New York Times* 25 Jan. 2015: BR9. Print.

All the Old Knives

Author: Olen Steinhauer (b. 1970)
Publisher: Minotaur (New York). 304 pp.
Type of work: Novel
Time: December 2006, October 2012
Locales: Carmel, California; Vienna, Austria

Olen Steinhauer adds a new twist to the spy genre with this intelligent and intriguing tale about two former lovers and CIA colleagues who reunite for dinner six years after experiencing a horrific terrorist incident together in Vienna, Austria.

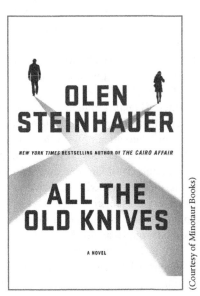

(Courtesy of Minotaur Books)

Principal characters:

HENRY PELHAM, a CIA operative working in Vienna

CELIA HARRISON FAVREAU, his former lover and colleague, a retired CIA agent and housewife living in Carmel

WILLIAM "BILL" COMPTON, a retired CIA commander, Celia's former boss

GENE WILCOX, a CIA data processor

ILYAS SHISHANI, a Chechen radical and Islamic terrorist

AHMED NAJJAR, a CIA courier

In the opening acknowledgments of *All the Old Knives*, Olen Steinhauer writes that he conceived the idea for the spy novel after watching the 2010 television adaptation of Christopher Reid's book-length poem *The Song of Lunch* (2009). Remaining faithful to the basic premise of Reid's poem, the fifty-minute BBC-*Masterpiece* film stars Alan Rickman and Emma Thompson as two unnamed former lovers who reunite for lunch fifteen years after the end of their relationship. On the strength of their performances, Steinhauer became inspired to write an espionage thriller with the same conceit.

Like the film, *All the Old Knives* focuses on two former lovers who rendezvous at a restaurant years after parting ways. Similarities with the film, however, mostly stop there. In the film, Rickman plays an unnamed, middle-aged book editor and failed poet; Thompson's character left him for another writer whose career has flourished. When the two former lovers dine at an old haunt in London's fashionable Soho district, Rickman bitterly and boozily muses on the failure of their relationship and what his life has become. The film is almost entirely composed of interior monologues voiced by Rickman's character.

Steinhauer's novel, in contrast, centers on Henry Pelham, a Central Intelligence Agency (CIA) agent based in Vienna, Austria, and his former flame and colleague, Celia Favreau, née Harrison, who has retired from the agency to raise a family in the "leafy utopian outpost" of Carmel-by-the-Sea, California. The novel is set primarily in a restaurant in Carmel on Tuesday, October 16, 2012. There, Henry and Celia convene to tie up loose ends from a terrorist incident that occurred on the tarmac of the Vienna airport—the Flughafen Wien—in 2006. Steinhauer's novel is told in alternating first-person perspectives between Henry and Celia, and takes place over only a few hours, with much of the plot unfolding through flashbacks.

All the Old Knives opens as Henry is flying to Monterey, just a short drive from Carmel. Though fatigued from spending the previous fifteen hours in the air, Henry reveals that he has been unable to sleep on airplanes ever since the 2006 Vienna airport disaster—known simply to those in the agency as Flughafen. Readers later learn that Islamic terrorists took 120 airplane passengers hostage as collateral for the release of militants from German and Austrian prisons; following a botched rescue attempt, the terrorists released sarin gas into the plane's ventilation system, killing themselves and every passenger on board. Henry has set up a dinner date with Celia to help wrap up an internal investigation into the incident—which, according to new intelligence gleaned from Ilyas Shishani, a Chechen Islamist radical being held at the US military prison in Guantanamo Bay—may have been aided by a source within the US embassy in Vienna, where Henry and Celia were then stationed. In true spy fashion, Henry does not initially disclose the true purpose for their dinner, however, instead telling Celia in an e-mail that he will be in her "neck of the woods" for a "company thing."

From the novel's outset, it is apparent that Henry still harbors strong romantic feelings for Celia and, like his male counterpart in *The Song of Lunch*, is bitter over the way things ended. Following Flughafen, Celia, for reasons as yet unknown, abruptly left the agency and walked out on her yearlong relationship with Henry, even though the two had initiated plans to move in together. Just months after fleeing Vienna, Celia married Drew, a retiree "with no apparent charms," moved to Carmel with him, and had two children in quick succession. Celia's sudden transition to a mundane Carmel housewife baffles Henry, who suspects she is pretending to be someone she is not.

For Steinhauer, Carmel serves as an effective setting of intrigue. Known for its beautiful white-sand beach, perfectly manicured, cypress tree–lined streets, posh art galleries, and quaint English-style cottages, the upscale seaside village offers residents and tourists an illusory respite from the harsh realities of the outside world. According to Henry, it is the perfect make-believe backdrop for Celia's new life. Upon first arriving, Henry finds himself "in the middle of an idealized vision of a seaside village, rather than the real thing." Carmel's artificiality mirrors the duplicitous nature of CIA operatives, and the village is used as a cover for the many deceptions and double-dealings that Henry and Celia engage in throughout the novel. At one point, Celia even tells Henry: "Welcome to California. Don't take any of us at face value."

Nevertheless, when Henry meets Celia at the Carmel restaurant, he initially keeps their conversation light. Henry updates Celia on his love life and her former colleagues, while Celia expounds on the joys and perils of wifedom and motherhood. After several glasses of wine, Henry eventually works the pending Flughafen investigation into the conversation. In an effort to downplay its seriousness, Henry falsely tells Celia that the international police organization Interpol is running matters, not the CIA. Early on, readers learn that Henry has taken over the investigation from a young CIA career climber named Larry Daniels to prevent a potential scandal for the agency. He has since interviewed everyone associated with the disaster, except for Celia.

When Celia starts filling in the gaps for Henry, the novel shifts to her perspective, giving readers insight into her character. Celia's narrative begins on the morning of the Flughafen disaster, at which point, she is on the verge of moving in with Henry. Unlike smitten Henry, however, she has serious doubts about their relationship. Worried by the perpetual threat of disappointment and failed expectations, Celia wonders whether marriage, which she likens to a "death spiral of endless power plays," will ever be possible for them. As CIA operatives, Celia and Henry have made a living lying and deceiving others, and Celia thinks they have "become too jaded about the human race" to consider pursuing anything more serious. Their tenuous situation provides Steinhauer with ample opportunity to explore the dynamics of how spying can affect personal relationships.

As Celia ruminates on her relationship with Henry, she relates details from the day of the Flughafen incident. From morning to night, Celia and her CIA colleagues at the US embassy work local networks, investigate leads, and float theories about the unfolding hijacking. Among other things, they learn that the four Islamic militants are part of Aslim Taslam, a terrorist organization consisting of former members of Al-Shabaab, an al-Qaeda affiliate based in Somalia, and that they were likely directed by Shishani. More information is eventually gleaned from Ahmed Najjar, a CIA courier fortuitously aboard the hijacked plane, who surreptitiously sends a series of text messages to the agency, setting in motion an attack and rescue plan. Those plans are later called off, however, at the urging of Ahmed, whose identity, the agency determines, may have become compromised.

Olen Steinhauer is the author of The Bridge of Sighs series, the Milo Weaver trilogy, and The Cairo Affair *(2014). His novel* The Nearest Exit *(2010), the second installment of the Milo Weaver trilogy, won the 2010 Hammet Prize for best literary crime novel.*

After most of her colleagues have gone home for the night, Celia sticks around in the office of her boss and mentor William "Bill" Compton to reanalyze Ahmed's text messages. When Celia finds a telling grammatical flourish in Ahmed's last message, she determines that he had indeed been discovered. She subsequently pores through the embassy's phone records to see if someone there gave Ahmed up. When Celia discovers that a mysterious call was made from Compton's office earlier that evening, she keeps the revelation to herself. Readers learn that Henry is fully aware of this secret and that it is the real reason for his trip. Readers also learn that Celia cares deeply for Bill and are led to speculate, like Henry, whether she is covering up for him.

Steinhauer shifts perspectives between Henry and Celia once more before conflating their perspectives in the novel's final section. Celia's later sections center on her children and her deep concern for them. Some of the novel's most haunting episodes, in fact, are recurring nightmares Celia has about defending her children from the murderous hijackers. Flashbacks in Henry's sections, on the other hand, feature his interviews with Bill Compton, now one year retired from the agency and living in

London, and Gene Wilcox, the CIA data processor who provided Celia with the phone records. They also shed light on his troubled past. In particular, Henry's prior stint as a CIA field agent in Russia and his experience of handling the (real-life) 2002 Nord-Ost siege, also known as the Moscow theater crisis, plays an important contextual role in the novel.

On the surface, *All the Old Knives* stands in stark contrast to Steinhauer's other more elaborately plotted novels, which include the Milo Weaver trilogy and the stand-alone thriller *The Cairo Affair* (2014). However, it is no less complex. Throughout the novel, Steinhauer utilizes all the traditional tropes of the spy-fiction genre, as Henry and Celia try to match each other in spy-craft wits. Major revelations and Henry and Celia's true motives are withheld until the novel's ambiguous end via plot twists, red herrings, and cliffhangers. Meanwhile, short, tautly written chapters and fragmented chronology help to sustain the suspense and keep readers guessing. The novel's care-ful pacing and masterful construction impressed critics. Art Taylor, writing for the *Washington Post*, proclaimed the novel "a splendid tour de force," with "as hearty a helping of suspense" as the most adrenalin-packed espionage thrillers, while crime novelist Paula L. Woods commented for the *Los Angeles Times* that Steinhauer "ex-pertly navigates on a much broader stage with an aplomb reminiscent of the best of [Len] Deighton and John Le Carré."

Still, at the heart of *All the Old Knives* is the dinner between Henry and Celia, and as many critics observed, the novel never loses sight of its premise. In her *New York Times* review, Janet Maslin called the novel a "sneaky little gem" and wrote that Steinhauer "sustains the difficult balancing act of melding a heart-racing espionage plot with credible dinner table conversation." Much of the novel's action takes place at the dinner table, and as wine flows freely between its protagonists, readers receive subtle hints about machinations that are bubbling beneath the surface. Though the idea of a narrative unfolding over a single dinner has appeared before in various literary forms, from the aforementioned *Song of Lunch* to Herman Koch's acclaimed family drama *The Dinner* (trans. 2013; *Het Diner*, 2009), Steinhauer succeeds in adding a new twist to the spy thriller, and the most avid readers of the genre should appreciate this intimate and sly probing of the human condition.

Chris Cullen

Review Sources

Graff, Keir. Rev. of *All the Old Knives*, by Olen Steinhauer. *Booklist* 1 Jan. 2015: 43–44. Print.

Maslin, Janet. "In Olen Steinhauer's 'All the Old Knives,' Exes Recall Love and Blood." Rev. of *All the Old Knives*, by Olen Steinhauer. *New York Times*. New York Times, 1 Mar. 2015. Web. 2 Oct. 2015.

Taylor, Art. "Spy vs. Spy: Olen Steinhauer's Thriller 'All the Old Knives.'" Rev. of *All the Old Knives*, by Olen Steinhauer. *Washington Post*. Washington Post, 8 Mar. 2015. Web. 2 Oct. 2015.

Woods, Paula L. "Olen Steinhauer's New Novel Reunites Spies with a Shared History." Rev. of *All the Old Knives*, by Olen Steinhauer. *Los Angeles Times*. Los Angeles Times, 20 Mar. 2015. Web. 2 Oct. 2015.

Among the Ten Thousand Things

Author: Julia Pierpont
Publisher: Random House (New York). 336 pp.
Type of work: Novel
Time: Present
Locales: New York; Rhode Island; Jamestown, Virginia; the western United States

Among the Ten Thousand Things, Julia Pierpont's debut novel, is a nuanced exploration of the effect of infidelity on a family. Pierpont's narrative traces the emotional ebb and flow of the various members as they grapple with what has happened and its aftermath.

Principal characters:
KAY SHANLEY, an eleven-year-old girl
SIMON SHANLEY, her fifteen-year-old brother
DEB SHANLEY, her mother, a former dancer
JACK SHANLEY, her father
THE OTHER WOMAN, Jack's former mistress

(Courtesy of Random House)

Among the Ten Thousand Things is a novel about the unraveling of a family. It begins when the doorman gives Kay a package for her mother as she enters the elevator. Because the package is not firmly wrapped, and because there is something pink peeking out that just *might* be a present for her, Kay opens the box. It unleashes consequences of Pandora-like dimensions. Although she is not entirely familiar with all the words in the printed e-mails that fill the box, Kay learns that her father has been having an affair for the past six months. Enclosed with the printouts is a handwritten letter addressed to Deb, Kay's mother. In the letter Jack's unnamed mistress explains that their affair ended because Jack no longer wanted her, and she cannot figure out why. In her conclusion, she compares Jack to dirty water and September 11, pointing out that if she and Deb had gotten cancer from either one, they would seek a settlement. She then asks Deb what she has settled for.

The question is a good one and underscores the uncertainty that Deb faces as she decides what to do. She already knew about the affair. She does not want to appear to be the bad one to her children. She does not want to break up her life and her marriage. She knows Jack well enough to know that he will not only go on as if this never happened but also give her excuses as to why it is either not such a big deal or was actually a good thing. Which, indeed, he does.

Meanwhile, the children are completely unsettled by what they discover in the box. When Kay read through the contents, she was alone. Her mother knew immediately that something was wrong when she saw Kay. Indeed, Kay avoided her, going "quickly to her room, head down to hide her face. There was that little guy in her throat, the one that hurt when she wanted to cry." Kay lets her mother believe she is crying about the trouble her friends have given her that afternoon. The reader knows, when Deb asks Kay where it hurts, that this is an answer that is beyond Kay's ability to articulate. Kay decides the safest thing to do is to hide the box. She cannot go to her father because she knows instinctively that her mother would not be able to live with him if she knew about the box. He would have no choice but to hide it.

After school the next day, Kay shares the contents with Simon. At fifteen, he is getting ready to explore his own sexuality. He is also a bit high that afternoon. Learning of his father's behavior in explicit detail unsettles him but leaves him with no doubt about calling his mother in to see the contents of the box. His disbelief is multiplied by the fact that his mother does not pore over the contents of the box. He is furious with both his father, for obvious reasons, and his mother, although he is not sure why. The reader cannot help but wonder what the ultimate effect of the box will have on Simon.

Deb takes the box and has to fight the impulse to hide it. She knows that her children will not view her as the victim for long. In fact, within the course of this novel, Kay will come to hate her mother for the way in which she natters at her father over his flirtations with yet another waitress. All Deb can do by that point is leave the diner. "'Please would you just excuse me a minute.' [Deb says.] She went outside, chiming the bells again, meandering unstraight lines. Jack and Kay and Brenda with the coffee pot watched her, but Deb, through the window, appeared to be looking for something dropped.'" The reader is left to realize that this is what Deb will be settling for, the resentment of her daughter and the search for what her life might have been, if she decided to stay with Jack.

For her part, at eleven, Kay is not sure what exactly it is that her father did other than cheat on her mother. However, she understands enough to begin to write X-rated *Seinfeld* fan episodes that explore infidelity. When her classmates the Haber twins snatch the notebook with her work, their taunting brings her social life to a new low. In addition to Kay's humiliation, the twins tell their mother about Kay's writing. She then tells Deb. What could be sustained in the closed sphere of family cannot be tolerated in the full light of day. Deb takes the kids to Rhode Island for the summer as a result.

The implications of Jack's affair play out over the remainder of the novel. There is never a point where the ground is truly solid again. Each member of the family is affected in a slightly different way and to a slightly different degree. Deb, who, for better or worse, views herself as a mother first, tries to hold herself and the kids together. Jack continues his flirtations and denial. Jack's career begins an unhappy slide. Deb is left searching for what is left of the potential that she happily left behind when she married and had children.

When a family emergency occurs, it seems only natural that Jack comes to be a part of it. After all, he and Deb share these children, if nothing else. No matter the many ways in which Jack has hurt Deb, and the children in the process, he is always going to be their father. The interesting point for the reader is that Deb accepts this, angrily yelling at the current man in her life that he is not worried enough because the missing child is not his. His reaction is to leave. Ironically, it is Jack who knows just where to find the missing child.

The result of this uncomfortable and highly charged reunion is a tangle of emotions and allegiances that make it clear that nothing will be what anyone in the family had thought they had, even if it had never been real. Perhaps there is a chance for a new normal, the reader might think, but Pierpont makes it clear that it could just as easily be the case that there is not. It is a story that has been told many times before, and it is a tribute to the strength of Pierpont's writing that her narrative is utterly compelling.

Among the Ten Thousand Things was highly anticipated and eagerly greeted. Meredith Turits reports for *Vanity Fair* that Pierpont's MFA thesis adviser at New York University, Jonathan Safran Foer, gave Pierpont encouragement and advice as she developed the novel, and agent Elyse Cheney worked with the first-time writer on the book before it went to auction. Once at auction, the rights to the novel sold for six figures before Pierpont had graduated from her MFA program, and the novel went on to become a *New York Times* best seller.

In her review for the *New York Times Sunday Book Review*, Helen Schulman describes *Among the Ten Thousand Things* as "a novel about a family blown apart and yet still painfully tethered together." Once the children read the box's contents, it is particularly painful to watch them try to cope with what they surely wish they had never known. Not all reviewers found the plotline to be compelling, however. Rayyan Al-Shawaf for the *Miami Herald* writes, "Julia Pierpont's debut novel squanders a suspenseful opening" as "these characters and their travails become achingly boring in no time at all." Yet other reviewers thought highly of the characters, especially Kay and Simon. Sarah Lyall likens them to Holden Caulfield and other characters in the category of "best fictional alienated-children-of-New York."

Julia Pierpont is a graduate of New York University's MFA program. Her debut novel, Among the Ten Thousand Things, *sold at auction for a six-figure sum before her graduation and became a New York Times best seller.*

Among the Ten Thousand Things is strong, even, and "written by a blazingly talented young author whose prose is so assured and whose observations are so precise and deeply felt that it's almost an insult to bring up her age," which is twenty-eight, according to Schulman. However, even those who agree with the strength of Pierpont's writing disagree about her use of an unusual literary device: revealing the ending just shy of the middle of the book. Maureen Corrigan for NPR finds the glimpse into the future "smart," while Lyall seems less convinced, writing that "it has the leaden sting of inevitability and cannot help dampening what is still to come. The die is cast, she seems to be saying. There is no going back."

Gina Hagler

Review Sources

Corrigan, Maureen. "Infidelity Is Steeped in Suspense in 'Among the Ten Thousand Things.'" Rev. of *Among the Ten Thousand Things*, by Julia Pierpont. *NPR*. NPR, 23 July 2015. Web. 5 Jan. 2016.

Lyall, Sarah. "Review: In 'Among the Ten Thousand Things,' Julia Pierpont's First Novel, a Family Struggles." Rev. of *Among the Ten Thousand Things*, by Julia Pierpont. *New York Times*. New York Times, 22 July 2015. Web. 6 Jan. 2016.

Schulman, Helen. Rev. of *Among the Ten Thousand Things*, by Julia Pierpont. *New York Times Sunday Book Review*. New York Times, 7 July 2015. Web. 15 Jan. 2016.

Shawaf, Rayyan al-. Rev. of *Among the Ten Thousand Things*, by Julia Pierpont. *Miami Herald*. Miami Herald, 7 Aug. 2015. Web. 15 Jan. 2016.

Turits, Meredith. "How Julia Pierpont's Debut Novel Sold for Six Figures before She Graduated." *Vanity Fair*. Condé Nast, 6 July 2015. Web. 15 Jan. 2016.

Zeidner, Lisa. "'Among the Ten Thousand Things': A Family Torn Apart by Infidelity." Rev. of *Among the Ten Thousand Things*, by Julia Pierpont. *Washington Post*. Washington Post, 2 July 2015. Web. 18 Jan. 2016.

Ancillary Mercy

Author: Ann Leckie (b. 1966)
Publisher: Orbit (New York). 368 pp.
Type of work: Novel
Time: Thousands of years in the future
Locale: Athoek system, Radchaai Empire

(Cover design by Kirk Benshoff; Illustration by John Harris.)

Ancillary Mercy *is the final book in the Imperial Radch space opera trilogy by American author Ann Leckie.*

Principal characters:
Breq, the sole surviving ancillary of the starship *Justice of Toren*
Anaander Mianaai, Lord of the Radch, an interstellar ruler with a divided consciousness
Seivarden, a lieutenant on the *Mercy of Kalr*
Tisarwat, a former embodiment of
    Anaander Mianaai serving as one of Breq's lieutenants
Mercy of Kalr, Breq's starship, which has artificial intelligence

Although Ann Leckie's Imperial Radch trilogy initially appears to be anchored in the familiar science-fiction tropes of intergalactic warfare and the ascension of intelligent machines, upon further reading the series quickly proves to be more nuanced and original than many other well-established novels of the genre. In addition to its swashbuckling plot and fantastical futuristic technologies, the Imperial Radch trilogy is unique in the perspective it assumes on the issue of identity. The final installment in the trilogy, *Ancillary Mercy* (2015), continues Leckie's groundbreaking body of work by exploring the significance of consciousness and personhood through emotionally complex characters, many of whom are not human.

    Preceded by *Ancillary Justice* (2013) and *Ancillary Sword* (2014), *Ancillary Mercy* concludes the story of Fleet Captain Breq in her quest to take down the intergalactic tyrant Anaander Mianaai. Leckie begins the series' third installment just days after the events of *Ancillary Sword* and with the bare minimum of backstory, ensuring that *Ancillary Mercy* is better appreciated as part of the trilogy rather than as a standalone novel. This is exacerbated by the complexity of the world that Leckie has created. *Ancillary Mercy* is set in Radchaai Empire, a collection of human-occupied planets ruled for three thousand years by the Lord of the Radch, Anaander Mianaai. It is Mianaai's militant expansionist agenda that has resulted in the cultural and governmental subjugation of thousands of foreign peoples. Many of these conquered people are turned into "ancillaries," humans implanted with technology that allows them to be controlled by the artificial intelligence (AI) of the starship to which they are assigned.

Once people become ancillaries, their former identities are completely erased. Essentially appendages of their ships, they gain a collective or hive consciousness with their ship and ancillary colleagues.

As an author, Leckie builds her characters around multilayered, abstract iterations of identity that challenge conventional storytelling. This is particularly evident in the protagonist, Breq, who was once an ancillary until her ship, *Justice of Toren*, was destroyed by Mianaai. As the sole survivor, Breq is the last remaining fragment of her ship's consciousness and therefore the human embodiment of *Justice of Toren*. Ultimately, Leckie establishes, Breq is both a ship and an officer. While she has the appearance of a human, she does not have the mind of one. This does not mean she is without emotion, however. Breq's journey is fueled by her desire to avenge the destruction of *Justice of Toren* and one of its officers, Lieutenant Awn, whom she loved. During this endeavor, Breq learns that Anaander Mianaai has created and spread hundreds of embodiments of herself throughout the Radchaai Empire that are linked through telepathic implants. As Breq attempts to kill as many Mianaais as she can, she learns that there are two factions of these clones—one that advocates for the continued military expansion of the empire and another that wants peace and reform. Caught in the middle of this civil war, Breq joins forces with the reformists. In turn, they make her fleet captain and commander of the ship *Mercy of Kalr* before assigning her to protect the Athoek system and its people.

Leckie's depiction of AI is original and multidimensional. Technologies with the capacity for AI are neither cold and mechanical nor overtly human. Instead, they are portrayed as being somewhere in between. *Mercy of Kalr* is a prominent character of *Ancillary Mercy* and is often referred to by Breq as "Ship." Ship not only has its own personality and feelings, but cares deeply about its officers. It communicates with Breq telepathically or by using its ancillaries as mouthpieces. The sentience of Ship and other vessels are thanks to their "AI-cores," which can be replaced or destroyed by humans. Athoek Station, where the *Mercy of Kalr* is docked for most of *Ancillary Mercy*, is also sentient and works to do everything in its power to keep the people living on it safe. Athoek Station proves to be a hero in this effort as it is a particularly tumultuous time within the Radchaai Empire and the civilians have never been at greater risk. Not only are warships from the militant Mianaai faction making their way to Athoek Station, but a mysterious stranger named *Sphene* has been discovered there. To further the precariousness of the Station's safety, Translator Zeiat, a representative of the powerful and potentially dangerous Presger alien race, has arrived to Athoek Station with unknown intentions.

Ancillary Mercy is similar to its predecessors in the fact that it has a complex and character-driven plot. Beyond the primary story line of Breq and her loyal officers attempting to destroy Mianaai once and for all, *Ancillary Mercy* has numerous subplots that follow supporting characters and their personal conflicts. One supplemental story line is that of Lieutenant Seivarden, Breq's second-in-command, facing the aftermath of a chemical addiction while trying to sustain a healthy romantic relationship with the lower-class Lieutenant Ekalu. Another follows Lieutenant Tisarwat as she attempts to overcome the psychological trauma of being a former Mianaai clone. While all of the story lines could become overwhelming and disparate, Leckie succeeds in balancing and uniting them by ensuring that the fight to be recognized as individuals remains at the heart of each character's conflict. The citizens of Athoek Station fight for their own cultural autonomy amid the oppressive Radchaai imperialist regime by staging protests. Most importantly, after thousands of years of being treated as disposable pieces of equipment, the ships, stations, and ancillaries within *Ancillary Mercy* are willing to both defy and directly fight Mianaai in order to be recognized as people.

(Mission Photo.org)

Ancillary Mercy has been described as a space opera, a reference that alludes to the novel's setting, themes, and melodrama. Although the central story line of the Imperial Radch trilogy fits neatly into this designation, it is important to note that Leckie's prose and structure break away from the genre's literary conventions. This is primarily evident is the way in which Leckie indicates which character is speaking. In a world where AI is omnipresent, ships and stations often speak through humans. As it is not always clear to the reader or even the other characters which consciousness is actually speaking, Leckie often uses Breq's internal dialogue to clarify. When *Mercy of Kalr* speaks through Seivarden, for example, Breq will first state that Seivarden is speaking and then note that she is almost certain that it is in fact Ship speaking.

Ann Leckie is an American science-fiction author. Her debut novel, Ancillary Justice *(2013), won the Nebula Award, the Hugo Award, and the Arthur C. Clarke Award.*

The most dramatic way in which Leckie deviates from literary stylistic norms, however, is in her use of pronouns. As the Radchaai do not differentiate gender, Breq refers to everyone around her as with the default "she" pronoun. Consequently, readers never know the gender of the characters. In interviews, Leckie has said that this stylistic decision was a point of contention with her editors, most of whom claimed that it would make the book unpublishable. Despite their warnings, Leckie's use of exclusively female pronouns has been met with widespread acclaim with critics, who have noted that it provides for a thought-provoking reading experience. Without gender or detailed physical descriptions, characters are ultimately differentiated by their interests, feelings, and relationships with one another.

In addition to the strength and originality of her literary style, Leckie's detailed vision of an alternate universe has been a point of praise among reviewers. Despite the Radchaai Empire being three thousand years old and distinctly foreign from contemporary Earth, Leckie has been successful in forging a believable culture and mythology. The intricacies of the Radchaai lifestyle, their military, and advanced technology are meticulously wrought. This is evident with the Radchaai starships, which are divided into the three classes of Justice, Sword, and Mercy, and ancillaries, who are recognized by their decade and number. In addition to these small details, Leckie has instilled the Radchaai Empire with a realistic economy and political landscape. Like fellow fantasy and science-fiction writers J. K. Rowling or Frank Herbert, Leckie is successful in creating a full, exciting fictional universe.

Since its 2015 publication, *Ancillary Mercy* has been declared a successful conclusion to its award-winning prequels. Leckie's debut novel, *Ancillary Justice*, was the recipient of numerous science-fiction accolades, including the Nebula Award, the Arthur C. Clarke Award, and the Hugo Award. Its sequel, *Ancillary Sword*, won the BSFA Award for Best Novel and the Locus Award for Best Science Fiction Novel. The reviews of *Ancillary Mercy* reflect a similar celebratory sentiment. Recurrent among the novel's myriad praises has been recognition for Leckie's skilled storytelling. Despite the number of complex story lines present within the novel, Leckie effectively wraps up each one while leaving the fictional universe and its characters open for future stories.

Given the steady escalation of the conflict between Breq and Mianaai throughout the trilogy, the lack of a lengthy, violent showdown in *Ancillary Mercy* could feel anticlimactic to some readers. However, Leckie's use of suspense and emotion prevents the last act of Breq's story from ever becoming boring. In her National Public Radio review, Genevieve Valentine writes that although *Ancillary Mercy* may not conform to the expectations that come after a powerhouse debut like *Ancillary Justice*, the novel deserves recognition as "a capstone to a series that shook genre expectations." Ultimately, what makes *Ancillary Mercy* an engaging read, despite its lack of protracted action sequences, is the characterization. The novel's cast of heroes are highly relatable as flawed and emotionally vulnerable individuals. It is their bravery, friendship, and willingness to confront the Lord of the Radch for the sake of justice that keeps the narrative consistently exciting.

Leckie's defiance of certain science-fiction norms in *Ancillary Mercy* has drawn some controversy. Especially polarizing have been Leckie's decision to forgo the standard white, male hero and the book's parallels to contemporary society. Some of the genre's traditionalist fans argue that science fiction should focus exclusively on the intergalactic experience and avoid any discussion of existing sociopolitical problems. The majority of critics, however, have commended Leckie for exploring identity in an unconventional manner that is relevant to the world today. Tammy Oler writes in her *Slate* review that because Leckie's work focuses on ordinary people and real societal issues it will "speak to the heart across the ages." Although there is political subtext to Leckie's writing that might be unappealing to some readers, *Ancillary Mercy* can also be enjoyed simply as a futuristic space adventure. With a quick-paced, unpredictable plot and a collection of unique characters, *Ancillary Mercy* ultimately proves to be an exciting addition to the science-fiction genre.

Emily E. Turner

Review Sources

Rev. of *Ancillary Mercy,* by Ann Leckie. *Kirkus Reviews* 1 Aug. 2015: 49–50. Print.
Rev. of *Ancillary Mercy*, by Ann Leckie. *Publishers Weekly* 7 Sept. 2015: 50. Print.
Oler, Tammy. "Oh, the Humanity." Rev. of *Ancillary Mercy*, by Ann Leckie. *Slate.*
    Slate Group, 4 Nov. 2015. Web. 3 Feb. 2016.
Valentine, Genevieve. "An Intergalactic Adventure Winds to a Close in 'Ancillary
    Mercy.'" Rev. of *Ancillary Mercy*, by Ann Leckie. *NPR Books*. NPR, 5 Oct. 2015.
    Web. 3 Feb. 2016.

The Arab of the Future
A Childhood in the Middle East, 1978–1984: A Graphic Memoir

Author: Riad Sattouf (b. 1978)
First published: L'Arabe du futur, 2014, in France
Translated from the French by: Sam Taylor
Publisher: Metropolitan Books (New York). 160 pp.
Type of work: Graphic novel, memoir
Time: 1978–84
Locales: Tripoli, Libya; Ter Maaleh, Syria; France

(Courtesy of Henry Holt & Co)

A graphic memoir written by cartoonist and filmmaker Riad Sattouf, The Arab of the Future *chronicles the author's varied childhood experiences growing up in Libya, Syria, and France.*

Principal personages:
RIAD SATTOUF, the narrator and main character
ABDEL-RAZAK SATTOUF, his Syrian father
CLÉMENTINE SATTOUF, his French mother

Turmoil in the Middle East continues to dominate the headlines. Following the collapse of the Ottoman Empire during World War I, Great Britain and France carved up the region between them, intending not to modernize and uplift the Middle East but to exploit it. This artificial division forged new nations without regard for ethnic and religious divisions among the people on the ground, and when the imperial powers finally withdrew, they left behind relative poverty and a power vacuum that fueled the internecine warfare that still troubles the region. Tyrants filled the political niche left by western Europeans and brought a new, brutal form of leadership that nevertheless conferred some measure of stability.

It was into this setting that Riad Sattouf was born. As a child, he possessed a unique perspective on the events he witnessed—events that he chronicles in *The Arab of the Future*, the first in a planned trilogy. A cartoonist by profession, Sattouf turns his pen to his own recollections of growing up in two different worlds, a cosmopolitan and modern France and the struggling Middle Eastern nations of Libya and Syria. Filled with cogent insights pulled from Sattouf's early childhood memories, *The Arab of the Future* sheds much light on the problems that plagued the Middle East at the end of the twentieth century, just as it provides some much-needed context to understand the problems that still engulf the region.

Sattouf's parents came from two very different traditions. His mother, whom he calls Clémentine in the book, was born and raised in France; his father, whom he names Abdel-Razak, was reared in Syria. (In an interview with Adam Shatz for the October 19, 2015, issue of the *New Yorker*, Sattouf pointedly declined to reveal his parents' real names.) Sattouf shows them meeting as college students studying at the Sorbonne in the early 1970s and commencing a whirlwind romance that culminates in marriage and two children. Early in the courtship, Abdel-Razak demonstrates unabashed admiration for France and desires nothing less than to see his benighted Middle East break from its prejudices and replicate the modernity found in the Western world.

The defeat of the Arab forces in the 1973 Yom Kippur War and the signing of the Camp David Accords change everything for Abdel-Razak. After that, he increasingly views the world around him through the lens of his upbringing. An expatriate who fled Syria for France in part to avoid compulsory military service, he soon finds himself an ardent pan-Arab nationalist who views the Western world with scorn and suspicion. His tone changes from trumpeting all things French to condemning university administrators as racists for not properly acknowledging the merits of his successful dissertation. As Abdel-Razak shifts his perspective, his wife stands by, tolerating her husband's tirades while caring for their infant son, Riad, born the same year that Abdel-Razak defends his dissertation.

With a successful end to his academic journey and a brand new addition to his family, Abdel-Razak does not stop and celebrate his good fortune, instead dwelling on injustices in the global community over which he has no control. When offered a job at England's prestigious Oxford University, a post his wife appears thrilled about, Abdel-Razak is disappointed because university officials spelled his name incorrectly in the letter. Not long thereafter, he tells his wife that he also applied for a position in Libya and that he has been offered a job there. He eagerly points out that the staff at the Middle Eastern university addressed him as "Doctor" and correctly spelled his name on the envelope. Without hesitation, he announces to his family that they are going to Libya.

As soon as the Sattouf family touch down in Muammar Qaddafi's communist Libya, they begin to realize how different things will be there compared to their life in France. From the start, Abdel-Razak makes every effort to embrace life in their new home, all the while championing the superior culture and lifestyle of the Arab world. Rarely does he express signs of discontent; after all, he grew up in relative poverty in Ter Maaleh, outside the Syrian town of Homs, so doing without is not new to him The scenes depicted in each cartoon frame clearly reveal the dilapidated state of the country's infrastructure, yet Abdel-Razak continually points out the country's glorious past and expresses his optimism for a better, richer future. Sattouf leaves little record that his father was disappointed by the state of affairs, though several panels do subtly indicate his father's repeated sense of humiliation or his defensiveness in the face of his wife's shock at local practices.

Clémentine is given far fewer lines, either because she was quiet by nature or, more likely, because Sattouf wanted to highlight his father's bombastic character. Nonetheless, in one-liners throughout the narrative, she repeatedly asks pointed questions or undercuts Abdel-Razak's assertions. Though clearly a devoted wife who willingly follows her husband as he bounces from job to job, country to country, Clémentine is disturbed by the casual violence around them in Syria and finally explodes in outrage at the killing of a dog.

Despite living in an ultrareligious environment, first in Libya and even more so when the family relocates to Syria, Abdel-Razak rarely mentions religion and instills only a few religious or superstitious beliefs in young Riad. Although he rails against the Jews and champions a decidedly pro-Arab perspective, he is never depicted as a devoted Muslim and makes only a halfhearted attempt to compel little Riad to commit Qur'an passages to memory—a doomed mission, given that his son cannot read Arabic.

Other cultural legacies of the region are more readily embraced in the Sattouf home. In an age when American children still played cowboys and Indians, Riad's Syrian cousins play Arabs versus Israelis. Their toy soldiers depict the Syrians in heroic battlefield stances, while the Israeli soldiers reveal the utmost duplicity, waving a flag of surrender in one hand and holding a dagger in the other—a powerful symbol designed to inculcate distrust at an early age. Such toys teach children to grow up hating the "enemy" in much the same way that generations of young people around the globe have been indoctrinated with intolerance: they grow up listening to their parents besmirch those who differ from them, and they play games that reinforce the stereotypes. Young Riad, with his fair skin and blond hair, was immediately set apart from his peers and subjected to anti-Semitic taunts and bullying, despite being Arab himself. He struggled to make sense of the world he inhabited and clearly internalized the hate and despair he saw around him. He might not have always understood what he witnessed, but he recognized the intensity with which people clung to their beliefs.

Riad Sattouf is a popular French cartoonist, screenwriter, and director who grew up in Libya, Syria, and France. He has worked as a columnist for the weekly magazines Charlie Hebdo *and* L'Obs. *His feature films include the comedies* The French Kissers *(2009) and* Jacky in the Women's Kingdom *(2013).* The Arab of the Future *is his first work to be translated into English.*

When the family relocates to Hafez al-Assad's Baathist Syria, the dynamics of the country, also governed by an all-powerful leader, are very similar to those they experienced under Qaddafi. The conditions in Syria are generally poor, but unlike in Libya, Riad's father is now in the land of his birth. If Abdel-Razak was excited about Libya, he is downright boisterous when it comes to showing his family around Syria. Despite his glowing praise, the cartoon frames make evident that the situation is far less idyllic than he describes. Even from the perspective of a child, the golden land that Riad's father promised falls far short of expectations. All around them is evidence that circumstances in Syria do not comport with Abdel-Razak's paradisiacal recollections or observations. And as much as Abdel-Razak wants to fit in with the Syrian people, it is clear that he no longer quite belongs. His mother still dotes on him, but he and his older brother Mohamed have a falling out, and much that would have been his, including a large tract of land, was sold after he went to study in France.

Each summer, the Sattouf family vacationed for extended periods in Brittany, France, visiting Clémentine's family and giving little Riad new sights and smells to experience. The first such vacation comes at the end of the volume. While in France, Clémentine is more relaxed, while Abdel-Razak is on edge, feeling unsafe either physically or metaphysically and adopting a self-defensive swagger. Yet as much as Abdel-Razak is guarded about his heritage, there is one thing he clearly respects about the Western world: the value placed on education. His vision of bringing education to the Arab world remains an integral part of him throughout Sattouf's account. In many ways, his life represents a turning away from the traditions of his homeland. As a child, his parents allowed him to attend school at a time when education was not compulsory; he, in turn, embraced the value of a classical liberal arts education and ended up reaching a terminal degree in his field of study. Near the close of this rather slim book, Abdel-Razak claims that Arab people only respect force and would be lazy bigots if given the opportunity. They need to be pushed and cajoled, he argues, and whatever form that prodding takes will be necessary to bring about an educated citizenry that would promote real reform in the Middle East. The Arab of the future, according to Abdel-Razak, is a well-educated citizen. Sattouf fittingly concludes the book with the family preparing to leave their French vacation—which Riad did not realize was only a vacation—and return to Syria, where a reluctant Riad will attend school.

In many ways, Sattouf's account reinforces, rather than dispels, perceptions of the Middle East as an intolerant place where ethnic, religious, and gender prejudices abound and corruption and violence are ongoing at all levels of society. The challenges confronting the region appear insurmountable, and Sattouf's book is filled with snippets of desperation alongside its message of hope and opportunity. As the title implies, the future of the region belongs to the young and the educated. Yet while suggesting the possibility of progress, the book simultaneously subverts that message by undermining its chief champion, Abdel-Razak.

The Arab of the Future received a mixed reception in France, where it was first published and where tensions between the ethnic French and citizens or residents of North African descent run high. Some critics have found the portrayals of life in the Middle East offered in Sattouf's book to be orientalist, reductionist, or even racist. Other readers, including many of North African or Middle Eastern extraction, have applauded Sattouf's depictions of rural life in Libya and Syria for their veracity. The publication of *The Arab of the Future* has been considered timely, coming at a time when the West feels increasingly threatened by Islamist militants in war-torn Syria. Two further graphic memoirs that will chronicle Sattouf's coming-of-age in France are planned; time will tell what influence the trilogy will exert on the Western audiences who read and respond to it.

Keith M. Finley, PhD

Review Sources:

Lalami, Laila. "World of His Father." Rev. of *The Arab of the Future: A Childhood in the Middle East, 1978–1984*, by Riad Sattouf. *New York Times Book Review* 18 Oct. 2015: 9. Print.

Lehoczky, Etelka. "Rage and Humor Alternate in *Arab of the Future*." Rev. of *The Arab of the Future: A Childhood in the Middle East, 1978–1984*, by Riad Sattouf. *NPR*. NPR, 29 Oct. 2015. Web. 31 Dec. 2015.

Wolk, Douglas. "Graphic Memoir *Arab of the Future* Takes a Look Back to the Author's Childhood in Libya and Syria." Rev. of *The Arab of the Future: A Childhood in the Middle East, 1978–1984*, by Riad Sattouf. *Los Angeles Times*. Tribune, 23 Oct. 2015. Web. 31 Dec. 2015.

Aurora

Author: Kim Stanley Robinson (b. 1952)
Publisher: Orbit (New York). 480 pp.
Type of work: Novel
Time: ca. 2500
Locales: An interstellar starship, the planet
Aurora, Earth

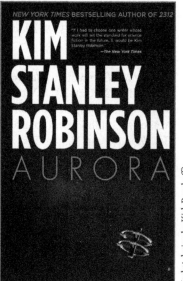

(Jacket design by Kirk Benshoff)

*Aurora is the story of a generational starship
and the people aboard. The novel explores
the practicality of space expeditions and colonization, as well as who bears the responsibilities and consequences of the success or
failure of such a voyage.*

Principal characters:
DEVI, the unofficial chief engineer of a star-
  ship headed for the Tau Ceti system
BADIM, her husband
FREYA, their daughter
ARAM, Badim's friend
JOCHI, Freya's friend
EUAN, Freya's friend
SHIP, an artificially intelligent quantum computer

Aurora is the story of a generational starship that has been launched from Earth in
response to an environmental disaster. The journey will last for several generations,
with the initial voyagers numbering approximately two thousand volunteers. The ship
they are traveling in is a complex affair of biomes in the form of twenty-four individual pods that mimic the twelve major various climactic biomes found on Earth.
The biomes are biologically diverse, and the crew must carefully manage many unexpected chemical reactions that can create problems, such as altered levels of important
trace elements.

As the decades fade away and several generations live and die on the voyage to
what is believed to be an inhabitable planet in the Tau Ceti system, the seventh and
presumably final generation of travelers is anxious to begin their work beyond the
confines of the ship. They know no other life because they were born on the ship, but
what makes this group unique is that they are going to be the first to leave the ship
and colonize a new planet. They listen to the feed from Earth, which is twelve years
behind, and they look forward to reporting back on their progress.

As they close in on their destination, things start going wrong on the ship. The
problems are relatively minor, but Devi, the ship's leader and chief engineer, recognizes that there is very little room for error in a system in which every water droplet

or grain of sand plays a vital role. Because of her ability to take a problem back to where it was first recognized before the reason for the problem is determined, Devi is the person on this ship whom most seek out when any kind of trouble occurs. As a result, she is in constant demand. Her daughter, Freya, often goes with her to meetings. Badim, who is Devi's husband and a doctor, acts as loving and caring sounding board. In a typical exchange, Devi demands, "We've been rats in a cage, two thousand at a time for seven generations, and for what? For what?" Badim replies, "What's it been? About fifteen thousand people, and a couple hundred years? In the big scheme of things it's not that many. And then we have a new world to live on."

While Badim gives Devi his full support, there are not many others on the starship who understand Devi or the full extent of the problems she grapples with. Because of this, she speaks to Ship, the artificial intelligence interface for the quantum computer. No one has programmed Ship; it has simply learned as events have unfolded. Even Devi is not sure just how Ship works, but she is certain that Ship is able to reason and will be capable of making decisions if and when it is absolutely necessary for the survival of those onboard. To help Ship develop intellectually, Devi instructs it to write the narrative of their journey. This is not an easy thing, and the reader is included in Ship's humorous observations and struggles. At one point Ship observes, "Eventually it became clear that no individual, couple, or group wanted to sacrifice the remainder of their lives to watching over the rest. To a certain extent it as an endorsement of our abilities as caretaker or cerebellum, a kind of gesture of trust, along with the more usual will to live, and a disinclination to starve in solitude."

When the ship does reach Aurora, what happens there is anything but what has been planned. Many critics and readers alike have felt that the result is a bit predictable, but the reaction of the travelers to this new reality and the outcome of their time on the planet is not, and this has dire consequences on the crew, forcing them to make a new set of decisions that are not foregone conclusions. One significant hurdle that the people on the starship must overcome is to understand and engage in the decision-making process is that they have never been forced, or even asked, to make any significant decisions for themselves. Every life-sustaining and life-altering decision was predetermined generations before or has been adjusted over time. The decisions they face outside the ship, however, are ones that will determine their fate and whether they survive or die. They are also unaware of their individual and cultural histories and have been living in ignorance of both.

Despite Devi's concern that Freya will not have a fulfilled life, Freya plays a major role in the discussion and decision-making process. She is a people person, which is a characteristic that her mother failed to recognize in her or value because of her focus on the mechanics of survival. Freya's skills are ultimately every bit as essential to the survival of the people onboard the starship as are Devi's, and as she grows to be a leader and gains more confidence in her abilities, the reader is shown through Freya's eyes the reality and human cost of this venture. By the time she lashes out in anger at an expert who has come to see the mission of generation starships as a sort of quixotic quest to spread the seed of humankind beyond the cradle of Earth, it is difficult not to empathize with her and feel that Freya has done precisely what needed to be done.

The generational starship story is a type of literary genre in itself, but Robinson brings new life to it by exploring the role of AI (artificial intelligence) in quantum computing. The AI in *Aurora* grows at an astonishing rate in both its intellect and its capacity to feel. Ship expresses its impressions of what love is, explaining (in a first-person plural voice), "We think now that love is a kind of giving of attention. It is usually attention given to some other consciousness, but not always. . . . At that point, the conscious-ness that is feeling the love has the universe organized for it as if by a kind of polarization. Then the giving is the getting. The feeling of attentiveness itself is an immediate reward."

(Sean Curtin)

Kim Stanley Robinson is a speculative science fiction author best known for his Mars trilogy. He has published nineteen novels and numerous short stories and has won numerous awards, including several Hugo and Nebula Awards for best novel, multiple Locus Awards, and a prestigious World Fantasy Award.

Freya's personal and emotional growth is just as astonishing. The reader first meets her as a teen who is considered intellectually slow, but it soon becomes clear that the en-tire group is slow, with each new generation being less capable than the last. No one is quite sure why or how far this will proceed. Even Ship is not certain what to make of the decline or how to reverse it. This is one of several instances where Robinson sub-tly incorporates the science of extended space travel and the balance of resources in a biome. Adam Roberts, reviewing the novel for the *Guardian*, wrote that Robin-son's writing is "superbly insightful on the way entropy actually works in complex systems. . . . Valves stick open, biome lakes wash away their beds and start to corrode the fabric of the ship, kilometer-long artificial lights blink out. In deep space, any of these glitches might lead to annihilation."

That sense of potential annihilation is pervasive, and it lingers in the growing list of things gone awry and the tension over how to make decisions that affect every indi-vidual in every biome. There is a growing realization that even the right decisions have unintended and far-reaching consequences. The overall question that *Aurora* drives readers to consider is, Who has the right to make decisions for future generations? It is a question that for many is simple and obvious: parents make the decisions that affect their children, and their children do the same for their children, and so on. But Rob-inson goes beyond such basic cultural traditions. When a culture or civilization must experience life and death as it journeys toward a better existence, who decides that the journey itself is enough to be the work of a lifetime, and at what cost?

By the time *Aurora* reaches its conclusion, it is difficult to view the colonization of space in quite the same manner. It is also difficult to overlook the strong environmental messages in the book. Readers are left with the thought that rather than leave behind what is destroyed and then live and die trying to recreate what once was, humanity should instead maintain, repair, and improve what already exists. This notion is illustrated in one of the ending scenes of the book, when Freya meets the "kindred souls" on a beach who are "expressing their love of that lost world by the seashore by rebuilding it."

By the time the citizens of the starship must make their most difficult decision, the reader is fully engaged by the strength of the manner in which Ship tells Freya's story. When the ultimate dilemma comes to the fore, as Alan Cheuse wrote for NPR, "it makes an already compelling plot, with its near-perfect marriage of the technical and the psychological . . . , even more compelling."

Gina Hagler

Review Sources

Alexander, Niall. "A Labour of Love: *Aurora* by Kim Stanley Robinson." Rev. of *Aurora*, by Kim Stanley Robinson. *Tor.com*. Macmillan, 10 July 2015. Web. 16 Jan. 2016.

Billings, Lee. Rev. of *Aurora*, by Kim Stanley Robinson. *Scientific American*. Nature Amer., 1 July 2015. Web. 16 Jan. 2016.

Cheuse, Alan. "*Aurora* Journeys in a New Direction." Rev. of *Aurora*, by Kim Stanley Robinson. *NPR*. NPR, 7 July 2015. Web. 16 Jan. 2016.

Doctorow, Cory. "Kim Stanley Robinson's *Aurora*: Space Is Bigger Than You Think." Rev. of *Aurora*, by Kim Stanley Robinson. *Boing Boing*. Happy Mutants, 2 Nov. 2015. Web. 22 Feb. 2016.

James, Thea. Rev. of *Aurora*, by Kim Stanley Robinson. *The Book Smugglers*. Book Smugglers, July 2015. Web. 22 Feb. 2016.

Roberts, Adam. "*Aurora* by Kim Stanley Robinson Review: 'The Best Generation Starship Novel I Have Ever Read.'" *Guardian*. Guardian News and Media, 8 July 2015. Web. 16 Jan. 2016.

Avenue of Mysteries

Author: John Irving (b. 1942)
Publisher: Simon & Schuster (New York). 480 pp.
Type of work: Novel
Time: 1970–2011
Locales: Oaxaca, Mexico; Hong Kong, China; Manila, the Philippines; New York, New York; Iowa City, Iowa; Lithuania

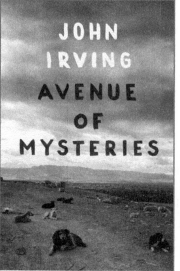

(Courtesy of Simon & Schuster)

John Irving returns to form with Avenue of Mysteries, *a complex, multifaceted novel about a Mexican American writer who, after falling into a drug-induced dream state during a trip to the Philippines, accesses his most beloved childhood memories in 1970s Mexico.*

Principal characters:

JUAN DIEGO GUERRERO, a retired middle-aged teacher and famous Mexican American novelist
LUPE, his sister, a mind reader and clairvoyant
EDWARD BONSHAW, his stepfather, an American missionary
FLOR, his "stepmother" and Edward's husband, a cross-dressing Mexican prostitute
RIVERA/EL JEFE, his caretaker, a Mexican dump boss
CLARK FRENCH, one of his former students, an American novelist
MIRIAM, a fan of his work
DOROTHY, Miriam's daughter, also a fan of his work
BROTHER PEPE, a Jesuit priest
THE GOOD GRINGO, an American hippie and draft dodger

In *Avenue of Mysteries*, John Irving's fourteenth novel, a famous fifty-four-year-old Mexican American novelist named Juan Diego Guerrero finds himself in the middle of a dilemma: he has frighteningly high blood pressure and has to take beta-blockers, in the form of Lopressor tablets, to keep his heart rate in check. The beta-blockers not only make him tired but also inhibit his dreams and memories. Such medical inconveniences are to be expected in middle age, but for Juan Diego, a man who lives inside his own head, they are, to say the least, diminishing. "The past was where he lived most confidently," Irving's omniscient narrator notes, "and with the surest sense of knowing who he was—not only a novelist."

Though Juan Diego has lived in the United States for the past forty years, he derives his strongest sense of identity from his upbringing in Oaxaca, Mexico. He ruminates endlessly on childhood memories both joyous and tragic and misses being

woken up by the "gentlest" of recurring
nightmares—one recounting the time he acquired his lifelong limp after a truck ran over
his right foot. When *Avenue of Mysteries*
opens, it is December 2010, and Juan Diego
has recently retired from his job as a writing
teacher. He is journeying to the Philippines
to fulfill a childhood promise and to reconnect with one of his former pupils, an "un-
stintingly earnest" American novelist named
Clark French. During a stopover in New
York City, his plane is delayed by a snow-
storm; as a consequence, he is accosted by
two women, Miriam and her daughter Dorothy, who are devoted fans of his work. While
getting to know his new travel companions,
Juan Diego forgets to take his beta-blockers,
triggering a bout of deep, lucid dreams.

*John Irving has authored fourteen nov-
els, five of which have been adapted into
feature-length films. He has been nominated for a National Book Award on
three occasions, winning in 1980 for his
best-selling novel* The World according
to Garp *(1978).*

At the beginning of *Avenue of Mysteries*,
the narrator states that Juan Diego lived two
lives at once, always in his mind, and that he
lived them on "parallel tracks." The novel is
built around this conceit, shifting back and
forth between Juan Diego's present-day trip to the Philippines and his childhood in
Mexico in the early 1970s. But indicative of Irving's style, those two story lines only
provide the framework for a much more complicated plot. From the Philippines, Juan
Diego will travel to a book festival in Lithuania honoring his life and career. Meanwhile, memories of his childhood in Mexico eventually give way to ones chronicling
his adolescence and emergence as a writer and teacher in Iowa. Along the way, readers meet a multitude of characters and encounter familiar Irving subjects such as sex,
death, fate, and religion, as Juan Diego attempts to uncover the "avenue of mysteries"
that has helped shape him into the man he has become.

Juan Diego had humble beginnings. He and his younger sister Lupe grew up as
dump kids in the Oaxaca neighborhood of Guerrero, a colony for families who worked
in the city's trash heap. Their mother, Esperanza, works as a cleaning woman for a
local order of Jesuit priests, but she moonlights as a prostitute. She does not live with
Juan Diego and Lupe and is largely absent from their lives. Instead, Juan Diego and
Lupe live with the dump boss, Rivera, also affectionately referred to as "El jefe."
Rivera is likely not Juan Diego's father and is certainly not Lupe's, but he raises the
children as his own, providing them with food and shelter.

Like other bizarre characters found in Irving's fiction, Juan Diego and Lupe are
not normal children. Though uneducated, Juan Diego has taught himself how to read
in English and Spanish by rescuing discarded books from dump fires. Meanwhile,
Lupe is a mind reader and clairvoyant. A "dark-eyed, feral-looking girl" with a "husky

falsetto," Lupe has a congenital laryngeal web and as a result speaks a language unintelligible to everyone but Juan Diego, who serves as her translator and interpreter. She also shares an unusual kinship with dogs and gets into heated debates about the superior sanctity of her namesake, the Lady of Guadalupe, over the Virgin Mary. Lupe invites comparisons to Owen Meany, the eponymous hero of Irving's best-selling novel *A Prayer for Owen Meany* (1989), who also speaks in a strange voice because of a damaged larynx.

These "miraculous ones," as Lupe refers to herself and Juan Diego, eventually catch the attention of Brother Pepe, a Jesuit priest. An avid bibliophile, Brother Pepe naturally becomes drawn to Juan Diego and further cultivates his thirst for the written word by giving him more books to read. When Rivera accidentally runs over Juan Diego's right foot, permanently displacing it toward a two o'clock position and giving him his aforementioned limp, Brother Pepe persuades Juan Diego and Lupe to live at the Jesuit orphanage in Oaxaca he helps run, Hogar de los Niños Perdidos ("Home of the Lost Children"). There, Juan Diego and Lupe draw sympathy from Edward Bonshaw, an American missionary from Iowa who has recently arrived in Mexico to complete his training as a priest.

Edward, who has a fondness for Hawaiian shirts and self-flagellation, first encounters Juan Diego and Lupe by accident: after picking up Edward at the airport, Brother Pepe takes a wrong turn and ends up in Guerrero. At first sight, Edward likens the dump—with its noxious smells, mountains of trash, feral dogs, and vagabond children—to a "vision of Hades." The scene is indeed hellish, but Irving tempers the dump colony with his usual brand of tragicomedy, bringing to life Juan Diego and Lupe's exploits through colorful, descriptive prose. Those exploits continue at the orphanage, including one involving a nameless American known only as the Good Gringo, a mescal-loving hippie who gets himself into trouble after shortchanging a Mexican prostitute during a drunken blackout.

The Good Gringo, Juan Diego learns, has spent three years on the lam evading the draft for the Vietnam War. He fears that he will meet the same premature fate as his father, who died in the Philippines during World War II. While sobering up at the orphanage, the Good Gringo makes Juan Diego promise him that he will visit the grave of his father, located at the Manila American Cemetery and Memorial, should anything happen to him. Juan Diego agrees, and when the Good Gringo dies under suspicious circumstances, he is bound by his promise.

Forty years later, Juan Diego finds himself fulfilling that promise on a flight to the Philippines by way of Hong Kong. The events that unfold in Juan Diego's present-day story are constantly interrupted by flashbacks, which increase as he experiments with his beta-blockers and other prescriptions, which include the sexual stimulant Viagra. The topic of sex has long been an Irving hallmark, and there is no shortage of it in this novel. During the course of his journey, Juan Diego has sexual encounters with both Miriam and Dorothy, who not only fight over him in the bedroom but also hijack his travel plans. At various points in the novel, however, readers are left to wonder whether Miriam and Dorothy even exist, as Juan Diego starts to lose his grip on reality. The two women appear and reappear seemingly out of nowhere and their likenesses never appear in photographs or mirrored reflections, suggesting they are of supernatural origin.

Competing for face time with Juan Diego is Clark French, his friend and former student. An author of popular but critically lambasted inspirational novels, French lives with his Filipino wife in Manila and has overzealously helped organize Juan Diego's trip to the Philippines. Upon reuniting, Clark, a devout Catholic, argues with Juan Diego over issues such as abortion and gay marriage and, at one point, even suggests Miriam and Dorothy are succubi. Their scenes together and subsequent ones in Juan Diego's present-day narrative, however, fail to carry the same emotional weight as the passages chronicling his past.

As Juan Diego makes his way around the Philippines, more memories from his past unfold. At the suggestion of a doctor, Juan Diego and Lupe leave the orphanage to become circus performers, joining Oaxaca's Circo de La Maravilla. The formerly celibate Edward, meanwhile, abandons the priesthood after falling in love with a cross-dressing Mexican prostitute named Flor. After a series of tragedies, Juan Diego is adopted by Edward and Flor, and the three relocate to Iowa City, Iowa. There, Juan Diego grows up to become a successful novelist and a teacher at the esteemed Iowa Writers' Workshop. During that time Edward and Flor are stricken with and die from AIDS. As the novel zooms back to the present and builds toward its conclusion, Juan Diego reflects on the impact they and others had on him as well as on his own mortality.

Avenue of Mysteries traces its origins to a trip Irving took with his friend, the late photographer Mary Ellen Mark, twenty-five years earlier. They had traveled to India to learn about the lives of child circus performers, and Irving wrote an original screenplay based on the experience. The screenplay was originally intended for Mark's husband, director Martin Bell, but after undergoing several incarnations, Irving adapted it into a novel. That novel, *A Son of the Circus* (1994), centers on a Bombay-born doctor, Farrokh Daruwalla, who returns to his birthplace to study circus dwarfs. After the novel's publication, Irving continued working on his original screenplay idea with Bell, eventually shifting the location of the story to Mexico, where Mark had also photographed child circus performers. *Avenue of Mysteries* is dedicated to both Bell and Mark, the latter of whom died in May 2015.

With a history as muddled and meandering as many of its thirty-two chapters, *Avenue of Mysteries* will likely throw readers into a tailspin. Characteristically, Irving crams loads of details onto every page, digressing on everything from women's breasts to green-tea muffins. Because all of those details are interwoven into a narrative where past and present worlds are presented simultaneously, it is often hard to draw the line between fantasy and reality. Most critics, including Tayari Jones for the *New York Times*, regarded the novel as inferior to some of Irving's other works, particularly *The World according to Garp* (1978), *The Cider House Rules* (1985), and *A Prayer for Owen Meany* (1989). Nevertheless, the novel contains many of the themes and elements that have helped shape Irving's reputation as a literary showman and should please his most avid fans.

Chris Cullen

Review Sources

Rev. of *Avenue of Mysteries*, by John Irving. *Kirkus Reviews* 1 Sept. 2015: 257. Print.

Rev. of *Avenue of Mysteries*, by John Irving. *Publishers Weekly* 7 Sept. 2015: 42. Print.

Burling, Alexis. Rev. of *Avenue of Mysteries*, by John Irving. *San Francisco Chronicle*. Hearst Communications, 5 Nov. 2015. Web. 17 Jan. 2016.

Charles, Ron. "John Irving's 'Avenue of Mysteries': One Writer's Beginnings." *Washington Post*. Washington Post, 28 Oct. 2015. Web. 17 Jan. 2016.

Jones, Tayari. "John Irving's 'Avenue of Mysteries.'" *New York Times Sunday Book Review*. New York Times, 25 Nov. 2015. Web. 3 Feb. 2016.

Magras, Michael. "John Irving's 'Avenue of Mysteries' Explores Familiar Territory." Rev. of *Avenue of Mysteries*, by John Irving. *Chicago Tribune*. Chicago Tribune, 19 Nov. 2015. Web. 17 Jan. 2016.

Barbara the Slut and Other People

Author: Lauren Holmes (b. 1984)
Publisher: Riverhead Books (New York).
272 pp.
Type of work: Short fiction
Time: 2010s
Locale: United States, Mexico

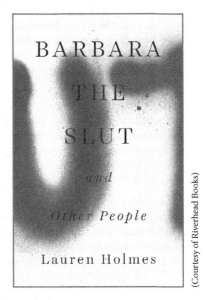

A collection of ten short stories about millennial characters who are struggling with life, sex, and family issues.

(Courtesy of Riverhead Books)

Principal characters:
LALA, a young woman who visits her mother
  to come out as gay
JASON, the only male narrator, who struggles
  with understanding a friendship
BRENDA, a law school graduate looking for
  her place in the world
PEARL, a woman who falls in love with a Swiss graduate student
JANE, a hearing-impaired woman who meets up with a high school crush
PRINCESS, a dog who observes her owners' relationship
BARBARA, a high school senior who has a brother with autism

In an interview with Kevin Nance for the *Chicago Tribune*, Lauren Holmes said that the stories in *Barbara the Slut and Other People* are intended to address gender equality and sexual politics. In this collection of stories about millennials who are exploring relationships and searching for a place to belong, she covers the differences between the ways men and women approach sexual relationships and the contrasts between gay and straight couples with a humorous touch. Ultimately, the way Holmes speaks to these issues is by making *Barbara the Slut* a book about sex. The result has garnered positive attention from numerous venues. It was named to *Village Voice*'s list of the "fifteen books you need to read in 2015" and was called a best book of the year by *Publishers Weekly*.

Overall response to the book has varied. While some reviewers have praised its characters, who often struggle with finding their place in the world, others have criticized them for being shallow and undeveloped. Some of the less likable characters include Brenda in the story "Desert Hearts" and Pearl in "Pearl and the Swiss Guy Fall in Love." Brenda has a law degree and has passed the bar, but she is not sure that she wants to practice law. Since moving in with her boyfriend, she has only applied to two law firms, neither of which has contacted her for an interview. Instead, she takes a retail job in a small store that sells sex toys to lesbians. She enjoys the job, which her boyfriend does not understand and her father deplores, but she is ultimately fired because she is not a lesbian. Brenda is relatable in her struggle with depression as her boyfriend moves on with his career while she purposely puts the brakes on in her own. Though she may not be a particularly sympathetic character for some readers, she is one of the more developed. Pearl is a teacher who is looking for love; she meets a Swiss graduate student on the Internet, and they begin a casual relationship. His strange compulsion about germs and his fear of her dog are only two of the issues that highlight the dysfunction in this relationship.

One of the most sympathetic characters in the collection is Lala from the first story, "How Am I Supposed to Talk to You." Lala's vacation to Mexico has a secondary purpose: she is planning to come out to her mother as a lesbian. Lala's mother does not know how to respond to her daughter, so the two part, both feeling unfulfilled. Though there are glimpses of brilliance in some of the descriptions in this piece, Lala comes off in the end as too lazy to actually stay

(Beowulf Sheehan)

Lauren Holmes has a bachelor's degree from Wellesley College and a master of fine arts degree from Hunter College. Barbara the Slut and Other People *is her first published book.*

and pursue a real relationship with her mother and too selfish to try to see how her mother may be doing her best to reestablish a relationship with her.

Some reviews have suggested that the characters in this collection are basically all the same. Most of the narrators and central characters are female, ranging from high school age to late twenties. Many of them are shallow and selfish, thinking only of their own desires and not considering the ways their actions may affect those around them. One notable exception is the titular Barbara, who cares deeply about her brother with autism.

All of the stories in this collection are concerned with sex in one way or another. Lala struggles with telling her mother that she is gay because of her fear of rejection. After this introductory piece, however, the stories revolve around sex. The second piece, "Weekend with Beth, Kelly, Muscle and Pammy," is the only story narrated by a man, and thus the only one that offers a glimpse of sex from a male perspective. It might be surprising to some readers that Jason's descriptions are not the most graphic. Jason's desire to have sex only with someone he actually cares for romantically is refreshing. He is in almost direct contrast with Natalie, the college student in "I Will Crawl to Raleigh If I Have To" who whines about spending a year with a boy whose biggest fault is that he has been too caring and attentive. He also contrasts with Barbara in the title story, whose junior year of high school is spent having one-night stands with as many boys as she finds desirable.

One question the stories raise is whether the characters take control of their sexuality or just take advantage of it. Some reviewers argue, for example, that Barbara is empowered by her approach to sexual activity. As a high school junior, she decides that she likes sex and becomes sexually active, but rather than letting boys control her, she calls the shots. She picks boys she is attracted to and she has sex with each boy just once. By her senior year, however, her priorities have shifted, and she focuses more on getting into Princeton than on pursuing boys. When she agrees to have sex with one of the baseball team captains, the other captain starts to pursue her, but an offhand comment about her autistic brother being "retarded" results in her shutting him down. Not surprisingly, the boy retaliates by spreading hateful comments. At this point, any control Barbara has had is lost. She is harassed by both boys and girls, and her joy over getting accepted into Princeton is overshadowed by a physical attack in the library. In an attempt to regain power, Barbara threatens the boy and his friends, but she has already been undermined and lost the control she worked to gain.

In "Pearl and the Swiss Guy Fall in Love," Pearl has very little control. She pursues a sexual relationship with a Swiss graduate student, but when he moves into her apartment for a short time, at her invitation, she realizes that she has lost all control. After he performs sexually in a way that dissatisfies her, she avoids him, but she does not ask him to leave. Her lack of action means she has to live with him for several weeks even though he disgusts her and she confuses him. Ultimately, if there is power in their awkward relationship, it is his; he gets a free place to stay while she locks herself in her room.

In "My Humans," Princess the dog tells the sad tale of Jenna and Mike. This couple picks the dog out from a shelter, and then the dog relates the dysfunction of an affair and the couple's breakup. While Princess spends most of her time slavering over disgusting smells, Mike plans to marry Jenna, who is off at college sleeping with her old boyfriend. Jenna may feel as if she has power in that choice, but she ruins her relationship with Mike, who is the better man.

One of the most interesting aspects of the stories is the use of varied first-person narration. The ever-changing personas of the stories keeps the reading fresh. The narrators are gay and straight, male and female, human and canine. Starting with the transition from the fearful lesbian Lala in the first story to the laid-back Jason in the second, Holmes keeps readers guessing what and how the next narrator will reveal. Princess the dog's perspective in "My Humans" has the potential for creative storytelling, but the dog's disgusting focus on smell may detract from the seriousness of the relationships. Jane, the hearing-impaired narrator of "Jerks," provides an insightful look into the way people behave when they do not realize someone is listening. Jane's point of view shows how shallow many people's behavior really is.

While the first-person perspective effectively draws readers into each narrator's experiences, it also limits some of the other characterization. Since readers can only see the story from the narrator's point of view, it is difficult to understand what Brenda's boyfriend or Jason's female friends, for example, are thinking or feeling. In particular, Jason's friend Beth has potential to be the source of more humor, and it is disappointing that readers cannot truly understand her motivations for being such a crude person.

Another aspect highlighted in several reviews is Holmes's use of humor. While some criticized the humor as too simple and obvious, there is some variation in the jokes. The irony of Barbara's situation when the school turns on her for her sexual exploits could be darkly humorous for more mature readers, while the gross humor of Princess eating a used tampon and salivating over bodily odors could appeal to those looking for something less serious.

Younger readers will likely find the stories in *Barbara the Slut and Other People* to be humorous and refreshing takes on their own experiences. However, the collection may leave older readers feeling unfulfilled and wondering at the maturity and motivations of the millennial characters who populate its pages.

Theresa L. Stowell

Review Sources

Rev. of *Barbara the Slut and Other People*, by Lauren Holmes. *Kirkus Reviews* 1 June 2015: 242. Print.

Rev. of *Barbara the Slut and Other People*, by Lauren Holmes. *Publishers Weekly* 13 Apr. 2015: 1. Print.

Tennant-Moore, Hannah. Rev. of *Barbara the Slut*, by Lauren Holmes. *New York Times*. New York Times, 31 July 2015. Web. 19 Jan. 2016.

Williamson, Eugenia. Rev. of *Barbara the Slut*, by Lauren Holmes. *Boston Globe*. Boston Globe Media Partners, 3 Sept. 2015. Web. 19 Jan. 2016.

Barbarian Days
A Surfing Life

Author: William Finnegan (b. 1952)
Publisher: Penguin Press (New York). 464 pp.
Type of work: Memoir

In Barbarian Days, journalist William Finnegan recalls how surfing has shaped his life. From his formative years in Hawaii in the 1960s and his youthful search for the perfect wave to his journalistic travels and his present home in New York City, the surfing life has beckoned Finnegan from every corner of the globe.

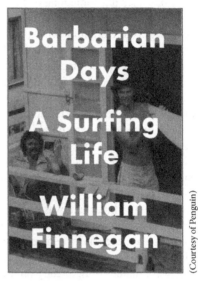

(Courtesy of Penguin)

William Finnegan is a well-regarded journalist, author, and longtime staff writer for the *New Yorker* magazine. He made a name for himself reporting on apartheid in South Africa, wars in Nicaragua and Bosnia, and the bleak underbelly of Southern California, but for years he harbored a terrible secret: he was a surfer. Not merely a person who had learned to surf on vacation in Costa Rica, or even a teenager who grew up during the birth of American surf culture in California and Hawaii and caught a few waves because he saw it in a magazine; Finnegan was, and still is, a hopeless addict. To paraphrase Finnegan, surfing for him is not merely a sport but a way of life.

Finnegan first came clean in 1992, when the *New Yorker* published his now-classic two-part essay "Playing Doc's Games," about San Francisco oncologist and surfing guru Mark "Doc" Renneker. The essay, which is included in *Barbarian Days: A Surfing Life*, chronicles Finnegan's relationship with Doc, a big-wave specialist and true surfing fanatic, as well as his own waning interest in the "path." Doc had arranged his entire life around chasing waves; Finnegan, then in his mid-thirties, was beginning to look at his life a little differently, questioning his own devotion to the fickle pleasures of surfing. The essay, as Thad Ziolkowski wrote in a review of *Barbarian Days* for the *New York Times*, was one of the first pieces of writing to truly render the sport, both technically and emotionally. Nonsurfers had captured some of the spark, he wrote, but got the "mechanics and ethos laughably wrong." Surfers themselves, when they began writing about the sport in the 1960s, wrote prose that was too "purple" or too steeped in terminology to appeal to a wider audience. "It came to seem that surfing, like some pagan mystery cult, might simply defy literary representation, remaining properly understood only by initiates who were too busy surfing to learn to write," Ziolkowski wrote. Finnegan's essay changed that, and now *Barbarian Days*, Finnegan's roving memoir about his complicated relationship with surfing and his quest for the perfect wave, elevates the discourse he established. By examining his own life through the lens of surfing, Finnegan shows in *Barbarian Days* that surfing is not merely something one does but something one is.

Finnegan grew up in Los Angeles and learned to surf at San Onofre, but *Barbarian Days* begins in Honolulu, where Finnegan's family moved when he was in the eighth grade. It was the early 1960s, and thanks to beach movies such as *Gidget* (1959) and the rise of *Surfer* magazine, surfing was becoming a national cultural movement. Finnegan wanted desperately to be good, and thanks in part to a dearth of friends at his tough new school, he was able to spend hours each day in the water. He cut his teeth at a spot near his house, on the southern tip of the island, called Cliffs. Finnegan writes that the break there was durable but "possessed a moody complexity." Cliffs was a lesson in intimacy that would dog Finnegan throughout his restless youth: it takes a long time to really get to know a wave (to get it "wired"), and some waves—like one in Fiji that Finnegan for years refused to name—suggest a spirit that is altogether unknowable.

For young Finnegan it was just as important to study other surfers as it was to study the quirks of the waves themselves. Perhaps it was the time or perhaps it was the place, but Finnegan, even as a young novice, stumbled upon a world that is small and exclusive. Many of the boys he met—he is careful to point out that all of the surfers at that time were male—were already on their way to surfing stardom in some capacity, but then again, surfing was not considered a sport, per se. Surfing was a secret club with its own celebrities, rituals, hierarchies, shorthand, and philosophy; relatively few people knew how to do it, and even fewer knew how to do it well enough to be called a surfer. Finnegan's early passion for surfing earned him entrée into this world, as well as his first true friends on the island: three brothers, one of whom was Glenn Kaulukukui, a local legend. Kaulukukui was Finnegan's first real hero on the board, and arguably the first to make him realize that he did not have the makings of a world-champion surfer himself. Kaulukukui was a true artist, Finnegan writes. He "moved with unusual elegance," and he embodied a particular variety of the surfer's ambivalence in the face of danger. "There was something else—call it wit, or irony—that accompanied his physical confidence and beauty, something bittersweet that allowed him, in all but the most demanding situations, to seem like he was both performing intently and, at the same time, laughing quietly at himself."

Still in Hawaii, Finnegan coveted a spot in the local surf club and entered his first surfing competition (he placed second), but this was the end of his career as a competitive surfer. As a twentysomething, dazzled by wanderers such as Jack Kerouac, Finnegan, board in tow, began a bohemian quest for the perfect wave. He had already skipped his high school graduation to trek across the continental United States and much of Europe and, in true Kerouacian fashion, had worked as a brakeman on the railroad. But these things were not enough, because they did not embody a higher purpose. He yearned for what he calls "back-to-nature" surfing: "The newly emerging ideal was solitude, purity, perfect waves far from civilization. Robinson Crusoe, *Endless Summer*. This was a track that led away from citizenship, in the ancient sense of the word, toward a scratched-out frontier where we would live as latter-day barbarians."

William Finnegan has been a staff writer at the New Yorker since 1987. His previous books include Crossing the Line: A Year in the Land of Apartheid *(1986) and* Cold New World: Growing Up in a Harder Country *(1998).*

Finnegan and his friend Bryan Di Salvatore, who would also go on to become a writer for the *New Yorker*, set off for the South Pacific, though their years-long journey ended up taking them all the way around the globe. Di Salvatore, like Finnegan, was a surfer and a writer, looking for direction in both disciplines. As portrayed by Finnegan, the two young men share literary enthusiasms and pretentions and attempt to embody the specific swaggering, macho ideal of a male writer. They learn the local drinking rituals in Guam. They hoof it across Australia in a beat-up car with a broken window, wrapping shirts around their noses and mouths to keep out the dust from the road, measuring the journey in "tinnies" (cans of beer). Finnegan develops a near-fatal case of malaria in Indonesia; then, while Bryan packs it in and heads home, Finnegan travels to apartheid-era South Africa, where he becomes a teacher at a black high school.

Amid the surfing, it is satisfying to watch Finnegan wrestle his youthful identity. For every pristine wave, there is a little letdown—domestic spats with Bryan, acute loneliness, the woes of hard-core traveling—that takes Finnegan down a peg and, simultaneously, brings him closer to the more mature, empathetic character he inhabits as an adult. The trip is often a slog, but there are moments of real transcendence. In Fiji, Finnegan and Di Salvatore persuade local fishermen to drop them on an uninhabited island called Tavarua, the site of the wave-that-shall-not-be-named. One particular ride on the wave, Finnegan writes, appeared to defy the laws of nature. "It felt like a runaway train, an eruption of magical realism, with that ocean-bottom light and the lacy white canopy. I ran with it."

Barbarian Days is not merely a coming-of-age story, though Finnegan's formative years take up most of the book's nearly five hundred pages. The book follows him into adulthood to Ocean Beach in chilly San Francisco, and then to the present day, catching waves off even-chillier New York City and Long Island. After he settles down, years and years after his trip with Di Salvatore, he comes across a photo in a magazine: an ad for a resort on Tavarua. Today, people can pay to surf there, both on Finnegan's magical realist break and another, farther out, called Cloudbreak. It is a poignant turn of events, a nod to Finnegan's early attitudes about nature as well as the pervasive nostalgia shared by a lot of surfers. Finnegan himself writes that, as a teenager, he had a "dystopian view" of the crowded beaches of Southern California, even as they were in their heyday. The "outing" of Tavarua was a real-time demonstration of the surfer's ideal-turned-dystopia: the lost paradise. Surprisingly, Finnegan pays the outrageous fee to return to Tavarua, and he has a grand time surfing it again (and again). But by this time, readers understand that while surfing has shaped Finnegan's identity, it has not become his entire identity. He is not above paying resort fees; nor, as he learns for himself in San Francisco, is he any longer above a crowded break. Finnegan is a pragmatist. He hates flowery comparisons between riding a wave and making love, because a wave, unlike a lover, is a natural killer with whom one shares only a moment. In other words, it is not an equal partnership.

Finnegan is also a technician. *Barbarian Days* overflows with surfing lingo and descriptions of geography, trade winds, and swells—"all surfers are oceanographers," he writes. His understanding of waves is more mathematical than mystical, which makes his more personal musings about the sport all the more affecting. "With me it's not a matter of packing up or staying on," he writes, "but rather of being always half poised to flee my desk . . . to throw myself into some nearby patch of ocean. . . . That cracking, fugitive patch is where I come from."

Molly Hagan

Review Sources

Bradley, Ryan. "William Finnegan Surfs the Meaning of His *Barbarian Days*." Rev. of *Barbarian Days: A Surfing Life*, by William Finnegan. *Los Angeles Times*. Tribune, 16 July 2015. Web. 22 Jan. 2016.

Dyer, Geoff. "One Hell of a Ride . . ." Rev. of *Barbarian Days: A Surfing Life*, by William Finnegan. *Guardian*. Guardian News and Media, 19 Aug. 2015. Web. 22 Jan. 2016.

Gregory, Alice. "The Riders of the Waves." Rev. of *Barbarian Days: A Surfing Life*, by William Finnegan. *New York Review of Books*. NYREV, 13 Aug. 2015. Web. 22 Jan. 2016.

Taylor, Kimball. "Along for the Ride." Rev. of *Barbarian Days: A Surfing Life*, by William Finnegan. *Surfer*. Enthusiast Network, 27 July 2015. Web. 22 Jan. 2016.

Ziolkowski, Thad. Rev. of *Barbarian Days: A Surfing Life*, by William Finnegan. *New York Times*. New York Times, 13 July 2015. Web. 22 Jan. 2016.

The Beauty

Author: Jane Hirshfield (b. 1953)
Publisher: Alfred A. Knopf (New York).
128 pp.
Type of work: Lyric poetry
Time: 1950s–2010s

(Courtesy of Alfred A. Knopf)

The Beauty is the latest collection of verse by acclaimed poet Jane Hirshfield. It deals in simple, accessible, but often very subtle phrasing and forms and addresses a wide variety of topics, showing the poet's familiarity with both everyday life and scientific facts.

Jane Hirshfield has long been an esteemed and popular poet, and it is easy to see why. Her works are accessible but not shallow, and her poems are easy to read but not always immediately easy to comprehend, thus provoking thought and rewarding multiple close readings. Although her poems usually deal with issues to which most readers can relate, they rarely do so in predictable ways. They are spare and well crafted, yet sometimes the sources of their effectiveness are so subtle that they are difficult to discuss. The mere fact that Hirshfield's latest volume is titled *The Beauty* is significant: many contemporary poets would not have wanted to risk a title so obviously traditional and potentially sentimental. The fact that Hirshfield is interested in beauty (and is actually capable of creating it, again and again) puts her a bit at odds with the kinds of poets who often seem more interested in mystifying and challenging their readers than in genuinely gratifying or communicating with them.

Hirshfield's poems are often short; some of the texts in this collection run less than twenty words. Their diction, moreover, tends to be simple and plain; most of the words are quite familiar from everyday use, and many of them are only a syllable or two in length. In appearance, tone, effect, and effectiveness, Hirshfield's poems often resemble those of William Carlos Williams. It would not be hard to imagine her writing about seemingly mundane topics, such as a white chicken beside a red wheelbarrow or eating some refrigerated plums, as Williams did.

This is not to imply that she is imitative, except to the extent that all the best poets imitate. Hirshfield has her distinctive interests, tones, and phrasing. One notices, for instance, a recurring tendency to allude to scientific facts in the midst of otherwise straightforward, lyrical ruminations. Another common theme is the poet's concern with the nature of the mind and of perception. Consider, for example, these lines from the brief lyric "My Task":

An idea appears.
It catches
against the edge of the bedside table.

Coffee on the wall.
Coffee on the marble tabletop.
Coffee on the sheets.

. . . .

Aplysia, marine snail of memory,
someone may someday find in your 20,000 neurons
this thought I have lost.

What makes this poem so effective? Note the abrupt opening line, which appears and ends as quickly as the idea it describes. No sooner is the idea there than it is interrupted—"it catches"—before it can be described in anything but the broadest, most general terms. The idea occurs to the speaker and is then lost never becomes precisely apparent to the reader. It is, in that sense, even more lost to the reader than to the speaker. Only one syllable is heavily accented in the poem's second line, the first syllable of the crucial verb. A mess occurs in an instant, and the poet mimics the brevity of the event in the brevity of the line. Likewise, she imitates the forcefulness of the event in the forcefulness of the isolated accented syllable. The third line—longer than the first two put together—then completes the simple narrative with which the poem opens.

In the shift from stanza one to stanza two, Hirschfield also creates a shift from the event to its consequences: coffee is literally everywhere, and again the speaker mimics, through the effects of sight and sound, the point she might otherwise have merely stated. The word "coffee" is used three times, each time at the beginning of a line, as if to emphasize the dark liquid's omnipresence. The fact that coffee begins with an accented syllable gives that word, and its triple initial placement, all the more force.

Jane Hirshfield is a prize-winning poet and the author of seven previous books of poetry. Her 2006 collection, After, was shortlisted for the T. S. Eliot Prize for Poetry, and her 2001 collection, Given Sugar, Given Salt, was a finalist for the National Book Critics Award.

Part of the effectiveness of this poem derives from the absolute familiarity of the event it describes. It is hard to imagine a reader who has not had a similar experience of spilling a beverage and making a mess. Yet no sooner is the reader "relating" to the speaker's plight than the speaker once more surprises. What, after all, is an "Aplysia"? The speaker immediately explains, but it is hard to know at first whether she is being strangely metaphorical or characteristically accurate. *Aplysia* is a genus of sea slugs, also known as sea hares. The fact that these animals possess only twenty thousand neurons makes them a favorite subject of study for neuroscientists seeking to understand how brains work.

This poem, then, is in some ways typical of Hirshfield's writing: the allusion is confusing at first but then, on further reading, seems absolutely appropriate, though oddly unfamiliar (at least to those less scientifically literate than Hirshfield). And further investigation makes the allusion even more appropriate: sea hares, in turns out, are known for releasing large clouds of ink and so are perfect symbols in a poem that is partly about the process of writing—of spilling ink, not just coffee.

"My Task" is in some ways a perfectly typical Hirshfield poem. The diction is simple and clear, although the allusion to the marine snail will catch most readers off guard, while also subtly implying the speaker's learning and intelligence. But the learning is not heavy-handed or overdone, and the intelligence is not unduly emphasized. The speaker is less interested in calling attention to herself than in faithfully reporting what happened and how she reacted. She uses words and syntax that almost anyone can understand. And if she sends readers briefly to the Internet or a dictionary, she thereby enhances their own knowledge rather than simply parading her own. All in all, this is a delicate, witty, ironically memorable performance—a poem about a lost idea that paradoxically sticks in the reader's mind.

Even more impressive, in some ways, is "My Skeleton," the poem with which the main section of *The Beauty* opens. Unfortunately, this printing of the poem seems to contain a serious typographical error. The version printed here opens as follows:

> My skeleton,
> who once ached
> with your own growing larger,
>
> are now,
> each year
> imperceptibly smaller,
> lighter,
> absorbed by your own
> concentration.

At first, these lines seem grammatically confused or incomplete, and a quick check of previous printings suggests that in fact a crucial word is missing. Previously published versions of this poem include the word "you" at the beginning of the second line—"you who once ached"—and when that word is inserted, the opening lines make perfect sense. It is possible, of course, that Hirshfield deliberately revised the poem, but the ambiguity created by the omission of "you" is so severe and pointless, and so unlike her writing in general, that a typo seems the most likely explanation. This is unfortunate, especially since, aside from an introductory lyric, this poem is the first thing one encounters in this superbly written book.

"My Skeleton" is a splendid meditation on such themes as aging, mutability, approaching death, and the interpenetration of the physical and the spiritual—topics that appear elsewhere, in different forms, throughout *The Beauty*. At one point in this poem, for instance, the speaker imagines the coming day when she will be dead and disassembled:

> Angular wristbone's arthritis,
> cracked harp of ribcage,
> blunt of heel,
> opened bowl of the skull,
> twin platters of pelvis—
> each of you will leave me behind,
> at last serene.

Here, as so often in Hirshfield's writing, the effectiveness of the sounds is notable. In every one but the last of the lines in this stanza, Hirshfield begins with a strongly accented syllable. Each line is forceful by itself, partly because of its brevity, and the accumulation of one forceful line after the other, in an ever-expanding catalog of body parts, gives the stanza an extremely powerful, almost chant-like rhythm. It somehow sounds like an Old English incantation, especially because of the poet's spare diction and the heavy stress on similar sounds, not to mention the fact that most of the words (many monosyllabic) are quite literally Anglo-Saxon in origin.

One notices, too, the wit of the phrasing here, especially in the metaphors—the "cracked harp," the "opened bowl," and especially the wonderfully alliterative "twin platters of pelvis." The speaker contemplates her eventual bodily dissolution bluntly and frankly, but also with great good humor. The sudden shift to simple iambic rhythm in the final brief line is wonderfully effective, partly because it contrasts so strongly with the preceding rhythms and thus signals a clear end to the ever-expanding list. But even that final line of the stanza, so apparently simple and lucid, raises intriguing questions: who (or what) will be "at last serene"? Will it be the speaker's soul, the speaker's skeleton, or somehow both?

In poem after poem in this collection, Hirshfield uses phrasing that seems quite simple on first reading but then blossoms out, adding one subtlety after another, the more closely one examines it. Unlike much other contemporary poetry, Hirshfield's work does not seem so immediately odd, forbidding, or bizarre that one feels little interest in trying to read it more than once (if even once). Instead, it is so immediately inviting that one reads it with pleasure again and again, each time noticing some detail previously overlooked. In this respect it reminds one of the work of such otherwise radically different poets as George Herbert or Philip Larkin, poets who also wrote plainly, but never without suggestiveness or substance. That is the kind of poet Jane Hirshfield is: one whose works, like theirs, are likely to last.

The Beauty, Hirshfield's eighth collection of poetry, was well received by critics, who praised the volume's sparse and simple language and the depth of its observations. In a review for *Shelf Awareness*, Jeanette Zwart wrote that the collection "reveals a poet at the height of her powers. . . . While many of these poems are brief, they are masterpieces in miniature." Zwart also praised the collection for rewarding contemplation and drawing out readers' individual reactions and interpretations. *The Beauty* was long-listed for the 2015 National Book Award.

Robert C. Evans, PhD

Review Sources

Rev. of *The Beauty*, by Jane Hirshfield. *Publishers Weekly*. PWxyz, 19 Jan. 2015. Web. 22 Dec. 2015.

Bonazzi, Robert. Rev. of *The Beauty*, by Jane Hirshfield. *World Literature Today*. U of Oklahoma, May 2015. Web. 22 Dec. 2015.

Hughes, Henry. Rev. of *The Beauty*, by Jane Hirshfield. *Harvard Review Online*. Houghton Lib. at Harvard U, 1 Dec. 2015. Web. 22 Dec. 2015.

McMichael, Julia. Rev. of *The Beauty*, by Jane Hirshfield. *San Francisco Book Review*. San Francisco Book Rev., 24 July 2015. Web. 22 Dec. 2015.

Rigsbee, David. Rev. of *The Beauty*, by Jane Hirshfield. *Cortland Review*. Courtland Rev., Spring 2015. Web. 22 Dec. 2015.

Beauty Is a Wound

Author: Eka Kurniawan (b. 1975)
First published: *Cantik Itu Luka,* 2002, in Indonesia
Translated from the Indonesian by: Annie Tucker
Publisher: New Directions (New York). 384 pp.
Type of work: Novel
Time: 1942–99
Locale: the fictional town of Halimunda, Indonesia, and environs

(Courtesy of New Directions)

Beauty Is a *Wound is a sprawling novel that explores Indonesian society, culture, traditions, customs, and beliefs through the exploits and relationships of several generations. One family endures the turbulence of the country's social and political upheavals during the twentieth century, through Dutch colonization, Japanese occupation, and independence.*

Principal characters:
DEWI AYU, the illegitimate daughter of a Dutch colonial plantation owner and a housemaid
ALAMANDA, her first daughter
ADINDA, her second daughter
MAYA, her third daughter
BEAUTY, her fourth daughter, who, unlike her sisters, is ugly
MAMA KALONG, a wealthy, middle-aged former prostitute who runs a brothel

Beauty Is a Wound is laid out in similar fashion to a rijsttafel—a Dutch colonial smorgasbord-like feast featuring dozens of examples of Indonesian cuisine—with something for any taste, for every appetite. There is salty language. There is sweet, tender romance. There are relationships that become bitter or turn sour. There is hot, unrequited lust. There is the spine-tingling chill of the supernatural.

The novel opens with a startling scene: Dewi Ayu, who died at the age of fifty-two and has been dead for twenty-one years, climbs out of her grave. Despite being a member of the walking dead, Dewi Ayu has retained her good looks, having chosen her time to die rather than let death overcome her. Though her skin, pale due to her half-European heritage, is wrinkled, her hair is still long and black, and she still retains traces of the legendary beauty that made her the city's favorite prostitute for more than thirty years. Dewi Ayu has resurrected herself to check on the condition of her extended family, and the supernatural incident launches a family saga set against the volatile backdrop of twentieth-century Indonesia.

At the center of the story is Dewi Ayu. In 1942, when she is the sixteen-year-old, well-educated, illegitimate daughter of a Dutch colonial cocoa grower named Stammler, the Japanese invade and occupy Indonesia. While the rest of the Stammler family flee, Dewi Ayu remains to protect the family estate, where a fortune in jewels has been buried. She and other Europeans are rounded up and placed in a prison camp. Though some captives succumb to starvation and disease, strong-willed Dewi Ayu survives by eating leeches, mice, lizards, and small crocodiles, and she helps other prisoners organize work groups, ration foods, and obtain medication.

After two years, the Japanese select twenty of the healthiest and prettiest female prisoners, including Dewi Ayu, and transport them to Mama Kalong's brothel, where they are to service Japanese soldiers. Dewi Ayu becomes pregnant by one of the soldiers and subsequently gives birth to a beautiful daughter, Alamanda. After the Japanese are driven out in 1945, the Dutch return with British allies to reassume control in Indonesia, spurring a national revolution for independence. While most of the other girls leave, Dewi Ayu remains at Mama Kalong's. During the uprising, Dewi Ayu is raped at the brothel by a guerrilla raider, becomes pregnant again, and ultimately gives birth to another beautiful girl, Adinda.

Dewi Ayu makes a bargain with Mama Kalong: she borrows money to buy back her family home, which was appropriated during the occupation and has been since acquired by someone else. Dewi Ayu hopes to find the hidden treasure and become independent again. However, the treasure has disappeared, so Dewi Ayu must stay at the brothel and work as a prostitute to repay her debt. She gives birth to a third beautiful daughter, Maya. Because of her beauty and skill, Dewi Ayu is the most popular prostitute in Halimunda, able to command high rates while servicing just a single customer per night before returning to her home and children. Late in life, she marries recluse Ma Gedik and, at age fifty-two, gives birth to a final daughter, named Beauty. Soon afterward, Dewi Ayu dies, never having seen her last child, who was born hideous.

Following the establishment of Dewi Ayu as a matriarchal figure, the focus of *Beauty Is a Wound* shifts to her children and the relationships they form. Her first three daughters marry men who represent the shifting forces that are shaping Indonesia's future. Alamanda marries the brutal guerrilla leader Shodancho, Maya marries a gangster named Maman Gendeng, and Adinda marries Comrade Kliwon, a communist and the leader of a fishermen's trade union who was previously in love with Alamanda. After Shodancho rapes and impregnates Alamanda, Kliwon places a curse on the unborn child, and Alamanda miscarries. Shodancho begins a campaign against communists in revenge for Comrade Kliwon's perceived curse on his prospective child and wipes out the whole Indonesian Communist Party—an incident that gives rise to a related subplot, that of gravedigger Kamino, who has to dig a mass grave for more than 1,200 dead communists. Shodancho captures Kliwon and schedules his execution, but Alamanda pleads for Kliwon's life, and Shodancho relents and releases him. Kliwon, spared from the fate of his comrades, drifts from job to job. Reacting to the Halimunda government's sale of coastal lands to developers, which prevents his fishermen friends from thriving, he reverts to his Comrade Kliwon persona. After organizing demonstrations and giving speeches, Kliwon is arrested, interned, and tortured for a time before being released.

Beauty Is a Wound concludes with a strange chain of tragic and unearthly events linking several secondary characters. Ultimately, Dewi Ayu learns that her entire life and the lives of her descendants and anyone connected to them have been plagued by an echo-voiced evil spirit seeking revenge for wrongs committed long before. It is because of the evil spirit's curse—to destroy her family's love and happiness—that Dewi Ayu cursed her own daughter Beauty, to make her so ugly that she could never marry and be happy. However, Beauty in her turn becomes pregnant, proving that someone is capable of loving her. For that reason, Dewi Ayu purposely chooses to die, so she can return from the dead, since only in nonhuman form is she able to stab the evil spirit to death.

Beauty Is a Wound was Eka Kurniawan's debut novel, first published more than a dozen years before it was translated into English. It is steeped in Indonesian myth and folklore, which is rife with ghosts, spirits, curses, revenge, magic, and other supernatural motifs. The history of the nation—a long-inhabited archipelago of more than seventeen thousand islands that, prior to independence, witnessed early Hindu and Buddhist civilizations, kingdoms, Islamic sultanates, and periods of colonization by the Portuguese, French, British, and Dutch—is an important element in the telling of the sweeping epic, which often shifts backward and forward in chronology.

The novel's sprawling history and elements of magical realism have drawn numerous comparisons to the celebrated Colombian writer Gabriel García Márquez, particularly his epic novel *One Hundred Years of Solitude* (1967). Other reviewers have noted similarities between the novel's fictional setting of Halimunda, with its dizzying array of interconnected characters, and the fictional Yoknapatawpha County, the setting of the vast majority of William Faulkner's novels, including *The Sound and the Fury* (1929), *As I Lay Dying* (1930), and *Absalom, Absalom!* (1936). However, translator Annie Tucker, writing for PEN America, listed several distinctly Indonesian influences on Kurniawan's writing, including wayang puppet theater, local folk tales, and popular Indonesian horror and martial arts genre fiction, noting that these influences make Kurniawan's novel fresh and exciting for Western readers. Other critics have commented on the underrepresentation of Southeast Asian fiction in general and Indonesian fiction in particular in the West, and many have hailed *Beauty Is a Wound* as a significant contribution to world literature.

*Journalist Eka Kurniawan has written numerous short stories, film scripts, and essays, as well as and a graphic novel. Cantik Itu Luka (*Beauty Is a Wound, *2002) was his debut novel, following the publication of his short-story collection Corat-coret di Toilet (*Graffiti in the toilet, *2000). His second novel, Lelaki Harimau (*Man Tiger*), was published in Indonesia in 2004. Both novels were translated into English in 2015.*

Critics have widely praised the novel's ambitious premise, with many reviewers noting that despite its frequent plot twists and wide range of characters, the storyline remains coherent and unified. Critic Sarah Lyall, in a review for the *New York Times*, remarked that "the winding roads the characters' lives take are too complicated to explain fully. But the book never spirals out of control, and Mr. Kurniawan does a masterly job of pulling together all the seemingly flyaway strands." Many readers may be uncomfortable with the novel's frequent scatological references or disturbed by its brutal descriptions of rape and murder. "There is much physical and sexual violence," wrote one reviewer for *Publishers Weekly*, "but none of it feels gratuitous—every detail seems essential to depicting Indonesia's tragic past. Upon finishing the book, the reader will have the sense of encountering not just the history or Indonesia but its soul and spirit."

Kurniawan's follow-up novel, *Man Tiger*, which was published in Indonesia in 2004 and translated into English in 2015, demonstrates his maturity as a writer. Employing many of the same motifs and techniques as in his first novel, *Man Tiger* likewise unfolds like a folktale and similarly links tragic events between two families connected over generations. However, the narrative is presented in a more straightforward, linear fashion, allowing the writer to tell his tale in less than half the length of his first novel. Though Kurniawan's second work, like the first, contains a strong supernatural element (hinted at in the title), most of the characters—two of whom appear briefly in *Beauty*—are portrayed as ordinary human beings. As a result, the story has fewer elements of magical realism and may be more satisfying for some readers.

Jack Ewing

Review Sources

Rev. of *Beauty Is a Wound*, by Eka Kurniawan. *Publishers Weekly*. PWxyz, Sept. 2015. Web. 14 Jan. 2016.

Deb, Siddhartha. "Where the Dead Refuse to Vanish." Rev. of *Beauty Is a Wound*, by Eka Kurniawan. *New Republic*. New Republic, 2 Sept. 2015. Web. 14 Jan. 2016.

Domestico, Anthony. Rev. of *Beauty Is a Wound*, by Eka Kurniawan. *SFGate*. Hearst Communications, 11 Sept. 2015. Web. 14 Jan. 2016.

Fasman, Jon. Rev. of *Beauty Is a Wound* and *Man Tiger*, by Eka Kurniawan. *New York Times*. New York Times, 9 Sept. 2015. Web. 14 Jan. 2016.

Lyall, Sarah. "*Beauty Is a Wound*, an Indonesian Blend of History, Myth and Magic." Rev. of *Beauty Is a Wound*, by Eka Kurniawan. *New York Times*. New York Times, 17 Sept. 2015. Web. 14 Jan. 2016.

Twyford-Moore, Sam. "Eka Kurniawan's *Beauty Is a Wound* Inspired by Indonesia's Past." Rev. of *Beauty Is a Wound*, by Eka Kurniawan. *Australian*. Nationwide News, 9 Jan. 2016. Web. 14 Jan. 2016.

Best Boy

Author: Eli Gottlieb (b. 1956)
Publisher: Liveright (New York). 256 pp.
Type of work: Novel
Time: 2011
Locale: Grable, New York and environs

(Courtesy of W.W. Norton & Co.)

Narrated by a middle-aged autistic man,
Best Boy *vividly illustrates many of the difficulties of diagnosing, managing, and treating mental conditions in general and developmental disorders in particular.*

Principal characters:

TODD AARON, a tall, normally placid fifty-four-year-old man with autism who resides at Payton LivingCenter

NATE AARON, his younger brother who lives in New York State with his family

BETH AARON, Nate's wife and the mother of their two preteen sons, Steve and Cam

TOMMY DOON, his new ill-tempered, brain-damaged, roommate who has a shaven head and green eyes

RAYKENE SMITH, a kindly African American woman, Todd's primary counselor at Payton

MIKE HINTON, a shady new staff member at Payton LivingCenter, who sports a mullet and a droopy mustache

MARTINE CALHOUN, a tall, thin young woman with an eye patch, a new resident at Payton

ANNIE APPLIN, the red-haired, freckled psychologist at Payton

SHERROD TWIST, the tall, low-voiced psychiatrist at Payton

Because of the autism that has affected him since early childhood—when the developmental disorder was poorly understood and inconsistently diagnosed and managed—*Best Boy* protagonist Todd Aaron might be presumed to be an unreliable narrator. However, despite somewhat distorted perceptions, a fragile emotional state that causes him to cry when sad or rock when happy, and a tendency to flash back to his childhood during moments of high stress, Todd is usually truthful. He is compulsively honest to the best of his abilities about what he thinks and feels and would rather say nothing than lie. He tries hard to keep a promise to his late beloved mother, Netta, to be a "Best Boy"—to do exactly as told, in hopes of hearing the song of happiness at the center of life that she mentioned. From the time he was eleven until he was thirteen, Todd was shuttled from institution to institution in an effort to achieve the proper balance of psychological help and beneficial environment. Finally, he lands at a facility in an undisclosed location about 745 miles west of the New York town where he grew up.

As the novel opens, Todd has settled in at Payton LivingCenter, where he is called the "village elder," since he has lived there for forty-one years. Following the death of their parents, Todd's younger brother Nate, who tormented Todd when they were children, has become Todd's guardian. Nate lives near the brothers' childhood home, with his wife, Beth, and their two sons. Nate seldom visits but calls often. Todd has wistful aspirations of someday leaving Payton, living alone, and driving a car.

A high-functioning resident, Todd enjoys listening to music and can remember every song he ever heard. He is frightened of animals, typewriters, and cash registers. He hates shaking hands but enjoys hugs. With gentle encouragement from his main counselor, Raykene Smith, he is capable of doing simple tasks on the campus grounds and works part time as a kitchen helper in a local high school cafeteria. In his free time, he secretly researches his condition in encyclopedias and via computer. He lives in a cottage with a nasty-tempered roommate, Tommy Doon. Tommy tries constantly to upset Todd. Todd resists by biting his own hand or practicing other methods, like using tunnel vision, to ignore Tommy's taunts. Todd takes medications every day, including Risperdal—an antipsychotic that quells irritability—to calm him, but the drug makes him almost immobile.

After the setting is established and several major characters are introduced, the plot of *Best Boy* is set into motion with the arrival of new staff member, Mike Hinton, supposedly an Iraq War veteran. Todd is instantly afraid of Mike, because in certain ways he resembles Todd's dead father, who used to cruelly beat his elder son. Todd's instincts prove to be on target. Before long, Mike manipulates Todd into covering for him while the two men are supposed to be tending the lawn, so Mike can ostensibly help pretty, sweet-natured, high-functioning Greta Deane study for her General Education Development (GED) test. Later, Mike brings candy and other treats to Todd and flies a remote-controlled camera-bearing toy drone to spy on Todd and other residents.

A further complication is introduced with the arrival of another high-functioning patient, Martine Calhoun, a tall, eye-patch-wearing young woman who has also been in and out of several different institutions. Todd is assigned to give Martine a tour of the campus—they are trailed and watched by Mike's drone—and the two residents begin to bond. As Martine is processed into Payton, she is dosed with Risperdal. Like

(© Francesco Capponi for Civitella Ranieri)

Eli Gottlieb, a 1999 Fellow of the American Academy in Rome, has written articles for such periodicals as the New York Times, Wall Street Journal, *and* Village Voice. *His first novel,* The Boy Who Went Away *(1997), earned him the 1998 McKitterick Prize. His second novel,* Now You See Him *(2008), was named a book of the year by the* UK Independent.

Todd, she hates the effects of the drug, and she teaches her new friend how to fake swallowing the pills. Todd eventually stops taking the antipsychotic drug for the first time in years and begins experiencing stomach cramps and anxiety. He also hatches a plan to run away from Payton and make his way back home.

Soon afterward, Greta overdoses on pills she had been saving. Because of Greta, Raykene questions Todd, telling him that Mike is not what he appears to be: his application is full of lies. Todd tells Raykene that Mike was with Greta and talks about the camera-equipped drone. Raykene comforts Todd, telling him nothing that happened is his fault. Mike leaves a threatening note for Todd, and the autistic man, frightened, runs away.

Todd slips away from the facility and begins walking along back roads in the direction of his old home. He does not get far before Mike approaches in a truck and again warns him to not talk about Greta. Later, Todd is found and returned to Payton, where he learns Greta has died. During a required session with psychiatrist Sherrod Twist, Todd is warned if he attempts to escape again, there will be serious consequences for him.

Todd and Martine reconnect during a memorial service for Greta, and Martine invites Todd to a dinner outing with her parents. The wealthy elder Calhouns arrive in a limousine, which drives them all to a fancy restaurant. There is considerable friction between Martine and her parents as well as tension between her mother and father, who drink great quantities of liquor and bicker throughout the meal.

Eventually, Nate reluctantly agrees to let his brother come home for an extended visit. On a previous occasion, several years earlier, Nate and his family flew out to see Todd, and it did not go well. While dining at a restaurant, both parents briefly left their small children in Todd's care. Todd, concentrating wholly on his meal, did not notice when the boys slipped out, ran into the street, and were nearly run over, causing a collision. The incident caused harsh recriminations between Nate and his wife, Beth, who had not fully realized the extent of her brother-in-law's disability and initially blamed Todd for the close call.

Now, Todd is entrusted to fly alone on a plane and lands safely without incident. The visit at his brother's unfolds as expected—Beth is especially welcoming, to make up for her unkind, heated remarks in the wake of the earlier family get-together—with a few setbacks. The family dog has to be confined because it scares Todd. The two boys, Steve and Cam, argue, and Todd wonders if the older boy, Steve, has inherited his uncle's disorder.

While in New York, Todd wants to visit his old family home down the street from Nate's house, and a tour is arranged by the current occupants. During the visit, Todd insists on squeezing into a tiny crawl space under the stairs, where he finds a box containing a letter addressed to him by his mother and an envelope full of pictures of Todd and his mother: Todd is smiling in every one of the photos. The fond parting letter from his mother, written while she was dying, reminds her favorite son that though people and things come to an end, love never dies.

Todd returns to Payton and settles into his routine again. He is put back on Risperdal and closely monitored to make sure he regularly takes the drug. Several people come and go, but despite the changes, Todd is happier than he has been in a long time. Though he has trouble remembering recent events and forgets new things, he recalls in vivid detail highlights from his youth and now has a whole wall of photos of himself and his smiling mother together to remind him daily of the best times from the past. Finally, he still has Raykene, another affectionate, constant, motherly figure, who is the living embodiment of unconditional love.

Best Boy is Eli Gottlieb's fourth novel, and like his debut, *The Boy Who Went Away* (1997), it addresses issues associated with autism. Many of the tropes in his earlier work—a mother who gravitates more toward the troubled child, sibling jealousy, the revelation of hidden secrets—are similarly explored in the later novel, this time from the point of view of an impaired individual who has reached adulthood. Todd's sometimes disjointed thoughts and often halting speech are childlike in simplicity, yet layered with meaning and perspicacity that suggest he has unplumbed depths of knowledge and ability. The off-center viewpoint lends fresh insight into the disoriented mental processes of a person who has autism, reinforced with information gleaned from research into the condition, as interpreted through a fictional adult patient. The result is a poignant, touching plea for understanding and humane treatment of people with this severe, widespread, and still greatly misunderstood disorder, which, as the narrator notes, is the "largest childhood epidemic in history."

Jack Ewing

Review Sources

Bauer, Ann. "'Best Boy' Review: An Unforgettable Novel Narrated by an Adult with Autism." Rev. of *Best Boy*, by Eli Gottlieb. *Washington Post*. Washington Post, 19 Aug. 2015. Web. 24 Dec. 2015.

Rev. of *Best Boy*, by Eli Gottlieb. *Kirkus Reviews* 15 June 2015: 1. Print.

Rev. of *Best Boy*, by Eli Gottlieb. *Publishers Weekly* 1 June 2015: 37–38. Print.

Chavez, Donna. Rev. of *Best Boy*, by Eli Gottlieb. *Booklist* July 2015: 29. Print.

Johnston, Bret Anthony. "High Functioning." Rev. of *Best Boy*, by Eli Gottlieb. *New York Times* 30 Aug. 2015: BR15. Print.

Sullivan, Patrick. Rev. of *Best Boy*, by Eli Gottlieb. *Library Journal* 140.9 (2015): 70–71. Print.

Between the World and Me

Author: Ta-Nehisi Coates (b. 1975)
Publisher: Spiegel & Grau (New York). 176 pp.
Type of work: Letters, memoir, history

Inspired by James Baldwin's classic 1963 book The Fire Next Time, *journalist Ta-Nehisi Coates began a letter to his teenage son that became a book-length essay and memoir about his intellectual coming-of-age.*

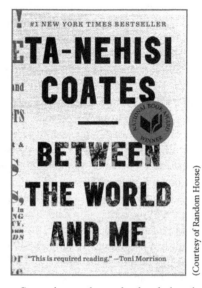

(Courtesy of Random House)

Ta-Nehisi Coates's epistolary memoir, *Between the World and Me*, begins after the nonindictment of Darren Wilson, the white police officer who shot and killed a black teenager named Michael Brown in Ferguson, Missouri, in 2014. Coates's fifteen-year-old son, Samori, to whom the book is addressed, was shocked and angry at the verdict. Coates was cynically resigned. "It was not my expectation that anyone would ever be punished," he writes. "But you were young and still believed." *Between the World and Me* is an argument for the value of black bodies—the tangibility of the word "body" as opposed to the word "life" is a touchstone of Coates's argument—and a chronicle of Coates's intellectual coming-of-age. It is also an extended explanation of why Coates chose not to comfort his son that night. Coates's first book, a memoir called *The Beautiful Struggle* (2009), told of his relationship with his own father, a former Black Panther and intellectual who taught at Howard University. Coates's father required an intellectual rigorousness from his sons, which he sometimes elicited through means of a stinging leather belt. In *Between the World and Me*, Coates wrestles with how to instill the same inquisitiveness in his own son while exploring the question of how to "live free in this black body."

Coates is a national correspondent for the *Atlantic* and one of the most prominent public intellectuals writing today. His essay "The Case for Reparations," a sweeping historical account of structural racism and exploitation in the United States, won the George Polk Award for Commentary in 2014. For that essay, Coates presented his own data and interviews alongside the work of Isabel Wilkerson, the author of the National Book Award–winning history *The Warmth of Other Suns* (2010), and that of a dizzying compendium of other thinkers, including historian Edmund S. Morgan and sociologist St. Clair Drake.

Coates's aforementioned intellectual rigor is his greatest gift to popular discourse. He is an accessible writer and a thorough journalist with an active Twitter following who is also deeply read in African and African American history. He is dissatisfied with examining singular events such as Ferguson in and of themselves, because he understands them as part of a larger history and, in some cases, as with his careful examination of the history of American real estate, as a part of a larger mechanism specifically constructed to oppress black people. In some circles, Coates is a divisive figure—not for his findings, but for what his findings imply. Conservative columnist David Brooks of the *New York Times* accused Coates and his book of distorting American history for his own purposes.

Michelle Alexander, author of the landmark *The New Jim Crow: Mass Incarceration in the Age of Colorblindness* (2010), also expressed some disappointment in the book in her review for the *New York Times*, finding fault not with Coates's history but with his relationship to that history. In her review, she draws attention to a widely quoted passage in which Coates tells his son, "Here is what I would like for you to know: In America, it is traditional to destroy the black body—*it is heritage*." Coates drew inspiration for his book from *The Fire Next Time*, a book of two essays by literary icon and African American intellectual James Baldwin. The book, published in 1963, was addressed to Baldwin's teenage nephew, in whom he tries to instill hope for a brighter future. Baldwin implores his nephew to rise up and be an instrument of change; Alexander argues that Coates, speaking to his son, says the opposite. "Rather than urging his son to awaken to his own power, Coates emphasizes over and over the apparent permanence of racial injustice in America, the foolishness of believing that one person can make a change, and the dangers of believing in the American Dream," she wrote.

Coates studied history at Howard University, a historically black college that Coates refers to in the book with affection and reverence as "The Mecca." Thanks to his father, Coates was already more familiar with African history than many of his peers, but he considers his time at Howard to be his great intellectual awakening. His account of this awakening—which coincides with his sexual awakening—is engaging. In one passage, Coates recalls watching his future wife smoke marijuana: "I was lost and running and wondering what it must be to embrace her, to be exhaled by her, to return to her, and leave her high." Coates's prose style is pleasingly fresh and loose, capable of expressing both youthful exuberance and deep sorrow. It can bring bodies out of the darkness of the past. In another passage, a riff on the origin of Samori's name and his role in the larger struggle for racial justice, he asks Samori to remember that each of his enslaved ancestors was a person with individual thoughts, hopes, and feelings. "Slavery is not an indefinable mass of flesh. It is a particular, specific enslaved woman," he writes,

> whose mind is active as your own, whose range of feeling is as vast as your own; who prefers the way the light falls in one particular spot in the woods, who enjoys fishing where the water eddies in a nearby stream, who loves her mother in her own complicated way, thinks her sister talks too loud, has a favorite cousin, a favorite season, who excels at dressmaking and knows, inside herself, that she is as intelligent and capable as anyone.

At Howard, Coates discovered the work of writers and artists such as prominent Black Arts Movement scholar Larry Neal, journalist George Padmore, poet Sonia Sanchez, and historian Manning Marable. He recalls walking into the library, choosing a handful of books at random, and sitting down to read them, taking copious notes in composition notebook. Coates devoted himself to learning with a religious fervor because he imagined the world's history as one long and unified narrative: when he knew it all, he would have all the answers, and the villains responsible for the unjust world of his youth would be exposed. But he quickly realized that his idols were often at war with one another and that the answers he sought would not come so easily.

At Howard University, Coates disabused himself of romantic ideas about African kings and came to adopt a richer understanding of black history and his own life. He also made many friends, including a man named

(Nina Subin)

Ta-Nehisi Coates is a national correspondent for the Atlantic. *He has received the National Magazine Award for Essays and Criticism, the Hillman Prize for Opinion and Analysis Journalism, and the George Polk Award for Commentary. His memoir,* The Beautiful Struggle, *was published in 2008.*

Prince Jones. Everyone loved Prince Jones; he was successful, charismatic, and a born-again Christian. Despite his atheism, Coates was drawn to Prince. Shortly after graduation, Prince was shot and killed by a police officer. Coates writes powerfully about Prince's murder; his account includes a discourse on injustice, the irrelevance of individual forgiveness, and the soul-as-body, which ignites all the ideas he gleaned from the books he read and connects them to the fearful education he earned growing up in Baltimore. It was an important moment in Coates's growth as a person. He describes feeling oddly distant from the mourners in his own private thoughts. The scene is reminiscent of the Richard Wright poem "Between the World and Me," from which Coates took his title and which serves as the book's epigraph. The poem's narrator is confronted—suddenly, violently—with the ghosts of the past, who tear at his skin and set him on fire. Their skin becomes his skin; their bones become his bones. Wright suggests that the narrator can never be entirely free of his ancestors' pain; the pain will present itself when least expected, just as the narrator stumbles upon the gruesome scene in a "grassy clearing": "And the sooty details of the scene rose, thrusting themselves between the world and me."

Prince Jones is not introduced to the reader until about halfway through Coates's book, but in many ways, he is the book's uniting force, one of the more painful reminders, for Coates, of the ghosts that separate him from the world. At the end of the book, Coates seeks out and interviews Prince's mother. It is as if Coates must grapple with his own relationship with Prince's death to connect himself more fully to his son's shock and hurt over the injustice surrounding the death of Michael Brown. Samori is of a wholly different generation than James Baldwin's nephew or even Coates himself. He is intimately familiar with white America, far more so than Coates was as a teenager. He is also accustomed to seeing black people in positions of power, even, Coates writes, black women on television with their natural hair. But evidence of progress can be deceiving. Samori cried when the Michael Brown's killer walked free. "And that cut me," Coates writes, "because, for all our differing worlds, at your age my feeling was exactly the same. . . . You still believe the injustice was Michael Brown. You have not yet grappled with your own myths and narratives and discovered the plunder everywhere around us."

In 1993, the literary theorist Edward Said gave a Reith Lectures series called Representations of the Intellectual, which were published in book form the following year. In the book's introduction, he defines an intellectual as a person who "tries to speak the truth to power." It is, he writes, "a lonely condition, yes, but it is always a better one than a gregarious tolerance for the way things are." Coates's message, as Alexander says, may not be entirely hopeful, but Samori is likely all too familiar with messages of hope; what he wanted was the truth.

Molly Hagan

Review Sources

Alexander, Michelle. Rev. of *Between the World and Me*, by Ta-Nehisi Coates. *New York Times*. New York Times, 17 Aug. 2015. Web. 16 Nov. 2015.

Hartman, Chris. "*Between the World and Me* Examines Race in America with Sharp Intellect, Gorgeous Prose." Rev. of *Between the World and Me*, by Ta-Nehisi Coates. *CSMonitor.com*. Christian Science Monitor, 13 Aug. 2015. Web. 16 Nov. 2015.

Lee, Adrian. "Ta-Nehisi Coates' Sledgehammer Words on Being Black in America." Rev. of *Between the World and Me*, by Ta-Nehisi Coates. *Maclean's*. Rogers Media, 14 July 2015. Web. 16 Nov. 2015.

McFadden, Syreeta. "An Urgent Wake-Up Call." Rev. of *Between the World and Me*, by Ta-Nehisi Coates. *Guardian*. Guardian News and Media, 14 July 2015. Web. 16 Nov. 2015.

Binary Star

Author: Sarah Gerard (b. 1985)
Publisher: Two Dollar Radio (Columbus, OH). 172 pp.
Type of work: Novel
Time: Present day
Locale: United States

Binary Star, *a short novel told from the perspective of a young woman struggling with eating disorders, is an exploration of codependence and self-destruction.*

Principal characters:
UNNAMED NARRATOR, the protagonist, a young woman
JOHN, her boyfriend, an alcoholic

(Courtesy of Two Dollar Radio)

In the study of astrophysics, a binary star is defined as a star system comprising two stars that are gravitationally bound and orbit a shared center of mass. In her novel *Binary Star* (2015), American author Sarah Gerard uses the analogy of this two-star system to illustrate the dysfunctional relationship between the unnamed narrator, a young woman who struggles with eating disorders, and her alcoholic boyfriend, John. Similar to a binary star, these characters are drawn and tied together by their mutual tendency for self-destruction.

Sarah Gerard has said that her best writing comes from a place that frightens her. It was for this reason that she, as a survivor of anorexia and bulimia, chose to write a story that forced her to revisit and address the physical and psychological suffering that accompanies eating disorders. Originally intending the book to be a personal memoir that expanded on her 2012 *New York Times* essay "From Hunger," Gerard ultimately decided to turn *Binary Star* into a work of fiction so that she would not have to worry about how she treated the characters, both of whom were originally based on real people. Throughout the novel, she uses different astrophysical concepts, laws, and terminology as metaphors for the human body and personal relationships. She focuses particularly on the phenomenon of a dying star, which in its last stages of death projects an increasing amount of colors and light. Gerard poses that, similar to stars, dying bodies and relationships also emanate a kind of doomed beauty.

The narrator of *Binary Star* is an unnamed woman whose identity Gerard reveals piecemeal throughout the novel. It eventually becomes clear that she is a student in her twenties studying astronomy at Adelphi University on Long Island. She has a mentor and occasionally teaches science at a high school where she is an intern. Although the details of her external life are spare, the descriptions of her internal struggle are prolific. She describes herself as a white dwarf, or dying star, with an ever-burning center

of hunger. This is an allusion to her anorexia and bulimia, which have reduced her to
ninety-eight pounds. Perpetually dissatisfied
with her appearance, she continues working
toward her goal weight of eighty-five pounds
through starvation.

Equal to the narrator's longing for a perfect body is her longing to be desired by
her boyfriend John. John, an alcoholic who
lives in Chicago, is erratic and unable to
hold a job or finish a degree. Gerard conveys their connectivity, the oneness of their
shared dysfunction, by drawing distinct
parallels between the two characters. John
self-medicates by mixing Dewar's whiskey
with antipsychotic medication; the narrator
self-medicates with sugar-free Red Bull and
diet pills. He promises to stop consuming
alcohol; she promises to stop purging food.
The substances he abuses put him into a deep
sleep; the substances she abuses keep her up
all night. In addition to describing the similarities of their afflictions, Gerard is effective

(Nina Subin)

*Sarah Gerard is a writer whose short
stories, essays, and criticisms have appeared in* The New York Times, *the*
Paris Review Daily, *the* Los Angeles
Review of Books, Bookforum, Joyland,
Vice, BOMB Magazine, *and other publications.*

in establishing the two characters' congruence through the narrative's literary style.
Gerard omits quotation marks and any written indicators of who is speaking, causing
each line of dialogue to feel connected to lines that precede and follow it. It is often not
clear which character is speaking; however, it does not matter because they are usually
saying the same thing in different words.

As there are three "dredge-ups" or stages in a star's death, Gerard organizes *Binary
Star*'s narrative into three parts. For a star, the first dredge-up occurs late in life, when
the hydrogen fuel at its core has been exhausted and new materials are brought to the
surface for the first time. The chemistry and physics of this event causes the star to turn
red. In the narrator's first dredge-up, she and John have been together for a little over
a year. In an effort to shed their old lives, the two decide to take a road trip together
around the perimeter of the United States. Several nights before she flies out to meet
John and begin their journey, the narrator calls him while high on Adderall to confess
that she is bulimic. They make a pact: he will not drink during the road trip and she will
not purge.

Gerard uses the subsequent events of the road trip to illustrate how the narrator's
relationship with John reinforces her illness. Once on their journey, the narrator does
not try to maintain her pact with John. After eating several donuts at a vegan donut
shop in Seattle, the narrator purges in the bathroom. Although John is upset, he too is
unable to keep his end of the bargain. The next day, the two stop at a "zine" distributor
in Portland where they buy a book about "veganarchism." When the employee offers

them a locally brewed beer, John accepts without hesitation. By having the two characters fail immediately, Gerard establishes the hopelessness of their situation. As neither character genuinely wants to get better, they enable each other's self-destruction.

As the road trip continues, John becomes increasingly engrossed in the revolution touted by the veganarchism book. Beyond this story line, however, the plot is mostly limited to brief moments of their failing relationship. Instead of focusing on events, Gerard uses the narrative to bring readers deep inside the mind of someone afflicted with an eating disorder. Through the narrator's thoughts, Gerard expounds on the obsession that accompanies anorexia and bulimia. This is largely demonstrated in the narrator's methodical approach to losing weight. She lists everything she consumes quantitatively, whether it is three grapes, two Hydroxycut diet pills, or one cigarette. Additionally, she keeps meticulous track of her weight and whether or not she purged after eating and if she was able to take diet pills afterward. The great amount of detail Gerard uses here suggests that she may be mining her own experiences as a survivor of eating disorders.

By describing the narrator's struggle in an authentic manner, Gerard makes it clear that the illness of eating disorders cannot be easily controlled. This removes blame from the narrator. To further exonerate those afflicted with eating disorders, Gerard points to possible causes. When the narrator and John make stops along their road trip, she buys celebrity gossip magazines and diet pills. These items could arguably be seen as both the catalyst and manifestation of her illness. In interviews, Gerard has said that while there are many books about characters with eating disorders, most tend to oversimplify the issue to being about women who think that they are ugly. Gerard demonstrates the complex psychology behind eating disorders by clarifying that while the narrator idolizes the thin celebrities in the gossip magazines, it is not just their beauty she wants. This becomes evident as she describes a long list of the different desires that cause her to starve herself, and the items include everything from wanting to "burn bright" to wanting to disappear and wanting to have an affair that keeps her up at night.

The second dredge-up begins at the end of the road trip. Gerard ensures that, like a dying star in its penultimate stage of life, the characters' relationship is teetering on the edge of collapse. By the last few days of their road trip, John's abuse of alcohol and pills has made him increasingly erratic and violent. Similarly, the narrator's eating disorders have begun the next level of destruction on her body. She considers briefly asking her mother for help, but instead chooses to try to win back John's attention.

The third dredge-up is the last stage of a dying star. For the narrator, it is the final phase in the destruction of her body and her relationship to John. In an effort to save their relationship, the two characters focus on their one remaining shared interest: veganarchism. John comes to New York City for the summer, and the two begin writing a manifesto for an anarchist group, which they name the *Students for the Liberation of Animals.*

The narrator and John's devotion to the vegan cause escalates when they begin planning an animal liberation act of protest. However passionate they may be about their mission, it is not enough to save their relationship. Similarly, the narrator's life is beyond repair. In a scene that is taken directly from Gerard's own experience as described in her essay "From Hunger," the narrator's mentor confronts her and tells her to get professional help. For the first time, she genuinely wants to get better. Unlike Gerard in real life, however, the narrator does not get help but seeks out another path.

As Gerard's prose breaks away from established writing conventions, *Binary Star* falls definitively in the genre of experimental fiction. The innovativeness of her storytelling most clearly begins with her choice to have an unnamed narrator tell the story in first person, present tense. Additionally, the narrative moves in a nonlinear fashion. This is facilitated largely by Gerard's decision to focus more on the internal dialogue of the narrator than the events of story. By keeping the sentences short, most no longer than a single line, Gerard creates a structure that looks and reads like poetry.

Binary Star has received overwhelmingly positive reviews by critics, most of whom have extolled its boldness, both in literary style and content. The most ubiquitous praise has been for Gerard's ability to transform the grim themes of addiction, eating disorders, and codependence into a beautiful narrative. In her *Los Angeles Times* review, Heather Scott Partington writes, "Gerard captures the beauty and scientific irony of damaged relationships and ephemeral lights." There has also been critical acclaim for the effectiveness of Gerard's simple prose, which Martin Riker in his *New York Times* review argues has a utilitarian ability to distill moments of despair and dislocation.

Although Gerard's writing is engaging, it occasionally tries too hard to make all of the different elements connect. Specifically, Jason Heller from *National Public Radio* points to Gerard's attempt to link the refusal to eat by vegans with anorexics' refusal to eat, an effort he describes as "strained." Additionally, her use of astronomy to describe personal and relational decay at times becomes complex and overwhelming. While not all of Gerard's analogies are perfect, the rest are conducted in such a skilled, affecting manner that it is easy to excuse any missteps. Gerard is not the first writer to tackle the issue of self-destruction, but she captures the feelings of longing, emptiness, and decay in a compelling, original way. Despite its occasional flaws, *Binary Star* is ultimately a moving examination of what it means to collapse.

Emily E. Turner

Review Sources

Rev. of *Binary Star*, by Sarah Gerard. *Publishers Weekly*. PWxyz, 8 Dec. 2014. Web. 15 Nov. 2015.

Heller, Jason. "'Binary Star' Is a Hard, Harrowing Look into Inner Space." Rev. of *Binary Star*, by Sarah Gerard. *NPR Books*. Natl. Public Radio, 15 Jan. 2015. Web. 15 Nov. 2015.

Norcia, Alex. "The Path to Destruction: On Sarah Gerard's 'Binary Star.'" Rev. of *Binary Star*, by Sarah Gerard. *Millions*. Millions, 23 Jan. 2015. Web. 15 Nov. 2015.

Partington, Heather Scott. "Sarah Gerard's Debut, 'Binary Star,' Radiates Beauty." Rev. of *Binary Star*, by Sarah Gerard. *Los Angeles Times*. Los Angeles Times, 8 Jan. 2015. Web. 16 Nov. 2015.

Riker, Martin. "Experimental Fiction." Rev. of *Binary Star*, by Sarah Gerard. *New York Times*. New York Times, 20 Feb. 2015. Web. 15 Nov. 2015.

Bone Gap

Author: Laura Ruby
Publisher: Balzer + Bray (New York). 368 pp.
Type of work: Novel
Time: Present
Locale: Bone Gap, Illinois

Laura Ruby's new novel Bone Gap *combines ancient myth, fairy tale, and midwestern realism to produce a story about friendship, betrayal, and learning to love someone for who they are.* Bone Gap *was a finalist for the National Book Award for Young People's Literature in 2015.*

(Used by permission of HarperCollins Publishers)

Principal characters:
FINN O'SULLIVAN, an eighteen-year-old boy whose dreamy demeanor has earned him nicknames like "Sidetrack" and "Moonface"
SEAN O'SULLIVAN, his older brother, a pragmatic EMT
PRISCILLA "PETEY" WILLIS, a fierce teenage beekeeper with a visage reminiscent of an actual bee
ROZA, a mysterious Polish transplant with a green thumb

One can find the town of Bone Gap, Illinois, on a map, but Laura Ruby's Bone Gap—the setting of her new novel of the same name—exists only in dreams. It is a strange place. The corn stalks talk (if you listen carefully); strange animals appear out of the ether; and if you are riding along at the right clip, you and your mare just might stumble through a "gap" into the world of the dead. Bone Gap looks like any small midwestern town, though, and its inhabitants are as neighborly, gossiping, and knowledgeable of one another's business as anyone might suspect.

Finn O'Sullivan is well known in the town. His mother Didi ran off with an orthodontist a few years ago, leaving Finn and his older brother, Sean, to fend for themselves. Sean, an aspiring artist in his early twenties, relinquished his college plans and became an EMT to support Finn, who is still in high school. The story of *Bone Gap* begins during Finn's junior year. Finn is a good-looking kid and is kind to others, but the people of Bone Gap make fun of him. He never seems to be quite all there, they say. He is not stupid, just dreamy—and he never meets anyone's eye. They call him names like "Moonface" and "Sidetrack." The Rudes, an interchangeable clan of brothers, do more than call Finn names; within the first few pages of the book, Finn is lying on the side of the road after an altercation with the Rudes, nursing a few broken ribs.

Things have been worse for Finn since Roza went away. Ruby unravels the mystery of Roza over the course of the book, but at the beginning it is clear only that Roza, a universally beloved Polish girl of mysterious origins, is gone and that people blame Finn for her disappearance. As *Bone Gap* progresses, Finn finds an ally in a girl named Priscilla, though she prefers to be called Petey, who is renowned for her beekeeping skills. People think Petey is strange, too, not because she is dreamy, but because her face looks like a bee. While Sean sulks over Roza, his great lost love, Finn and Petey discover that there is more to Roza's story than they thought, and that it has to do with the strange and mystical nature of Bone Gap itself.

Bone Gap was widely praised after its publication in 2015, and was named a finalist for the National Book Award for young people's literature. Before *Bone Gap*, Ruby was best known for her children's book *Lily's Ghosts* (2003), about a misfit teenager living in a haunted house, though she had written several other books for older teenagers, including *Good Girls* (2006) and *Play Me* (2008). Her novel *Bad Apple* (2009), about a teenage girl falsely accused of having an affair with her teacher, touches on the fairy tale tropes that drive the engine of *Bone Gap*, though *Bone Gap* could more accurately be described as magical realism. Bone Gap, however strange, is a realistically rendered place, whose gaps in reality provide a bridge to another, thoroughly magical, world. This other world, as it turns out, is holding Roza hostage. Roza's story is based on the Greek myth of Demeter, the goddess of corn and the harvest, and her daughter Persephone. Persephone is abducted by Hades, the lord of the underworld, and while she is gone, crops wither and die because of Demeter's grief.

Bone Gap is told from the perspective of various characters, including Roza, who the reader first meets trapped in a suburban mansion. It becomes clear that her prison is not just any house, but an enchanted one, with unbreakable windows and a monstrous, snarling guard dog. (The dog recalls Hades's own hound, Cerberus.) But even those precautions prove unnecessary—when Roza finally does escape, she is merely transported to another strange world. Roza's abductor is described as being made of stone, though he moves "like a cornstalk in the wind." His true identity is revealed later, as is Roza's backstory. Roza grew up with her grandmother in a small town in Poland. She is exceptionally beautiful, and men begin to pay attention to her at a young age. When one young boyfriend demands that she quit school to prove her devotion to him, Roza realizes the importance of breaking out on her own, and, with her grandmother's blessing, travels to Chicago as a foreign exchange student. The other Polish girls in her class are vain, but also desperate. They see their salvation in the form of an abusive Polish immigrant named Bob. Roza has bigger plans for herself, and for this, she is hated.

Laura Ruby is a novelist, essayist, and short-story writer, writing books for both young people and adults. Her works includes the story collection I'm Not Julia Roberts *(2007); an award-winning children's book called* Lily's Ghosts *(2003); and YA novels* Bad Apple *(2009),* Play Me *(2008), and* Good Girls *(2006).*

Roza studies botany and has an uncanny knack for making plants grow, and her professor, a kind, older fellow, offers her a job—she needs one to stay in the United States—in the university greenhouse. Roza is careful around the professor, despite his seemingly harmless interest in her. Ruby seems particularly in tune with Roza here, and in other passages where her young female characters navigate the attentions of men. Ruby captures the fear and frustration of constantly being on one's guard, unsure of which gifts or favors will require one to give something in return.

As it turns out, Roza's professor does require something for his small kindnesses, and that thing is Roza herself. When she is scheduled to return to Poland, he offers her a ride to the airport and drives her to rural Illinois instead. She escapes by jumping out of his moving car but he finds her, secreting her away in a magical place that the reader later learns is also the land of the dead. The form of this world seems to shift constantly into more and more outlandish settings, from the suburban mansion to a castle to a tiny Polish cottage to a spinning upside-down carnival (reminiscent of Ray Bradbury's 1962 novel *Something Wicked This Way Comes*). The scene changes make the internal logic of the world as a whole difficult to understand, rendering it less compelling than the strange but specific world of Bone Gap.

Some aspects of the world are only clear if one is familiar with the Persephone myth. For example, Roza refuses to eat anything more than bread and water during her imprisonment. The writer points this detail out several times, but it is not explained in the book itself; the reader can make sense of it only by referring to the myth. In that story, eating is a capitulation: eating the food of the underworld prevents one from returning to the world of the living. Persephone eats a few pomegranate seeds, and this act binds her irrevocably to her abductor. Similarly, Roza's story has no real-life translation. Petey and Finn navigate the real and fantastical while learning how to love one another despite their flaws. Their night journeys to the portal of the magical world are emblematic of their growing intimacy: their love is a place that no one but the two of them can truly know about. Roza's story is exciting, but because it lacks a similar metaphorical explanation, it also lacks urgency. Though she has been abducted by an all-powerful being, she never appears to be in serious danger; the reader is more afraid for her as a non-English-speaking exchange student navigating interactions with variously hostile men in the real world, because that is a conflict that has an understood consequence.

Despite its flaws, *Bone Gap* is refreshing for its focus on the particular challenges of being a young woman. Petey, who, like Finn, is eighteen years old, faces the mounting pressures of applying for college (Ruby nails the absurdity of the application process) while navigating boys, men, and sex. As Carol Memmott of the *Chicago Tribune* wrote, "sex looms large" in the novel, but the act is not always a sinister threat, as it is in Roza's case. Petey's "hip" mom is open about her daughter's budding sexuality, and the scenes between Petey and Finn are remarkably tender. Their interactions retain the excitement and naiveté of young lovers, but it is clear that both of them—unlike, perhaps, other teenagers in a rural, small town—have an educated and healthy view of intercourse.

Petey, meanwhile, is a delightfully prickly character, though her tough exterior has been honed by years of abuse. She is secure in her own abilities, particularly her knack with bees, but it seems that her every small confidence is undermined by the way people see her. She recalls one instance in which a group of boys spoke admiringly of her body as she passed down the street. When she turned around to see who the boys were, they told her to turn her face back around, accusing her of "ruining the view." Finn is devoted to her, though, and for a while, Petey is worried that his devotion is because of a peculiar disability that distorts his ability to see people as others see them. Finn's infirmity—revealed before the book's climax—is a physical manifestation of the dominant theme in *Bone Gap*. Small-town squabbles, gender stereotypes, and physical appearance hamper characters' abilities to see people as they really are. For the villains of the novel, Roza is merely beautiful, Petey is merely ugly, and Finn is merely stupid. But, like the town of Bone Gap itself, there is much more to them than meets the eye.

Molly Hagan

Review Sources

Barisich, Justin. "Mystery in the Midwest." Rev. of *Bone Gap*, by Laura Ruby. *Book Page*. ProMotion, 1 Mar. 2015. Web. 21 Jan. 2016.

Rev. of *Bone Gap*, by Laura Ruby. *Kirkus*. Kirkus Media, 10 Jan. 2015. Web. 21 Jan. 2016.

Rev. of *Bone Gap*, by Laura Ruby. *Publisher's Weekly*. PWxyz, 1 Mar. 2015. Web. 21 Jan. 2016.

Meloy, Maile. Rev. of *Bone Gap*, by Laura Ruby. *New York Times*. New York Times, 8 May 2015. Web. 19 Jan. 2016.

Memmott, Carol. Rev. of *Bone Gap*, by Laura Ruby. *Chicago Tribune*. Chicago Tribune, 25 June 2015. Web. 21 Jan. 2016.

Bonita Avenue

Author: Peter Buwalda (b. 1971)
Publisher: Hogarth (New York). 544 pp.
Type of work: Novel
Time: 1996–2007
Locales: Berkeley, California; Netherlands; Belgium

Bonita Avenue *is a generation's spanning novel about the Sigerius family and son-in-law Aaron Bever. Told from the perspectives of four characters, the novel explores the dark side and frailties of human nature in a digital age. The story is told in a fast-paced style that finds each chapter jumping between time periods in the narrative.*

BONITA AVENUE

PETER BUWALDA

A NOVEL

(Courtesy of Penguin Random House)

Principal characters:
SIEM SIGERIUS, former judo champion and renowned mathematician; one of four narrators
TINEKE SIGERIUS, his second wife and a narrator
JONI SIGERIUS, his stepdaughter and a narrator
JANIS SIGERIUS, his stepdaughter
WILBERT, his son
AARON BEVER, his judo protégé and Joni's husband

Journalist and first-time novelist Peter Buwalda is the author of the sprawling book *Bonita Avenue*, which immediately introduces readers to Siem Sigerius—a larger-than-life hulk of a man who was once considered an Olympic contender in judo before becoming injured. He is now enjoying a second career as a renowned mathematician and is about to meet his stepdaughter Joni's new partner, Aaron Bever.

Aaron is a slight man who works as a photographer for the local university where Siem teaches and who readers quickly learn has also taken a famous nude photo of Siem. The photo has only added to Siem Sigerius's legendary status, and Aaron is quickly welcomed into the family unit, which, from an onlooker's point of view, appears to be perfect. Buwalda uses the nakedness of the Sigerius patriarch as a metaphor for the entire Sigerius clan, which at first glance seems to be the picture of a sophisticated, intellectual family but, as Buwalda warns readers, is different under its veneer.

Readers are given the essential plot of the book within its first chapter: Siem discovers the secret pornographic website maintained by Aaron and Joni. Siem then has a breakdown. Aaron has a breakdown. Aaron and Joni move to the United States, and Siem ultimately commits suicide. What readers learn is the rest of the story is told through flashbacks with a present thread consistently woven through.

The title *Bonita Avenue* comes from the name of the street on which the Sigerius's lived in Berkeley, when Siem taught at the University of California. For two years, the family lived in harmony. When they returned to Europe, they experienced disastrous divorces, homicidal children, and scandal. At one point in the book, adult Joni revisits the house on Bonita Avenue. Marking one of the more poignant passages, her visit seems to amplify the disasters that the family met upon their return to the Netherlands. She explains that she once believed the years on Bonita Avenue to be the calmest, but in looking back on them as an adult, she has a new and different understanding of that time period. She wonders whether the family was in essence running away by returning to Europe.

Bonita Avenue is a novel that is interested in forms of escape—from modern life through pornography or substance abuse, through physical flight, and from the past. Buwalda focuses largely on the development of the Internet as a way to explore these themes and has said about his inspiration for this book in *Book Page*, "thinking about the abyss between the younger generation of the 1990s and 2000s and the older generation. For the first time in history, I think, because of the rise of the Internet, people from the older generation know less about the world, maybe even about wisdom, than the younger generation." He expands on this to consider the limitless access to pornography on the Internet; because of that, people have access to many more bodies than they ever had in previous generations. He wonders what this progression means for society and what the commodification of sex to this degree will lead to.

Flesh and the frailty of flesh are other themes within *Bonita Avenue*. Tineke appears naked just a few pages into the book when Aaron stumbles upon her obese form eating chocolate sprinkles in the family's kitchen late one night. Siem's grizzly cauliflower ear, developed after years of abuse in judo competition and practice, is described in precise detail on the first page. The abundance of flesh in the book is a backdrop for a sweeping story of the vulnerabilities of the human spirit and the consequences of succumbing to one's deepest desires. At one point, Aaron is on a commuter train and finds himself sitting directly across from Tineke, whom he has not seen in years since tragedy struck the family. Tineke has lost a great deal of weight, as if the horrible experiences she has been through have left her hardened. She barely recognizes Aaron when he follows her off the train, and the reader soon learns that she is no longer in touch with Joni and that Siem has died and the family is shattered.

Just as notable as the baring and abundance of flesh is its weakness. Siem bears this burden most heavily when he walks through a sliding glass door after the revelation of what will ultimately lead to his and his family's undoing. He is left to deal with his injuries alone while hiding naked in a wooded area in the suburbs, and readers are similarly meant to deal with the most gruesome of descriptions. The injuries Siem himself inflicts in the final act of the book are shocking, and perhaps Buwalda expects the reader to find a sense of irony in this.

Buwalda explores the pornography industry from both the inside and the outside. After being rejected by an undergraduate student with whom he has had a brief affair, Siem turns to a paid service that quickly becomes an obsession and ultimately and indirectly leads to his downfall and the downfall of his family. It seems that Buwalda is connecting the brutal force and speed with which that destruction happens to both Siem's obsession with the pornographic site and society's addiction to pornography. Later in the story, Siem's favorite daughter Joni has built an adult-entertainment empire of her own after fleeing to the United States. There she creates a character whose likeness is based on real-life porn star Sasha Grey. Going by the name "Joy," Joni is forced to hide her true identity even though she has become wildly successful. She tells people that she works for a company that makes sporting goods. Despite his moralizing, Buwalda does not seem to offer a final statement or solution regarding what he sees as the problem of pornography in modern society. The characters suffer and lives are ruined, but readers are not offered an alternative. In fact, Buwalda's writing could at times be considered sexist and clichéd in this respect. He offers little commentary, and rather than using the plotline to make a larger point about society and its problems, he uses these moments to describe the pornography in detail. The tone is one of naïve teenage excitement rather than of sophisticated or insightful commentary on the sex business. An epigraph closes the novel with a nod to the adult-entertainment industry with a quote from Sasha Grey, "Y'know, I am to you what a gladiator was to the Roman citizen."

Peter Buwalda is a Dutch journalist, critic, and novelist. He was a founder of the Dutch literary magazine Wah-Wah. Bonita Avenue *is his first novel.*

Buwalda's writing is frequently compared to novelists like Jonathan Franzen and Philip Roth. Like Franzen, Buwalda's writing is focused on realistic characters and settings. Also, as with much of Franzen's and Roth's works, small, seemingly normal incidents lead to the ultimate breakdown of the nuclear family. *Bonita Avenue* is most closely related to Franzen's *The Corrections* (2001). Buwalda's raw depictions of violence and sex are also reminiscent of the writing of Scottish novelist and playwright Irvine Welsh, as are his fast-paced plot and the atmosphere of tension created through structure and language. At times Buwalda's ambitious plot structure surpasses his skills as a writer, and the story suffers. And for many readers, one particularly troubling area in his writing is his treatment of race. For example, at one point in the novel, Siem goes to Shanghai for a conference and he and others use several racial slurs to describe their Chinese colleagues. This treatment resurfaces several times through the book, and many may find it surprising if not uncomfortable to read.

Though the book was widely praised in Europe, where it won multiple awards, reception in the United States has been more sedate. Tony Tulathimutte, for the *Los Angeles Review of Books*, said in his review, "Buwalda has a talent for the cutaway, [and] . . . this talent is especially useful as his novel is largely made of digressions that unfold in flashbacks from an inert present tense in which the estranged characters reflect on their past. . . . Though the present-tense scenes do feel like a drawn-out epilogue because the characters do little except sit around and feel wistful." Michael Upchurch said in the *New York Times*, "While the plot orchestration and lively character renderings of 'Bonita Avenue' are dazzling, Buwalda's go-for-broke style can be a hit-and-miss affair. Sometimes it's brilliantly on target. Sometimes it just feels overwritten."

Despite its problems with clichéd language, disordered plot, and sometimes-weak characters, *Bonita Avenue* is a strong debut novel from a promising writer. The brash, take-no-prisoners approach in which Buwalda writes proves encouraging for future works that will no doubt be at once refreshingly original and profound.

Melynda Fuller

Review Sources

Cummins, Anthony. Rev. of *Bonita Avenue*, by Peter Buwalda. *Telegraph*. Telegraph Media Group, 22 Apr. 2015. Web. 25 Jan. 2016.

Fallon, Claire. "The Book We're Talking About." Rev. of *Bonita Avenue*, by Peter Buwalda. *Huffington Post*. TheHuffingtonPost.com, 8 Jan. 2015. Web. 25 Jan. 2016.

McCartney, Tammy. Rev. of *Bonita Avenue*, by Peter Buwalda. *San Francisco Book Review*. San Francisco Book Review, 25 Mar. 2015. Web. 25 Jan. 2016

Tulathimutte, Tony. "Infornography." Rev. of *Bonita Avenue*, by Peter Buwalda. *Los Angeles Review of Books*. Los Angeles Review of Books, 14 Jan. 2015. Web. 25 Jan. 2016.

Upchurch, Michael. Rev. of *Bonita Avenue*, by Peter Buwalda. *New York Times*. New York Times, 14 Feb. 2015. Web. 25 Jan. 2016.

The Book of Aron

Author: Jim Shepard (b. 1956)
Publisher: Alfred A. Knopf (New York). 272 pp.
Type of work: Novel
Time: ca. 1937–42
Locale: Warsaw, Poland

(Courtesy of Alfred A. Knopf)

The Book of Aron *explores the Holocaust and one of its heroes, Polish doctor and writer Janusz Korczak, from the perspective of an ordinary child. Aron, a young boy growing up in Warsaw's Jewish ghetto, learns to survive in desperate times by stealing, smuggling, and even becoming an informer for local police. When Aron loses everything, he is taken in by Korczak, who runs an orphanage and offers hope and kindness to children trapped in the bleakest of circumstances.*

Principal characters:
ARON RÓŻYCKI, a.k.a. Sh'maya, the narrator and protagonist, a hapless, trouble-prone young boy
JANUSZ KORCZAK, a.k.a. The Old Doctor, a pediatrician, children's rights advocate, and head of an orphanage, based on the historical figure of the same name
LUTEK, one of Aron's friends, who steals and smuggles with him on Warsaw's streets
ZOFIA, a girl who becomes a member of a street gang
ADINA, a newcomer and later a member of the street gang
BORIS, a tough boy who becomes Aron's neighbor and a leader of their gang
MADAME STEFA, a Polish woman who works with Korczak in the orphanage
LEJKIN, a member of the Jewish Order Service who recruits Aron as an informer

In *The Book of Aron*, Jim Shepard, an author known for writing short stories that fuse historical and scientific fact with fiction, takes on the Holocaust and one of its heroes as seen through the eyes of Aron, a young Jewish boy caught up in a tragedy almost beyond his comprehension. Born into a poor and unlucky family in a Polish village, eight-year-old Aron, nicknamed Sh'maya (for "God has heard"), does poorly in school and generally fails to distinguish himself. He does, however, show an unexpected talent for staying alive in the most hostile of environments.

Aron, his parents, and his three brothers move from their village into Warsaw, where there is more work. Soon after Aron's tenth birthday, however, the Nazis invade Poland. Sanctions against Jews, combined with an epidemic of typhus, force Aron's family into tighter living quarters and an ever more precarious existence. One by one, Aron loses his family members to disease or deportations as living conditions go from bad to worse. It is a story that history knows, but Aron, the narrator, has no words for the Holocaust and little knowledge of the world beyond Warsaw's Jewish ghetto. Practical and self-centered, he focuses on surviving from day to day, evading soldiers and police, and scavenging, smuggling, and trading black-market goods for food. "Sh'maya only looks out for himself" is a taunt frequently leveled at Aron, an attitude contrasted with the idealism and self-sacrifice of Janusz Korczak, whom Aron first knows as the Old Doctor from a radio program and who later becomes his caretaker and mentor. Korczak, a doctor and writer of books for and about children, has many chances to leave Poland before and even after the Nazi takeover, but he chooses to stay and help orphaned children who have nowhere else to go. His kindness and quiet courage inspire Aron, even as the deadly net cast by the Nazis tightens around them.

Jim Shepard's short stories have been included in the Best American Short Story and Pushcart Prize anthologies, and his collection Like You'd Understand, Anyway *(2007) was a National Book Award finalist. His 2005 novel* Project X *won the 2005 Massachusetts Book Award for Fiction and an Alex Award from the Young Adults Library Services Association.*

Speaking at a public library reading of *The Book of Aron,* Shepard told the audience that he did extensive research on the life of Janusz Korczak, who is as well known and beloved in Poland as first president George Washington is in the United States. He found it difficult to approach such an iconic, larger-than-life figure directly, and so Shepard chose to create an ordinary, entirely fictional character whose life played out on the periphery of Korczak's world. As novelist Geraldine Brooks pointed out in the *New York Times,* Shepard's choice of narrator limited his style and vocabulary. In order to create a convincing voice for a young, poor, and haphazardly educated boy, the author had to forgo the wit, wordplay, introspection, and lyricism that characterize much of his fiction. Instead, Aron's voice is deceptively simple, authentic, and all the more effective for its understated description of atrocities. As a young boy, Aron has no sense of history and little knowledge of the world beyond the ghetto. He takes life as it comes, and his resilience helps him resist the despair to which others succumb. When German soldiers take his father and brothers to a "work detail," Aron, like his mother, waits for them to return. No one yet knows about the Nazi concentration camps; only toward the end of the novel do stories about death camps begin to emerge.

Outwitting the authorities becomes a kind of game for Aron and his friends as they respond to attempts to contain the ghetto and curtail smuggling with clever schemes to get themselves out and bring desperately needed food in. A passageway the smugglers use is known as the Immortal Hole because the smugglers reopen it every time the Germans try to seal it up. Aron and his gang of street kids classify the police as yellow (Jewish), blue (Polish), or green (German), based on their uniforms, and work out a system of bribery to evade arrest. They must evade not only the police and Nazi soldiers but also rival gangs. Daily life becomes more and more difficult as transportation services are cut and Warsaw's Jews are forced into a smaller area; families must cram together into small apartments, people wrap twine around their shoes to hold them together, epidemics rage, and decent food becomes almost impossible to find.

Just when it seems life cannot get worse, some new restriction or catastrophe is added to the burden. Aron's younger brother succumbs to tuberculosis; his father is brutally beaten by the Nazis; later, his father and his two older brothers are sent to work in a "labor battalion" and never return; and finally, his mother dies of typhus, a disease exacerbated by the ghetto's crowded and unsanitary conditions.

One factor in Aron's survival is his ambivalent cooperation with Lejkin, a member of the Jewish Order Service. During the Nazi occupation of Poland, Jewish councils (the Judenrat) and police forces were set up by the Germans to keep order in the ghetto, and this character may be based on the real-life Jakob Lejkin, who led the Jewish police in the Warsaw ghetto. Lejkin is aware of Aron's success as a smuggler and even asks the boy to bring him a bootjack. Later, he convinces Aron to serve as an informer about smuggling and other activities in the ghetto, so he can meet his quotas of arrests. Boris, the leader of Aron's smuggling gang, initially agrees that Aron should work for Lejkin, so they in turn can know what the police are planning, but he turns against Aron when Aron gives Lejkin information that results in Lutek, another member of the gang, being shot by the Gestapo.

After Aron's mother dies, Boris throws the orphaned boy out of their house, and Aron wanders the streets, sleeping in cellars and fighting with beggars for scraps of food. At the lowest point in his life, left without family or a single friend, he is rescued by Janusz Korczak. Aron has encountered Korczak before: while tending his younger brother, he listened to Korczak's radio program, *The Old Doctor*, and Korczak once intervened when Aron's gang was beating a younger child. Now Korczak finds a place for Aron at his orphanage, and he becomes a father figure to the boy as the two bond over their shared insomnia. As he follows Korczak on his rounds through the ghetto to raise money for the orphans and talks to him through the long nights, Aron evolves from a child who "only cares about himself" to a boy willing to do anything he can to save the heroic man who has shown him kindness.

In a Holocaust novel, a happy ending would probably be too much to expect. The real Janusz Korczak died in Treblinka, along with the orphans he refused to abandon. But Shepard offers a sliver of hope by ending Aron's story as he, Korczak, and the other orphans are waiting for the train that will take them to the death camp. Earlier, resistance fighters had told Aron and Korczak about mass killings at the concentration camp. If everyone was gassed, Korczak asks, then how did any survive to tell the tale? The resistance fighter explains that he, like some others, managed to escape from the train, tearing barbed wire from windows or kicking through floorboards. Aron imagines that he will do the same, climbing over other peoples' heads if he had to. Readers can imagine this fierce young survivor slipping away from the Nazis' grasp, living to tell the world Janusz Korczak's story and his own.

The Book of Aron met with a generally positive reception, although some reviewers found the novel too slight, overwhelmed by the gravity of its historical background. The reviewer for *Publishers Weekly*, for example, acknowledged Shepard's extensive research and the realistic background he was able to create for his characters but found the characters themselves one-dimensional and the plot underdeveloped.

Other reviewers greeted *The Book of Aron* with unreserved praise. Novelist Joshua Ferris, who reviewed *The Book of Aron* for the *Guardian*, praised Shepard both for his seamless integration of extensive research into a work of fiction and for his creation of an authentic voice for Aron, a "remarkable act of ventriloquism" that never slips to reveal the writer's more knowing voice. He notes Shepard's use of dark humor to undermine oppressive authority and connects it with the speech patterns of traditional Yiddish wit. *Kirkus Reviews* concurred, singling out the novel's well-researched background and "pitch-perfect" narrative voice for praise and noting Shepard's carefully paced portrait of life in the Warsaw ghetto as inconveniences escalate into horrendous deprivation and violence. The reviewer for *Kirkus* also found Aron's scrappy pragmatism an effective counterpoint to Korczak's idealistic heroism.

Ron Charles, in the *Washington Post*, hailed *The Book of Aron* as "a masterpiece," destined to join the ranks of essential Holocaust literature. Charles noted Shepard's deft handling of moral complexities and his use of an innocent voice, with its "child's concentration on the specific," to make the horrors of the Holocaust real and comprehensible in a way that statistics of millions of deaths cannot. He also lauded Shepard's portrait of Janusz Korczak as a personally flawed yet undeniably heroic man who gave hope to children living in the worst of times. Donna Seaman, in her *Booklist* review, agreed, calling *The Book of Aron* a "magnificent tour de force" that captures the resiliency of the human spirit through its portrayal of brave children fighting to survive in the face of war and genocide.

Kathryn Kulpa

Review Sources

Rev. of *The Book of Aron*, by Jim Shepard. *Kirkus Reviews* Mar. 2015: 152. Print.

Rev. of *The Book of Aron*, by Jim Shepard. *Publishers Weekly* 2 Feb. 2015: 31. Print.

Brooks, Geraldine. "From Shtetl to Ghetto." Rev. of *The Book of Aron*, by Jim Shepard. *New York Times Book Review* 24 May 2015: 14. Print.

Charles, Ron. "*The Book of Aron*, by Jim Shepard, Is a Masterpiece." Rev. of *The Book of Aron*, by Jim Shepard. *Washington Post*. Washington Post, 28 Apr. 2015. Web. 23 Dec. 2015.

Ferris, Joshua. "A Testament of Love during the Holocaust." Rev. of *The Book of Aron*, by Jim Shepard. *Guardian*. Guardian News and Media, 1 July 2015. Web. 23 Dec. 2015.

Seaman, Donna. Rev. of *The Book of Aron*, by Jim Shepard. *Booklist* 15 Apr. 2015: 32. Print.

Book of Numbers

Author: Joshua Cohen (b. 1980)
Publisher: Random House (New York). 592 pp.
Type of work: Novel
Time: Present day
Locale: New York

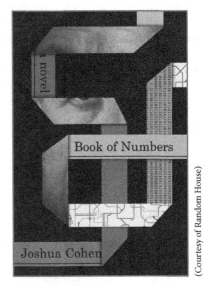

(Courtesy of Random House)

Book of Numbers *is an exploration of the modern age of technology. This novel engages the reader in an examination of what it means to be truly transparent on both sides of any interaction in the Internet age.*

Principal characters:

JOSHUA COHEN, a failed novelist who has been contracted to ghostwrite the autobiography of a tech billionaire named Joshua Cohen

JOSHUA COHEN, also called the Principal, a phenomenally wealthy and successful man who founded the Internet search firm known as Tetration

MOE, the Principal's partner and Hindu engineer

DIETMAR KLUG, a German translator

AARON, ghostwriter Cohen's agent

Book of Numbers is a work told in a breathless, headlong rush to an uncertain destination. At its heart, it is the story of a struggling novelist named Joshua Cohen who is contracted to ghostwrite the autobiography of a billionaire tech guru named Joshua Cohen. In fact, it is an exploration of society at the point when a technology is still considered new by those who were there at its start, but for the greater part of a newer generation it is simply the way things have always been.

In keeping with the premise of a novel observing fundamental societal change, ghostwriter Cohen thinks—a lot, and about a lot of things, with a fast-forward motion that manages to meld details with a style that is urgent. It is not a book most readers would choose to curl up with on a cold winter night or select for a beach read. It is an ambitious tale of a writer struggling to find his center and get his shot at writing a major work, set against the reality of the increasingly dominant role the Internet and digital technology is taking in daily life. It presents itself as a jumble of expectations, linguistic styles, and characters.

A few of those characters keep the book from being completely claustrophobic, but not by much. Ghostwriter Cohen's wife, who is seeking a divorce, is included, along with the young woman he now has his eye on. There are also friends who have a variety of opinions about what he should be doing with his life, as well as his agent, Aaron.

It is clear, however, that once ghostwriter Cohen meets up with the Principal and embarks on a trip to various far-flung places as he interviews the Principal for his autobiography, the heart of the narrative has been reached. Unfortunately what follows is a long diatribe describing the history of Tetration—an Internet search company that is eerily similar to Google. It seems the Principal is getting ready to take off for parts unknown and live the life of a recluse—perhaps as a result of having created a technology that leaves nothing private—and before he does, he wants this book to be written.

The Principal will be instantly familiar to any student of the current age as a stereotypical dot-com billionaire. He speaks in tech jargon, is focused on something just out of sight, and articulates in a "better keep up" style that does not suffer fools. For his part, the book's real-life author Joshua Cohen is clear that tech guru Joshua Cohen is most definitely ripped from real life and based upon the actual tech gurus of our age. He says in an interview with Kyle Chayka for *Rolling Stone* that tech guru Joshua Cohen was created when "I took a little piece of [Steve] Jobs, took a little piece of [Jeff] Bezos, took a little piece of [Mark] Zuckerberg." All that was needed was a pair of thin-rimmed round glasses. Author Joshua Cohen added those, and the portrayal was complete.

Book of Numbers is an ambitious work. Whether the book is brilliant, or if it even succeeds, is a point of digression among reviewers. In his review for the *Boston Globe*, Max Winter noted, "There will be a point at which you realize *Book of Numbers* is a brilliant book." He then goes on to recount several such instances, including one in which "you first encounter the book's subject-within-a-subject, also named Joshua Cohen, the inventor of a Google-esque search engine called Tetration, who speaks in a blend of Orwell's newspeak, New Age gibberish, technical jargon, and our current patois." If this leaves readers feeling less than inclined to open the book, they are not alone.

Dwight Garner wrote in his review for the *New York Times* that it is at just this same point that "Mr. Cohen loses control over his novel. . . . Joshua Cohen, the billionaire, is simply not as alive as Joshua Cohen, the flailing novelist. We're not invested; the billionaire is a head in a jar. *Book of Numbers* stalls out for long passages as he relates the story of Tetration's founding. After a hundred or so pages, you begin to think: Forget the data, hand over your findings."

Garner also remarked, "The author's heart is not in this stuff. *Book of Numbers* is instead a wheeling meditation on the wired life, on privacy, on what being human in the age of binary code might mean. The narrator thinks, 'I'd forgotten just how much of myself I'd outsourced, offshored, externalized.'" Surely that is a commentary on modern times, even as it falls short of a ringing endorsement for this current work. It speaks to a view of the world that informs Joshua Cohen's work—real-life author Joshua Cohen, that is. Garner further observed, "The book isn't cold, yet it never finds an emotional tone to match its intellectual one."

It is not all tech speak and hurried worry. There is one interchange that speaks to the way that tradition and modernity intersect and must be reevaluated in this technological age. The changes brought about by the Internet and cloud computing, for instance, require a new look at the meaning of long-standing proscriptions and customs.

Cohen delivers this in the form of an online exchange on a Jewish "Ask the Rabbi" website. The questioner points out that, according to tradition, using the Tetragrammaton—the four-letter Hebrew name of God—requires that the medium on which it is used be destroyed and asks what must happen when the Tetragrammaton is written on a computer? The questioner closes his question with a traditional phrase, updated for modern technology "May your site go from strength to strength, b'ezrat HaShem." The rabbi responds with an interpretation that takes the spirit and meaning of the original statement and brings it to the modern time. "In a computer file, the Name of God, like any other word, exists only as a binary series of numbers, as 1s and 0s signifying the sequence of the letters—they are NOT the letter themselves." When the word is printed on paper or written by hand, that medium must be destroyed. In closing he assures the questioner that "Onscreen, the Name of God is not even represented, but just perpetually refreshed. Light is beamed at the screen approximately 60x/second. In its every manifestation, then, the digitized Name is purely symbolic, and so, by the standards of Jewish law, lacks permanence. HaShem's light, by contrast is everlasting."

For some, this passage brings to mind the question of just why this book is entitled *Book of Numbers*, given that there is a book in the Torah called Numbers. In Numbers, the Israelites wander in the desert. They will be able to return to the Promised Land once the last person who has memories of their time as slaves has died. Author Joshua Cohen has alluded to the time when those who do not remember a time before the Internet will populate the world. Perhaps the title alludes to a time when digital technology will be seen as much a part of life as the seasons—a ubiquitous but ultimately utilitarian aspect of daily life. Then again, there are few people who view the Internet as a gift given in fulfillment of a covenant.

Joshua Cohen is the author of four novels and several books of short stories. The Village Voice *named his novel* Witz *to its list of the best books of 2010, and the* New Yorker *named his short-story collection* Four New Messages *to its list of the best books of 2012.*

Whatever the rationale behind the novel's title, ultimately *Book of Numbers* is another book in a line of recent releases that received reviews in which the author was lauded but the book itself was not. Each of these novels had a high page count and was widely anticipated. Each was consistently reviewed as not living up to its promise or ambition. The authors of these novels, including Garth Risk Hallberg (*City on Fire*) and Julia Pierpont (*Among the Thousand Things*), were nevertheless lauded by critics for having great promise and vision. Such is the case with Joshua Cohen the author. Garner wrote, "Mr. Cohen has enormous gifts, almost terrifying ones. At this point he's like the apprentice wizard who accidentally blows up the supermarket while trying to coax a tin of herring into levitation. His magic is serious."

In agreement with this view, Steven Poole wrote in his review for the *Guardian*, "*Book of Numbers* comes with a blurb by the critic James Wood, which is interesting for what it doesn't say: 'He certainly can write!' Cohen certainly can write. And an editor who had the time might have found the decent shorter novel buried somewhere within these pages." *Book of Numbers* is sprawling, challenging, and timely and will appeal to readers who like difficult and high-minded works of fiction. However, it will likely be off-putting and overwhelming for readers who are looking for lighter fare.

Gina Hagler

Review Sources

Chayka, Kyle. "The Great American Internet Novel Is Here: Inside 'Book of Numbers.'" *Rolling Stone*. Rolling Stone, 21 July 2015. Web. 18 Jan. 2016.

Garner, Dwight. "'Book of Numbers,' by Joshua Cohen, Is Narrative as Rich as the Web." *New York Times*. New York Times, 7 June 2015. Web. 18 Jan. 2016.

Hendrix, Jenny. "The Original Online." Rev. of *Book of Numbers*, by Joshua Cohen. *Slate*. Slate Group, 6 July 2015. Web. 18 Jan. 2016.

Poole, Steven. "The Guru and the Ghostwriter." Rev. of *Book of Numbers*, by Joshua Cohen. *Guardian*. Guardian News and Media, 3 July 2015. Web. 18 Jan. 2016.

Winter, Max. Rev. of *Book of Numbers*, by Joshua Cohen. *Boston Globe*. Boston Globe Media Partners, 30 June 2015. Web. 18 Jan. 2016.

Zeidner, Lisa. "Joshua Cohen's 'The Book of Numbers,' and the Birth of the Internet Age." *Washington Post*. Washington Post, 10 June 2015. Web. 18 Jan. 2016.

Boys in the Trees

Author: Carly Simon (b. 1945)
Publisher: Flatiron Books (New York). 384 pp.
Type of work: Memoir
Time: 1948–83
Locales: United States, Europe

Carly Simon shares personal stories about her family, her music, and her relationships ranging from her childhood through the end of her marriage to James Taylor.

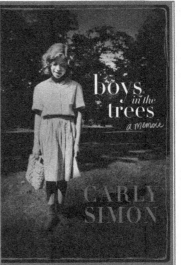

(Courtesy Flatiron Books)

Principal personages:
CARLY SIMON, author, composer, and singer
RICHARD "DICK" SIMON, her father, a founding partner of Simon and Schuster Books
ANDREA SIMON, her mother
LUCY SIMON, her older sister who performed with her as the Simon Sisters
JAMES TAYLOR, her husband from 1972 to 1983

Carly Simon is a singer, composer, and legend. *Boys in the Trees*, a memoir based on her early childhood through the end of her marriage to James Taylor, shares many of the stories and secrets of her family life, her love life, and her career.

The first portion of Simon's autobiography shares stories of her childhood and often conflicting relationships with her parents. She was the third daughter of publisher Richard Simon, one of the founders of Simon and Schuster. Simon felt lifelong distance between her father and herself because she felt that he wanted a son. Richard Simon's struggles with depression and mental health issues were more likely the basis of his separation from the family, a connection that Simon began to understand as an adult with similar problems. Toward the end of his life, she began to see her father the way others saw him; she visited his office one day and found that, due to his physical and mental health issues, he had lost his position in the company he had worked so hard to establish. As young child, she deeply admired her mother, Andrea, but that would change and their relationship would become more complicated.

Simon's early years were ideal; she was always surrounded by family and friends. Simon, her parents, her older sisters Joey and Lucy, and her younger brother, Peter, lived in a building which also housed apartments for her grandmothers, various aunts, uncles, cousins, and family friends. Social gatherings were common, and the family was, on the surface at least, happy. Performances were common as both Andrea Simon's brothers and Dick Simon himself were musically talented. The children often wrote, produced, and performed summer plays. The constant influence of music would become Simon's salvation when she developed a stutter that still incapacitates her at times. To help with the stammer, the family made it a game to sing simple everyday phrases like "pass the butter."

Simon continued to feel part of a happy family until she realized that her parents' relationship was no longer idyllic. When Simon was eight, Andrea hired a nineteen-year-old tutor and companion for Peter, Ronny. Ronny's presence confused Simon, especially when an affair that she did not quite understand began between Andrea and Ronny. Her frustration over her mother's relationship with Ronny was compounded by its taking place right under her father's nose and her mother continuing to nurse her father when he had a debilitating stroke. The very civilized face of their marriage that was presented to the children and public would misguide Simon's own relationships for years. Though she did not understand the nature of

(Heidi Wild)

Singer-songwriter Carly Simon has won multiple awards, including three Grammy Awards. Her musical career has spanned over five decades.

the relationships between the adults in her life, she knew that life had changed. She tells readers, "Later on, I would realize that it was Ronny who had stolen her away, but back then all I knew was that if Daddy had never been mine, Mommy wasn't mine anymore either." Her father's health issues, which led to his death in 1960, and her mother's emotional absences confused the young girl, leaving her to wonder where she belonged in the family. This uncertainty that would plague her into adulthood.

Andrea's affair with Ronny was not the only misconduct to happen in the Simon household. Starting when she was seven, Simon was subjected to years of sexual abuse at the hands of a neighboring boy named Billy. Though Simon takes on a self-accusatory tone about this abuse, suggesting that her innocent flirtation with the boy contributed to the molestation, she expresses annoyance that her mother's response to the news was to merely banish him for a month. Her mother's lack of response hurt Simon. Andrea would further injure her third daughter's emotional well-being by disinheriting her because Andrea did not feel Simon needed the money after she rose to fame.

Broken into three parts, the memoir moves from her childhood into a review of Simon's professional and romantic life after her father's death in 1960. The middle portion of the book answers many of the relationship and professional questions readers may have. Her professional singing career started in a folksong duo, known as the Simon Sisters, with her sister Lucy. The two traveled to Europe to perform and produced a record together before Carly went out on her own. Though Simon experienced some anxiety during their performances, she was always comforted by the presence of her older sister. While enjoying a burgeoning career during the 1960s, Simon was also enjoying the sexual freedom that marked that decade. In *Boys in the Trees*, Simon shares the details of her affairs, both long and short term. She seems to have genuinely cared for each man with whom she became involved, even if it was only for a night or two. The list of her lovers seems, at times, to cover many of the major names of the film and music worlds, including a brief flirtation with Sean Connery, whom her sister Lucy pursued more heavily. She had a short-term affair with singer Cat Stevens, for whom she opened; with actor Warren Beatty, whom she confesses is one of the men she was thinking about when she wrote "You're So Vain;" and with actor Jack Nicholson, who confessed in her bed that he was planning to marry another woman. Her most long-standing relationships, however, included singers Mick Jagger and James Taylor. Though she argues that she never had a sexual relationship with Jagger, the two were friends and she tells readers that their sexual chemistry was actually stronger than the act.

In 1971, she produced her first solo album, *Carly Simon*, which featured the hit single "That's the Way I've Always Heard It Should Be." Though she won a Grammy for best new artist as a result, she underplays the importance of that work, partially because she was in a relationship with James Taylor at that point. Much of her career is pushed aside in favor of delving into her relationships throughout the book.

Simon's relationship with James Taylor is the focus on the final third of the book. Though the two had met briefly as young teens, they only renewed their acquaintance in the early 1970s. Almost as soon as they became reacquainted, their love affair started in earnest. Taylor moved into Simon's New York apartment, and the two worked together when they were not separated by their individual recording and touring requirements.

The importance of this relationship is evidently still vital to Simon, as she confesses at one point, "These days, I'm anxious for Ben and Sally, our two children, to believe their father was happy with me. Obviously, not all of me, and not everything, but that there was enough good in me, and in the two of us, that James would not want to exclude me from his memories." Comments like this, sprinkled throughout the narrative, show how the power Taylor held over Simon's still-fragile ego during their marriage and in the years after its end further complicated her struggles with depression. She continuously questioned why Taylor would want to be with her and where she fit into his life.

Taylor's personality and drug use often left Simon feeling unnecessary in his life. He was often distant, especially after drug detox programs. Ironically, alcohol led him back to her, but she understood that his reliance on chemical substances affected their marriage, leaving her feeling left out on a regular basis. Another aspect of being an outsider is revealed in her paradoxical discussion of his family. At several points in the memoir, she calls her relationship with his parents and siblings "skin-deep," yet at other points, she hints at a more intimate connection with his mother, Trudy. For example, early in Simon's relationship with Taylor, she took on a craft project, making a needlepoint pillow for her mother-in-law.

The ever-present depression, anxiety, and self-esteem issues that plagued Simon throughout her life were not absent in her relationship with Taylor. His own depression issues challenged the marriage in many ways as well, compounding Simon's concerns about her own worth. Toward the end of their marriage, after she found out about a long-standing affair that he had been having, she even experienced an anxiety attack on stage. Her sister Lucy, who was in the audience, helped her through the situation, and Simon continued the concert with the support of her family and fans.

The memoir draws to a close as Simon's marriage to Taylor ended. She provides a few notes about her life after Taylor, but readers are left wondering what has happened in the ensuing years. Another potential problem some readers may have with the memoir is that Simon occasionally wanders back and forth in time. Nonchronological asides appear throughout the piece, but her ability to jump back into the story of the moment makes the experience feel like an intimate conversation. Many critics also found that Simon was excessively verbose at times, to the point that her descriptions (particularly those about Taylor) became cloying. While many noted this as a negative aspect of the book, it did not detract from the quality of the rest of the book and the grace with which Simon relates her storied life.

Theresa L. Stowell

Review Sources

Rev. of *Boys in the Trees: A Memoir*, by Carly Simon. *Kirkus Reviews*. Kirkus Media, 1 Dec. 2015. Web. 28 Jan. 2016.

Cohen, Howard. Rev. of *Boys in the Trees*, by Carly Simon. *Miami Herald*. Miami Herald, 1 Dec. 2015. Web. 28 Jan. 2016.

Juris, Carolyn. "Branching Out." Rev. of *Boys in the Trees*, by Carly Simon. *Publishers Weekly*. PWxyz, 7 Dec. 2015. Web. 28 Jan. 2016.

Maslin, Janet. "Review: In Carly Simon's Memoir, Few Secrets Left Untold." Rev. of *Boys in the Trees*, by Carly Simon. *New York Times*. New York Times, 26 Nov. 2015 Web. 28 Jan. 2016.

Sullivan, James. Rev. of *Boys in the Trees*, by Carly Simon. *Boston Globe*. Boston Globe Media Partners, 23 Nov. 2015. Web. 28 Jan. 2016.

Bright Dead Things

Author: Ada Limón (b. 1976)
Publisher: Milkweed Editions (Minneapolis). 128 pp.
Type of Work: Poetry
Locale: United States

(Courtesy of Milkweed Editions)

Bright Dead Things is the latest collection of verse by the prize-winning poet Ada Limón, author of three earlier volumes of poetry. Her latest poems are often set in Kentucky and deal with such topics as love, death, and familial relationships.

Ada Limón's new book, *Bright Dead Things*, is full of poems characterized by precise details and clear syntax. They are usually accessible, welcoming works rather than strange, forbidding, self-involved, or self-indulgent ones. For instance, the opening poem, "How to Triumph Like a Girl," begins with these four lines:

> I like the lady horses best,
> how they make it all look easy,
> like running 40 miles per hour
> is as fun as taking a nap, or grass.

Such phrasing can seem undistinguished, but even lines like these have their charms, as in the combination of assonance and alliteration in "I like the lady"; the wit of following "lady" with "horses"; the firm, brief assertiveness of the opening line; and the unexpected arrival of the final phrase ("or grass"). The last two words break the pattern of eight-syllables-per-line and seem intriguingly out of place amid four lines focusing either on movement or the lack thereof. The speaker of these four lines seems down-to-earth and unpretentious, and this appealing impression continues to the end of the work. This feeling is enhanced by a growing sense of the speaker's humor and that she genuinely enjoys life and the simple joys of living.

Limón's poems also have an alluring sense of adventure, specifically those that recount the speaker's (clearly resembling the author's) move from New York to Kentucky. Thus, a poem called "During the Impossible Age of Everyone" seems almost archetypal as it alludes to the process of moving from a former home to an unfamiliar new location and beginning a new life with one's partner. In fact, many of Limón's poems have a strong narrative impulse. They are almost always spoken by a clearly visible "I," and, as they proceed, they develop into a kind of coherent story about the speaker's move, her new environment, her new discoveries, her loving relationship with her unnamed partner, and the impressions all these experiences make on her observant eyes and thoughtful mind.

The book displays a variety of forms, from short, unrhymed lyrics that look quite traditional on the page, to brief square blocks of rhythmic prose and long, loose, and somewhat unshaped narratives. Some of these latter works arguably go on too long; some readers will prefer the short, tight works. But in practically all the poems in this volume, readers are likely to find striking phrases and intriguing individual passages. Take, for instance, the closing lines of the short prose poem titled "Mowing": "I'm thinking about people and trees and how I wish I could be silent more, be more tree than anything else, less clumsy and loud, less crow, more cool white pine, and how it's hard not to always want something else, not just to let the savage grass grow."

(Jude Domski)

Ada Limón is a California-born poet, a graduate of New York University, and the author of a number of collections of verse. These include Lucky Wreck *(2006),* This Big Fake World *(2006), and* Sharks in the Rivers *(2010).*

The phrase "less crow, more cool white pine" seems especially vivid and memorable, because of both the imagery and the sound effects (for example, a comma after "cool" would have weakened the rhythm). The balance of colors, the balance of "less" and "more," and the striking metaphor "less crow" all contribute to the force of the phrasing. Limón's book is full of moments like this, in which she shifts suddenly from the prosaic into a higher register, into something more hauntingly lyrical. Limón has a sharp eye for beauty and is not embarrassed to use it. Yet her writing rarely seems treacly or sentimental; she can write about dogs, horses, love, and lovemaking without losing her balance. This is partly because the speaker has a healthy sense of humor, about both general aspects of life and herself. By the time most readers finish the book, they will probably have come to like this speaker as one likes an interesting new friend.

The further one progresses through *Bright Dead Things*, the more one finds to admire. For instance, Limón is especially effective in using both lists and anaphora (as in the repeated "There's" of "The Quiet Machine")—techniques that, in both cases, contribute to the strong sense of formal coherence, topical variety, and pulsing rhythm of her works. Her poems often involve unexpected, sometimes witty twists, as in "I Remember the Carrots." Also, sometimes (but rarely) she uses obscenity when it seems appropriate (as when describing passionate sex in "The Tree of Fire"). Often she evokes a vivid sense of place ("State Bird" is just one example) and an equally strong sense of the events of real life, whether those are personal or social (as in "How

Far Away We Are" and "Downhearted"). Anyone alive and even remotely alert during the past few years will know the specific historical events to which she alludes, but the allusions are typically phrased so broadly that the poems will not seem past their shelf life ten years from now.

Sometimes Limón deals with major topics, such as belief (or disbelief) in God, as in "Miracle Fish" or "What It Looks Like to Us and the Words We Use," but she never does so in an aggressive, hectoring way. The speaker seems to be either an atheist or an agnostic, and, in fact, "What It Looks Like to Us" concludes in a way reminiscent of Wallace Stevens's great poem "Sunday Morning." Sometimes the speaker deals with death, as in a striking series of works describing the slow, painful, passing of her stepmother. In these poems Limón shows just how blunt she can be. At one point, for example, the speaker mentions needing towels to clean away a "tumor's foul, black spit-up." That final term seems unrelentingly sharp and impossible to forget. Suddenly the dying stepmother seems connected, as she dies, to her days as a baby, when towels were needed to wipe away "spit-up" of an altogether different kind.

After the stepmother passes away, the speaker offers these lines, which reveal the kind of subtlety Limón often achieves:

> No one wants to be remembered
> for their death, or rather,
> I don't. So why do I remember hers
> and remember hers?
> I think I did everything right.

In this stanza are many of Limón's trademark conventions: clear phrasing, simple syntax, and continuing personal focus, with the strong emphasis on "I." Yet this excerpt also includes an assertion and then a quick qualification, suggesting Limón's ability to see at least two sides to the situation; she seems modest as both a person and a poet. Also present, in the third and fourth lines, is her typically effective use of repetition. Finally, in this stanza is an example of her often effective use of line breaks, so that the fifth line stands by itself, following a pause, with the subtle equivocation implied by the simple word "think." In such lines, Limón suggests moral depth and a willingness to question herself and to ponder right and wrong. The poems on the stepmother's death are some of the most haunting, and honest, works in a book full of honest thoughts and responses.

If one had to choose a single short poem to exemplify Limón's typical traits of style and theme, "State Bird" might be the one:

> Confession: I did not want to live here,
> not among the goldenrod, wild onions,
> or the dropseed, not waist-high in the barrel-
> aged brown corn water, not with the million-
> dollar racehorses, nor the tightly wound

round hay bales. Not even in the old tobacco
weigh station we live in, with its heavy metal
safe doors that frame our bricked bedroom
like the mouth of a strange beast yawning
to suck us in, each night, like air. I denied it,
this new land. But love, I'll concede this:
whatever state you are, I'll be that state's bird,
the loud, obvious blur of song people point to
when they wonder where it is you've gone.

This lyric—indebted to the sonnet form in its fourteen lines addressed to a loved one—exhibits many characteristic features of Limón's verse: an abrupt opening and straightforward assertion followed by rich specific details; the effective use of listing and anaphora; and evocative sound play, as in "brown," "wound," and "round." One notices, too, Limón's typical emphasis on a couple's loving relationship, the ways she plays with both assonance and alliteration (as in line 9), and the modesty of the speaker (as in lines 11–14). The final lines also exhibit her typical sense of humor, darkened by just a hint of potential loss (or at least separation) in the final word. The poem's first two sentences are long (consuming roughly five lines each), but then the work pivots on a brief, emphatic, six-word sentence ("I denied it, / this new land"), one weighty with combined assonance and alliteration. Then the work winds to its conclusion in another meandering sentence. Throughout all these sentences the tone is colloquial, even conversational: one notes the repeated use of contractions and how a poem that began by emphasizing the speaker concludes by emphasizing the person she loves.

Limón's book has garnered strong reviews. Brandon Amico for the *Los Angeles Review* says the poems "mov[e] with terrific force and speed, without sacrificing a terrific eye for detail and image," while Linda Ashok for the *Rumpus* states, "the works wear complexity on their sleeves with reassuring accessibility on their face." The collection is full of skillful and smooth-flowing poems, and longer works especially worth reading include "How Far Away We Are," "Torn," "In the Country of Resurrection," "The Wild Divine," and the immensely humorous "Service," which balances the seriousness of the other poems. In short, Limón is a poet of great range, able at once to ponder love and death with real tenderness and then joke about urinating in a junkyard like a proud pit bull. *Bright Dead Things* is a rewarding work in numerous ways. It will make many readers look forward to Limón's next collection.

Robert C. Evans

Review Sources

Amico, Brandon. Rev. of *Bright Dead Things: Poems*, by Ada Limón. *Los Angeles Review*. Los Angeles Review, 2015. Web. 30 Nov. 2015.

Ashok, Linda. Rev. of *Bright Dead Things: Poems*, by Ada Limón. *Rumpus*. Rumpus, 30 Sept. 2015. Web. 30 Nov. 2015.

Rev. of *Bright Dead Things: Poems*, by Ada Limón. *Publishers Weekly* 17 Aug. 2015: 48. Print.

Huston, Karla. Rev. of *Bright Dead Things: Poems*, by Ada Limón. *Library Journal* 1 June 2015: 107. Print.

Zaccagnino, Danielle. Rev. of *Bright Dead Things: Poems*, by Ada Limón. *Front Porch Journal*. Texas State U, 2015. Web. 30 Nov. 2015.

The Buried Giant

Author: Kazuo Ishiguro (b. 1954)
Publisher: Alfred A. Knopf (New York). 336 pp.
Type of work: Novel
Time: Early Middle Ages
Locale: Southern England

In his seventh novel—his first in ten years— Kazuo Ishiguro takes readers on an allegorical journey through medieval England during the dark period after both the Romans and King Arthur had departed.

Principal characters:
AXL, an old Briton
BEATRICE, his wife, the mother of his grown son
WISTAN, a brave Saxon warrior, sent on a mission
EDWIN, a Pictish youth being trained by Wistan
GAWAIN, an old British knight, nephew of King Arthur
FATHER JONUS, a wise old monk, skilled at healing

At the beginning of *The Buried Giant*, Kazuo Ishiguro sets up a "you-and-I" relationship between the implied reader and the narrator. The reader is at least an honorary English person, comfortably at home in the idealized countryside of fields and hedgerows. The narrator reminds the reader that life was not always so neat and simple: the hills and plains, foggy terrain, of England were once wild lands where humans ventured at their peril, ogres and pixies were "everyday hazards," and people had much else to fear.

In one such area, Axl and Beatrice, an elderly couple, live in a small development that is closer to a rabbit warren than a gated community. They live at the end of a tunnel, far from their village's central fire. They have lost status in the community as well as their youth and energy. They have even lost the privilege of having a candle to light their way. More to their dismay, however, they and their neighbors have lost all memory of anything beyond the immediate reality. They cannot even remember their son's name, his face, or his reason for leaving the village. Perhaps he was driven into exile. One day Beatrice, whose name means "blessed" and suggests that she is nominally Christian, makes an important announcement to Axl: "There's a journey we must go on, and no more delay."

These words are embossed on the cloth cover of the North American edition and may remind some readers of the words that Death speaks to Everyman in the medieval morality play commonly titled *Everyman*: "Thou must take a long journey." For Beatrice and Axl, the journey is not to Heaven, but to their long-lost son and to their memories. They have no address for him and no map to guide them, but Beatrice knows the first stop they must make because she travels there with other women selling herbs. Even though that stop is a village of the invading Saxons (Beatrice and Axl are Britons descended from the ancient people of England), Beatrice is following her vision; meanwhile, Axl is determined to help the woman he calls his princess.

The couple soon finds that they are not the only ones on a quest. In the Saxon village, they meet a wandering warrior named Wistan and an orphaned boy named Edwin, who is considered to be cursed because he was bitten by a "monster" and is still wounded. The four travel toward a promontory where Beatrice plans to seek medical advice from a wise old monk, while Axl hopes to get directions from the abbot. On the way, they meet two other questers, Sir Gawain of Arthurian lore and his faithful steed Horace. After escaping a trap set by the abbot and a leader of Britons in the area, the characters find that their separate quests have converged. They all seek a "she-dragon" named Querig, whose breath creates the pervasive fog in which people lose their memories. Wistan and Gawain have been charged by their different kings: Wistan by a British king in the east of England who wants the dragon dead, and Gawain by the late King Arthur in the west, who wants the dragon cared for. Axl and Beatrice have yielded to the pleas of children whose parents have forgotten about them; these children, guided by the mythical Welsh heroine Branwen, want to poison the dragon.

Born in Japan but raised and educated in England, Kazuo Ishiguro has written seven novels. The Remains of the Day, *his third novel, won the prestigious Man Booker Prize (1989) and was made into a feature film (1993).*

These plot details develop over the first three of four sections or "books." The characters meet in the first, are separated in the second, and discover their converging quests in the third. In the fourth book, the characters meet again and somehow remember that the lives of Axl, Gawain, and Wistan intersected during the time of Arthur and Merlin. Their destinies have become fused in the transition from England's past to its future.

The third book is framed by chapters that offer Gawain's private reveries as he talks to himself and his horse. Readers will be reminded that the story is set in the time of the anonymous romance of *Sir Gawain and the Green Knight*, which emphasizes chivalry. More distantly, the novel possesses echoes of the ending of the Anglo-Saxon epic *Beowulf*, where the death of the dragon coincides with the death of the hero and his court. There are echoes, too, of Sir Thomas Malory's *Le Morte d'Arthur*, in which King Arthur dreams, not long before his death, of riding the Wheel of Fortune from the heights to the depths.

The events in the novel occur at a time between the departure of the Romans in 410 CE and the arrival of the Normans in 1066. The events occur *in illo tempore*—"in those times," as scholars like to say of a past that is largely mythic. If the legendary King Arthur led the resistance to invading Saxons in the early sixth century CE, if Axl and Gawain were his young allies and Wistan was his foe, then their quests must occur before the century ended, in the year 600. By that point, there was an uneasy truce between Britons and Saxons, and their once separate developments were growing closer together. By this point, the aging dragon Querig has retired to high ground that must have once been a sacred spot for the Britons. At this spot the giant of the book's title lies buried, though who or what he was in life remains uncertain. Perhaps he was only a chalk man, drawn on the landscape like the Cerne Abbas Giant of Dorset. He nonetheless belonged to the mythic England of dragons and ogres.

The final chapter is narrated by a boatman who meets Axl and Beatrice as they rest below the hill where they saw the dragon's lair and the giant's cairn. Axl says Beatrice must be dreaming that they are at the island where their son has gone, but the boatman assures them that she is right and offers to ferry them over, one at a time. Having met another boatman at the start of their journey, they know that boatmen have their tricks and can leave travelers stranded. But they trust this one, who takes Beatrice first.

As the novel closes, the allegory is clear. The journey for Beatrice is to the island of the dead, where she will join her son and will be joined by the faithful Axl. But there are other journeys to be had in post-Arthurian England. Young Edwin has yet to learn the ways of the warrior, which are also the skills needed to understand the land that Saxons and Britons now share. Edwin has lost his mother, who belonged to the still more ancient tribe of Picts and spoke to him in their mother tongue. The Welsh children who sent Axl and Beatrice to the giant's cairn must learn to fend for themselves in a land devoid of the ancient heroes and heroines.

As the child of a family that immigrated to England from Japan only a few years after World War II, Ishiguro is familiar with the seismic shifts in countries that long seemed unchanging and unchangeable. His first novel, *A Pale View of Hills* (1982), tells the story of a Japanese woman who has moved to England, where she lives alone, far from the family and friends of her youth. His second, *An Artist of the Floating World* (1986), is set in Japan and focuses on a man, once a promising artist, whose life has been changed by the war and who struggles to find his identity in the postwar world. His third, and best known, novel, *The Remains of the Day* (1989), is set in a great English country house that is forced to close after the war and focuses on the adjustments that must be made by its former occupants. Similar themes of loneliness, artistic vision, and search for identity fill his other novels, which range from detective fiction, *When We Were Orphans* (2000), to dystopian fiction, *Never Let Me Go* (2005). While *The Buried Giant* moves into new territory for Ishiguro, seemingly closer, at least superficially, to fantasy and literary romance than his other works, it touches many of the author's abiding concerns. Contemporary concerns about immigrant populations, civil wars, ethnic cleansing, family breakups, and attempts at reconciliation—at home and abroad—are all addressed in the seemingly simple allegory.

Critics have mostly responded favorably to *The Buried Giant*. Tom Holland for the *Guardian* noticed parallels to studies of Arthurian figures by J. R. R. Tolkien, author of the *Lord of the Rings*. Alexandra Alter for the *New York Times* observed that, while the novel is "the weirdest, riskiest, and most ambitious" of Ishiguro's work, it touches on "hallmark themes" such as memory and its distortion, loss, and attempted recovery. Sabine Peschel for *Deutsche Welle* asked Ishiguro if he was trying to walk the fine line between remembering the past, as is stressed in German education today, and concentrating on the future, as other countries urge their children. He responded that it is dangerous both to remember too little and to remember too much. His goal, he said, is to promote mutual understanding and respect. That is exactly what one finds in the novel's fourth book, as the two old warriors, Wistan and Gawain, meet for the last time.

Thomas Willard

Review Sources

Alter, Alexandra. "A New Enchanted Realm." Rev. of *The Buried Giant*, by Kazuo Ishiguro. *New York Times* 20 Feb. 2015: C19. Print.
Holland, Tom. "Kazuo Ishiguro Ventures into Tolkien Territory." Rev. of *The Buried Giant*, by Kazuo Ishiguro. *Guardian*. Guardian News and Media, 19 Feb. 2015. Web. 8 Dec. 2015.
Rich, Nathaniel. "The Book of Sorrow and Forgetting." Rev. of *The Buried Giant*, by Kazuo Ishiguro. *Atlantic*. Atlantic Monthly Group, Mar. 2015. Web. 8 Dec. 2015.

The Cartel

Author: Don Winslow (b. 1953)
Publisher: Alfred A. Knopf (New York).
640 pp.
Type of work: Novel
Time: 2004–12, 2014
Locales: Mexico, southern United States, Guatemala

Don Winslow describes in graphic detail the workings of the Mexican drug trade and the savagery associated with the struggle for dominance among the country's drug cartels, and he dramatizes the personal tragedies of innocent victims caught up in the violence.

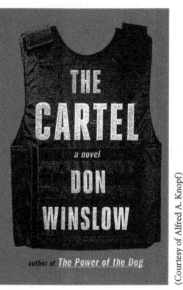

(Courtesy of Alfred A. Knopf)

Principal characters:
ADÁN BARRERA, the leader of the Sinaloa drug cartel
MAGDA BELTRÁN, his mistress and business partner
ARTURO "ART" KELLER, an agent with the US Drug Enforcement Agency
MARISOL CISNEROS, a physician and Keller's girlfriend
EDDIE RUIZ, an American involved in the Mexican drug trade
HERIBERTO OCHOA, the leader of the Zetas, a Mexican drug cartel
LUIS AGUILAR, Mexico's assistant attorney general for organized crime
GERARDO VERA, the head of Mexico's federal investigative agency
JESÚS BARAJOS (ALSO KNOWN AS "CHUY" OR "JESUS THE KID"), an American teen involved in the drug trade
PABLO MORA, a journalist based in Juárez

On July 12, 2015, news sources around the world reported the escape of convicted Mexican drug lord Joaquin "El Chapo" Guzmán from a Mexican prison where he was serving his sentence for a long list of felonies that should have kept him behind bars for years. The incident brought back into focus the United States' longest-running war: the War on Drugs. In the following weeks, details of the elaborate plan to get Guzmán out of what was supposedly a maximum-security prison revealed once again the corruption that plagues Mexico's law-enforcement system. Guzmán's escape also pointed up the inability of the United States to deal effectively with the ongoing problem of narcotics trafficking in Mexico that feeds a ready market north of the Rio Grande.

Guzmán's successful breakout may have struck some, however, as an instance of life imitating art. Only weeks before Mexico's most notorious drug lord slipped behind a screen and down a tunnel to freedom, a similar escape had been described in detail—in *The Cartel*, a newly released novel by veteran crime writer Don Winslow.

Although *The Cartel* can be read as a stand-alone novel, it is an extension of Winslow's 2005 book *The Power of the Dog*, which traces the relationship between Sinaloa drug-cartel boss Adán Barrera and US Drug Enforcement Agency (DEA) agent Art Keller. The latter's pursuit of his archenemy continues in *The Cartel* when Barrera escapes from a Mexican prison and begins to reestablish himself as *El Jefe de Jefes*— "the boss of bosses"—kingpin of all drug trafficking in Mexico. Barrera's efforts to secure control over the various regional cartels is opposed by several of their leaders, including the Tapia family and Heriberto Ochoa, leader of the Zetas. Much of the novel describes the shifting alliances among these families and government officials, many of whom are in the pay of the cartels. Keller makes his own alliances with the few people in the Mexican government whom he thinks he can trust: Luis Aguilar, assistant attorney general in charge of prosecuting drug crimes, and Gerardo Vera, head of the country's investigative agency. Even these relationships prove troublesome, as corruption seems to invade every aspect of Mexico's local, regional, and national governing agencies.

Although Keller is in Mexico in an official capacity, sent by the DEA to help the Mexican government capture leaders of the drug trade, his pursuit of Barrera has the characteristics of a personal vendetta. Barrera, too, wants to settle a score with Keller, placing a $2 million bounty on his head. Yet in this bizarre world of shifting loyalties, the two eventually find themselves working together to eliminate what at the moment seems a greater threat to the country: the Zetas, who emerge as the worst of the criminal groups. Their open use of terror tactics—senseless killing of innocent civilians, maiming, burning, dismemberment, and a host of torture tactics—let the population and the Mexican government know that Ochoa's forces intend to emerge victorious no matter the cost.

Running parallel to the main story are ones involving several of the second-tier players in the drug trade, most notably Americans Eddie Ruiz and Jesús "Chuy" Barajos. Both are lured south of the border to pursue their fortunes. Ruiz, a disgruntled twenty-six-year-old denied opportunities for making his fortune legitimately in south Texas, rises from street punk to minor drug lord in Mexico. Barajos, nicknamed Jesus the Kid, commits his first murder on behalf of the cartel at age eleven and by sixteen emerges as one of the cartel's most vicious assassins. Winslow also introduces two strong women into the narrative. Magda Beltrán, a former Mexican beauty queen, becomes Barrera's mistress while incarcerated at the same prison where Barrera is being held, and she parlays that relationship into a lucrative business opportunity as his partner and later as an independent entrepreneur. Marisol Cisneros, a physician who left Mexico City to practice in a rural area near the northern city of Juárez, serves both as Keller's love interest and as a model of the heroic citizen who stands up to the cartels, placing herself—and unfortunately, her friends and associates—at risk.

Winslow concentrates a portion of the story on the violence plaguing Juárez, the city across the Rio Grande (or Río Bravo, as the Mexicans call it) from El Paso, Texas. There, journalist Pablo Mora tries valiantly to report on the dozens of murders carried out by warring cartel factions, often risking his own life in the process. The murders of several journalists and people close to Mora offer Winslow an opportunity to explore the human dimensions of the national scourge. A certain macabre irony emerges from the book as the cartels vie for dominance and the brutality and senseless carnage becomes so commonplace that, as reporter Pablo Mora observes, the absence of murders, not their commission, is news. The warring factions tout their ability to protect the citizens of their territory; some even make public statements about their honor, insisting that they do not kill innocent women and children. Winslow also exposes the United States' role in perpetuating these drug wars, dramatizing the knotty bureaucratic and diplomatic issues that arise as a result of American attempts to squash the drug trade while maintaining good relationships with their neighbors to the south. He also exposes the ties between the Mexican drug trade and international terrorism, and links between drug trafficking and legitimate business interests (including those of US businesses) in exploiting Mexico's natural resources, particularly oil and natural gas.

Don Winslow is the creator of the Neal Carey and Boone Daniels mystery series. Several of his of seventeen novels have been nominated for various mystery and crime awards and adapted for film. In 2012, he received the Raymond Chandler Award for excellence in the crime and mystery genres.

The novel ends with a battle in the Guatemalan jungle that promises to put an end to Ochoa's bid for domination and Barrera's efforts to bring the drug trade under his control. As the conclusion to a work of fiction, the ending offers some closure, and the epilogue suggests that the survivors have managed to make some sort of separate peace. Yet anyone reading *The Cartel* carefully, aware of the historical events on which Winslow bases his fictional account, understands that the real story is far from finished. The chilling implications of the narrative linger long after the informed reader turns the last page.

The Cartel has been compared to Mario Puzo's *The Godfather* (1969), a generational saga of Italian Mafia families fighting for control of illicit trade in New York City. Acclaimed crime writer James Ellroy has called it "the *War and Peace* of dope-war books." While its characters are fictional, many of the events Winslow describes seem little more than retellings of real incidents that have occurred within the past two decades. Although Winslow acknowledges that *The Cartel*, like its predecessor, is based on extensive research, he believes his decision to write a novel is justified on both aesthetic and political grounds. In *a Los Angeles Times* interview published shortly after *The Cartel* was released, Winslow told fellow novelist Ivy Pochoda that he believes fiction can be more effective than journalism in describing the horrors of Mexico's drug wars: "Journalism can give the facts, but fiction can tell the truth."

Winslow shares this sentiment with Ernest Hemingway, who made a similar statement more than half a century earlier. The similarities between these writers go beyond a belief in the power of fiction; like Hemingway, Winslow employs a spare style that focuses on events and delivers the grim facts of warfare among rival criminal gangs that highlights its senselessness yet simultaneously captivates readers' interest. Winslow sketches his scenes like a Japanese artist, deftly providing just enough details about setting to anchor his action in the geography of the region in which these brutal drug wars are fought. What is alarming is that one is likely to begin to sympathize with some of the drug lords and their lieutenants, to applaud their courage and their capacity to stay out of harm's way—and beyond the reach of the few honest law-enforcement officials who want them put in prison for life. Even more frightening, readers are just as likely to admire Winslow's putative "good guy," Art Keller, even to the point of overlooking the extralegal acts of violence in which he routinely engages. Winslow is adept at making heroes of these outlaws, some of whom carry out crimes against enemies (and allies) that would make a medieval torturer blush. At the same time, the mind starts to become numb to the tragedy that the drug wars have caused. Body counts dehumanize the atrocities, masking the fact that every number represents a human life taken away to satisfy the desires of drug lords for power and wealth—drug lords who almost always remain far removed from the bloodshed.

The Cartel is more than a work of fiction; it is simultaneously a political statement indicting the powerful who profit from the chaos and mayhem. Winslow makes the point explicitly through Mora, whose final posting on the blog he runs secretly calls out everyone responsible for this national tragedy. "This is not a war on drugs," he insists. "This is a war on the poor." Speaking for "the powerless, the disenfranchised . . . the victims of this so-called 'war on drugs'"—and for the journalists who "tried to tell the story" but were "silenced" and "blinded"—Mora tells "the rich, the powerful, the politicians, the *comandantes*, the generals," the Mexican government and the US president and Congress, Mora says, "You are all the same. You are the cartel. And you are guilty." Equally chilling is Keller's succinct observation at the end of the novel: "People don't run the cartel; the cartel runs people." The bleak conclusion is that, unless there is some seismic shift in the political landscape, the cartel—the unholy alliance between criminals, governments, and big business—is likely to go on operating no matter who is said to be in charge.

Laurence W. Mazzeno

Review Sources

Miller, Laura. "The System: A Sprawling Novel about the War on Drugs." Rev. of *The Cartel*, by Don Winslow. *New Yorker*. Condé Nast, 6 July 2015. Web. 7 Dec. 2015.

Maslin, Janet. "A Drug War, Long and Brutal." Rev. of *The Cartel*, by Don Winslow. *New York Times* 19 June 2015: C21. Print.

Wolff, Carlo. "The Combatants from 'The Power of the Dog' Return in Brilliant Sequel." Rev. of *The Cartel*, by Don Winslow. *Pittsburgh Post-Gazette*. PG Publishing, 12 July 2015. Web. 7 Dec. 2015.

Challenger Deep

Author: Neal Shusterman (b. 1962)
Publisher: HarperCollins (New York). 320 pp.
Type of work: Novel
Time: Present day
Locale: New York

(Used by permission of HarperCollins Publishers)

Challenger Deep describes a boy's struggles after he begins to experience symptoms of schizophrenia. Shusterman wrote the novel to help open a dialogue about mental illness and reduce its stigma. The illustrations are by his son, Brendan, who was diagnosed with schizoaffective disorder as a teenager.

Principal characters:
CADEN BOSCH, a fifteen-year-old boy and talented artist who is experiencing symptoms of schizophrenia
MACKENZIE, his younger sister
SHELBY, his friend
THE CAPTAIN, a man in charge of the pirate ship imagined by him
THE PARROT, the captain's talkative sidekick
GIRL, a patient at Seaview Hospital's psychiatric unit

Challenger Deep is the story of a boy who is trying to reach Challenger Deep, the deepest point in the ocean. The story was inspired by Shusterman's son, Brendan, who began experiencing symptoms of schizoaffective disorder as a teenager and described his experience to Shusterman as being at the bottom of the ocean, screaming, where nobody could hear him. The reader becomes aware of Caden's mental illness slowly as it unfolds in his first-person narration that includes both reality and delusions.

At first Caden is anxious. The reader knows this because he reminds himself that the sprinklers hissing down the street are not snakes. He tells himself that the dolphins in the mural he painted for his little sister are not plotting something deadly. And he fears that the Captain will be there soon. The reader learns more about the captain as Caden's account of his journey with the Captain is juxtaposed with his increasingly unsettling behavior in his everyday life.

The reader cannot be entirely sure what is real and what is not, especially since the novel is written in present tense, with chapters from Caden's day-to-day experience alternating with chapters about his time as an artist on a ship traveling to Challenger Deep. It becomes clear to the reader, after Caden tells his father that he is certain someone who does not know him and has never threatened him is going to kill him, that something is going terribly awry. As Caden's friends and family become more concerned, the reader does, too.

Caden is an artistic boy who has always sketched. Drawings that are attributed to him are included throughout the book, and the reader can see that his ability to draw recognizable objects becomes increasingly compromised as the story progresses. His friend Shelby notices and comments on it as well. Caden's sister, Mackenzie, is also deeply concerned about her brother. She comes home from school to find him listening for termites that he is sure are destroying the house. When he tells her this, she says, "You can hear termites?" The thought horrifies her. Caden's behavior becomes more and more strange. The things he does make no sense to the people in his life. In fact, the reader knows they make no sense to Caden, either.

Events reach a decision point when Caden, rather than attending track practice, spends his time walking around aimlessly. One day he walks barefoot in a parking lot, his feet blistered and bloody, and tells a woman he sees that there is a worm inside her heart. He asks her for help but she pushes him away, threatening to call the police. Another woman comes to him and he pleads, "Please just make it stop. Please just make it stop." She offers, kindly, to call someone for him, but the thought of her calling his parents gets him up on his feet to find his way home. Not long after, his father, whom Caden can tell has been crying, tells Caden it is time to take a trip. In reality, Caden is committed to Seaview Memorial Hospital's psychiatric unit, leaving the reader both concerned for Caden's well-being and relieved that he will finally be in a facility where he can get the care he needs.

Yet the situation does not markedly improve after Caden enters treatment. His hallucinations include his fellow patients, his therapist, and the staff at the unit. It is difficult to discern whether he is making any progress. When he has bad reaction to a medication change, it is impossible to tell at first whether Caden has moved beyond reach or if it is simply a matter of adjusting his medication again. The reader cares because, ultimately, Caden is an extremely likable person. Even when he is most confused and disoriented, he remains concerned about his sister and the people around him. This deeply caring part of Caden seems to be the core of who he is, and readers will become invested in Caden and his recovery process.

Throughout his treatment, his family stands by him and offers him the support that they can. His younger sister comes to visit him when she is allowed. His friends come when they can, too. It is clearly painful for them, and the reader cannot help but share their pain because it is difficult to be sure at any given moment whether Caden knows that he has not been abandoned by his family and friends. Only the fact that he hesitates to

Neal Shusterman is an award-winning author who has written a number of fiction and nonfiction books. His novel The Schwa Was Here *received the 2008 California Young Reader Medal. He is also the author of the novels* The Dark Side of Nowhere *(1997),* Downsiders *(1999),* Full Tilt *(2003), and* Unwind *(2007).*

join the Captain at the bottom of Challenger Deep leaves the reader with hope that Caden's rational mind is still intact despite the delusions—calling out but not yet heard.

The use of first-person narration in this novel is highly effective. It gives the reader no choice other than to join Caden in the fluctuating, confusing, and competing emotions he experiences. When he is agitated, the language unsettles the reader as well. When he is confused and lost, the reader is right there, trying to distinguish between hallucination and reality. It effectively conveys to the reader the experience of struggling with an undiagnosed and untreated mental illness.

Challenger Deep also makes the point that not all therapists and facilitators are equally adept at gaining and keeping a patient's confidence. Dr. Poirot, in particular, is not a favorite of Caden's from the start. Caden observes, "Dr. Poirot has a cheat sheet that tells him everything about you. Even things you don't know yourself. How can you even begin to trust such a person?" On the other hand, Caden's group-therapy leader, Carlyle, seems far more approachable. "I'm not here to brainwash you," he tells Caden. "I'm just here to help you speak your mind."

The subject matter of *Challenger Deep* is profoundly unsettling. The way in which Shusterman switches between lucid observation, delusion, and observation of events within a distorted sense of reality succeeds in moving the reader well off center. Nevertheless, the novel is not plodding and heavy. It is actually funny in many places, leaving the reader to wonder if Holden Caulfield of J. D. Salinger's *The Catcher in the Rye* (1951) might have done better if he had had a better sense of humor.

Caden can see humor in his situation even when things are at their worst and the Captain is pushing Caden as hard as he can to join him at the bottom of the ocean. Caden can see that the choices he has before him are not choices he would really like to make. This levity—or his capacity to maintain a wry outlook on life—keeps the book, and the reader's emotional response to it, in a range that compels readers to move forward to see what will happen next. The reader may be upset to join Caden in a place where his logic is profoundly flawed and the way out is unclear, but that does not mean the reader will want to leave him before the end of the novel.

A critic for the *Kirkus Reviews* praised the book's portrayal of mental illness, writing, "Caden's disorientation and others' unease also make the story chillingly real. Except in the heights of Caden's delusions, nothing is romanticized—just off-kilter enough to show how easily unreality acquires its own logic and wit." *Challenger Deep* is not an easy read. In a review for the *Horn Book*, Deirdre Baker wrote that "this novel is a challenge to the reader from its first lines: author Shusterman takes us into the seemingly random, rambling, and surreal fantasies. . . . The disorientation Shusterman evokes through the first-person narration requires some patience, but it's an apt, effective way to bring readers into nightmarish anxiety and despair—and out of it."

Shusterman's son had a similar experience to Caden with a sudden onset of schizoaffective disorder as a teen, and he described it to Shusterman. The illustrations that are included in the novel are by Shusterman's son, which he drew during the onset, diagnosis, and treatment of his mental illness, paralleling Caden's experience in the novel. While not a memoir, the novel does draw heavily on the experience of losing oneself in this disorder and fighting to come back to a new normal.

Shusterman teamed with his son to write this novel, using his son's experience to inform the body of the work, as well as his artwork to accompany the work. The way in which the artwork varies throughout Caden's story is a strong, unspoken metaphor for the progression of his illness and his subsequent recovery process. These sketches give the reader an entrée into an additional, unspoken level of understanding his struggle. The novel draws heavily on Brendan's description of his experiences of losing himself during the onset of mental illness. A critic for *Publishers Weekly* stated that this collaboration is powerful and "crucial to the novel's credibility."

Challenger Deep received the National Book Award for young people's literature. Shusterman accepted the award with his son at his side. The judges described the book as "poetic, compassionate, and thrillingly inventive" and hailed it for affirming "the power of narrative to describe the indescribable." The greatest achievement of this book is in the way Shusterman has made it possible for the reader to share Caden's growing detachment from reality while also deeply caring for and connecting with Caden. Considering that the reader meets Caden as he is already experiencing symptoms of mental illness and that the reader learns about Caden only through the events Caden is able to communicate, it is remarkable that the reader is not only able to sense Caden's family's concern but share it as well.

Gina Hagler

Review Sources

Baker, Deidre. Rev. of *Challenger Deep*, by Neal Shusterman. *Horn Book*. Horn Book, 10 Mar. 2015. Web. 5 Jan. 2016.

Rev. of *Challenger Deep*, by Neal Shusterman. *Kirkus*. Kirkus, 20 Jan. 2015. Web. 10 Jan. 2016.

Rev. of *Challenger Deep*, by Neal Shusterman. *Publishers Weekly*. PWxyz, Apr. 2015. Web. 10 Jan. 2016.

The Children's Crusade

Author: Ann Packer (b. 1959)
Publisher: Scribner (New York). 448 pp.
Type of work: Novel
Time: 1954–2008
Locale: Portola Valley, California

Ann Packer's The Children's Crusade *offers a stirring examination of family reality and dysfunction in a California home where four children grow to adulthood in the shadow of their benevolent father and distant mother.*

Principal characters:
BILL BLAIR, the fun-loving family patriarch, a pediatrician
PENNY BLAIR, his wife, a disaffected mother and artist
ROBERT BLAIR, their first child, a doctor
REBECCA BLAIR, their second child, a psychiatrist
RYAN BLAIR, their third child, a private-school teacher
JAMES BLAIR, their troubled youngest child

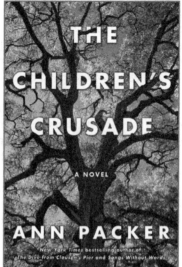

(Courtesy of Scribner)

The countless movies, books, and television sitcoms that take the dysfunction of family life as their subject tend to emphasize either uproarious laughter or incredible tragedy. Rarely is the story merely a snippet of life, a window into the day-to-day minutia of the lived experience. Ann Packer's novel *The Children's Crusade* offers yet another discourse on the family that embraces a formulaic approach of exploring childhood problems that have profound impact on the adults who emerge from the experiences. In *The Children's Crusade*, the line between good and bad is not as clear as it appears at first glance. The book, like life itself, tends to dwell in shades of gray.

Of all of the figures that exist in Packer's work, the family patriarch, Bill Blair, comes across as the most sympathetic and, in many ways, the least realistic character. A Korean War veteran who returns to Northern California after the conflict, Blair soon marries, and he and his wife plan a family that would include three children. It does not take long to see that the "picture-perfect" family has some serious problems. Each of the Blair children is spotlighted in the narrative, which includes alternating retrospectives highlighting poignant episodes from their childhood and musings from their adult lives, as well as sections told in omniscient perspective. The one thing that they all seem to agree on is the centrality of their father to the family unit. The children adored the man, who despite his busy work as a pediatrician, still found time to spend with his offspring. There is no hint of anger in any of the stories told about Bill—he is too perfect. A character such as Bill, who remains universally heralded throughout the story, is difficult to conceptualize. In literature, individuals are often exalted, yet usually only for dramatic effect in preparation for their fall. With Bill, the fall never arrives. Throughout the novel, he makes each of his children feel special, even his troubled fourth child, James. The reader gets the sense that his household would have been pure paradise were it not for the presence of his rather sullen wife, Penny.

The matriarch of the Blair clan, Penny, is an ever-present force in the book, yet one who remains on the periphery of the family unit. The children remember her as quick-tempered, lashing out at all transgressions, whether big or small. She clearly did not spend much time with the children. If her husband's mantra is "children deserve care," hers might be "keep your distance." The children learned to steer clear of her as much as possible, although they did make several abortive attempts to launch a "crusade" to integrate their mother more fully into family activities. The crusade is something only referenced in passing with the children, who forged the idea, seemingly not interested in seeing it through. Since the kids had Bill, who gave them complete attention, it is unsurprising how easily they forgot their mother. Penny sat back and stewed, or at least that is the way her children chose to remember her.

The memories of warm and affectionate Bill contrast sharply with the distant and often disinterested Penny. Just as with Bill's characterization, the reader waits for the real Penny, who was the victim of some unspoken evil, to appear, but this never happens. Penny becomes more understandable as the story goes on but does not become a more sympathetic character. Where Bill makes his world the nurturing of the children, Penny has harbored dreams of being an artist that were disparaged by her parents and subsumed when she married Bill and devoted herself to the raising of children. Bill lives the life he wanted; Penny, however, is trapped in a prison that she has struggled to escape, much like many other women in the 1960s and 1970s. Just when she thought she was free following the birth of the three Rs—Robert, Rebecca, and Ryan—she found herself pregnant again. The birth of the fourth child, James, fundamentally altered the marital union between Bill and Penny. Central to the discord were James's frequent outbursts.

For Penny, the whirlwind of activity and lack of self-censorship in her youngest child was simply too much and drove a wedge between her and Bill. Regardless of James's transgressions, Bill always seemed able to talk him down and to calm him. And true to form, Bill could not stay mad at his son. This quality made him a number-one dad to his children while also making him an annoyance to Penny, who took Bill's failure to discipline his children as her cue to withdraw from the family unit. Eventually, she moved outside of the main house into a shed that Bill had expanded into an art studio (and eventual cottage) for his increasingly estranged wife. Although she came into the main house during the daytime, she abandoned the family as soon as Bill returned home to work on her art. The tension in the Blair home was palpable, and as the children grew, they increasingly recognized that something was not quite right with their parents. Among the children, Penny is rather unfairly labeled as the sole reason for the family's problems.

The three Rs in the Blair family all become successful members of the community, with Robert entering the medical profession, Rebecca becoming a psychiatrist, and

Ryan making his way as a teacher. Then there is James, the free-spirited one who, despite a stormy relationship with his mother rooted in the knowledge of her loathing, has more in common with Penny than the other children. The last of the Blair children to leave the house, James's antics brought him much difficulty and his parents much anguish. When he finally moved out, he bounced from job to job and place to place before invariably ending up on the couches and in the spare bedrooms of his more successful and stable siblings. Although they always welcomed the wayward James, they all wished for him to grow up. Indeed, the artistic Penny, under different circumstances, would probably have found much to admire in her youngest son; after all it was Penny who took a gamble later in life by giving up on her marriage and relocating to an artist enclave in Taos where she could pursue her muse uninhibited by the naysayers in her family. James, in many ways, has followed his own inner voice from the start and refused to be pigeonholed by society or by his family. The irony is that James was permitted to be a free spirit by his compassionate father, whereas his mother, Penny, considered Bill—and, by extension, James—the very reason she was so unhappy. As the plot develops, more and more of James's antics are brought to light, including his rather distasteful fascination with the 1978 Jonestown Massacre. The novel leaves the impression that something terrible would be revealed, that James would commit a transgression that would forever wrench the family apart. But he never does. Youthful indiscretions are certainly plentiful, but his antics do not seem all that different from the foibles that befall countless teens. James is certainly less self-directed than his siblings, but little is presented in the book to account for the disdain Penny has for her son, save for the fact that he was never wanted. Considering this, it is difficult to find anything redeeming about Penny, especially because even after he leaves the home, her contempt for James remains long after she could reasonably assert that his presence is keeping her from her calling.

Best-selling author Ann Packer has written two collections of short stories and several novels, including The Children's Crusade *and the widely heralded* The Dive from Clausen's Pier *(2002), which garnered her the Kate Chopin Literary Award.*

In a book filled with vivid prose and often tense descriptions of family discord, Packer's work tends to fall short in character development. The three Rs come across as rather flat, while the book's hero, Bill, is too good to be true, a character who lacks a weakness and thus a human dimension. James and Penny, who at various points in the book seem the most human, are never permitted to fully blossom into relatable characters. James does at least appear to get his life on track as the book closes, as he reverses course on what likely would have been yet another disastrous decision involving a married woman with whom he was having an affair. The book terminates thereafter, depriving readers of the chance to see how James turns out. *The Children's Crusade*, however, was never meant to follow a standard narrative in which good triumphs over evil and in which all of the story lines are neatly tied up at the end. Rather Packer's work reflects the narrative of real-life families with problems drawn from history. Both Bill and Penny had tempestuous relationships with their parents. As a father, Bill strove to nurture his children in a manner dissimilar to the way in which he was raised. Penny also sought a different example for her kids, yet she fell short of the mark. The Blair children in turn take a crack at child rearing, and their offspring will no doubt live an existence shaped in every way by Bill and Penny. Such is the cycle of real life, in which story lines are rarely concluded but continue on generation after generation. If Packer's work achieves nothing else, it reveals a slice of reality that all have experienced. For this, *The Children's Crusade* is worth a look.

Keith M. Finley, PhD

Review Sources

Corrigan, Maureen. "'The Children's Crusade': A Heavily Plotted Family Saga to Dive into and Savor." Rev. of *The Children's Crusade*, by Ann Packer. *Fresh Air*. NPR, 14 Apr. 2015. Web. 31 Dec. 2015.

Kitamura, Katie. "The Prodigal Son." Rev. of *The Children's Crusade*, by Ann Packer. *New York Times* 12 Apr. 2015: BR11. Print.

Maslin, Janet. "Uh Oh, Mom Has Another Art Project." Rev. of *The Children's Crusade*, by Ann Packer. *New York Times* 16 Apr. 2015: C1. Print.

Sampson, Hannah. Rev. of *The Children's Crusade*, by Ann Packer. *Miami Herald*. Miami Herald, 1 May 2015. Web. 31 Dec. 2015.

China Rich Girlfriend

Author: Kevin Kwan
Publisher: Doubleday (New York). 400 pp.
Type of work: Novel
Time: 2012–13
Locales: Beijing, Shanghai, and Hangzhou, China; London, England; Hong Kong; Cupertino, Santa Barbara, Montecito, and Los Angeles, California; Singapore; New York, New York; Venice, Italy; Paris, France

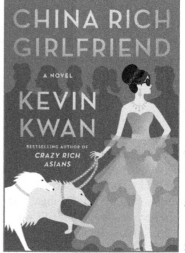

(Courtesy of Penguin Random House)

The sequel to the best-selling Crazy Rich Asians *(2013) and the second entry in a planned trilogy,* China Rich Girlfriend *continues the chronicle of relationships, activities, and aspirations of a group of fabulously and ostentatiously wealthy Asians as they maneuver to compete in status and influence.*

Principal characters:
NICHOLAS "NICKY" YOUNG, a history teacher at New York University
RACHEL CHU, his fiancé and later wife, a teacher of economics
ASTRID TEO LEONG, his cousin, the mother of a five-year-old
SU-YI YOUNG, his grandmother, a wealthy widow who owns the estate of Tyersall Park in Singapore
ELEANOR YOUNG, his mother, Eddie Cheng's aunt
EDISON "EDDIE" CHENG, his cousin, a Hong Kong private banker
MICHAEL LEONG, Astrid's husband, the recently wealthy founder of a tech company
CHARLIE WU, Astrid's friend and former lover, now the head of Wu Microsystems and a married father of two
BAO GAOLIANG, a Chinese politician and heir to a large pharmaceutical firm
BAO SHAOYEN, Bao Gaoliang's wife
CARLTON BAO, their wastrel son, a graduate student at Cambridge University
CORINNA KO-TUNG, a mousy, middle-aged art consultant
COLETTE BING, Carlton Bao's sometime girlfriend, a young and popular fashion icon
RICHIE YANG, a racing enthusiast, a suitor of Colette's and the son of one of the richest men in China
JACK BING, Colette's father, a billionaire
KATHERINE "KITTY" PONG, a.k.a. Mrs. Tai, a social-climbing former porn actor and soap-opera star
BERNARD TAI, Kitty's husband, a future heir to billions

China Rich Girlfriend literally opens with a bang. Early one September morning in 2012, a new Ferrari traveling at a high speed through the streets of London crashes into a store, injuring the driver, young Carlton Bao, and killing his female passenger. Immediately, private banker Edison "Eddie" Cheng, who handles the accounts of the well-heeled Bao family, flies in from Hong Kong with Carlton's mother, Bao Sha-oyen, to initiate an expensive cover-up. Meanwhile, wealthy Eleanor Young is also in London, holidaying with three female friends. Eddie enlists the aid of "Auntie Elle" in taking care of Mrs. Bao while he arranges payoffs for Carlton's mishap.

The scene shifts to Hong Kong in early 2013, where twenty-four priceless seventeenth-century Qing dynasty silk scrolls are being auctioned by Christie's. Among those participating in the spirited bidding are Kitty Pong, a former actor married to a billionaire, and Astrid Leong, wife of a newly wealthy entrepreneur. Kitty wins the scrolls for a price of $195 million.

The scene shifts again, this time to Cupertino, California, on February 9, 2013, where the Chu family has assembled for Chinese New Year's Eve. Rachel Chu, raised by single mother Kerry, is now engaged to New York University professor Nick Young, scion of the rich Young family. The couple's romance was the cause of Nick's estrangement from his mother, since Rachel comes from a humble, middle-class family. Rachel and Nick have visited China in a futile search for Rachel's father.

Meanwhile, Eleanor Young visits the Baos at their $15 million condo in Singapore, where Carlton recovered after undergoing extensive plastic surgery following his accident. Also in Singapore is Astrid, recently moved into a nine-thousand-square-foot home to accommodate her husband's collection of vintage cars. Astrid keeps in touch via e-mail with former lover and faithful friend Charlie Wu, owner of a profitable tech company. Eleanor and Astrid attend a Chinese New Year's gathering at Su-Yi Young's estate, where Eleanor learns from Astrid's young son that Nicky and Rachel are engaged to be married soon in Los Angeles. Astrid warns Nick that his mother knows about the forthcoming wedding. Eleanor asks a family friend with connections to a Norwegian billionaire to persuade Nick to marry into a wealthy family, lest his grandmother change her will to prevent him from inheriting the vast family estate, Tyersall Park in Singapore. Nick ignores the advice.

Kevin Kwan published his widely acclaimed debut novel, Crazy Rich Asians, *in 2013. The novel was optioned for a film adaptation, with Kwan as an executive producer.*

In Hong Kong, Kitty makes an egregious social faux pas and is afterward shunned at an exclusive club. Art consultant Corinna Ko-Tung takes Kitty under her wing and, for a fee, begins making over her dress, habits, and manners to help her gain entrance into high society. A major obstacle to overcome is Kitty's husband, living in California with the couple's daughter. Bernard has had extensive plastic surgery and is psychologically unhinged. Astrid Leong and Charlie Wu also run into one another in Hong Kong. Astrid is preparing to fly to Los Angeles to attend Nick and Rachel's wedding. Charlie, who still has feelings for Astrid, decides to fly there too.

While preparing for their wedding, Rachel and Nick learn that Eleanor is on her way to California. Eleanor arrives at the wedding in spectacular fashion, in a rented helicopter. She begs Nick's forgiveness, gives the union her blessing, and announces she has, via a private detective, found Rachel's father: he is Bao Gaoliang, a Chinese politician and billionaire. Nick and Rachel honeymoon in Shanghai, China, and they are scheduled to meet the Baos. Shaoyen, however, refuses to meet Rachel: she has lost face because her husband's previous affair and illegitimate daughter brought shame to her family, which may ruin his political life and destroy their son's future.

Rachel and Nick wait in a private room at a plush restaurant for the Baos to arrive. Instead, they are greeted by Colette Bing, Carlton's sometime girlfriend, and Colette's assistant, Roxanne Ma. The honeymooners meet Carlton, who closely resembles his half sister. Colette, Nick, and Carlton all bond over having studied in London. The four attend many parties together, but Nick and Rachel still do not meet with the elder Baos. They end up at the thirty-acre private retreat of Colette's, where Nick and Rachel finally meet Rachel's father, Bao Gaoliang. They also meet Richie Yang, the son of another billionaire. Also there is Jack Bing, Colette's father and one of the richest men in China. Jack tells Colette that Richie wants to marry her, though she is uninterested in Richie. On a whim, Colette uses the Bings' luxuriously appointed private Boeing 747 to transport Rachel, Nick, and more than twenty others to Paris for a week-long party and shopping spree. Richie Yang shows up in Paris and proposes to Colette with a gigantic diamond ring, which precipitates a fight between Richie and Carlton. The two rivals make a ten-million-dollar wager on an illegal drag race through Paris, repeating the event that led to the earlier tragedy in London, but Rachel persuades Carlton to call off the race.

Astrid, attending an event in Venice, Italy, learns from the family housekeeper of her husband's cruelty to their five-year-old son, Cassian: Astrid's husband, Michael, locked Cassian in a closet for hours after he accidentally scratched a vintage car. The couple have a phone conversation about child rearing that degenerates into a bitter exchange about money. Charlie Wu calls Astrid and is appalled to learn of Michael's treatment of her son. Charlie later composes a long e-mail to Astrid, confessing his love for her, but does not send it.

After returning to Singapore, Astrid sees an article about her husband in a magazine and is infuriated to find it contains private information about her family. She and Michael have an angry confrontation. Astrid's wealthy father, Harry Leong, meets with Michael to tell him he has bought the entire print run of the magazine and had it pulled and pulped. Astrid solicits Charlie Wu's help in finding out who bought Michael's first company, thus making her husband a millionaire. Charlie has a major dilemma: it was his firm, through a shell company, that purchased Michael's enterprise at a loss. Astrid learns who made the sale from her father and realizes that Charlie did it out of love for her.

Back in Shanghai, the elder Bings tell Colette that they are disappointed she did not accept Richie's proposal, which Jack orchestrated. Jack threatens to cut off Colette's accounts if she does not do as ordered. She refuses, and her father makes good on his threat.

Still on honeymoon in China, Rachel falls deathly ill. She has been deliberately poisoned with a drug the Bao family manufactures, and Carlton thinks his mother is responsible. Ultimately, the real culprit is exposed, and Rachel is given an antidote, recovers, and is finally welcomed into the Bao home.

Though relationships among characters are sometimes confusing—everybody seems related in some way to everybody else—*China Rich Girlfriend* humorously illuminates the habits and foibles of unimaginably rich Asians. Conflicts between old and new money and between the rich of mainland China and those elsewhere in Southeast Asia are especially highlighted. The third-person omniscient viewpoint—spiced up by text messages, phone conversations, and print clippings—permits the narration to travel wherever the plot demands and keeps the pace lively. Frequent footnotes translate expressions from various dialects (Hokkien, Cantonese, Mandarin), explain slang, give further information about specific places or items, and often contain snarky editorial comments, adding to the fun.

Like Kwan's previous novel, *Crazy Rich Asians* (2013), *China Rich Girlfriend* contains numerous scenes of extravagant wealth. Bao Shaoyen, for example, has an entire room filled with $100,000 customized Hermés designer handbags to give as gifts. Another wealthy woman has a room lined with mirrors where friends can see what they look like wearing items from a collection of priceless jewelry worth hundreds of millions of dollars.

Characters, ranging from the ordinary to the oddball, are a particular strength in the novel. The author saves his sharpest satirical cuts for the globe-hopping status seekers who think nothing of flying halfway around the world on the spur of the moment to attend a trendy event, buy a precious bauble, spend obscene amounts to purchase an entire high-fashion wardrobe, or dine on exotic delicacies, all in the name of highly visible one-upmanship. At the same time, many of the fabulously wealthy are saved from stereotyping by exhibiting moments of extreme frugality. One wealthy matron collects complimentary shampoos from hotel rooms, samples free foods at supermarkets, and uses grocery coupons; another gathers up packets of condiments from restaurants and always flies economy class. Such insights make these characters not just memorable but real and human.

Jack Ewing

Review Sources

Chu, Arthur. Rev. of *China Rich Girlfriend*, by Kevin Kwan. *New York Times*. New York Times, 10 July 2015. Web. 29 Jan. 2016.

Herborn, Daniel. "Kevin Kwan Continues His Satires of the Fabulously Wealthy." Rev. of *China Rich Girlfriend*, by Kevin Kwan. *Sydney Morning Herald*. Fairfax Media, 1 Aug. 2015. Web. 29 Jan. 2016.

Lee, Nicole. "The Opulence and Drama of the Asian Jetset in 'China Rich Girlfriend.'" Rev. of *China Rich Girlfriend*, by Kevin Kwan. *Los Angeles Times*. Los Angeles Times, 19 June 2015. Web. 29 Jan. 2016.

Circling the Sun

Author: Paula McLain
Publisher: Ballantine Books (New York).
   Illustrated. 384 pp.
Type of work: Novel
Time: Early twentieth century
Locale: British East Africa, Kenya Colony

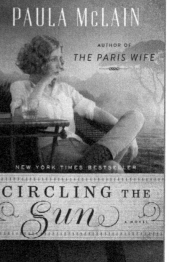

(Courtesy of Penguin Random House)

This historical novel reimagines the early life of Beryl Markham, who was raised in Africa. It closes with her famous flight west across the Atlantic Ocean; Markham was the first person to make this flight successfully.

Principal characters:
BERYL CLUTTERBUCK MARKHAM, horse trainer
   and aviator
CHARLES CLUTTERBUCK, her father, a horse
   breeder and trainer
CLARA CLUTTERBUCK, her mother
DICKIE CLUTTERBUCK, her older brother
DENYS FINCH HATTON, her lover, a big-game hunter and aviator
LORD DELAMERE, a British leader

The life of Beryl Markham so intrigued Paula McLain that she set aside the book she was working on about Georgia O'Keefe to write a historical novel about Markham's life, *Circling the Sun.* The novel focuses on one of several women assuming nontraditional roles in what was known as British East Africa and the Kenya Colony, a British crown colony, during the 1920s and 1930s. Told in the first person, the book is divided into three major sections with a total of sixty-two short chapters. Each part is separated by a black-and-white photograph of an African scene: elephants walking, with a mountain in the background; horses running in front of another mountain; and trees in front of a snow-capped mountain. The book's endpapers show a map of the Kenya Colony in the 1920s. A prologue and epilogue of the famous 1936 flight bracket the main narrative. The novel moves in strict chronological order, covering Markham's life from just before she was four years old, when her mother abandoned her, until her transatlantic flight in 1936, when she was thirty-four.

Perhaps the most famous work on the same era is *Out of Africa* (1937), the memoir by Danish writer Baroness Karen Blixen, who took the pen name Isak Dinesen. Like Dinesen, McLain is careful to present Africa as a character itself. Just as *Out of Africa* begins with mention of the coffee farm that Dinesen owned, the opening paragraph of this novel describes the view from the farm on which Markham grew up. "Behind us, the Rongai Valley sloped down and away, bordered on one side by the strange, high Menengai Crater, which the natives called the Mountain of God, and on the other by the distant Aberdare Range, rounded blue-gray hills that went smoky and purple at dusk before dissolving into the night sky." After Markham's father, Charles Clutterbuck, sold the farm to pay debts, the family moved to South Africa to start over. Markham studied to become a licensed racehorse trainer and received her license at the age of eighteen.

Markham was part of a love triangle with Dinesen and Denys Finch Hatton. She was the younger woman vying for Finch Hatton's love as he pulled away from Dinesen, whose coffee farm was failing. Flying was not Markham's first love, but something she pursued to draw Finch Hatton's attention and join in his interests. Even after she received her pilot's license, however, she continued to train racehorses.

McLain's novel makes several significant departures from Markham's own memoir, *West with the Night*, published in 1942. For example, McLain's novel omits some of Markham's love affairs, while Markham's memoir does not mention her three marriages or her affair with Finch Hatton. Nor did Markham reveal that her mother, Clara Clutterbuck, had abandoned her when she was four to return to England with Markham's older brother Dickie and a colonel, which Markham only learned of decades later. McLain was drawn to this particular aspect of Markham's life, in part because it mirrored her own experience. Like Markham, McLain was abandoned by her mother at four, and reconnected with her mother at twenty.

McLain's Markham is full of questions about her life and her decisions. She receives a request from her mother, who was returning to Africa after the death of her second husband, to locate lodging for her. McLain's Markham wonders, "Had her going changed everything, and now she was returning? It didn't make sense. Why would she think she could find her feet in Kenya, a place she couldn't get away from quickly enough? And how had she summoned the nerve to ask for my help? How was any of this my responsibility?"

The novel presents a more introspective heroine than does Markham's memoir. Markham presents herself almost completely outwardly focused, concentrating on her horse training, flying, and big-game hunting. She does not admit to any deep thinking, doubts, or questions; rather, she depicts herself as a woman of action. Of course, the characters of both the memoir and the novel are created and reveal only as much as their creator chooses to reveal.

In addition, the Markham of the novel is insecure, especially about her lack of education. "Denys and Karen were each so intelligent . . . and together they might make me feel a fool. Would it have killed me to stay at school for a few years and glean some knowledge that had nothing to do with horses or farming or hunting with Kibii?"

Another potential difficulty for readers who prefer to hew close to reality is the amount of dialogue in the novel; naturally, these conversations had to be invented. They do function to move the plot forward, as good dialogue should, but nearly every page contains some conversation between one or more characters. These conversations vary in plausibility. They can feel slightly off, particularly the ones between Markham and any of her male partners. Denys Finch Hatton is an obsession from her teenage years. Texture is added to the romance, because Markham and Dinesen were rivals for the love of Finch Hatton, a man who did not believe in commitments such as marriage. McLain also portrays a kind of friendship between the two women, perhaps beyond what is historically warranted. She also grants Markham guilt over her love affair with Finch Hatton—though not enough to end the affair for Blixen's sake.

After Markham accepts Finch Hatton's offer to return with him to Ngong, ending up in his bed as she had hoped though perhaps guiltily, she asks, "If you had another life to live, would you change anything?" He responds, "I don't know. Maybe our mistakes make us who we are. . . . The only thing I'm really afraid of is shrinking away from life, not reaching for the *thing* . . . . you know?" The constructed response may simply be a shortcut to reveal Finch Hatton's preoccupation with himself; Alexandra Fuller describes him in her review for *New York Times Sunday Book Review* as "a narcissistic woman slayer."

Paula McLain is the author of two collections of poetry and a memoir. Her first historical novel, The Paris Wife (2011), about Ernest Hemingway's first wife, was a New York Times best seller.

McLain is one of several contemporary women writing about women who married and/or supported famous men, particularly in the late nineteenth and early twentieth centuries. Gaynor Arnold's 2009 work on Charles Dickens's wife, *Girl in a Blue Dress*, and Nancy Horan's 2008 work *Loving Frank*, about Frank Lloyd Wright's companion, as well as her *Under the Wide and Starry Sky*, about Robert Louis Stevenson's wife, published in 2014, are others in this category. Melanie Benjamin's novels on Alice Liddell, *Alice I Have Been*, published in 2010, and Anne Morrow Lindberg, *The Aviator's Wife*, published in 2013, are also popular examples.

It is unlikely that any of these novels by women about strong women will be accepted into the literary canon of the academy or win national prizes. They are classed as "women's fiction," rather than literary fiction, which says more about institutional sexism in publishing than their popularity or value. All of them have required intense research. McLain herself traveled to Kenya to gather firsthand impressions. Although the intervening decades have dramatically changed the land and culture from the British protectorate of Markham's day, the book was doubtless improved by McLain's immersing herself in the sounds and smells of Africa as she retraced Markham's steps. Being in the places where Markham had been, even with the intervening decades, added a certain depth to the novel.

Detailing her research, McLain mentions not only Markham's memoir but also a collection of works on Africa and other memoirs, including one by Bror Blixen (Baron Bror von Blixen-Finecke, Karen Blixen's husband and cousin), which helped her conjure the British East Africa and Kenya Colony of the 1920s and 1930s. *The Lives of Beryl Markham*, a scholarly biography written by Errol Trzebinski that McLain consulted, was published in 1993 and followed publication of two other works on Africa. Trzebinski lived in Kenya and was able to interview Markham and others of her social set.

Trzebinski and McLain differ on the question of authorship of *West with the Night*. The former holds, with evidence, that Markham's third husband, Raoul Shumacher, was the ghostwriter of the book. He was a Hollywood scriptwriter, whereas Markham had little formal schooling. In a rebuttal in her author's note, McLain writes, "Beryl was so reluctant to talk about herself, even people who believed they knew her quite well in later life were often surprised to learn she knew anything about flying or horse racing or could write more than a postcard. But the overwhelming evidence attests that Beryl had shown her publisher a large portion of the book (eighteen chapters out of twenty-four) before she ever met Raoul."

The novel closes with the 1936 flight, just as *West with the Night* does. Dramatic ending though it is, it may leave the reader wondering what else Markham, who lived another fifty years after that event, had accomplished. An author's note at the conclusion of the novel does provide a few updates.

While the book is very readable, some critics have taken exception to elements of the novel. Jocelyn McClurg, writing for *USA Today*, sounded a negative note. "Markham, the narrator, remains oddly inert, enigmatic. Where is the jaunty Katharine Hepburnesque heroine we crave and expect? This Beryl is given to mundane musings like this one about marriage: 'People did this every day. Why, then, did it feel so strange and wrong for me?'" Yet McClurg admits the novel "shines a bright light on an intriguing woman who has hidden in the shadows." Alexandra Fuller, who grew up in and has written about Africa, also took McLain to task. She likened the book to McLain's earlier novel about Hadley Hemingway—a book she found unreadable—stating, "The formula seemed suspiciously similar—people behaving badly in settler-era Kenya rather than people behaving badly in Jazz Age Paris." Nonetheless, McClurg predicted that *Circling the Sun* will become a best seller, just as McLain's first historical novel did.

Judy A. Johnson

Review Sources

Bissell, Sally. Rev. of *Circling the Sun,* by Paula McLain. *Library Journal* 19 May 2015: 71–73. *Literary Reference Center.* Web. 21 Oct. 2015.

Fuller, Alexandra. Rev. of *Circling the Sun,* by Paula McLain. *New York Times.* New York Times, 31 July 2015. Web. 27 Oct. 2015.

Labrise, Megan. "Bestseller Paula McLain Circles the Sun with the Woman Who Stitched Her Name on the Sky." *Kirkus Reviews* 15 July 2015: 24. *Literary Reference Center.* Web. 21 Oct. 2015.

McClurg, Jocelyn. "Beryl Markham Gets Moment in the 'Sun.'" Rev. of *Circling the Sun,* by Paula McLain. *USA Today.* Gannett, 1 Aug. 2015. Web. 21 Oct. 2015.

Seaman, Donna. Rev. of *Circling the Sun,* by Paula McLain. *Booklist* 1 June 2015: 59. *Literary Reference Center.* Web. 21 Oct. 2015.

City on Fire

Author: Garth Risk Hallberg (b. 1978)
Publisher: Alfred A. Knopf (New York).
944 pp.
Type of work: Novel
Time: 1976–77
Locale: New York City

City on Fire *is a sprawling tale of New York City in the 1970s. Told from multiple points of view, this novel paints a gripping picture of a troubled time, intertwining a mystery in the process.*

(Courtesy of Alfred A. Knopf)

Principal characters:
WILLIAM HAMILTON-SWEENEY, the estranged heir to a wealthy banking family
REGAN HAMILTON-SWEENEY, his sister
MERCER GOODMAN, his boyfriend, a teacher at a private school for girls and an aspiring novelist
KEITH LAMPLIGHTER, Regan's cheating husband and an unsuccessful money manager
SAMANTHA "SAM" CICCIARO, the target of an attempted murder
CHARLIE WEISBARGER, Sam's friend
NICKY CHAOS, an anarchist and the leader of Ex Nihilo
AMORY GOULD, a successful networker and businessman
RICHARD GROSKOPH, a journalist

City on Fire employs multiple points of view to re-create New York City of the 1970s. Each major character lends a voice to the growing body of knowledge of the city at that time. Each brings the reader along into the minutiae of his or her life, creating a collage of individual photographs seen through various sets of eyes rather than a panoramic overview from one independent, omniscient source. The result is an in-depth understanding of the characters, as well as journey down the winding paths they take to reach their united experience during the blackout of July 1977.

The characters themselves come from a wide variety of disparate backgrounds. William Hamilton-Sweeney, described as "a kind of genius for not noticing what he didn't want to notice," is a ne'er-do-well white man of wealth. Regan Hamilton-Sweeney is a divorced mother who is estranged from her brother, William. She looks very much like him. She is also extremely wealthy. William's black boyfriend Mercer observes, "She had that comely young-mother thing—her skirt probably cost more than Mercer's entire wardrobe—but it was more than that that made her look familiar." When the reader first meets her, she is visiting Mercer at school to ask if he could deliver a letter to William.

Keith Lamplighter is a wealth manager who works long hours at Lamplighter Capital Associates and has missed most of the events in his children's lives. Standing in line at the supermarket on New Year's Eve, he regrets the opportunities he has missed with his kids. Hallberg brings the poignancy alive for the reader when he writes of a little girl tugging on her mother's scarf: "That could have been his scarf-end, once. That could have been his hand feeling for the quarter he surely would have come up with had this been his little girl. But he'd believed he had better things to do."

Garth Risk Hallberg is a writing professor at Sarah Lawrence College. He published the novella A Field Guide to the North American Family *in 2007, and his debut novel,* City on Fire, *in 2015. His essays, stories, and book reviews have been widely published in newspapers and magazines.*

William's current partner, Mercer Goodman, is a Southern boy who has come to New York to teach in Greenwich Village and write a novel. He quickly tires of correcting people when they tell him that they of course know Atlanta. He is from the small town of Altana, Georgia, but he simply leaves it at that. He and William make an unlikely couple, and as the couple carry home a Christmas tree, Mercer is "acutely aware of he must appear: a corduroyed and bespectacled brother doing his best to backpedal, while at the far end of the tree, a bedheaded whiteboy in a motorcycle jacket tried to yank the trunk forward and to hell with the shopping cart."

Sam Cicciaro is a tough, punk rebel who skipped sixth grade and attended New York University with Charlie Weisbarger and his friends. She has been in a relationship with Keith Lamplighter. She is asked to meet him on New Year's Eve. "We have to talk," she said. "I'm not pregnant, so you know. But it's important."

Charlie is a thin guy who is not quite comfortable with the people Sam hangs out with. When he accompanies her to a club, he is nervous about getting in and does not want to shake hands with the bouncer because, in addition to being uncomfortable with the place, "he was a little scared of black people in general, and in particular of this man who, if he'd taken the notion, could have snapped Charlie over his knee like kindling." He meets Sam on New Year's Eve, thinking they will celebrate together, only to have her tell him she has to run uptown for an hour and will be back.

As the lives of these characters lead up to a unifying event on New Year's Eve, the reader learns about failed marriages and relationships, attempts at rock stardom and literary fame, and youthful ambition dulled by the tedium of daily life. All of this is set against the somewhat forbidding setting of New York in the 1970s—a time when few people stepped in Bryant Park and no one thought of Times Square at night as a good place to take the kids. The economy was in tatters, violent crime was more than a statistic, and the idea of New York City as the place to make your name was losing its cachet.

Against this backdrop, Sam is shot on New Year's Eve and lingers in a coma. The detective assigned to the case is facing forced retirement and working without the resources he needs. The disparate cast of characters, coming from all walks of life, pursue their individual goals, only to wind up crossing paths on the night of the blackout of July 1977. All is resolved as this night reveals the clues that are vital to the resolution of the crime.

Hallberg received a $2 million advance for this novel. That is significant because it ensured not only that the novel was eagerly anticipated but also widely reviewed. While the reviews were unanimously congratulatory on Hallberg's sparkling writing and remarkable potential, few critics found that *City on Fire* had lived up to its promise.

There are multiple reasons for the disappointment in this epic work. One is that the book, at more than nine hundred pages, is far longer than it needs to be. Ron Charles, reviewing the novel for the *Washington Post*, argued that at least two hundred pages could have been cut without losing anything of value. Other reviewers found that the switching points of view allowed for a close look at the disparate lives—and inner lives—of the characters. However, many felt this format resulted in a jumbled mosaic rather than a cohesive tapestry that depicts New York at that time.

In his review for the *New Yorker*, Louis Menand cited two noteworthy shortcomings of *City on Fire*. The first was that "contrary to what newcomers to the city may imagine, New York is a place where circles almost never intersect, except transactionally—at a co-op meeting and parent-teacher conferences, or on jury duty." As a result, Menand found it highly implausible that such disparate people would have lives that overlapped to such an extent in the actual city of New York as they do in the novel.

The other is that many of the major events of the 1970s in New York—the brouhahas between the New York Yankees' George Steinbrenner, Billy Martin, and Reggie Jackson; the terror that gripped the city during the Son of Sam hunt; the mayoral campaign between Mario Cuomo and Ed Koch—are ignored. They may not have been important events to the individual characters in *City on Fire*, yet they were decade-defining events for New Yorkers as a whole, and it feels like an oversight that Hallberg never alludes to these events in the novel's nearly one thousand pages.

Furthermore, several reviewers argued that the voices of the point-of-view characters did not vary. They all tended to use the same diction, regardless of the character's social class or education. In her review for the *Guardian*, Sandra Newman wrote, "Unfortunately, these characters are all uncannily alike. In their abundant interior monologues, they tend to fall into Hallberg's voice, a nostalgic, glimmering chandelier of a thing with a tendency to cross the line into self-indulgence."

Reviews have compared Hallberg to Tom Wolfe, Charles Dickens, and Marcel Proust. In each case, critics have hailed Hallberg's writing and raw talent. In fact, the highest praise appeared in a review for the *New York Times*, in which critic Frank Rich wrote that "Hallberg is the natural novelist that Wolfe was not." He also wrote of Hallberg's talent, "There are also passages of true beauty, none more so than the nearly 150-page climax. . . . It's a tour de force of narrative crosscutting and chiaroscuro scene-painting reminiscent of the infernal Hollywood riot, the figurative 'Burning of Los Angeles,' that caps Nathanael West's *The Day of the Locust*."

While disappointed in the novel in many ways, Rich summarized what so many other reviews stated:

> In the end it is the largeness of Hallberg's spirit rather than the size of his sometimes patchy canvas that matters most anyway. *City on Fire* may not be as good as it is ambitious, but in the tradition of other precocious New York debuts since time immemorial, it is radiant with the possibility that its author will do something great.

Readers who manage to finish this tome will likely look forward to subsequent novels by Hallberg as he hones his craft and focuses his talent.

Gina Hagler

Review Sources

Charles, Ron. "The 'It' Novel of the Year." Rev. of *City on Fire*, by Garth Risk Hallberg. *Washington Post*. Washington Post, 5 Oct. 2015. Web. 25 Jan. 2016.

Hoel, Erik P. "*City on Fire* Proves How Culturally Dominant Television Has Become." Rev. of *City on Fire*, by Garth Risk Hallberg. *Atlantic*. Atlantic Monthly Group, 21 Oct. 2015. Web. 25 Jan. 2016.

Menand, Louis. "The Time of Broken Windows: New York from Punk to Trump." Rev. of *City on Fire*, by Garth Risk Hallberg. *New Yorker*. Condé Nast, 12 Oct. 2015. Web. 23 Jan. 2016.

Newman, Sandra. "A Promising Debut, but No Masterpiece." Rev. of *City on Fire*, by Garth Risk Hallberg. *Guardian*. Guardian News and Media, 22 Oct. 2015. Web. 26 Jan. 2016.

Rich, Frank. Rev. of *City on Fire*, by Garth Risk Hallberg. *New York Times*. New York Times, 8 Oct. 2015. Web. 23 Jan. 2016.

Ulin, David L. "Can Garth Risk Hallberg's 'City on Fire' Sustain the Weight of Author's Intentions?" Rev. of *City on Fire*, by Garth Risk Hallberg. *Los Angeles Times*. Los Angeles Times, 8 Oct. 2015. Web. 26 Jan. 2016.

Counternarratives

Author: John Keene (b. 1965)
Publisher: New Directions (New York). 320 pp.
Type of work: Short fiction
Time: 1600s to the present
Locales: Various

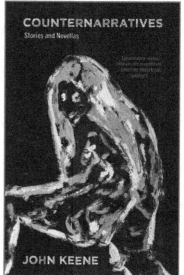

In Counternarratives, *a collection of thirteen short stories and novellas, John Keene reimagines black history through revised accounts of colonization, slavery, war, and black resistance from the seventeenth century to the present. Both employing and subverting forms and genres including historical documents, textbooks, slave narratives, diaries, and gothic fiction, Keene suggests that black resistance to white supremacy has long pulsed just below the surface of the historical register.*

(Courtesy of New Directions)

Principal characters:

BURUNBANA, a slave *in seventeenth-century Brazil*
DOM JOAQUIM D'AZEVEDO, a Portuguese priest
CARMEL, a mute slave from a Haitian coffee plantation
EUGÉNIE, her teenage mistress
JIM, a former slave
XAVIER VILLAURRUTIA, a Mexican poet and playwright
LANGSTON HUGHES, a Harlem Renaissance poet, playwright, novelist, and activist

John Keene's sweeping short-story collection *Counternarratives* opens with epigraphs from James Baldwin, Fred Moten, and Audre Lorde, twentieth-century radical thinkers and writers who worked to bring attention to the structural oppression of African Americans, in addition to advocating for women, LGBTQ people, students, and the working class. By invoking these three writers at the opening of his collection, Keene aligns himself with the black radical tradition, a twentieth- and twenty-first-century resistance movement influenced by early radical thinkers such W. E. B. Du Bois and sometimes, though not always, informed by Marxist theory. This tradition seeks to critique systemic racism and white supremacy in its many and evolving forms, from slavery to Jim Crow laws to contemporary mass incarceration of young African American men. Keene also aligns himself with the experimental tradition in poetry and fiction, one in which Baldwin, Moten, and Lorde all participated. The very title of Keene's book, *Counternarratives*, asserts the author's commitment to a literature of resistance.

Keene's stories and novellas, his title signals, will counter the hegemonic tradition of narrative itself.

Keene's commitment to the black radical tradition and black experimentalism predates *Counternarratives*. His first book, *Annotations* (1995), is a lyrical, highly experimental novel about a black man's coming-of-age and sexual awakening. Keene has long been a member of the Dark Room Collective, an African American writers' group founded in 1988 by poets Thomas Sayers Ellis and Sharan Strange, many early members of which went on to become major literary voices. In 1996, two members of the collective, Cornelius Eady and Toi Derricotte, founded the Cave Canem Foundation, a renowned nonprofit writers' center for African American poets. Keene himself is a graduate fellow of the Cave Canem writers' workshop. Collectives such as Dark Room and Cave Canem have helped produce a new wave of creative writing and poetry by African American authors, work that often delves deep into history to explore the complex of power relations and forms of structural oppression that have led to the social conditions facing African Americans living today.

In *Counternarratives*, Keene brings together thirteen stories that span from the seventeenth century to the present, chronicling the ways in which black lives have been shaped by the Atlantic slave trade and the Middle Passage, during which millions of Africans were forcibly transported as slaves across the Atlantic Ocean to the Americas. The Atlantic slave trade lasted for three centuries, from the early 1500s to the mid-1800s. Keene's stories are set on multiple continents, reflecting the expansive reach of the trade. Keene experiments with different formal and genre traditions, including slave narratives, gothic fiction, speculative fiction, epistolary narratives, diary entries, newspaper stories, and history texts, among others. At the same time, he actively questions and undermines these formal and genre traditions by transforming them and giving voice to black figures who have often been marginalized or even erased by history's traditional narratives. Sometimes his style feels archaic, incorporating historical documents and leading readers to feel as though they are reading a very old text from a white history book. But Keene then surprises his readers by subverting these stylistic conventions, challenging them to imagine a history of buried narratives and black resistance just below the surface of history's official register.

In two pieces that appear early on in *Counternarratives*, "On Brazil, or Dénouement: The Londônias-Figueiras" and "A Letter on the Trials of the Counterreformation in New Lisbon," Keene describes altercations between Portuguese colonists and black slaves in Brazil. In the latter story, the slave Burunbana stands up to a Portuguese priest, Dom Joaquim D'Azevedo. Burunbana demands that the priest address him by his real name rather than his Christian one, João Baptista. At a critical turning point in the story, which until this point has been focused on D'Azevedo, the priest looks Burunbana in the face and sees him for the first time. The story merges a historical documentary style with a kind of magical realism.

Other pieces in Keene's collection also employ a seemingly dry historical narrative style at the outset only to later undermine it. In an ambitious novella titled "Gloss on *A History of Roman Catholics in the Early American Republic, 1790–1825*; or, The Strange History of Our Lady of the Sorrows," Keene begins with what appears to be a chapter from an academic history book, but then he departs from the chapter itself and moves into a lengthy footnote. To the reader's surprise, the novella takes place entirely within this single footnote. "Gloss" begins with a detailed, objective history of Carmel, a young slave girl who is sent from a coffee plantation in Haiti to a convent in Kentucky with her teenage mistress, Eugénie. Carmel is mute, at first communicating only through pictures and hand gestures. In many ways, her life is dictated by the whims of Eugénie, who is domineering and often physically abusive. Carmel experiences only brief moments of reprieve. But at the convent, Carmel gradually begins to develop a sense of her own power. Readers first encounter Carmel's voice through diary entries, which she pens at first in nearly incomprehensible pidgin English; gradually her English improves until, at a certain point, readers realize that Carmel's first-person voice has achieved mastery of Standard English. Readers also stand witness as Carmel wields increasing power over herself and the people around her. By the end of the novella, she has achieved full agency, and even a kind of supernatural power.

Carmel's individual story points toward its historical context: the Haitian Revolution (1791–1804), in which slaves rebelled against and eventually overturned French rule of the colony then known as Saint-Domingue and abolished slavery. Ironically, as "Gloss" moves from a footnote in a history book to Carmel's personal narrative—from ostensibly objective to subjective account—its wider social and historical significance becomes increasingly apparent. As Keene explained in an interview with Blake Butler for the website *Vice*, he is particularly interested in what he described as the "movement from objectivity to subjectivity," and he actively explores that movement in a number of the stories collected in *Counternarratives*.

John Keene is a graduate fellow of the Cave Canem writers' workshop and a member of the Dark Room Collective. His previous works include Annotations *(1995) and the poetry collection* Seismosis *(2006), as well as a translation of Brazilian writer Hilda Hilst's novel* Cartas de um sedutor *(1991;* Letters from a Seducer, *2014). He is associate professor and chair of African American and African studies at Rutgers University–Newark.*

In "Rivers," Keene imagines the untold tale of Jim, the runaway slave, from Mark Twain's *Adventures of Huckleberry Finn* (1884). This story, narrated from the perspective of Jim, appears in the second section of *Counternarratives*, titled "Encounternarratives." A freed Jim, now the owner of a tavern in St. Louis, happens to run into Huck Finn and Tom Sawyer, by now both grown men. During their encounter, Jim considers telling Huck and Tom about all the details of his life and what has happened to him, but he decides against it. Then, when the Civil War begins and Jim enlists in the Union Army, Jim runs into Huck once again, this time on the battlefield.

In another story, "Blues," the Mexican poet and playwright Xavier Villaurrutia visits New York during the Great Depression. Villaurrutia, an openly gay man, was a member of Los Contemporáneos (the contemporaries), a group of writers who wrote poems, short stories, and plays intended for Mexico's emerging middle class. "Blues" tells of a meeting between Villaurrutia and the influential Harlem Renaissance poet Langston Hughes. At a restaurant, the two poets talk about their backgrounds, the city, and poetry. Eventually Hughes brings Villaurrutia back to his room, where their cordial encounter develops into something much more. The story's clauses are separated by ellipses rather than end punctuation; as a result, the encounter reads like a single, breathy sentence, or perhaps as a fluid piece of blues music, the ellipses building momentum and creating an erotic, dreamlike atmosphere. From the outset, readers sense that something sexual might happen in this imagined encounter between the two poets, and the experience of reading the story is heightened by anticipation of the consummation of their mutual erotic longing for one another.

Together, the stories and novellas of *Counternarratives* make a powerful argument for the continuity of history and the interconnectedness of not only forms of structural oppression and racism but also resistance movements. Keene gives fictional voice to both imagined and real black historical figures, modeling innovation in storytelling through his experimentation with punctuation, form, style, and genre. But perhaps more than anything, what Keene's *Counternarratives* achieves is a demonstration of how fiction cannot just make but also unmake stories and the cultural hegemony that they impose.

A. Lewandowski

Review Sources

Rev. of *Counternarratives*, by John Keene. *Kirkus Reviews* 1 Apr. 2015: 236. Print.

Rev. of *Counternarratives*, by John Keene. *Publishers Weekly* 30 Mar. 2015: 46. Print.

Johnson, Brad. Rev. of *Counternarratives*, by John Keene. *Quarterly Conversation* Fall 2015: n. pag. Web. 17 Feb. 2016.

Nelson, Max. Rev. of *Counternarratives*, by John Keene. *Bookforum*. Artforum Intl., 8 July 2015. Web. 17 Feb. 2016.

Smallwood, Christine. "New Books." Rev. of *Counternarratives*, by John Keene; *Suite Vénitienne*, by Sophie Calle; and *Mislaid*, by Nell Zink. *Harper's Magazine*. Harper's Mag., May 2015. Web. 17 Feb. 2016.

West, Adrian. Rev. of *Counternarratives*, by John Keene. *Music & Literature*. Music & Lit., 17 June 2015. Web. 1 Feb. 2016.

Crow Fair

Author: Thomas McGuane (b. 1939)
Publisher: Alfred A. Knopf (New York).
288 pp.
Type of work: Short fiction

*In his latest collection, author Thomas Mc-
Guane presents seventeen new, mostly comic
stories about the misadventures of Montana
men.*

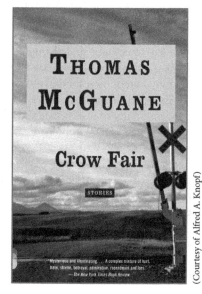

(Courtesy of Alfred A. Knopf)

Thomas McGuane once said that although he
studied the tradition of comic literature and
started his career wanting to be a comic novelist, he soon began to feel that the episodic
structure of the American picaresque novel,
so popular in the nineteenth century, was
not appropriate for contemporary writing.
More recently, when speaking about his collection of short stories, *Crow Fair*, he said
that it has taken him a long time to know enough about writing to really write short
stories; whereas the novel is a flexible and accommodating form, he said, short stories are more restrictive and demanding. Many of the seventeen short stories in *Crow
Fair* show McGuane straddling the divide between the rambling, comic picaresque
style of his early novels and his more recent effort to rein things in. These stories,
most of which were originally published in the *New Yorker*, are clearly meant to be
"about" something, rather than just raconteur rambles intended to elicit guffaws from
his readers.

The opening story, entitled "Weight Watchers," is about a Montana man whose
mother puts him in charge of taking care of his father after she kicks the old man out
for being obese. The first-person narrator notes that "as an only child, [he] was the
sole recipient of [his] parents' malignant parenting." Once, when the boy was in fifth
grade, his mother glued his father to the toilet seat with superglue. Another night, he
heard a noise and sneaked downstairs to find his father on his knees, licking pie filling from a mixer beater while his mother looked down at him. Of the latter scene, the
narrator muses, "The extraordinarily stern look on my mother's face . . . disturbs me
to this day." Although people have told him he comes from a dysfunctional family, he
says that as a child, he viewed his parents distantly, "as an anthropologist might view
them," deciding that they had become "locked into something . . . so exclusive as to be
hermetically sealed to everyone else." The narrator, in a voice typical of McGuane's
stories, says that he took advantage of his parents' self-absorption to exercise his freedom and that, perhaps as a result of their dysfunction, he knows he will never marry
and cannot imagine sharing his home with another person. "Weight Watchers," like

most of the stories in this collection, ends suddenly and arbitrarily. In fact, there is no place for the story to go; it must either go on and on or just stop, and McGuane chooses the latter. He concludes with the narrator saying he has always enjoyed the idea of nonexistence, but the story does not justify any such highbrow philosophic generalization. Instead, it seems primarily one of those loose, comic riffs that McGuane exploits in his picaresque novels.

In "The House on Sand Creek," the house in question—to which the narrator and his wife, Monika, move when they are first married—comes complete with skinned coyote carcasses piled on the front step and a dead horse hanging from its halter on the front porch. Monika soon leaves and goes back to her parents in Bosnia-Herzegovina, taking up with another man and a baby. The narrator becomes friends with a retired electrician named Bob who calls himself a "former cowboy," prompting the narrator to suggest that "[Bob's] facial movements ha[ve] more in common with those of Soupy Sales than John Wayne." Indeed, the narrator, who also has that now-familiar Thomas McGuane voice, seems proud of his "ability to wittily point out things like this."

When Monika returns with an African baby named Karel, the tone is philosophically flippant, as usual. After the narrator and Monika have sex, he "drift[s] off into postcoital tristesse" while she "raid[s] the icebox." Some time passes, and Monika returns to architecture school, while Bob begins to spend more time with the narrator as he cares for Karel. Then Bob kidnaps the baby, although it is not clear why. But never mind—Mom and Dad get the child back, even though he subsequently stays over at Bob's more often than not, which, the narrator says, he hopes will grant him and Monika "some room to work things out." This is a story that depends on the comic voice of the narrator, who is not as witty as he thinks he is.

"Grandma and Me" features somewhat the same voice, only more so. This not-so-nice narrator looks after his ninety-three-year-old blind grandmother's property while working as a teaching assistant at a preschool and tending bar two nights a week. He says that "in families like [his], grandmothers loom large as yetis." The story centers on an incident in which the narrator takes his grandmother on a nature jaunt and sees a body float downstream. When he calls the sheriff's office on his cell phone, he finds out the body is a depressed "jilted groom" who jumped into the canyon upriver. This whets his curiosity, and he sneaks off, leaving his grandmother alone on the riverbank, to check on the floating body, thinking it must hold the answers to some of life's mysteries. When he gets back, his grandmother is gone, so he takes the time to eat his lunch while trying to "collect [his] thoughts and ward off hysteria." After he finds out that someone has returned her home, he goes back to the preschool where he works and tells a four-year-old boy that in ten years he will "be sniffing airplane glue from a sandwich bag." Once again, it is the voice of the narrator that makes this a readable picaresque piece, if not a unified or meaningful short story.

Thomas McGuane is the author of ten novels, three works of nonfiction, and two other collections of short stories.

"On a Dirt Road" focuses on another not-very-likable character who prides himself on his clever remarks, such as calling an acquaintance an "oxygen thief" because one "can hardly breathe around him." The story centers on a disagreement between the narrator and his wife about a dinner arrangement with the aforementioned oxygen thief. The husband declines and goes to visit the new neighbors instead, where he soon realizes that the neighbor's wife, Nell, has something wrong with her, "big-time." "Retarded," he thinks when he sees her in a pile of Lego pieces, "but healthy otherwise and rather pretty." He later finds out that Nell, a former Miss Utah runner-up, was struck by a hit-and-run driver. He observes that Nell is "mentally challenged, underappreciated, and ha[s] a killer body" and that "a guy could get into a world of hurt with such mixed signals." But his problems are just starting; he begins to suspect his wife is having an affair, and his mind fills with an image of her as "random and dangerous as a Scud missile." The story ends with the narrator having a comic encounter with his wife over a bowl of popcorn and a pizza menu as they teeter on the brink of marital fallout.

"A Long View to the West" is about a man named Clay, who runs an unprofitable used car lot, and his father Bill, who tells stories, one in particular about Robert Wood and some wild horses. Clay comments on the story in italics throughout as his father tells it, although the story sounds more written than spoken, with natural oral syntax and diction. Indeed, McGuane's story only exists for the sake of Robert's story as told by Bill to Clay, and Robert's story is ultimately rowdy but inconsequential.

"Prairie Girl" forsakes the typical McGuane picaresque voice in favor of the somewhat more serious and straightforward story of a prostitute named Mary Elizabeth who becomes a bank president. She does so by marrying a gay man who is vice president of a bank owned by his father and who trains Mary in banking skills. In an unadorned manner, leaving the jokes and witty remarks aside, McGuane tells the story of the birth of Mary's son, her husband's leaving her for a gay lover, and her taking over the bank. There is no real point to all this, except a novelistic telling of the life of an intelligent and ambitious young woman. "The Good Samaritan" also temporarily forgoes the picaresque voice and the supposedly witty remarks to tell the story of a hired man who turns out to be a con artist who steals a multimillion-dollar painting. Also somewhat less comically picaresque is "Canyon Ferry," about a father who takes his son ice fishing; when a storm hits, although the boy seems to enjoy it, he claims afterward that he was frightened, creating a long-lasting rift between he and his father.

In "River Camp," two brothers-in-law, Tony and Jack, go on a fishing trip with a guide who seems more than a little mentally unbalanced. Tony, a surgeon, is being divorced by his wife, Jack's sister. Here, the typical McGuane "witty" voice returns; at one point, Tony describes Jack's wife as a woman who has "gone into a rapid glide toward what could be identified at a thousand yards as a frump, and at close range as an angry frump." The trip is supposed to be an attempt to recapture a time when the two men were just boyhood friends. Much of it recounts episodes from their past relationship, interspersed with the increasingly strange behavior of the guide, Hewlitt. Things come to a head when Hewlitt begins scourging himself with willow switches and tells them he has "spent [his] entire life as a liar and an incompetent." He begins a long listing of his past misfortunes—how the treatment of his wife's eating disorder and his daughter's "hoity-toity" wedding took all his money, and how the wedding caterer poisoned all his guests, several of whom sued him. Hewlitt then recounts how he "took a crash course in wilderness adventures," which put him where he is today. When Hewlitt, who is the only one who knows the way out of this wilderness, dies and the bears eat all their food, Tony and Jack pile into the boat and get swept into a wave of rapids, never to be seen again. Just another story in McGuane country, where men get caught in comic nightmares of errors and incompetence.

The title story, "Crow Fair," is told by one of two brothers who must put their mother in a rest home. The narrator, Earl, recalls that when they were growing up, their mother was "a queen"—the kind of woman who was a Cub Scout den mother, who volunteered at her sons' school, who "read good books and understood classical music." Earl and his brother, Kurt, always said they hoped she had cheated on their father, but they knew that she, "the queen of [their] town," was above such things. Much of the story focuses on the brothers visiting their mother, whose dementia worsens as she obsessively tells embarrassing stories of her past. Earl remembers when he was a child and their mother took them to the Crow Fair. When he begins to suspect there was something going on between his mother and their guide at the fair, Roland White Clay, he gets the man's phone number and arranges for him to come to the rest home to see her. Earl tells Kurt that their mother had a romantic retreat with White Clay while their father was recuperating from gallbladder surgery, but it is all a story Earl invents to give his brother a gentler interpretation of the choices their mother made when she was younger. This is perhaps the most serious story in this collection of mostly comic monologues from Montana mountebanks.

Although not widely reviewed, *Crow Fair* elicited strong praise from Stefan Beck in the *Christian Science Monitor*, who wrote that McGuane's "deep appreciation for the human comedy" brings to mind "the grotesques of . . . Flannery O'Connor." In a review for the *New York Times*, Atticus Lish argued that McGuane elevates his "bluff Western comedy of masculinity" to the level of "fable or myth"—a dubious claim that may better apply to more complex "Big Sky" writers such as Annie Proulx and Rick Bass than to the party animal once nicknamed "Captain Berserko."

Charles E. May

Review Sources

Beck, Stefan. "*Crow Fair*: Thomas McGuane's New Short Story Collection Examines the Dark Side of the Human Comedy." Rev. of *Crow Fair*, by Thomas McGuane. *CSMonitor.com*. Christian Science Monitor, 20 Mar. 2015. Web. 25 Nov. 2015.

Rev. of *Crow Fair*, by Thomas McGuane. *Kirkus Reviews* 1 Jan. 2015: 28. Print.

Rev. of *Crow Fair*, by Thomas McGuane. *Publishers Weekly* 20 Oct. 2014: 29. Print.

Lish, Atticus. Rev. of *Crow Fair*, by Thomas McGuane. *New York Times*. New York Times, 27 Mar. 2015. Web. 25 Nov. 2015.

Mort, John. Rev. of *Crow Fair*, by Thomas McGuane. *Booklist* 15 Nov. 2014: 22. Print.

A Cure for Suicide

Author: Jesse Ball (b. 1978)
First published: 2015
Publisher: Pantheon (New York). 239 pp.
Type of work: Novel
Time: Present day
Locales: A series of villages

A Cure for Suicide *is Jesse Ball's fifth nov-el. In this dystopian work, Ball explores the nature of identity, memory, the ability to re-create oneself, and the consequences of well-intentioned actions.*

(Courtesy Pantheon Books)

Principal characters:
THE CLAIMANT, a man who undergoes many changes of identity over the course of the novel to escape painful memories
RANA, source of his pain
THE EXAMINER, the woman helping him to learn all he must to function again
HILDA, a woman who loves him, and with whom he falls in love
THE INTERLOCUTOR, the person who decides who will be permitted to have the cure for suicide
THERESA, his first examiner

As *A Cure for Suicide* begins, the reader is introduced to the claimant, a man who is a patient of sorts under the care of a woman referred to only as "the examiner." The claimant is suffering from some sort of amnesia that has left him with the understanding of a young child. The job of the examiner is to teach him to call by name simple objects such as a chair, a table, and the floor, and to learn their function.

The claimant and the examiner are in the Process of Villages, a series of villages where patients, such as the claimant, are reintroduced to what is considered to be normal life. The reader soon learns that the claimant's amnesia was caused by an injection given to eradicate all traces of memory or identity. The claimant eventually understands enough to question why he is there. The examiner tells him he has asked the question she has been expecting, nearly to the minute of the right time to do so. She explains that the claimant was so sick that he nearly died, but that he sought help before it was too late, and that is why they are there together. She states that they will work together to make him better. Yet the rest of the claimant's questions go largely unanswered and the reader is equally disoriented and confused.

One of the first tasks the claimant must complete is to learn how to listen to a story. The stories are filled with things he does not understand. "That is not important. It isn't important that you understand what I say. What's important is that you behave as a human being should when someone is telling a story. So, listen properly, make noises at appropriate times, and enjoy the fact that I am speaking to you." The examiner goes on to inform him that most communication is meaningless and the value of it is the emotional connection that is made during the telling and the listening. The claimant accepts this explanation, but he does begin to question the examiner, particularly after he meets Hilda at a party the examiner takes him to. They fall in love, and Hilda suggests that they should not trust the examiners. She asks him to escape, but he does not go.

As the story progresses the reader learns this particular claimant is difficult to reboot: the injections he receives are not having the desired long-term effect. The first evidence of this occurs early on, when the claimant settles into a routine after the first shot and begins to have dreams. He sketches the dreams and describes them to his examiner. She recognizes that he is dreaming about events in his former life and tries to convince him that he is dreaming of things that she has suggested to him. This seems to work until he tries to harm himself. Once this happens, the process must be started again.

Ultimately, the claimant moves around the Process of Villages several times and with different examiners. For each new start he is given a new identity and profession. He adjusts to that part of the program well enough, but part of him resists annihilation. Each time the process fails, another injection to restart it is required. Each new injection is a health risk.

Indeed, the cumulative effect of these restarts is that the claimant is significantly impaired. He will never function as well as he did originally. In the case of the Process of Villages, "It wasn't that the process made the brain function less well. It only removed a capacity for action. Each time, a person became less likely to follow an intuition, or take up an idea or a challenge." It seems that the cure results in a perpetual ennui bordering on a deep depression.

One of the themes of this work is the value, or lack thereof, of life to human beings. Ball writes, "If animals excel us, defeat us in one thing, it is this: they all want their lives. Life is given to each one of them separately, and they all want it. We do not." Through the experience of the claimant, Ball wonders at what point the pain of experience becomes so great that death is viewed as a relief. Ball also wonders if there were an alternative to death—the permanent end of our individual existence—whether or not such a process would be preferable. Would it really be better to continue on as someone else?

Another question that arises from this work is why it would be preferable to carry on without knowledge of one's prior existence. The claimant will become a new person with new memories, but if he were truly to forget all that had occurred before, could he take satisfaction in carrying on? Through the claimant, Ball grapples with questions of the functions of memory and identity and how they inform each other.

A Cure for Suicide not only speaks to both the value of life to human beings and the satisfaction of carrying on but also addresses what price is too high to pay for a new start. Laura Collins-Hughes observed in her review for the *Boston Globe*, "Oblivion is the whole idea. Not death, but erasure of memory—a scrubbing so pervasive that everything has to be learned again: how to walk, how to eat, how to perceive the world." With this total amnesia comes the opportunity to begin totally anew. On one hand, escaping the most painful memories of a lifetime is a tempting proposition, but played against the slightly wooden, unanimated individual the claimant becomes, it is difficult to see how this would be the better than anything other than a cure for suicide.

Resilience is another theme of *A Cure for Suicide*. An individual whose mind has been erased so cleanly that it cannot recall the name or purpose of a chair, for example, should not be able to dream of things that happened in an earlier time. Yet that is what happens. The claimant is left groping for the meaning that goes with these images. When he cannot put the meaning to the images he is left with unendurable pain. How is it possible that these memories still exist? This experience leads the reader to wonder if humans are so tied to experience that some experiences are impossible to expunge.

Jesse Ball is an American poet and novelist. His work is well represented in national journals and The Best American Poetry 2006. *He received a National Endowment for the Arts Creative Writing Fellowship in 2014.*

The nature of independence and resilience is brought forcefully to the reader's attention one other time. Seemingly, someone who has been scrubbed more than once should have an obedient heart. After all, the point of the Process of Villages is to return the claimants to a pseudosociety in which they function without the ability or will to act on intuition. The claimant's journey mimics the wish of many readers—to hit a reset button and start anew. And yet, this is not a cut-and-dried process. There is great feeling at the heart of this novel. Sarah Gerard writes in her review for the *New York Times*, "There is yearning at the core of *A Cure for Suicide*, and in that yearning is the reason for carrying on when doing so feels impossible. Ball asks whether, given the chance to shed our pain and start over with the mind of a child, we would want to do so—to what extent pain informs identity, and what parts of us would remain were we to shed that pain."

Reviewers have had high praise for the writing in *A Cure for Suicide*. Charles Finch, for example, for the *Chicago Tribune* called the book, "one of the finest things that Ball has ever written, a magical, gripping burst of emotional history, which interrogate the book's ultimate subject, suicide and the desire for oblivion." The only portion of the book that is subject to disagreement is when Ball tells the story of the love that results in the claimant's wish for a cure, which several reviewers described as an ultimately banal intrusion.

Critics also praise Ball for writing a work of dystopian literature that does not fit totally into the mold of the genre. Jason Sheehan, for example, writes in a review for *NPR*, "*A Cure for Suicide* is missing pretty much every trope and crutch that makes for proper dystopia by today's standards." What Ball does have, Sheehan goes on to note, is "Zombies. Lots and lots of zombies." These zombies are a reference to the people who exist after the Process of Villages—those who are "made zombie-ish. . . . For not quite belonging. For the weight of the sorts of memories we all want erased."

Gina Hagler

Review Sources

Collins-Hughes, Laura. Rev. of *A Cure for Suicide*, by Jesse Ball. *Boston Globe.*
Boston Globe Media Partners, 18 July 2015. Web. 20 Jan. 2016.
Finch, Charles. Rev. of *A Cure for Suicide*, by Jesse Ball. *Chicago Tribune.* Chicago
Tribune, 16 July 2015. Web. 20 Jan. 2016.
Gerard, Sarah. "'A Cure for Suicide by Jesse Ball.'" Rev. of *A Cure for Suicide*, by
Jesse Ball. *New York Times.* New York Times, 24 July 2015. Web. 20 Jan. 2016.
Harrison, M. John. "*A Cure for Suicide* by Jesse Ball Review—Enticingly Macabre."
Rev. of *A Cure for Suicide*, by Jesse Ball. *Guardian.* Guardian News and Media, 8
Oct. 2015. Web. 20 Jan. 2016.
Richardson, Owen. "Book Review: A Cure for Suicide a Philosophical Fantasy?"
Rev. of *A Cure for Suicide*, by Jesse Ball. *Sydney Morning Herald.* Fairfax Media,
16 Aug. 2015. Web. 20 Jan. 2016.
Sheehan, Jason. "'Cure' Hits the Reset Button on Suicidal Minds." Rev. of *A Cure
for Suicide*, by Jesse Ball. *NPR.* NPR, 12 Aug. 2015. Web. 20 Jan. 2016.

Dead Wake
The Last Crossing of the *Lusitania*

Author: Erik Larson (b. 1954)
Publisher: Crown (New York). 448 pp.
Type of work: History
Time: May 1915
Locales: New York City; Atlantic Ocean; Washington, DC; London, England

Dead Wake: The Last Crossing of the Lu-sitania *details the final days of the luxurious British ocean liner, one of the world's largest ships, prior to its sinking on May 6, 1915, off the coast of Ireland after being hit by a torpedo fired from a German U-boat. Among the drowned passengers were a significant number of Americans, and the incident helped propel the previously neutral United States into participation in World War I.*

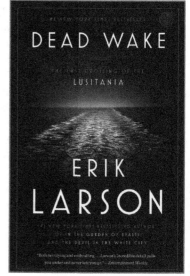

(Courtesy of Penguin Random House)

Principal personages:

WILLIAM THOMAS TURNER, captain of the Cunard cruise ship Lusitania

WALTHER SCHWIEGER, commander of German submarine U-20

WOODROW WILSON, president of the United States, 1913–21

WINSTON CHURCHILL, first lord of British Admiralty, 1911–15

WILHELM II, last German emperor and king of Prussia, 1888–1918

CHARLES EMELIUS LAURIAT JR., wealthy Boston bookseller, a passenger on the Lusitania

THEODATE "THEO" POPE, spiritualist and pioneering female architect, a passenger on the Lusitania

WILLIAM REGINALD "BLINKER" HALL, director of naval intelligence for British Admiralty, 1914–19

JOHN ARBUTHNOT "JACKY" FISHER, first sea lord of British Admiralty, 1904–10 and 1914–15

The year 2015 marks the one hundredth anniversary of the sinking of the British ocean liner RMS *Lusitania*. A timely new reexamination of the tragedy, Erik Larson's *Dead Wake: The Last Crossing of the Lusitania* commemorates the centennial of the incident that ultimately contributed to events of global proportion.

The book is divided into five parts, each dealing with a particular aspect of the incident; taken together, they support the author's central thesis that an incredible series of coincidences combined to cause a deadly catastrophe of far-reaching consequences. If any one of several factors contributing to the disaster had been prevented, Larson suggests, the sinking might never have occurred. If the *Lusitania*, with its complement of American passengers, had not been sunk, the United States, under isolationist president Woodrow Wilson, might never have entered World War I. Without American participation from 1917 on, the course of the war might have been significantly different, and the history of the world in the century since the ship went down could have been drastically altered.

Part 1, "Bloody Monkeys," provides a lengthy background that unfolds in cinematic fashion, with extended montages giving way to jump cuts that illuminate various facets contributing to the premise of the story. This ambitious segment of the book incorporates a broad sweep of information in the process of arranging props, assigning roles to players, and establishing the settings of scenes. The *Lusitania*'s captain, William Turner, an experienced sailor, is introduced, as is his counterpart, *U-20* commander Walther Schwieger, who eagerly embraced the early 1915 proclamation of Germany's total commitment to submarine warfare. Certain passengers and crew who figure prominently are profiled, creating apprehension for readers who, though aware of the ultimate fate of the ship, may not know who will live and who will die. Pertinent facts are provided about the ship, a veteran of more than two hundred transatlantic crossings—unlike the similarly enormous and equally doomed liner RMS *Titanic*, victim of a collision with an iceberg on its maiden voyage three years earlier. President Wilson is depicted as distracted by contemporary events—the war abroad, domestic recession, labor strikes—as well as his grief over the recent death of his first wife and his budding romance with his new love interest (and eventual second wife), Edith Bolling Galt. The machinations of the British Admiralty's secret decoding service, Room 40, which Larson hints may have manipulated events for their own Machiavellian purposes, seem especially sinister. Part of the manipulation may have entailed the British Admiralty, under then–first lord and eventual prime minister Winston Churchill, requisitioning another ship in New York Harbor, the *Cameronia*. That ship's passengers and baggage were transferred to the *Lusitania*, causing a two-hour delay, without which the larger vessel would probably have crossed the Atlantic to dock safely at port in Liverpool, England.

The drama is set into motion in part 2, titled "Jump Rope and Caviar." This portion of the book alternately follows the movements of the *Lusitania* and the *U-20* as they begin their rendezvous with destiny. The leisure activities of pampered first-class passengers as they enjoy the spacious, luxurious amenities of the cruise liner are starkly contrasted with the cramped quarters aboard the German U-boat. Early submarines, readers learn, were essentially fragile, vulnerable metal tubes. Totally blind except at periscope depth, reeking with unpleasant odors that could turn fatal, and loaded with torpedoes that more often than not failed to perform adequately, U-boats required crewmen to serve as ballast, running back and forth to assist in the danger-fraught process of diving or ascending. Glimpses are shown of

Journalist, author, public speaker, and teacher Erik Larson has written numerous articles for such periodicals as the New Yorker *and the* Atlantic, *as well as several nonfiction books. He won a 2004 Edgar Award for best true crime for* The Devil in the White City *(2003).*

other elements on the periphery of the main action: British warships cruising in the vicinity where the tragedy played out, messages about U-boats coming and going from Room 40, and major figures at work or play in world capitals (Wilson and Galt in Washington, Churchill meeting with officials in London and Paris, and the US ambassador communicating with the German Foreign Office in Berlin). An important consideration is also introduced: the ship's cargo. According to the official manifest, this included clandestine quantities of volatile metallic powders and thousands of cases of artillery shells and rifle ammunition, a fact Germany later used to justify the attack on the ship.

One of the shortest sections, part 3 describes the actual meeting of the *Lusitania* and the *U-20* in the Irish Sea, up to the moment when the submarine fires a single torpedo at the liner and it impacts against the hull. The section title, "Dead Wake," refers to the name of the visible track of a torpedo in the water. Part 4, "The Black Soul," describes in vivid detail the catastrophic effects of the torpedo striking below the waterline of the *Lusitania* and the reactions of various passengers and crew as the ship begins listing heavily to starboard. According to survivors' accounts, there was a second explosion shortly after the first that created a larger hole in the ship, hastening the sinking. Unlike previous authors writing about the demise of the *Lusitania*, who had variously attributed the subsequent blast to a second torpedo (the U-boat captain's log denies this) or the ignition of coal dust from the mostly empty ship's bunkers (dampness from condensation would have prevented this), Larson believes the explosion was the result of thermal shock from cold seawater coming in contact with extremely hot steam from the ship's boilers.

Of almost 2,000 people on board, nearly 1,200 passengers and crew were killed, including 123 Americans. Much of the rest of part 4 is concerned with the reasons for such a heavy loss of life. The gaping holes caused the ship to sink in just eighteen minutes. Because of the severe list, lifeboats on the stricken side hung too far away for passengers and crew to board easily, and many were launched incorrectly, spilling occupants into the ocean; lifeboats on the opposite side dangled over the decks, and were therefore useless. Many passengers died because they had donned lifejackets incorrectly; others perished from hypothermia after floating for hours in fifty-five-degree water while waiting for rescue by a flotilla of small boats from Queenstown, Ireland, twelve miles away. The bodies of several hundred of the dead were never recovered.

The fifth and final section, "The Sea of Secrets," concerns the aftermath of the tragedy. Ironically, Captain Turner, who in longstanding tradition had determined to go down with his ship, survived by a fluke of fate. He was subsequently blamed by British Admiralty for the disaster but was eventually absolved of responsibility following a trial, though Churchill, in a later memoir, continued to blame him for the loss of the ship. In Larson's view, the Admiralty contributed to the sinking by neglecting to inform the *Lusitania* of the presence of a submarine along its sailing route and by failing to provide a military escort following Germany's well-publicized intentions to conduct U-boat warfare. The author introduces the suspicion that, based on the opinions of maritime experts of the day and in conjunction with the many odd happenstances leading to the tragedy (delay in departing, bad weather that necessitated reduction of the ship's superior speed, a torpedo that actually worked, and other factors), Britain purposely left the *Lusitania* in jeopardy in order to sacrifice American lives and thereby to draw the United States into World War I.

If such was indeed the intention, it succeeded—but only after a delay of nearly two years. Immediately after the *Lusitania* sinking, President Wilson, still courting his future wife, engaged in an angry exchange of letters with Kaiser Wilhelm II rather than asking Congress for a declaration of war. This had little effect until midway through 1916, when, after many other submarine attacks, Wilhelm forbid U-boat attacks on large passenger ships. Wilson continued his letter-writing campaign and was reelected in late 1916. The United States did not enter the war until April 1917, triggered by the resumption of German U-boat attacks on US ships, which changed the mood of the nation from neutrality to hostility. Public opinion was particularly inflamed following the disclosure of the so-called Zimmerman Telegram, a secret message from Germany (intercepted and decoded by British intelligence) offering an alliance with Mexico in exchange for Germany's help in reclaiming former Mexican territory in the southwestern United States.

Dead Wake is an exhaustively researched book containing many pieces of interesting trivia, backed up by more than fifty pages of notes and bibliographic references. Critics praised Larson's consistent ability to provide such depths of detail while maintaining a narrative that Jean Zimmerman, in a review for National Public Radio, described as "thrilling, dramatic and powerful." Though much of the work treads territory covered by dozens of previously published examinations of the disaster, it makes a solid case that large historical events are often the result of small factors converging at a particular point in space and time. This latest release continues the author's series of nonfiction offerings with a similar thematic approach, including *Isaac's Storm: A Man, a Time, and the Deadliest Hurricane in History* (1999), *The Devil in the White City: Murder, Magic, and Madness at the Fair That Changed America* (2003), and *Thunderstruck* (2006).

Jack Ewing

Review Sources

Davenport-Hines, Richard. "How Were 1,198 Deaths Allowed to Happen?" Rev. of *Dead Wake: The Last Crossing of the Lusitania*, by Erik Larson. Guardian. Guardian News and Media, 7 May 2015. Web. 17 Dec. 2015.

Shribman, David M. Rev. of *Dead Wake: The Last Crossing of the Lusitania*, by Erik Larson. *Boston Globe*. Boston Globe Media Partners, 14 Mar. 2015. Web. 17 Dec. 2015.

Sides, Hampton. "Erik Larson's Dead Wake, about the Lusitania." Rev. of *Dead Wake: The Last Crossing of the Lusitania*, by Erik Larson. *New York Times*. New York Times, 5 Mar. 2015. Web. 17 Dec. 2015.

Zimmerman, Jean. "A Tale of Two Captains on a Tragic Journey in Dead Wake." Rev. of *Dead Wake: The Last Crossing of the Lusitania*, by Erik Larson. *NPR*. NPR, 10 Mar. 2015. Web. 17 Dec. 2015.

Death and Mr. Pickwick

Author: Stephen Jarvis (b. 1958)
Publisher: Farrar, Straus and Giroux (New York). 802 pp.
Type of work: Novel
Time: Contemporary setting; late 1700s to mid-1800s
Locale: London, England, and its environs

Death and Mr. Pickwick follows the investigative work of two literary sleuths as they uncover information supporting their claim that Charles Dickens stole credit for creating The Pickwick Papers *from the book's original illustrator, Robert Seymour.*

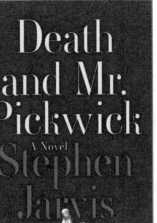

(Courtesy of Farrar Straus & Giroux)

Principal characters:
MR. INBELICATE, a modern researcher
INSCRIPTINO, a.k.a. Scripty, his research assistant
ROBERT SEYMOUR, a famous nineteenth-century caricaturist and illustrator
CHARLES DICKENS, a young up-and-coming writer
JOHN FORSTER, Dickens's friend and adviser

Charles Dickens's rank among the most well-known and admired writers in the English-speaking and English-reading world is beyond debate. His books are classics that are found on the shelves of public and private libraries; his novels have been translated into television, movie, and stage adaptations. His very name has become synonymous with the themes and the landscapes that he brought to life. "Dickensian" refers to plots that unfold in Victorian England, touching on many of the negative aspects of the time—poverty, social injustice, child labor, street crime—as well as some of the uplifting and comical motifs that he presented, such as orphans reunited with long-lost relatives, good-natured housekeepers, and goodwill and hope in the face of distress. Suffice it to say, Dickens's reputation and his work have endured. But what if his fame and notoriety came about because of an unapologetic, unabashed literary theft? Would this revelation cast doubt upon his entire body of work, making any and all of his subsequent writings the result of possible fraud?

Author Stephen Jarvis addresses the notions of intellectual property and creative theft in his 2015 debut novel, *Death and Mr. Pickwick*. Critics were impressed by his ability to endow such a dense subject with an abundance of wit, intrigue, humor, and facts. Indeed, Jarvis's consideration of the "facts" is what separates this undertaking from literary conjecture or a hypothetical detective novel. Jarvis has done a herculean amount of research into the life and times of illustrator Robert Seymour, the man whom he credits in the novel's preface with being the real creator of Samuel Pickwick.

According to Jarvis—and to his two fictional modern-day literary sleuths, Mr. Inbelicate and his assistant, Scripty, who piece together and re-create the dire incidents of 1836—artist Robert Seymour was a man at the top of his game professionally. He was considered one of the nation's most talented illustrators,

As a reporter for the Daily Telegraph, *Stephen Jarvis made his reputation writing about learning trapeze, walking on hot coals, and other unusual weekend activities.* Death and Mr. Pickwick *is his first novel.*

able to capture the haughty dignity of the aristocrat as well as the full-bodied joviality of more down-to-earth fellows. Seymour was so in demand that he was able to convince two publishers, Edward Chapman and William Hall, to publish his notion of a fictional gentlemen's club and its members' often hilarious and misguided adventures.

Seymour was to create four comic engravings per month as illustrations for serialized installments of *The Posthumous Papers of the Pickwick Club*. He felt that his illustrations set the tone, conveyed the spirit of the undertaking, and introduced readers to the sprawling cast of characters. He was simply in need of a writer—and, in his mind, any writer would do—who could provide enough text to fill up the twenty-four pages. This writer would function as the fictional "editor" of the piece, pretending that he was whipping these made-up reminiscences into printable, readable shape. The writer who was hired in this mercenary capacity was a young man who had enjoyed success as a parliamentary journalist. Tired of reportage, he had begun to try his hand at fiction. His pseudonym was Boz; his actual name was Charles Dickens.

Not much is actually known about the brief working relationship between Seymour and Dickens, which lasted for two installments of *The Pickwick Club*. What is known is that after a meeting in April 1836, wherein Dickens expressed his dissatisfaction with Seymour's deathbed scene of a pantomime actor, the artist went home, worked on correcting the illustration plate, and then killed himself. Stephen Jarvis and his fictional sleuthing counterparts have worked meticulously to restore Seymour's achievements and give him credit for the Pickwick craze.

The Pickwick craze itself is one of the most illuminating components of the book, as well as one of the most puzzling. For most modern readers, Dickens is hailed for his characters Oliver Twist, David Copperfield, and Ebenezer Scrooge; even Nicholas Nickleby is just a footnote in many readers' minds. The rotund and exuberant Samuel Pickwick is not a member of that top tier of beloved and revered Dickensian characters for contemporary American readers. However, according to Jarvis's novel, in late 1836, Pickwick and his illustrated exploits kicked off a blitz of merchandising and marketing that would make George Lucas and Steven Spielberg envious. Pickwick's likeness was immediately recognized and sought out by all members of British society:

> Mr Pickwick was *there*, in front of everyone, like a real person, not as a hazy mist of head-hidden words: every man, woman and child had exactly the same image of Mr Pickwick in his or her consciousness. When a dustman talked of Mr Pickwick, a lord could know exactly who was meant because of the pictures. *Your* Mr Pickwick was *my*

Mr Pickwick, was a *universal* Mr Pickwick—a being of fiction, a man-created man, was suddenly recognised by all. This was unprecedented in human affairs.

Obviously, having a character that is so relatable, and so cherished by so many members of the public, is a boon for Boz, and Jarvis's Dickens rides that response to greater and greater heights. With the death of Seymour, a new artist is hired by the publishers, the number of illustrations is reduced, and the number of words is increased, all at Dickens's insistence. His career is launched into the stratosphere, and his good friend John Forster advises him to downplay the contribution of Seymour: "I want you to consider the two views of Dickens. . . . One view is—the great novelist, who produces the immortal work, Pickwick. Another view is—the man who works from a structure and suggestions provided by a caricaturist."

This calculated whisper in the ear influences Dickens until the end of his life. With each retelling of his early days and his earlier works, he significantly erases any input and any measurable involvement from Robert Seymour. Not only does Dickens deny the man his artistic acknowledgment, but he also deprives Seymour's widow and family an appropriate cut of the royalties and payments that the Pickwick craze produced. This is a very unflattering portrait of Charles Dickens, a man who has long been associated with the benevolent and philanthropic message of *A Christmas Carol* (1843). Readers will have to make up their own minds about how culpable Dickens was in this squelching of Seymour's role in the origin of Pickwick. Jarvis's researcher characters maintain that the Pickwick tale is a major "literary hoax."

Many reviewers have applauded Jarvis for his meticulous research and for his narrative talents. He weaves scraps of unearthed material into a huge, vivid tapestry that re-creates the London that Dickens wrote about and lived in. Jarvis paints a portrait of the hitherto relatively unknown Seymour as a man who was, deep down, unsure of himself, despite his great commercial success. Portrayed in the novel as a closeted gay man, Seymour learns to keep much of his private thoughts and affairs just that— private. By killing himself so early in the Pickwick process, he abdicates having his participation properly noted and celebrated. Besides denying his family the monetary gains from his creation, he places himself in the dustbin of the forgotten. His accomplishments would have remained there if not for Stephen Jarvis, who has exhumed his career and imagined his fictional biography.

Detractors of Jarvis's book do not deny that there might be some questionable business regarding the origin of Pickwick. Dickens maintained that the first illustrations he saw of Samuel Pickwick did not match how the public came to view him and that he had Seymour fatten up the character to become the rotund gentleman who captured England's imagination. Even if that were not true, and Pickwick was portly from the very first picture, Dickens still went on to write several episodes of the gentlemen's club's escapades after Seymour's suicide. Most literary scholars grant that Dickens created the character of Sam Weller, the most popular of the series, who did not appear until the tenth serialized episode. Critics of *Death and Mr. Pickwick* point to Dickens's prolific output to suggest that his firm standing should not be eroded because of this allegation of perhaps taking too much credit, rather than plagiarism or thievery.

The background stories of how a work of art comes into existence are very rarely revealed. It is usually a secret known only to the artist, or to the artists when there is a collaboration. With Jarvis's depiction of Charles Dickens as an opportunist and a self-promoter, it is understandable why the origin of Pickwick was never fully or consistently told. Yet *Death and Mr. Pickwick* does not banish all the mystery and shadows that surround the creation of Charles Dickens's first hit and Robert Seymour's last success. Instead, it explores the artistic process, both the inspiration to create in the first place and the forces, real or imagined, that cause artists to decide that their days of creating are better left behind.

Stephanie Finnegan

Review Sources

Kirsch, Adam. "*Death and Mr. Pickwick*: A Marvelously Dickensian Novel about the Creation of *The Pickwick Papers*." Rev. of *Death and Mr. Pickwick*, by Stephen Jarvis. *Christian Science Monitor*. Christian Science Monitor, 16 July 2015. Web. 15 Feb. 2016.

Miller, Lucasta. "Thrilling Search for Mr. Pickwick and Those Who Made Him." Rev. of *Death and Mr. Pickwick*, by Stephen Jarvis. *Independent*. Independent News and Media, 17 May 2015. Web. 15 Feb. 2016.

Upchurch, Michael. Rev. of *Death and Mr. Pickwick*, by Stephen Jarvis. *New York Times*. New York Times, 17 July 2015. Web. 15 Feb. 2016.

Zimmerman, Jean. "*Death* Uncovers the Secret History of Mr. Pickwick." Rev. of *Death and Mr. Pickwick*, by Stephen Jarvis. *NPR*. NPR, 24 June 2015. Web. 15 Feb. 2016.

Delicious Foods

Author: James Hannaham (b. 1968)
Publisher: Little, Brown (New York). 384 pp.
Type of work: Novel
Time: 1970s–1990s
Locales: Louisiana, Minnesota

James Hannaham's second novel, Delicious Foods, *takes its title from a fictitious farm that exploits down-on-their-luck workers. The story focuses on Eddie and his crack-addicted mother, Darlene, who work for the farm and try desperately to escape their plantation-like surroundings.*

(Courtesy of Little Brown and Co.)

Principal characters:
EDDIE, a seventeen-year-old African American boy who has lost both of his hands
DARLENE, his mother, who became addicted to crack after the violent death of her husband
SCOTTY, the voice of Darlene's addiction to crack cocaine
NAT, Eddie's father and Darlene's late husband, who was murdered by a gang of white men

When the reader first meets Eddie Hardison, the central character of James Hannaham's ambitious second novel, *Delicious Foods*, he has no hands. His forearms, haphazardly bandaged with terry cloth and rubber cables, are looped through the steering wheel of a stolen Subaru, and he marvels at a road sign announcing that he is indeed in Louisiana (his mother always guessed that was where they were), where he has spent some six years performing back-breaking labor for a mysterious farm called Delicious Foods. Hannaham's tale careens out of the gate and raises a question that the author spends the remainder of the book answering: just how did seventeen-year-old Eddie lose his hands? Structurally speaking, as Ted Genoways pointed out in his review of the book for the *New York Times*, Hannaham's *Delicious Foods* is a bumpy ride, but its contents, like the fruits of the horrible farm itself, are rich and plentiful.

Once Eddie is safely settled in St. Cloud, Minnesota, where he finds success as the locally revered "handyman with no hands," Hannaham puts his story in reverse, jumping back in time to reveal Eddie's backstory as well as that of his mother, Darlene. Chapters toggle between mother and son, but—in the most innovative and successful quirk of the book—Darlene's story is narrated by Scotty, the voice of Darlene's crack addiction. Scotty is by turns savagely funny and menacing. Scotty clings to Darlene with a lover's passion while cruelly ridiculing her for the lengths to which she will go for a hit. Hannaham balances Scotty on a razor's edge: the character becomes neither a caricature nor a cheesy public-service announcement on the dangers of crack. In fact, Scotty—arguably the most complicated character in the book—steals the show.

Delicious Foods is not Scotty's story, however. The novel is an exploration of race, exploitation, and power told through the lens of a modern-day plantation. One could mistake *Delicious Foods* for a dystopian novel set in a fictional world in which slavery still exists in the twenty-first century in the deepest recesses of the American South under the cover of complicated corporate arrangements. Yet however dystopian the novel's setting may seem, *Delicious Foods* is actually based on the true story of a farm called Bulls-Hit in Hastings, Florida. In 2012, the *Tampa Bay Times* reported that Bulls-Hit lured drug-addicted, homeless black men with promises of a good job and fair pay (one man said he was enticed by the prospect of a camp where he could recover from his drug addiction) but ended up being a nightmare of modern-day slavery.

Darlene's fictional story cuts close to the ones reported in the *Tampa Bay Times*. In *Delicious Foods*, Darlene, working as a prostitute to fund her drug habit, sees an approaching van out of the night like a gift from God. A woman disembarks and hands a brochure to Darlene, who has just had her teeth kicked in by a prospective john. She offers Darlene a job on a farm, where she will get to live in a luxury condo with a pool. Darlene is so desperate she does not even let the woman finish her spiel. When she boards the bus, she is thrilled to discover people lighting up their pipes with her new employer's encouragement. As Scotty puts it, "One [of] the brothers passed the pipe up front and Darlene sucked it like it's a pacifier. She thinking how we could spend time together, but she also gonna have real, honest-to-God work at a place where they understand our relationship and ain't try to stop it or make her stay away from me. Too good." But when Darlene gets off the bus, she does not see a condo or a pool, just a filthy chicken coop with some rusted bunk beds at the back. The place is infested with bugs, and there is only one toilet. When Darlene protests, Jackie (one of Darlene's new bosses) insists that the place looks better in the daylight, but if she really wants to leave, all she has to do is pay for the ride and a bed for the night—and for that hit of crack she took on the bus. Darlene has been at Delicious Foods for less than fifteen minutes, but according to Jackie, she already owes six hundred dollars.

Like Bulls-Hit, the Delicious Foods farm enslaves its workers by keeping them in debt. Darlene and her cohorts—which soon include Eddie—are paid a pittance, but with fees for beds, food, drugs, and even working equipment, that money goes right back to the farm. Hannaham does a good job of framing the arrangement through the eyes of those who live it. Darlene hates the farm. She is an intelligent woman; she knows that what is happening to her is wrong, but her desire to continue her relationship with Scotty, her fear, and a general sense of moral failing aided by the degradation she endures at the hands of her bosses keep her complicit in the farm's scheme. In fact, when she first has the opportunity to leave Delicious Foods entirely, she chooses to stay, opening up a host of complicated questions about desire for authority and the power of addiction.

It is important to note, that like the men at Bulls-Hit, Darlene was not always in such dire straits. She grew up on a farm and went to college in Louisiana in the 1970s, where she met Nat, a charming basketball player. Nat was dating Darlene's charismatic best friend. When Nat's girlfriend finds out about his affair with Darlene, she leads their former friends in a campaign of intimidation that eventually drives Darlene and Nat to a different school. After graduation, idealistic Nat suggests they move to the small town of Ovis, Louisiana, to register black voters. They set up a general store that becomes the hub of the black community, but Nat's political organizing raises the hackles of the Ovis's white supremacist residents. One night, Nat goes to the store for a bottle of Tylenol for Darlene and encounters a group of white men. The men torture Nat and set him and the store on fire. Practically catatonic with grief, Darlene starts using drugs after suffering through an encounter with her husband's killers. Darlene and Eddie's backstory—Eddie was a child when his father was murdered—serves to underscore an

(Ian Douglas)

James Hannaham is a novelist, journalist, and performer. His first novel, God Says No, *was published in 2009. He is also an associate professor of writing at the Pratt Institute in New York City.*

important thematic component of Hannaham's novel about the various mechanisms of oppression and how institutions (or impromptu coalitions such as Darlene's friends or Nat's murderers) can conspire against an individual, and how the anonymity of a group can lead people to commit crimes more heinous than they would by themselves.

Given the moral or corporate authority, characters in the book behave heinously. Under the cover of shady Delicious Foods, a man named How, a former exploited farm worker and gang member, metes out the most cruel punishment, but he understands how small indignities suffered over time can most effectively wear a person down. He deliberately miscalculates workers' pay and then docks them more money when they call him on it. "But if you complained," Scotty says, speaking for Darlene, "How would go, You think a big diversified grower that has contracts with Birds Eye and Chiquita and Del Monte needs to skim five bucks off the paycheck of a little piddling serf like you? And you would shut your trap, 'cause on balance you needed the money more than that tiny moment of self-respect. Except that them tiny moments would start glomming together like little oil droplets in a contaminated stream."

Delicious Foods was highly anticipated based on the success of Hannaham's 2009 debut novel, *God Says No*, and has been widely praised. The *New York Times* named it to its list of the "100 Notable Books of 2015." Ron Charles, in a review of the novel for the *Washington Post*, wrote that it contained some of "the sharpest, wittiest, most unsettling cultural criticism I've read in years." Darlene and Eddie suffer but are also redeemed through forgiveness (for one another, not Delicious Foods), but Hannaham also has his eye on wider circles of good intentions and apathy, from the lawyers that vow to help Darlene bring Nat's killers to justice but drift away after losing the first trial to the consumers who unwittingly buy the literal fruits of slave labor. "Sometime Darlene took off one of her gloves and put her fingers up on the sticky watermelon skins," Scotty says, before Eddie joins her at the farm. "She deliberately leaving fingerprints, hoping somebody gonna dust that damn melon for evidence and let her son know where she at."

Delicious Foods, as Charles put it, is not *The Jungle*—the 1906 novel by Upton Sinclair that uncovered the harsh working conditions of the meatpacking industry—for modern agriculture workers. At its heart, *Delicious Foods* is less about places like Bulls-Hit than it is about systematic racism, exploitation, and oppression. At every turn, Darlene is made to believe that she is in control of her own destiny, when in reality her destiny is largely shaped by forces beyond her control. Hannaham may not offer any easy answers (or easy-won outcomes) for his characters, but that is what makes his story so riveting.

Molly Hagan

Review Sources

Charles, Ron. "Novel Will Make You Think Twice about Those Beautiful Fruits at the Store." Rev. of *Delicious Foods*, by James Hannaham. *Washington Post*. Washington Post, 17 Mar. 2015. Web. 15 Dec. 2015.

Dean, Michelle. "A Novel Where Crack Narrates." Rev. of *Delicious Foods*, by James Hannaham. *Guardian*. Guardian News and Media, 16 Mar. 2015. Web. 15 Dec. 2015.

Genoways, Ted. Rev. of *Delicious Foods*, by James Hannaham. *New York Times*. New York Times, 3 Apr. 2015. Web. 15 Dec. 2015.

Rev. of *Delicious Foods*, by James Hannaham. *Publisher's Weekly*. PWxyz, Mar. 2015. Web. 15 Dec. 2015.

Weinman, Sarah. Rev. of *Delicious Foods*, by James Hannaham. *Maclean's*. Rogers Digital Media, 21 Mar. 2015. Web. 15 Dec. 2015.

Did You Ever Have a Family

Author: Bill Clegg
Publisher: Gallery/Scout Press (New York).
304 pp.
Type of work: Novel
Time: Present
Locales: Litchfield, Connecticut; Moclips,
Washington

June Reid lives a quiet life in Litchfield, Connecticut, with her boyfriend, Luke. But on the morning of her daughter's wedding day, a gas explosion kills June's entire family and changes her life forever. Did You Ever Have a Family *follows June in the months after her family tragedy as she seeks answers, grieves, and begins to imagine how she might move on.*

(Courtesy of Gallery Books)

Principal characters:
JUNE REID, a fifty-two-year-old art dealer who lives in a country house in Connecticut
LOLLY REID, her daughter, who was to be married on the day she was killed
LUKE MOREY, her handsome thirty-year-old boyfriend who was imprisoned for a
   crime he did not commit
LYDIA MOREY, Luke's mother, a longtime working-class resident of Litchfield
WILL LANDIS, Lolly's kindhearted fiancé whose family is from Moclips, Washington
CISSY, a housekeeper at the Moonstone Motel and member of the Quinault tribe in
   Moclips

Bill Clegg's debut novel, *Did You Ever Have a Family* (2015), is a story about family tragedies. It is told from the perspectives of many characters whose lives are loosely interconnected. At the center of the novel are two women: June Reid, an affluent fifty-two-year-old divorcée who worked as an art dealer in New York and London and has moved to her country house in the small town of Litchfield, Connecticut; and Lydia Morey, a longtime working-class resident of Litchfield whose life becomes entangled with June's when her son, Luke, becomes romantically involved with June. At the outset of the novel, a gas explosion on the day that June's daughter, Lolly, is to be married to Will Landis destroys June's home and kills her entire family: Luke, Lolly, Will, and June's former husband, Adam. In the pages that follow, Clegg explores not only the depths of June and the other characters' grief, but also the tragedies, triumphs, and chance circumstances that bring them together.

The novel opens in the aftermath of the tragic gas explosion that has killed June's family. June is "for the first time in her life, alone." June recounts some of the details of the tragic day as she packs up her Subaru and starts driving west, leaving behind the East Coast and Litchfield, the town in which she had spent weekends for more than two decades and lived for several years. In the chapters that follow, readers are introduced to several minor characters who are peripherally connected to June and her family and who begin to fill in the details about the Reids and the Moreys. Edith, a local townsperson who had been creating the flower arrangements for Lolly's wedding, discloses town gossip about June and her young boyfriend, "that doomed Luke Morey."

Edith speaks to readers as though in secret, and in this way, readers become like fellow townspeople and spectators in the story, witnessing the tragedy from the sidelines. Rick, the owner of Feast of Reason, a local café and caterer in Litchfield, tells readers about being tasked with making Lolly's wedding cake and catering the event. Rick also provides readers with further insight into

(Christian Hansen)

Bill Clegg is the author of the memoirs Portrait of an Addict as a Young Man *(2010) and* Ninety Days *(2012). He has written for the* New York Times, Esquire, New York Magazine, *and the* Guardian. Did You Ever Have a Family *is his debut novel.*

June and Luke's relationship and Luke's difficult past. A former classmate of Luke, Rick recalls growing up with the talented athlete and how Luke's promising life was torn apart by a drug conviction and prison sentence. Rick recounts Luke's struggle to restart his life after getting out of prison, performing odd jobs, and how Luke seemed "too big, too handsome, too *something* for the likes of us." Rick also provides readers with a glimpse into Luke's family history. Readers learn that Luke was the illegitimate son of Lydia, who was desperate to get out of her abusive marriage to Earl Morey. Hated by the Moreys, Luke lived much of his life as an outcast in Litchfield.

While minor characters such as Edith and Rick function to provide readers with essential information about the Reid and Morey families without figuring prominently in the novel's plot themselves, there are other minor characters who do figure prominently and return repeatedly. For example, Rebecca and Kelly are a lesbian couple who manage the Moonstone Motel on the Pacific coast in Moclips, Washington. When June shows up one day at the Moonstone in the wake of her family tragedy, Rebecca and Kelly—along with Cissy, the housekeeper—decide to look after their mysterious guest about whom they know next to nothing. What readers soon learn is that Rebecca and Kelly's lives have been rocked by tragedy, too. Cissy, a member of the Quinault tribe in Moclips who grew up in the area, takes a particular interest in June, bringing her homemade soups and checking on her daily. Readers eventually learn that Cissy knew Will Landis as a child. Will also grew up in the Moclips area. In fact, Will proposed to

Lolly at the Moonstone Motel while the two were on a trip visiting his hometown. It is this fact that brought June to the West Coast in the first place.

The mysteries of Clegg's *Did You Ever Have a Family* unfold gradually. As readers encounter the novel's long cast of characters, they begin to ask a series of questions: Why was June Reid the only person not asleep in her house in the early hours of her daughter's wedding day when the fatal explosion occurred? How did June's boyfriend, Luke, a seemingly nice, put-together young man with a landscaping business, end up with a prison sentence when he was barely out of high school? What knowledge do the women of the Moonstone Motel harbor about Will, Lolly, and June? And most important, what caused the gas explosion that destroyed June's and Lydia's entire lives in a single moment? Clegg reveals the answers to these questions and others with precision and subtlety. The novel is a mystery, but first and foremost it is a drama, one that explores the nature of the grieving process. Clegg reminds readers of this fact through close attention to his characters' histories—their hardships and the particular conditions of their lives. With compassion and care, Clegg braids together his characters' stories, demonstrating how the meaning of "family" can change in an instant and, moreover, be transformed in and through the process of survival. While family ties are broken and lost over the course of the novel, they are also established anew. Intimacies and trusting relationships crop up in unexpected places as the novel's characters struggle to find truth and meaning amid disaster.

Critics have praised *Did You Ever Have a Family* for its unflinching exploration of the grief and healing processes in the aftermath of tragedy. Clare Clark for the *Guardian* states that "from the ashes of the fatal blaze Clegg has drawn a tale of prodigious tenderness and lyricism." Clegg's characters confess what they know or think they know in down-to-earth, plainspoken voices, despite the difficulty and gravity of their subject matter. In this way, Clegg points toward the way in which the people of Litchfield and Moclips could be any of us. Tragedy strikes when one least expects it, and tragedy's victims are most often ordinary people just going about their lives, doing their best with what they are dealt.

Reviews of Clegg's debut have been mixed. While many critics laud the novel, which was long-listed for the Man Booker Prize, for its emotional depth and character studies, some have critiqued it for its oftentimes clichéd prose and loose narrative ends. While the novel strives to depict authentically the atmosphere, temporality, and felt experience of grief, it often ends up resorting to platitudes, or what Dwight Garner for the *New York Times* described as "greeting card homilies." Readers might also find themselves asking whether they actually need quite so much backstory about certain characters. For example, it is unclear why readers require such detail about Rebecca's difficult childhood in Worcester, Massachusetts. While the novel aspires to be an emotionally charged drama, the plethora of characters, each with their own story to tell, ends up diffusing the central dramas of the story: June's and Lydia's.

Notably, Clegg works to develop a diverse array of characters—many of whom identify with underrepresented racial, ethnic, and class groups. He explores how tragedy affects their lives and their chances for survival in different ways. The characters of *Did You Ever Have a Family* are not only white but also black and Native American;

not only affluent but also working and middle class; and not only straight but also gay. Clegg's attempt to explore how socioeconomic status and racialization affect one's ability to navigate hardship is commendable and necessary. But, in the end, the primary character with whom readers are asked to sympathize is June Reid: a slim, blond, affluent woman who made her career in the elite art world. Moreover, Clegg often ends up reinscribing stereotypes about African Americans and African American families, Native American people, and marijuana use among teens.

Did You Ever Have a Family is perhaps most compelling in its exploration of how chance happenings can both destroy one's life in an instant and offer one the possibility of redemption. Clegg makes clear that the tragic events of the lives of June and Lydia lack reason or explanation. It is this nearly unbearable fact with which both June and Lydia must learn to live. It is also this fact that enables the two women to take new risks and begin to develop new bonds, radically challenging their understanding of concepts such as trust, family, and love.

A. Lewandowski

Review Sources

Currie, Janette. "Did You Ever Have a Family, by Bill Clegg—Book Review: Bereavement Counseling." Rev. of *Did You Ever Have a Family*, by Bill Clegg. *Independent*. Independent, 19 Sept. 2015. Web. 1 Feb. 2016.

Clare, Clark. "Did You Ever Have a Family by Bill Clegg Review—A Quiet Novel of Devastating Power." Rev. of *Did You Ever Have a Family*, by Bill Clegg. *Guardian*. Guardian News and Media Limited, 21 Aug. 2015. Web. 1 Feb. 2016.

Collins-Hughes, Laura. "'Did You Ever Have a Family' by Bill Clegg." Rev. of *Did You Ever Have a Family*, by Bill Clegg. *Boston Globe*. Boston Globe Media Partners, 5 Sept. 2015. Web. 1 Feb. 2016.

Garner, Dwight. "Review: Bill Clegg's 'Did You Ever Have a Family' Heaps One Tragedy upon Another." Rev. of *Did You Ever Have a Family*, by Bill Clegg. *New York Times*. New York Times, 8 Sept. 2015. Web. 1 Feb. 2016.

McAlpin, Heller. "Bill Clegg's 'Did You Ever Have a Family' Finds Solace amid Tragedy." Rev. of *Did You Ever Have a Family*, by Bill Clegg. *Los Angeles Times*. Los Angeles Times, 4 Sept. 2015. Web. 1 Feb. 2016.

Dietland

Author: Sarai Walker (b. 1972)
Publisher: Houghton Mifflin Harcourt (New
York). 310 pp.
Type of work: Novel
Time: Present day
Locale: New York City

(Courtesy Houghton Mifflin Harcourt)

The debut novel of author Sarai Walker, Dietland *explores the effects of the beauty industry and gender inequality on American
women.*

Principal characters:
PLUM KETTLE, the narrator
VERENA BAPTIST, the manager of the Cal-
liope House, a feminist collective
LEETA, the face of a feminist vigilante group
MARLOWE, a writer working from the
Calliope House

Alicia "Plum" Kettle is unlike most heroines of mainstream fiction. This is especially
evident in Plum's physicality. At three hundred pounds, Plum is fat, a quality that is
typically designated only to benign, matronly female characters in secondary roles. As
a narrator and protagonist, Plum defies literary conventions not only in her appearance
but also in the fact that she is a complex and compelling person. In interviews, author
Sarai Walker has stated that her decision to create the character of Plum was largely
in response to the dearth of fat heroines in literature. Plum's story, *Dietland* (2015), is
an in-depth look at the reality of being an overweight woman in modern society that
blends unflinching realism with satire and fantasy to reclaim the word "fat."

From the beginning of the narrative, Walker presents Plum Kettle as vulnerable and
unhappy. When Plum is first introduced, she is living a small, reclusive life in Brooklyn. With no real friends, her days are spent working a mindless job for *Daisy Chain*,
a magazine for teenaged girls. Her job, which she conducts from a café near her apartment, requires her to respond to the hundreds of daily emails sent to the magazine's editor, Kitty Montgomery. In these "Dear Kitty" emails, teenaged correspondents make
desperate requests for help with serious issues regarding their lives, bodies, and happiness. It is Plum's duty to masquerade as Kitty and provide each email with a personal
response. While Plum does not find the work stimulating or particularly enjoyable, her
intentions in helping the girls who write to Kitty are genuine.

Walker ensures that Plum is a relatable character through her internal dialogue.
When she is not working, Plum is fantasizing about a future when she is thin. As
a three-hundred-pound woman, Plum is conspicuous. Everywhere she goes people

stop, stare, and make disparaging remarks about her body. Consequently, Plum avoids public places and interpersonal relationships. After years of failed dieting, Plum has scheduled a weight-loss surgery that will shrink her stomach to "the size of a walnut." She believes that it is only when she loses weight that her true life as Alicia, her actual first name, can begin. In Plum's mind, Alicia is thin and beautiful and therefore worthy of love. Here, Walker taps into the human tendency to idealize what could be rather than embracing what is. Plum believes that all of her unhappiness stems from her weight when in fact there are more serious, complex problems at hand.

Plum's plans to become Alicia are derailed one day when she notices that a girl in bright tights and army boots is spying on her. The girl, whom she later learns is named Leeta, effectively changes the trajectory of Plum's life by introducing her to Verena Baptist. The founder of a feminist collective known as the Calliope House, Verena feels responsible for Plum after learning that she was a member of her mother's Baptist Diet empire. As restitution for the damage she believes the Baptist Diet inflicted on Plum's self-image, Verena comes to Plum with a proposal that becomes the impetus to the central story line of *Dietland*: if Plum seriously considers not going through with the weight-loss surgery, Verena will give her twenty thousand dollars. All Plum has to do is endure what Verena dubs the "New Baptist Plan," which comprises a series of existential exercises. If by the end of the New Baptist Plan, Plum wants to go ahead with the surgery, she is still entitled to the twenty thousand dollars.

By addressing the issues surrounding her sense of beauty and self-worth, Plum embarks on a journey of personal transformation. This transformation, however, deviates significantly from the "chick-lit" tropes to which *Dietland* ostensibly belongs. With meticulous execution, Walker ensures that Plum's growth as a character sharply contrasts the clichéd makeovers endured by heroines in mainstream romantic comedies. Under Verena's guidance, Plum does not magically become conventionally attractive or find a man who falls in love with her despite her physicality. Instead, she learns to identify the sources of her unhappiness and accept herself. Essentially, Plum learns to start living her life.

Walker denotes Plum's transformation throughout the novel through several stylistic cues. The most noticeable is the shift in the way that she describes food and hunger. In the beginning of the novel, Plum describes food by listing each food item she has eaten and the calories it comprises in parentheses. As her transformation ensues, however, she stops counting calories. Her feelings of shame toward food and perpetual hunger are replaced with feelings of satiation as she allows herself to enjoy eating. Additionally, she learns to embrace the word "fat" rather than seeing it pejoratively.

While self-acceptance may be one of the central themes of *Dietland*, it is presented in a wholly original way. Walker's interpretation of self-acceptance is not a platitude; it does suggest that once women learn to love themselves they will be loved by men. Instead she urges women to look toward the wellspring of their self-loathing: the misogynistic media and beauty industry. Through the story of Plum, Walker suggests that in order to be happy, women should focus on changing the world rather than their bodies. This message becomes particularly clear when Walker begins interspersing Plum's first-person narration with brief third-person accounts of a feminist terrorist group.

Known collectively as Jennifer, the vigilante group attacks women's oppressors. Jennifer's acts of revenge are presented in a surrealist manner and are accompanied by subversive humor. Rapists are thrown from helicopters, imams are forced to tell Muslim men to pour acid in their eyes rather than require their women to wear burkas, and fraternity houses are burned down. As Jennifer begins to spark a revolution, Plum discovers a radical side of herself that becomes increasingly difficult to quiet.

Although Plum's physicality and unhappiness may seem extreme, Walker presents her plight as being universal. In the beginning of the novel, the "Dear Kitty" emails are depicted as a collective cry for help. Like an endless sea, these emails pour into Plum's inbox by the thousands every week. Most of the writers are girls who believe that there is something inherently wrong with them because of the impossible standards established and advertised by the beauty industry. Others become depressed or end up hurting themselves simply because they are unable to achieve physical perfection. Another way in which Walker entrenches female universality into *Dietland*'s core message is through the Jennifer group. The character of Leeta eventually becomes the face of Jennifer in a manner similar to how Che Guevara became the face of the Cuban Revolution, and subsequently Jennifer becomes symbolic of all women. Additionally, the name Jennifer is intended to convey a sense of Everywoman. Walker clarifies this by stating that Jennifer was the most popular girls' name in the United States throughout the 1970s and 1980s.

As a writer, Walker has a talent for balancing suspense with comedy and original scenarios. She succeeds in delivering a thought-provoking story without being heavy-handed or cloying in her message. Furthermore, Walker is unwavering in her approach to uncomfortable, often taboo issues. She works to reclaim the word "fat" and explores all of the ugliness the word represents. She openly criticizes society for its shallowness and cruelty toward those who do not fit the mainstream ideal. Furthermore, Walker uses inflammatory language and ideas to provoke

Sarai Walker has an MFA in creative writing from Bennington College and a PhD in English from the University of London. She is a former magazine writer and editor of Our Bodies, Ourselves *(2005).* Dietland *(2015) is her first novel.*

both her characters and readers. A significant catalyst to Plum's awakening is when a Calliope House resident named Marlowe introduces her to the *F——ability Theory*, a book that encourages women to reject the idea that their worth is based in how sexually attractive they are to men. It is through these radical ideas that *Dietland*'s narrative influences become clear. Conceptually, *Dietland* emulates Chuck Palahniuk's novel *Fight Club* (1996) and the film *Thelma and Louise* (1991). In her acknowledgments, Walker states after seeing the 1999 David Fincher–directed adaptation of *Fight Club* in theaters she felt a need to create a similar revolutionary story for women. Ultimately, with *Dietland*, she succeeds in crafting a compelling call to arms for women against unrealistic beauty standards and misogyny.

Reviewers frequently praised Walker's ability to balance satire with a strong message. In a review of the novel for *Entertainment Weekly*, Isabella Biedenharn compared Walker's prose to subversive feminist sketch comedy, ultimately declaring *Dietland* a "thrilling, incendiary manifesto disguised as a beach read." Similarly, a critic for *Kirkus Reviews* described the narrative of *Dietland* as hilarious and surreal. In regard to its success in raising consciousness about society's acclimation and passivity toward sexism, Annalisa Quinn for NPR wrote that *Dietland* was successful in identifying and exploring the anger that so many women share toward the prevalence of misogyny, declaring the novel, "a complicated, thoughtful, and powerful expression of that anger."

While provocative and entertaining, *Dietland* is not without its shortcomings. For one, readers have cited Walker's use of violence as more disturbing than effective in driving the plot. It is important to note that the violent acts of *Dietland* are intended to be surrealist rather than realistic. Walker is employing provocation in an effort to spark discussions about real issues. Furthermore, although Jennifer's violent acts of revenge may be horrifying to some readers, the catalysts to their actions are arguably more disturbing in that they happen every day. Sexual assault, honor killings, body shaming, and the media's exploitation of women's bodies are ubiquitous realities. An additional criticism of *Dietland* has been directed toward the way in which Walker splices Jennifer's terrorist acts throughout Plum's story. In her otherwise positive review for the *Guardian*, Lydia Kiesling described these breaks in the narrative as "structurally inelegant" and argues that it ultimately gives the novel a patchwork quality. Although the shift in literary style in which the anecdotes of Jennifer's terrorist acts are written may take some readers out of the story, they are ultimately effective as vessels to essential plot points. As a whole, *Dietland* is a comical, thought-provoking novel that is highly engaging in the delivery of its message.

Emily E. Turner

Review Sources

Rev. of *Dietland*, by Sarai Walker. *Kirkus.* Kirkus, 26 May 2015. Web. 11 Jan. 2016.

Donnelly, Elisabeth. "Is Dietland 2015's Most Surprising Book about Women?" Rev. of *Dietland*, by Sarai Walker. *New York Magazine.* New York Media, 31 Dec. 2015. Web. 11 Jan. 2016.

Kiesling, Lydia. "Gleefully Censorious of 'Rape Culture.'" Rev. of *Dietland*, by Sarai Walker. *Guardian.* Guardian News and Media, 11 June 2015. Web. 11 Jan. 2016.

Quinn, Annalisa. "Fat is Not a Four Letter Word in 'Dietland.'" Rev. of *Dietland*, by Sarai Walker. *NPR Books.* NPR, 27 May 2015. Web. 11 Jan. 2016.

Eileen

Author: Ottessa Moshfegh (b. 1981)
Publisher: Penguin Press (New York). 272 pp.
Type of work: Novel
Time: December 1964 and the present
Locale: A suburban town in Massachusetts

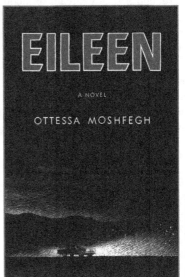

(Courtesy of Penguin)

Ottessa Moshfegh burnishes her reputation as one of the literary world's brightest new voices with Eileen, *an unsettling coming-of-age noir about a lonely young Massachusetts woman whose life is forever changed when she becomes drawn into a bizarre crime.*

Principal characters:
EILEEN DUNLOP, a twenty-four-year-old secretary at a correctional facility for teenage boys
REBECCA SAINT JOHN, her colleague, a social worker
CHARLES DUNLOP, her father, a retired police officer, and an alcoholic

The term "noir," as its name suggests, conjures images of bleak settings, shadowy characters, and dark themes. Whether it be the cynical, world-weary private detectives and mysterious femme fatales of the hard-boiled literary genre, or the self-destructive characters in noir fiction, noir protagonists are often depicted as running away from or reflecting on something that occurred in their past, which almost always involves some kind of crime, usually murder. Written in the noir tradition, Ottessa Moshfegh's sophomore novel, *Eileen*, focuses on the titular character who becomes involved in a crime that forever alters her life. The novel is less a crime story than a coming-of-age tale about a young woman who breaks free from the shackles of repressive familial and societal norms.

In typical noir fashion, Moshfegh's novel unfolds largely in flashback and is set against a cold and wintry New England backdrop. It is told from the first-person per-spective of Eileen Dunlop, a woman in her seventies who looks back to a fateful week in her life five decades earlier. When Eileen begins narrating her story, it is 1964 and the week before Christmas. She is twenty-four years old and works as a secretary at Moorehead, a private prison for teenage boys outside Boston, Massachusetts. (Moore-head is the surname of a terrible landlord Eileen once had.) She lives alone with her father, Charles, a retired police officer, in a three-story colonial in a suburban Mas-sachusetts town only referred to as "X-ville."

The street the Dunlops live on is tree-lined and tidy, but their home is devoid of any of the Christmas warmth and cheer exuding from other houses on the block. Eileen and her father lead a squalid existence characterized by dirt, dust, dilapidated furniture, and a steady stream of alcohol. Eileen has a sister, Joanie, who is four years older and who has been estranged from the family for years, and her mother died when Eileen was nineteen. Since then, she and her father have silently agreed to stop celebrating Christmas.

In her mother's absence, Eileen has become her father's caretaker, but not in the traditional sense. Instead of cooking and cleaning up after him, she is charged with fetching him bottles of gin on a daily basis. Cruelly demanding, emotionally abusive, paranoid, and delusional, Eileen's father has few, if any, redeeming qualities. He relentlessly insults Eileen about her appearance, and when he is not lying in a drunken stupor in the shabby armchair he keeps in the kitchen, he staggers around the house with a gun for protection against imaginary "hooligans" and "mobsters." Eileen, though, spends much of her time avoiding him in an unfinished attic that doubles as her bedroom. She nevertheless assures readers only pages into the novel that her story is not about how awful her father is but rather about how she escapes from her miserable, soul-shattering life.

Ottessa Moshfegh won the 2013 Plimpton Prize for Fiction from the Paris Review for her stories "Disgust" and "Bettering Myself." Her debut novel, McGlue (2014), received the inaugural Fence Modern Prize in Prose. She was a Wallace Stegner Fellow at Stanford University from 2013 to 2015.

Notwithstanding her father's daily barbs, Eileen already has a low opinion of herself. Mired in self-obsession, she analyzes every aspect of her body and life. Thin with small green eyes, light brown hair, and a wan complexion, Eileen looks like an average girl, or as she puts it, one "you'd expect to see on a city bus," but she sees herself as "the worst—ugly, disgusting, unfit for the world." She hides her self-hatred with an inscrutable exterior that she refers to as a "death mask" and channels her anger through dark obsessions and perverse fantasies. She reads books about murder and death, wears her dead mother's clothes, imagines being stabbed by falling icicles, and keeps a dead field mouse in the glove compartment of the run-down Dodge Coronet she drives to work each day.

For Eileen, it is only fitting that her home away from home is a prison. At Moorehead, she is constantly ridiculed and badgered by her two colleagues, "both awful middle-aged women with stiff hairdos" and likely, she imagines, "disgusting husbands." During brief work breaks, she feeds her narcissistic tendencies by looking at her reflection in the mirror above the coffee station. She passes the rest of her time fantasizing about a prison guard named Randy, whom she also stalks on weekends. Eileen's fantasies also involve some of the adolescent inmates, including Leonard "Lee" Polk, a teenager imprisoned for killing his father, an X-ville cop who had once served with her father. Moshfegh has said that the Polk character, who readers learn will serve more than just a cursory role in the story, was based on a real-life case that helped inspire the novel.

As the novel progresses, Eileen reveals other peculiar fixations and habits, such as her addiction to laxatives and penchant for stealing. She is also a virgin and an admitted prude who has never had a meaningful relationship. She believes that her first sexual experience will be by force, but she secretly hopes it will be with someone handsome like Randy. Despite Eileen's twisted and off-putting notions, Moshfegh manages to hold the reader's interest with carefully placed hints about plot developments that will happen later in the story. Seemingly unimportant details, such as casual mentions of basements, guns, and sleeping pills, become significant as the novel slowly burns toward its violent climax.

Eventually, Moshfegh introduces the character of Rebecca Saint John, a Harvard-educated social worker who is hired as Moorehead's new director of education. Tall, redheaded, beautiful, and mysterious, Rebecca instantly captivates Eileen, who sees her as her ticket out of X-ville. Randy becomes an afterthought, as the two become fast friends. "Meeting Rebecca was like learning to dance, discovering jazz," Eileen says. "It was like falling in love for the first time." Eileen falls in love with Rebecca but not in a sexual way; at one point, she affirms that she is not a lesbian. Nevertheless, like all femme fatales, Rebecca is not who she seems to be, and Eileen soon becomes her accomplice in a bizarre crime that ultimately leads to her Christmas escape.

Though Rebecca plays a defining role in her life, Eileen offers little more than superficial details about her. Throughout the novel, Eileen makes it clear that this is her story and her story alone. Moshfegh is unsparing in her portrayal of Eileen's self-obsession: she bids farewell to her decaying X-ville home by kissing her own reflection in the bathroom mirror. Because Eileen holds all the cards of her story, she conveniently picks and chooses what episodes she wants to include or omit. She makes only brief references to the many events that occur in her life during the fifty-year period after her story takes place. Among other things, readers learn that Eileen has since had numerous affairs, gone through at least two marriages, and established a new identity and life for herself in New York City. She also shares some harrowing details from her adolescence, like the time she was once drunkenly groped by her father, but thanks to Moshfegh's careful plotting, she never veers too far off from the story and always circles back to the fateful week in question.

At times, however, Eileen is, by her own admission, an unreliable narrator. Similar to her debut novella, *McGlue* (2014), about a drunken nineteenth-century sailor who struggles to piece together events leading up to a murder he may have committed, Moshfegh plays with the concept of memory in *Eileen* by exploring how people choose to remember things. During some of her recollections, Eileen expresses uncertainty about specific details that she may or may not have added, but she also brazenly embellishes other moments in her life for dramatic effect. Embellishments aside, readers will likely not find it difficult to be seduced by Eileen's whimsical narration, thanks to Moshfegh's formidable talents as a prose writer. Recounting Rebecca's arrival to work one day, Eileen describes her "bustling in from the frigid morning snowdrifts," whirling "off her coat as though in slow motion," and shaking it "like a bullfighter as she strode up the corridor toward me, hair rippling behind her, eyes like daggers shooting down straight through my heart to my guts."

However, such passages, which are rife throughout the novel, repeatedly call into question the believability of Eileen's septuagenarian voice. Imaginative and penetrating, Moshfegh's prose soars off the page, but it also often fails to reflect that of a woman seemingly tempered by worldly experience. Lydia Kiesling for the *Guardian* observes that Eileen writes with "the grandiose coltishness befitting the young woman whose early life she narrates." Meanwhile, certain plot developments in the novel, like the arrival of Rebecca, come off as contrived and implausible, or as novelist Lily King puts it in her *New York Times* review, "feel pasted in from another book." The novel's long-awaited payoff, when it comes, will also likely be regarded by some readers as anticlimactic.

Moshfegh's narrative choices are nonetheless the product of genre conventions, and as a whole, they do little to affect the overall power of the novel, which received mostly laudatory reviews. By keeping the novel rooted in the noir tradition and incorporating elements from various other genres like gothic fiction and the psychological thriller, Moshfegh effectively lures the reader into what is ultimately a dark and unsettling character study. Eileen is not only held captive by her father but also by the patriarchal, repressive society of the early 1960s, and however repulsive she may be at times, readers are left to understand her motives and sympathize with her plight.

Moshfegh has drawn comparisons to such noted American authors as Flannery O'Connor and Shirley Jackson, and many critics agree that she is at her best when traversing the landscape of the perverse. *Eileen* undoubtedly showcases Moshfegh's literary strengths, and though not for the squeamish or faint of heart, the novel will draw readers willing to venture into the sordid, twisted mind of one of the most memorable characters to hit the literary world in years.

Chris Cullen

Review Sources

Anderson, Patrick. "'Eileen' Review: A Lonely Young Woman Finds a Friend—Then Trouble." Rev. of *Eileen*, by Ottessa Moshfegh. *Washington Post*. Washington Post, 6 Sept. 2015. Web. 12 Jan. 2016.

Rev. of *Eileen*, by Ottessa Moshfegh. *Publishers Weekly*. PWxyz, 11 May 2015. Web. 9 Feb. 2016.

Kiesling, Lydia. "Eileen by Ottessa Moshfegh Review—An Odd Double of Plath's Bell Jar." Rev. of *Eileen*, by Ottessa Moshfegh. *Guardian*. Guardian News and Media, 20 Aug. 2015. Web. 9 Feb. 2016.

King, Lily. Rev. of *Eileen*, by Ottessa Moshfegh. *New York Times*. New York Times, 14 Aug. 2015. Web. 12 Jan. 2016.

Williamson, Eugenia. Rev. of *Eileen*, by Ottessa Moshfegh. *Boston Globe*. Boston Globe Media Partners, 15 Aug. 2015. Web. 12 Jan. 2016.

Zimmerman, Jean. "'Eileen' Is Dark, Damaged Fun." Rev. of *Eileen*, by Ottessa Moshfegh. *NPR Books*. NPR, 23 Aug. 2015. Web. 12 Jan. 2016.

The Empty Form Goes All the Way to Heaven

Author: Brian Teare (b. 1974)
Publisher: Ahsahta Press (Boise, ID). 98 pp.
Type of work: Poetry
Time: Present
Locale: Philadelphia

In The Empty Form Goes All the Way to Heaven, *Brian Teare chronicles his experience living with a debilitating chronic disease. To cope, he turns to visual art, meditation practice, and alternative medicine in order to gain insight into the nature of suffering and the limitations of the body.*

(Courtesy of Ahsahta Press)

In Brian Teare's fifth full-length poetry collection, *The Empty Form Goes All the Way to Heaven,* the Lambda Award–winning poet writes about his experience living with a chronic, debilitating illness. In the book, Teare reflects on the artwork of Agnes Martin (1912–2004), an abstract expressionist painter who worked with lines and grids and is particularly known for her six-feet-by-six-feet gridded canvases. Martin's work is sometimes associated with the landscapes of New Mexico, and her color palettes are often subtle and limited. She also wrote essays in which she discussed her beliefs in perfection, freedom, and nonattachment, as Teare highlights in the preface to his book. He quotes Martin's statement that the grid came to mind for her one day when she was thinking about innocence.

While the pages of Teare's book are not gridded, they are nearly square in shape, and his poetic forms call attention to the horizontal and vertical flows of text on the page through the use of columns, spacing, and varying line length. Most of his poems are just one page long, invoking Martin's gridded canvases and inviting readers to view the poems as if they were works of visual art. But Teare does not simply adopt or adapt Martin's grid. Instead, his poems remain critical of Martin's practice by allowing for asymmetry, ambiguity, and disruption on the canvas of the page. In the end, Teare maintains a critical relationship with the artwork of Agnes Martin and asserts himself to be a different kind of thinker and artist.

In many ways, *The Empty Form Goes All the Way to Heaven* is an exploration of spiritual practice. Teare's poetry, like Martin's art, is influenced by Buddhism. The book often references Buddhist teachings, such as patience in suffering. One might read the book as the practice of patience, one that Teare slowly adapted and refined as a means of enduring the debilitating symptoms of his illness. Teare relates the teachings of Buddhism to his own lived experience. For example, he writes, in a moment of sudden clarity, "I no longer believe that [suffering] is bad / I only believe it is suffering . . . and it means nothing at all." Through meditation practice, Teare reaches the conclusion that suffering is ultimately meaningless. It is not redemptive; rather, it is simply something that mortal bodies must endure.

The first poem in Teare's book is an ekphrastic one. *Ekphrasis* is a Greek word meaning "description." An ekphrastic poem is one that describes and reflects on a work of visual art. In this poem, titled "watercolor and graphite on paper, fifteen by fifteen inches," the poet describes the color, texture, and surface of one of Martin's paintings and meditates on his own body's relationship to it. He then relates the form of the Martin painting to his experience of illness. Just as Martin's grid is contained by the canvas, Teare's poem is contained by a rectangular frame and limited to the space of the page. The poem ends abruptly at the bottom of the page, as if reaching a canvas's end. Teare's chosen form becomes a metaphor for the sick body. Just as the poem contained by the limited space of the page is rife with unresolved tensions, so does the sick body, sometimes suffering from inexplicable pain, experience the limitations of its own mortal form.

The poems that follow are often arranged in multiple columns. These pages invite the reader to navigate the poems in different ways. For example, in a poem titled "With these rectangles I didn't know at the time exactly why," about taking a bath, the reader might read straight across the page, moving from the left column to the right one, or straight down, following a single column. Reading straight across, disregarding spacing, produces the lines

> nice image linoleum
>
> for nausea how small
> washing hot
> my body
> one end has become
> to the other

Reading straight down through a single column, on the other hand, produces the lines

> nice image
>
> for nausea
> washing hot
>
> one end
> to the other

Teare is an experimental poet, and readers who are familiar with his work will understand that these lines are not necessarily representative. One might point out how moving one's eyes from one column to the next mimics the sloshing motion of water in a tub. In this light, both reading and bathing, two seemingly ordinary and sometimes mindless daily activities, become disorienting, even nauseating. Through his experimentation with form, Teare is able to evoke the experience of illness through poetry.

Later in the book, in a poem titled "We are not the instruments of fate nor are we the pawns of fate we are the material of fate," Teare writes that his "body [is] so illegible no one can read it." He had difficulty obtaining a diagnosis for his chronic illness, and this experience of being undiagnosable, or "illegible," led to feelings of shame. Later in the same poem, he discusses how there is no language for his pain; even his poetry cannot describe it to his satisfaction. Once again, he insists that poetry is not representative. Instead, Teare writes, "I've had to find a form able to do what I mean / I mean I've had to fashion a form that pains." His poem about feeling nauseated while bathing, a poem that evokes the experience of nausea itself

(Ryan Collerd)

Brian Teare is the author of five full-length books and several chapbooks. He is a former Stegner Fellow and the recipient of poetry fellowships from the National Endowment for the Arts, the MacDowell Colony, the Fund for Poetry, the Marin Headlands Center for the Arts, and the American Antiquarian Society.

through its disorienting columns, is a good example of this "form that pains." In reading the poem, readers sense what it might be like for the poet to experience his symptoms. For Teare, poetry can both convey illness and serve as a mechanism for enduring it. Arguably, the book is a practice of endurance—of enduring the space of the page, the indeterminacy of poetic language, and "painful" forms and language that do not necessarily culminate in lyric musicality.

The anti-lyrical moments of *The Empty Form Goes All the Way to Heaven* mark a departure from much of Teare's earlier work. His collection *Companion Grasses* (2013), for example, contains poetry that is more aligned with the lyric tradition. Lyric poetry is often thought of as poetry about personal feelings that leads to insights and epiphanies, or, alternatively, poetry that is musical. In *Companion Grasses*, Teare's gaze is more often turned outward on the natural habitats of California, where he used to live. His forms in that collection often reflect the shapes or attributes of regional plant species, culminating in internal rhymes and delicate, precise imagery. The book is elegiac, ultimately setting meditations in and on nature alongside personal reflections and realizations, and in this way keeps with the romantic lyric tradition inaugurated by William Wordsworth and Samuel Taylor Coleridge.

Teare has discussed how his earlier work draws from the insights of mid-century objectivist poets such as Charles Olson, who practiced "composition by field" and treated the space of the page as an open field for experimentation and collage. In *The Empty Form*, however, he treats the page not as an open field but as a limited grid, a much more constrained space, and turns his gaze from the natural world outside of him to the interior world of his body. *The Empty Form* is about the absolute limit that is the body, and how poetry about embodiment and illness must reflect the often painful experience of being contained by a single, suffering body.

The Empty Form Goes All the Way to Heaven is also a critique of the American medical system. In the eyes of modern medicine, Teare is just another patient, and an uninsured one at that. When the doctors are not easily able to diagnose his illness, Teare is shuffled from one doctor to the next and given more tests. Because the system cannot classify him with a disease name, it does not know what to do with him. The poet's language of the clinic and the hospital provides brief glimpses of white hospital sheets and intravenous needles. Notably, humans are mostly absent from his descriptions. Teare depicts Western medicine and the Western clinic and hospital as sterile, alienating places where bodies are triaged, treated, or simply handled, and then turned out once again onto the streets. Teare writes of leaving one clinic feeling dizzy after having a significant amount of blood drawn. His days are measured in terms of walks to and from clinics.

Meanwhile, Teare's symptoms continue to worsen. He is vomiting and losing weight. Ordinary activities, such as eating and having sex, no longer bring him pleasure. Yet Teare writes in spite of his bodily dysfunction. Arguably, one of the book's achievements is that it inaugurates a poetics of dysfunction. Teare writes about waiting for years for his pain to become meaningful. What he learns by the end of the book is that "there's no salvation in it." This final claim is in reference to Agnes Martin's last painting, but metaphorically, as readers who have arrived at this point in the book will understand, "it" also refers to suffering. Here is the essential connection between art and pain: while neither art nor pain will redeem, both will certainly transform. And this endurance of the visceral, transformative experiences of both art and pain is simply a part of being alive.

The Empty Form Goes All the Way to Heaven marks an important contribution to the literature of chronic illness and disability. It is an unflinching and exacting exploration of both art's and the body's forms of being in the world amid what is often unbearable difficulty and incomprehensible suffering.

A. Lewandowski

Review Sources

Bartlett, Jennifer. Rev. of *The Empty Form Goes All the Way to Heaven*, by Brian Teare. *Wordgathering* Dec. 2015: n. pag. Web. 11 Feb. 2016.

Conoley, Gillian. Rev. of *The Empty Form Goes All the Way to Heaven*, by Brian Teare. *On the Seawall*. Ron Slate, 9 Nov. 2015. Web. 11 Feb. 2016.

Rev. of *The Empty Form Goes All the Way to Heaven*, by Brian Teare. *Publishers Weekly*. PWxyz, 7 Dec. 2015. Web. 11 Feb. 2016.

Hoffert, Barbara. Rev. of *The Empty Form Goes All the Way to Heaven*, by Brian Teare. *Library Journal* 15 Nov. 2015: 91. Print.

Fates and Furies

Author: Lauren Groff (b. 1978)
Publisher: Riverhead Books (New York).
400 pp.
Type of work: Novel
Time: Late 1960s–present
Locales: Florida, New Hampshire, New York City

Lauren Groff's third novel, Fates and Furies *views a marriage through a mythic lens.*

Principal characters:
LANCELOT "LOTTO" SATTERWHITE, an aspiring actor and golden boy from Florida who makes a name for himself as a playwright
MATHILDE YODER, his beautiful wife with a mysterious past
ANTOINETTE, his wealthy, calculating mother

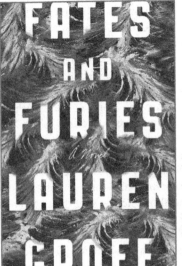

(Courtesy of Riverhead Books)

In Greek mythology, furies are female deities of vengeance. As the poet Hesiod imagined them in his *Theogony*, the furies sprang from the blood of the earth goddess Gaia's castrated husband. It is an appropriate origin story—though it is never mentioned in the book—for Lauren Groff's purposes in *Fates and Furies*, a novel about the bloodlust that lurks in a seemingly happy marriage.

Groff is an award-winning novelist and short-story writer whose last book, *Arcadia* (2012), followed a man through his life, from his childhood growing up in a 1970s hippie commune to his adulthood in 2018. *Fates and Furies* employs a similarly sweeping view of time, beginning in sultry Florida in the 1960s, before Lancelot "Lotto" Satterwhite, the book's protagonist, was even a gleam in his mother's eye. Antoinette, who will be his mother, is fiery, with brilliant red hair and "switchback curves." She lands a job as a costumed mermaid, donning a sequined tail and smiling at strangers from a tank behind paned glass. Groff compares her to both the original Little Mermaid—of the darker folkloric version, who gives up her tongue and tail for love and immortality of the soul—and the mythical sirens, female sea creatures who lure ships into rocks with their beautiful songs. Antoinette—like the novel's other central female character, Lotto's wife, Mathilde—embodies both sacrifice and vengeance. Both women give up parts of themselves to better serve Lotto in his chosen endeavors, but their desire to help him curdles their regard for themselves and for one another. *Fates and Furies* is about marriage, but specifically about heterosexual relationships and gender. Sometimes the theme sticks in the craw—why are all the women so cruel to one another? Why are they so tolerant of Lotto's affable narcissism? Groff explores these questions and others, but the fruits of her exploration are only intermittently satisfying.

The novel is split into two sections. The first, told from Lotto's perspective, is titled "Fates." The fates, in most stories, are also women, though they are merely all-knowing rather than malevolent. They flit in and out of this part of the book, interjecting in brackets, as when Lotto is born as the eye of a hurricane passes over the house: "[From the first, a wicked sense of timing.]" Lotto is as lucky as his name implies. He is materially privileged—his father, Gawain, is a bottled-water magnate—but he is also blessed with a social magnetism that draws women to him like moths to a flame. After his father dies of an aneurysm at age forty-six, Lotto rebels, and a run-in with the police lands him in a New Hampshire boarding school at the age of fourteen. He will never again see his mother in the flesh. At first, Antoinette pushes the boy away for his own good; bad elements exist in Florida, and she does not want

(© Megan Brown)

Lauren Groff is an award-winning short-story writer and novelist. Her previous books include The Monsters of Templeton *(2008),* Arcadia *(2012), and a collection of short stories called* Delicate Edible Birds *(2009). Her third novel,* Fates and Furies, *has been short-listed for the 2015 National Book Award.*

her son getting caught up in them again. Her tough love breeds resentment, however, and when Lotto, by now an aspiring actor, meets and promptly marries Mathilde in college, he alienates Antoinette by starting a new life without her. Cut off from the family fortune, he and Mathilde move to New York City as starving artists.

After whiling away his twenties, bouncing between one unsuccessful audition and the next, Lotto has a drunken epiphany: he was meant to write plays, not act in them. With Mathilde as his manager, Lotto becomes a celebrated playwright. This chapter of Lotto's tale moves away from his domestic life to explore his creative life. His collaboration and companionship with a young composer named Leo Sen provides a beguiling interlude before Lotto dies, as his father did, at the age of forty-six. His death concludes the "Fates" section of the novel. The second section, "Furies," is told from Mathilde's point of view.

In a November 2015 interview with Kevin Nguyen for the *Oyster Review*, Groff explained that she originally conceived *Fates and Furies* as two separate novels. As she imagined them, both novels would describe the same marriage, but from two radically opposite spousal points of view. She decided to keep the conceit but publish the "novels" as one. Indeed, Mathilde's section, "Furies," is too sparse to be considered a novel in its own right. Lotto's view is clearly the dominant one; Mathilde's story merely fills in the blanks. Part of the problem is that Lotto seems to take very little interest in his wife. In "Fates," he describes her as a saint because she lives her life in his service. Her past is totally unexamined, and Lotto appears to take it for granted, as one reviewer pointed out, that her life began when she met him. Even friends of the couple remark on Mathilde's enigmatic nature: she is beautiful, distant, unyielding. But then again, perhaps "enigmatic" is the wrong word. Mathilde does not so much provoke questions as repel them. She is the negation of a character, leaving Lotto's story unbalanced and strange.

When it is her turn to speak, Mathilde's story does little to define her outside of her relationship with Lotto. A traumatic childhood leaves her angry and deeply lonely. After marriage, she devotes herself to Lotto to such an extent that Groff suggests his success was the product of a vast conspiracy orchestrated on his behalf. (In addition to resorting to blackmail to finance the production of his first play, Mathilde rewrites his celebrated scripts in secret. Apparently, Lotto is too self-absorbed to notice the changes.) Antoinette, of course, is complicit in this conspiracy, but like many aspects of Mathilde's story, the particulars of their relationship, or lack thereof, are bewilderingly melodramatic. Lotto's story is characterized by the excitement of young love, scenes of domestic intimacy, and the melancholia of middle age. Mathilde's story is characterized by secret identities, private investigators, a stolen painting, sexual exploitation, and revenge. It is disappointing that Mathilde's story requires so many outlandish devices to be considered interesting, as if complexity of character (as opposed to complexity of plot), rooted in a few well-explored life events, were not enough. Her thirst for vengeance and deceit strains credulity—obviously intentional, but to what end is unclear—and overshadows a more nuanced story about a very lonely girl who tries to feel less alone by marrying a man she loves. It seems as though Groff set out to write her twin novels with the intention of exploring how difficult it is for two people, even two happily married people, to truly know one another. This is not a book about two people who think they know one another but do not; this is a story about two people who have no desire to know one another, and because of that, the reader has no desire to know them either.

The story in *Fates and Furies* may be disappointing, but Groff's prose is dazzling. Her writing has been described as "lyrical," but the word is too languid to capture the allure of her work. Her choice of words is sharp; she can cut to heart of an image with such precision and clarity that it takes the reader's breath away. In one early pivotal scene, young Lotto and his no-good friends are inspired to dig a gaping hole in the beach. The pill-fueled digging becomes its own fevered purpose, a ritual of its own:

> Moon rose blowsily, pissing white on water. Michael gathered driftwood, started a fire. Gritty sandwiches long in the past. Hands blistered to blood. They didn't care. . . . One by one, they guessed aloud about what Lotto had meant by this sculpture: nautilus, fiddlehead, galaxy. Thread running off its spindle. Forces of nature, perfect in beauty, perfectly ephemeral, they guessed. He was too shy to say *time*.

Near the end of his life, Lotto works on an opera about Antigone, the daughter-sister of Oedipus who is locked in a tomb and left for dead by her uncle Creon. Lotto imagines that the gods cursed Antigone with immortality. Left alone in her tomb for thousands of years, Antigone is unable to die until she humbles herself before the gods—something she explicitly refuses to do. In the present day, she falls in love with a construction worker through the wall of her tomb. They sing to one another through the wall that cannot be broken until he dies a mortal death. The opera's plot is revealing of the book's central conceit: the juxtaposition of the ephemeral and the ancient, the mythic and the real. If only the book were as elegant a metaphor as Lotto's opera.

When the reader first meets Lotto and Mathilde, hours after they are married, they are simply "two people . . . coming up the beach." Mathilde is "fair and sharp in a green bikini, though it [is] May in Maine and cold"; Lotto is "tall, vivid," with "a light flicker[ing] in him that caught the eye and held it." A few pages later, in a bracketed interjection, Groff writes, "Suspend them there, in the mind's eye: skinny, young, coming through dark toward warmth, flying over the cold sand and stone." Lotto and Mathilde never quite extricate themselves from that first image. Who are they? Even when the novel is over, it is difficult to say.

Molly Hagan

Review Sources

Black, Robin. Rev. of *Fates and Furies*, by Lauren Groff. *New York Times*. New York Times, 8 Sept. 2015. Web. 22 Oct. 2015.

Corrigan, Maureen. "*Fates and Furies* Offers a Tour-de-Force Plot, Minus Compelling Characters." Rev. of *Fates and Furies*, by Lauren Groff. *NPR*. NPR, 22 Sept. 2015. Web. 18 Nov. 2015.

Miller, Laura. "Strange Bedfellows." Rev. of *Fates and Furies*, by Lauren Groff. *Slate*. Slate Group, 16 Sept. 2015. Web. 29 Oct. 2015.

Wood, James. "Scenes from a Marriage." Rev. of *Fates and Furies*, by Lauren Groff. *New Yorker*. Condé Nast, 2 Nov. 2015. Web. 18 Nov. 2015.

The Fifth Season

Author: N. K. Jemisin
Publisher: Orbit (New York). 512 pp.
Type of work: Novel
Time: Fantastical present
Locale: The Stillness (fictional world)

The Fifth Season is the first novel in N. K. Jemisin's forthcoming Broken Earth series. It takes place in an apocalyptic world in which people called orogenes are able to control the plates of the earth by the strength of their will.

(Cover design by Lauren Panepinto; Cover photo © Arcangel-Images.)

Principal characters:

ESSUN, an orogene from Tirimo; she is pursuing her husband, Jija, who has killed their young son, Uche

HOA, a mysterious and not-quite-human youth who joins her on her quest

DAMAYA, a young girl born to modest farmer Stills; when her orogeny becomes apparent, she is carted away to live at the Fulcrum

SCHAFFA, Damaya's sinister Guardian

SYENITE, a four-ringed orogene; a good soldier of the Fulcrum

ALABASTER, Syenite's mentor; he has ten rings and his power makes him slightly unhinged

The first unfamiliar word a reader will need to learn in N. K. Jemisin's intricately-wrought new novel *The Fifth Season* is *orogene*. In Jemisin's world, orogenes are people who, due to a mutation, can control the plates of the earth at will. Their power is instinctual; baby orogenes can cause a shake when they cry. Stills—people of the Stillness (the name of the world) who do not have this awesome power—fear orogenes. Sometimes, when a backwater "comm" (or community) discovers a "rogga" (a slur for orogene) among them, even if it is a child, they kill it. Damaya, one of the central characters in Jemisin's novel, is lucky to avoid such a fate, though after discovering her nascent powers, her once-loving parents have locked her in a barn and refuse to look her in the eye. A man named Schaffa comes to take her away for good. Schaffa is Damaya's Guardian—a Still with specific orogene-quelling powers who claims total control of their charges—and he is taking her to the Fulcrum, a totalitarian school for young orogenes. Orogenes are useful, even necessary, to life in the Stillness because they quell the constant, wrathful shakes of the earth (in this world, the earth itself is intent on killing everything in it, all the time), but because the Stills do not understand orogeny, they exploit orogenes, and insist on treating all of them—from the most powerful and many-ringed Fulcrum orogene, to seven-year-old Damaya—like second-class citizens.

The second word readers will need to learn in Jemisin's book is *season*. For as long as history can remember, the earth has been plagued by "seasons," occurring every few thousand years. A season is akin to the period during which the dinosaurs went extinct, or the fall-out of a nuclear war. Lasting anywhere from a few years to a few centuries, a season means death; only the hardiest survive. However, Jemisin makes clear that this season, the one during which the book begins, will be the last.

Jemisin's previous books have been both popular and critically acclaimed. She has been nominated for the Hugo Award and the Nebula Award (the highest honors in the science fiction and fantasy genre), and in 2015, the *New York Times* named *The Fifth Season* one of its one hundred notable books of the year. In general, critics praised Jemisin's ability to shift between viewpoints relatively seamlessly and viewed the novel as a promising start to the new series. Jemisin, who is also a political blogger, explores themes of power and oppression in her work. Her first novel and the first of her Inheritance trilogy, *The Hundred Thousand Kingdoms* (2010), takes place in a matriarchal barbarian society where men are treated the way women are in the real world. Jemisin specifically creates stories that defy some of the fantasy genre's most enduring yet unspoken tropes—Tolkien-esque settings based on English medieval lore, white male heroes, and a world order that is inherently good challenged by a dark power. Instead, Jemisin creates multiple cultures in her novels; her heroes are black women; and the oppressed—from the enslaved gods in *The Hundred Thousand Kingdoms* to the orogenes in *The Fifth Season*—rise up to create a new world order.

There are three central characters in *The Fifth Season*: Damaya, the young orogene; Syenite, a twenty-something, four-ringed cog in the Fulcrum machine; and Essun—whose chapters are written in the second person—a forty-something woman on a quest to find her husband who has killed her young son, Uche, as the season begins. Essun has done a good job of hiding her orogeny in her small comm, including, it is implied, from her Still husband, Jija, who beat their boy to death when he discovered his powers. Essun's story takes place in the book's present, at the beginning of the season to end all seasons. Propelled by her animal grief, Essun destroys her comm and takes to the road in search of Jija, who has run off with their daughter, Nassun, a ten-year-old who also has orogene powers. In her quest, Essun has the help of a strange homeless boy named Hoa, who is inexplicably able to track Nassun with his mind. The world crumbling around Essun mirrors the emotional cataclysm that has taken place inside of her. It is the upending of her own life, more so than the onslaught of the season, that forces Essun to reevaluate her place in the world.

Syenite, on the other hand, is confident in her place—at least when the reader first meets her. She has made the best of her status as an orogene. She has been good, has obeyed her elders and her Guardian, and holds her self-control as a hard-won prize. Syenite demonstrates her obedience by accepting the undesirable task that falls to talented orogene women in the Fulcrum—selective breeding. Her mentor asks her to pair up with a man named Alabaster. One of the most powerful orogenes at the Fulcrum, Alabaster wears ten rings. After losing his son, he burns with a wrath as dark as

Essun's—as the reader soon finds, Alabaster has lost a number of his own children—and makes clear his contempt for the system that Syenite holds dear. Jemisin handles Syenite and Alabaster's relationship in a satisfyingly unexpected way. The couple becomes more emotionally intimate over time, but their story is not a love story. In fact, the thing that brings them together is not their offspring but their sexual desires. Their love for one another is, later, expressed through their mutual love for one man. While attempting to conceive a child, Syenite and Alabaster embark on a routine journey to a coastal comm that has requested a Fulcrum orogene to clear its harbor of coral. On the way, Syenite discovers the horror that the Fulcrum inflicts on its node maintainers— orogenes charged with the thankless task of maintaining far-flung fault lines—as well as the secrets of the mysterious obelisks that float among the clouds, left from a previous civilization. The combined knowledge changes the course of her destiny.

(Laura Hanifin)

N. K. Jemisin is an award-winning au-thor of science fiction and fantasy novels. Her previous works include the Inheri-tance trilogy and the Dreamblood books.

With its emphasis on rocks, it is appropriate that the scope of *The Fifth Season* is geologic in its scale. Seasons that occurred thousands of years in the past are spoken of as if they had happened only a few years before by stonelore, the collection of stories that dictate how humans can survive a season. The people of the Stillness hold stonelore very dear, but Jemisin invites the reader to question their unthinking submission, raising questions about the real lessons of history and blind submission to authority. Jemisin pointedly writes, "The lorists tell stories of what happens when people— political leaders or philosophers or well-meaning meddlers of whatever type—try to change the lore. Disaster inevitably results."

With her intricate tapestry of lorists, orogenes, Stills, and stone eaters—nonhuman beings that look like statues and munch on crystals—Jemisin's world-building is truly impressive. The novel comes with a glossary of terms and past seasons, and cryptic excerpts of stonelore close every chapter. (To wit: "Winter, Spring, Summer, Fall; Death is the fifth, and the master of all.") However, Jemisin's writing is not as arcane as this level of detail would suggest. She writes with a loose hand, tossing off fragments and slang, directly invoking the reader in the manner of an ancient storyteller. For example, this is how Jemisin introduces Essun's backstory, addressing her as "you," after a short piece of exposition: "Back to the personal. Need to keep things grounded, ha ha. The woman I mentioned, the one whose son is dead. She was not in Yumenes, thankfully, or this would be a very short tale. And you would not exist."

The choice to write Essun's story in the second-person makes her pain wrenchingly immediate; the reader feels the urgency of her quest because the reader literally *is* her, is also the "you," but the most effective stylistic choice in *The Fifth Season* is the structural twist Jemisin reveals about three-quarters of the way into the novel. Early pages of the book are difficult to follow because Jemisin throws the reader into her world with few tools to understand it. But the aforementioned twist is demonstrative of Jemisin's technical skill. Though it does not seem so at first, every line of *The Fifth Season* has a pay-off. Jemisin's joke about "grounding" her narrative rings true: *The Fifth Season* is successful largely because of its emotional core. Damaya, Syenite, and Essun live in a very strange world, but their problems are familiar and relatable. The novel is about oppression and survival, but it is also about identity and maintaining one's sense of self in the face of hatred, horror, and grief.

Molly Hagan

Review Sources

Heller, Jason. "*Fifth Season* Embraces the Scale and Complexity of Fantasy." Rev. of *The Fifth Season*, by N. K. Jemisin. *National Public Radio*. NPR, 4 Aug. 2015. Web. 8 Dec. 2015.
Rev. of *The Fifth Season*, by N. K. Jemisin. *Publishers Weekly*. PWxyz, 1 Aug. 2015. Web. 7 Dec. 2015.
Novik, Naomi. Rev. of *The Fifth Season*, by N. K. Jemisin. *New York Times*. New York Times, 6 Aug. 2015. Web. 8 Dec. 2015.

Finders Keepers

Author: Stephen King (b. 1947)
Publisher: Scribner (New York). 448 pp.
Type of work: Novel
Time: 1978–2014
Locales: New Hampshire; Northfield, Ohio

A haunting exploration of the power of literature, Finders Keepers *focuses on two bibliophiles who are profoundly affected by the works of a famous reclusive author. Stephen King combines elements of horror, suspense, and drama in this sequel that sees the return of retired detective Bill Hodges and his fellow investigators, Holly Gibney and Jerome Robinson.*

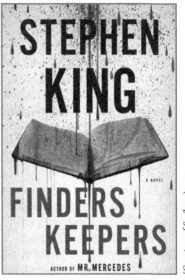

(Courtesy of Scribner)

Principal characters:
PETE SAUBERS, a book-loving high school student
MORRIS BELLAMY, a deranged fan of reclusive American author John Rothstein
JOHN ROTHSTEIN, an iconic and reclusive American author
TINA SAUBERS, Pete's younger sister
ANDREW HALLIDAY, a rare-book dealer and Morris's friend
BILL HODGES, a retired police detective and private investigator
HOLLY GIBNEY, Bill's assistant
JEROME ROBINSON, Bill's next-door neighbor and fellow investigator
BARBARA ROBINSON, Jerome's younger sister, Tina's friend

The year is 1978, and renowned American writer John Rothstein, the author of a trilogy of novels featuring the antihero Jimmy Gold, is whiling away his retirement on a remote farm in New Hampshire. While in the midst of a pleasant dream about his first wife, he is awakened by three balaclava-clad intruders who are distinguished from each other by their red, blue, and canary-yellow masks. They believe that Rothstein is in possession of a small fortune and have broken into his house in hopes of stealing it from him. They eventually discover a large safe containing dozens of bank envelopes filled with cash and more than 150 moleskin notebooks. Rothstein tells them to take the cash but to leave the notebooks, insisting they are of no value.

As the robbery unfolds, Rothstein notices something peculiar about the man in yellow, who repeatedly addresses him as "genius" and seems more educated than his partners. Mr. Yellow, as Rothstein calls him, is quickly revealed to be Morris Bellamy, a pallid twenty-three-year-old man with distinct yet disturbing red lips. Morris is more a deranged fan of Rothstein's work than he is a robber, and he is adamant that he be told why Rothstein has not published anything in eighteen years, why he retreated from public life, and why he changed the character of Jimmy Gold from a rebellious nonconformist in his first two novels to, in Morris's opinion, a sellout who work in advertising in the third and final book. Despite retiring into seclusion, Rothstein has continued to spend his days writing, and Morris believes the notebooks contain a treasure trove of unpublished works, including a long-rumored fourth Jimmy Gold novel that may offer a more satisfying conclusion. Still, Morris feels that Rothstein has betrayed his fans, and after the cantankerous author taunts him, Morris shoots him in the head.

Rothstein's cold-blooded murder is the starting point for *Finders Keepers*, an engrossing suspense thriller by Stephen King that revisits some of the themes the horror master first explored in his classic best-selling novel *Misery* (1987). *Finders Keepers* is the sequel to *Mr. Mercedes* (2014), which won the 2015 Edgar Award for best novel, and the second installment in a planned trilogy featuring retired police detective Bill Hodges.

In *Finders Keepers*, King reintroduces Hodges and his team—Jerome Robinson, Hodges's smart seventeen-year-old neighbor, and Holly Gibney, the cousin of Hodges's deceased girlfriend—but not until the second of the novel's three parts. Instead the first part of the novel focuses on Morris Bellamy and a teenage Rothstein fan, Pete Saubers, whose father was injured in *Mr. Mercedes*. Their stories comprise the entire first section of the novel and are told in alternating chapters that jump back and forth in time between Morris's past and Pete's present. Like *Misery*, which tells the story of a homicidal nurse who tortures and holds her favorite author hostage so he can write a new book more to her liking, *Finders Keepers* provides King the opportunity to explore the author-fan relationship.

> *Stephen King has written more than fifty best-selling books, many of which have been adapted into successful films. Finders Keepers is the sequel to King's detective thriller* Mr. Mercedes *(2014), which won the 2015 Edgar Award for best novel.*

After murdering Rothstein, Morris kills his two partners, not only to eliminate them as witnesses but also to increase his chances of reading Rothstein's notebooks, which are "the kind [Ernest] Hemingway had used." Morris then drives back to his childhood home in Northfield, Ohio, where he picks up a secondhand trunk in which to store the notebooks and the approximately $24,000 in cash. He buries the trunk under a tree in the woods behind his house. It is revealed that Morris considers his literary obsession with Rothstein to be comparable to the star-crossed romance between Shakespeare's Romeo and Juliet; Morris felt jilted after the conclusion of Rothstein's Gold trilogy, so now he watches over the notebooks like a possessive lover. However, Morris never gets to enjoy them or the money, as he is soon arrested and sentenced to life in prison for a previous vicious and violent crime.

Pete Saubers and his family also live in Northfield, Ohio, and are introduced to the reader after Morris has been in prison for more than thirty years. The year is 2009, and Pete's family is struggling to make ends meet after his father, Tom, was laid off from his job. Pete's family soon moves to a less expensive section of Northfield and coincidentally settle in Morris's childhood home. Pete's parents fight constantly about money and are on the verge of divorce, so when Pete discovers Morris's old trunk while seeking refuge in the woods during one of his parents' fights, he starts anonymously sending them $500 each month.

By 2013, Pete, now a high school sophomore, has developed his own love of literature, largely sparked by Rothstein's fiction. In the years since he started sending his parents money, he has secretly stashed and read through all of the author's notebooks, which contain not one but two more Jimmy Gold novels, among other unpublished literary treasures. For Pete, the latter two Gold novels were life-changing. Rothstein's notebooks take on new meaning and purpose for Pete, however, when the money from the bank envelopes runs out. Although Pete's parents have new jobs and seem to have recovered financially, they still do not have enough money to send Pete's younger sister, Tina, to an expensive private school that many of her friends are attending. Among those friends is Barbara Robinson, Jerome's younger sister, who also appears in *Mr. Mercedes*. To realize his sister's wishes, Pete devises a new scheme to sell the notebooks on the black market.

As Pete sets his scheme in motion, Morris is released from prison after thirty-five years. Morris reenters a world that has become foreign to him, "one where movies show on bloated screens called IMAX and everyone on the street is either wearing phones in their ears or staring at tiny screens." King fans will find it hard not to compare Morris's experience to that of the character Red in the author's novella *Rita Hayworth and the Shawshank Redemption*, which was published in his 1982 short-story collection *Different Seasons* and later adapted into an Academy Award–winning film. Almost sixty years old, Morris, like Red, is not the same young man he was when he entered prison, and he struggles to adjust to life outside of it. Unlike Red, however, Morris is far from rehabilitated: he is still maniacally driven to unearth Rothstein's notebooks, which have been a "maddening constant" during his long stint inside.

When Morris discovers that his trunk has been pillaged, he quickly reverts to his homicidal former self. He initially believes an old friend, a Northfield rare-book dealer named Andrew Halliday, is responsible, but when he tracks him down, Andrew reveals Pete as the culprit. Readers are already aware that Andrew initially conceived the idea of stealing Rothstein's notebooks. After the mysterious money runs out, Pete approaches Halliday and tries to sell him a small sampling of Rothstein's unpublished manuscripts. Pete's increasingly erratic behavior and gaunt appearance, however, raise concerns in Tina, who, through the help of Barbara, reaches out to Bill Hodges for help.

Hodges appears in this second installment as a healthy sixty-six-year-old who has started a private investigation firm he calls Finders Keepers. He runs the firm with Holly Gibney, who, despite her "Asperger's-like tics," is a brilliant researcher. When Hodges and Holly's services are sought out by Tina, Jerome has returned home from Harvard University for summer break, and the trio is reunited. The novel's blistering third act follows their attempts to save Pete and his family before Morris gets to them, culminating in a signature King climax filled with nail-biting tension, white-knuckle suspense, and a steady but not overwhelming stream of violence. Though Hodges and his sidekicks are reduced to secondary characters in *Finders Keepers*, King offers hints to readers that they will take on bigger roles in the finale of this trilogy, titled *End of Watch*, which is due out in 2016.

Finders Keepers is both an examination of how literature influences readers and a paean to great authors and their works, to reading, and to the lost art of storytelling. King peppers the novel with numerous literary allusions, as characters quote and refer to such famous writers as Shakespeare, Hemingway, Robert Frost, D. H. Lawrence, Mark Twain, T. S. Eliot, and John D. MacDonald. Readers will find it apparent that King largely modeled Rothstein after the famously reclusive author J. D. Salinger. Despite a cursory mention of *Catcher in the Rye* (1951), Salinger's name never appears in the book, but King gives readers more than enough details to draw undeniable parallels between the two, including Rothstein's secluded New Hampshire retreat, his trove of unpublished manuscripts, and his aversion to answering fan mail. At one point, King includes a fictional letter from Rothstein to Salinger contemporary Flannery O'Connor.

The thought of being in possession of a famous author's unpublished manuscripts will likely generate excitement among even the most moderate of readers. But who is actually reading these days? Throughout the novel King wistfully reflects on the so-called death of the book and the act of reading in general in a rapidly advancing technological world dominated by e-readers and mind-numbing smartphones. Morris and Pete, however different they may be, are exceptions to the norm, and while King's book may not change people's lives to the extent that Rothstein's books changes theirs, *Finders Keepers* offers proof that the power of storytelling and the written word is alive and well. As many critics agreed, Morris rivals some of King's most haunting characters, and this page-turning thriller will surely pique readers' interest in the author's own collection of unpublished works, which is rumored to be as prolific as his output.

Chris Cullen

Review Sources

Rev. of *Finders Keepers*, by Stephen King. *Publishers Weekly* 20 Apr. 2015: 54. Print.

Knoop, Doug. "*Finders Keepers*: Stephen King's Sequel to *Mr. Mercedes* Is a Nail-Biter." Rev. of *Finders Keepers*, by Stephen King. *Seattle Times*. Seattle Times, 31 May 2015. Web. 6 Oct. 2015.

Lippman, Laura. Rev. of *Finders Keepers*, by Stephen King. *New York Times*. New York Times, 27 May 2015. Web. 6 Oct. 2015.

Romeo, Nick. "Stephen King Revisits Psychotic Fandom in *Finders Keepers*." Rev. of *Finders Keepers*, by Stephen King. *Boston Globe*. Boston Globe Media Partners, 18 June 2015. Web. 6 Oct. 2015.

Truitt, Brian. "King's *Finders* Is a Definite Keeper." Rev. of *Finders Keepers*, by Stephen King. *USA Today*. USA Today, 1 June 2015. Web. 6 Oct. 2015.

The First Bad Man

Author: Miranda July (b. 1974)
Publisher: Scribner (New York); 304 pp.
Type of work: Novel
Time: 2013
Locale: Los Angeles

The First Bad Man is the first novel by artist and filmmaker Miranda July. It follows a middle-aged woman named Cheryl Glickman as she battles a bullying houseguest and finds love in an unexpected place.

Principle characters:
CHERYL GLICKMAN, a single woman in her
    early forties
CLEE, the daughter of her employers
PHILLIP BETTELHEIM, a member of the board
    at her work
KUBELKO BONDY, a mysterious yet instantly recognizable soul that she encounters in
    various small children

THE FIRST BAD MAN A NOVEL BY MIRANDA JULY

(Courtesy of Scribner)

Cheryl Glickman, the protagonist of Miranda July's debut novel *The First Bad Man*, likes living alone because she has a system. She needs the system because, in her view, it is all too easy to let the dishes pile up in the sink, so that one must eat using dirty dishes, which in turn makes one so depressed that one cannot bathe or leave the bedroom; eventually, one starts urinating "in cups because they're closer to the bed." Thus, a good system can be a real lifesaver, as far as Cheryl is concerned. Hers begins in the kitchen: she only uses one set of dishes. She also "carpools" objects around her house, so as not to have to repeat the same action twice. "Putting new soap in the bathroom? Maybe wait until the towels in the dryer are done and carry the towels and the soap together," Cheryl advises. Cheryl, a middle-aged woman living in New Agey Los Angeles, has thought deeply on such matters, and so her house is immaculate. However, contrary to what she tells the reader, her emotional life is not. Cheryl suffers from "globus hystericus," the clinical term for the feeling of having a lump in one's throat; only Cheryl's is there all the time. She seeks out a chromotherapist (a therapist who adjusts bodily vibrations using colors) who recommends a daily dose of red—but the red hardly helps. The chromotherapist was Phillip Bettelheim's idea, Phillip being a member of the board at Open Palm, a company that peddles self-defense videos, where Cheryl works. Phillip is wealthy and comically arrogant, but Cheryl does not think so—she has been in love with him for years. When she leaves the office of Dr. Broyard, the chromotherapist, she calls Phillip to tell him that Dr. Broyard was "phenomenal." "This had been my plan," Cheryl confides to the reader after successfully getting the word out, "to use the same word that he had used to describe my necklace at the fundraiser." Needless to say, he does not get the connection.

July paints Cheryl's particular brand of loneliness with humor and skill. Cheryl is a pushover who works for a self-defense company; a no-nonsense woman who believes that the soul of a baby named Kubelko Bondy occasionally appears to her in the form other people's babies and loves her more than its real parents. The elements of her tale, as award-winning writer Lorrie Moore wrote in her positive review for the *New York Review of Books*, are admittedly "bonkers," but, Moore cautions, to call July "quirky," as many critics have, is to ignore her unusual artistry. July, who is also a filmmaker, artist, actress, and dancer, is insistently inventive. Her characters cry out to be loved in ways that are variously embarrassing, horrifying, ridiculous, and strange. In a capsule review for the *New Yorker*, a critic wrote that July succeeds in making Cheryl both "achingly familiar and repulsively alien"—a description that fits every other July character too.

July published a book of short stories called *No One Belongs Here More than You* in 2007. *The First Bad Man* is her first novel, though it retains elements found in her other work. July is a skilled crafter of intimate moments of self-observation. As the book begins, Cheryl is driving to and arriving at the chromotherapist's office. As always, she is acutely self-aware, imagining that she is in a movie in which a woman visits a chromotherapist's office. "I strolled through the parking garage and into the elevator, pressing 12 with a casual fun-loving finger. The kind of finger that was up for anything," July writes. "Once the doors had closed, I checked myself in the mirrored ceiling and practiced how my face would go if Phillip was in the waiting room." July also excels at puncturing moments of self-posturing or self-delusion. When Phillip flirts with Cheryl by grabbing her necklace and pulling her toward him, she reflects: "An outsider . . . might have thought this moment was degrading, but I knew the degradation was just a joke; he was mocking the kind of man would do something like that." She says of a young girl's shirt: "She wore a blouse with diagonal pastel stripes that looked like it was from the 1980s; it was a joke about how silly the time before she was born was."

Cheryl's self-absorbed idyll is violently interrupted within the first few pages of the book, however, by a twenty-year-old woman named Clee. Clee is the daughter of Cheryl's employers, Carl and Suzanne. They tell Cheryl that Clee is an aspiring actor and needs a place to stay while she finds her feet. This turns out to be untrue, though Clee's true purpose is revealed obliquely later. She is described as looking like the actor Scarlett Johansson, but she is dim and a bully and her feet smell terrible. Clee camps out on Cheryl's couch and drags out all the dishes, eviscerating Cheryl's "system" within the first twenty-four hours of her stay. More significantly, she has thrown a wrench in Cheryl's plans to show Phillip "some heat," and Cheryl resents her for it. To make matters even worse, Clee is physically imposing; sometimes, when the two women are in the kitchen, she slams Cheryl up against a wall. These altercations then take a strange turn. Cheryl starts watching the self-defense-as-fitness DVDs she has been peddling for the past twenty years and turns the techniques on Clee. They develop a rough and wordless rapport, grappling in every room of Cheryl's house nearly every night. Miraculously, the lump in Cheryl's throat disappears.

In part, Cheryl is acting out against Phillip, who brought her to his penthouse only to confess to her his love for a sixteen-year-old girl named Kirsten. He wants Cheryl's blessing to consummate the relationship. So while Cheryl and Clee—who is now also watching the DVDs—act out their intimate struggle, Cheryl is also receiving explicit text messages from Phillip detailing his transgressions with Kirsten, but pledging not to consummate the relationship until Cheryl gives her approval. Cheryl and Clee's wrestling becomes more erotic, if only inside Cheryl's head. She is plagued by images of various men, starting with Phillip, having sex with Clee—suppressing her own attraction to her houseguest. But when Clee announces she is pregnant, the character of their relationship changes. They are no longer adversaries who express their intolerance for one another through consensual violence, but more like mother and daughter.

In her acknowledgements, July thanks her agent for telling her when she considered having children, "you will have a baby AND you will write a novel." This is significant, because, quite unexpectedly given the novel's early trajectory, motherhood and motherly love is the most powerful theme in the book. Clee insists that she wants to have the baby at Cheryl's house (she hates hospitals) and Cheryl becomes her de facto birthing coach. Of course, on the day the baby comes, there are complications. The midwife is driving from Idaho, and something is not right with the baby.

Miranda July is an artist, filmmaker, short-story writer, and novelist. Her films include the award-winning dramedy Me and You and Everyone We Know *(2005) and* The Future *(2011). She published a book of short stories called* No One Belongs Here More than You *in 2007;* The First Bad Man *is her first novel.*

A swath of the book takes place inside the hospital, with Clee's as-yet-unnamed baby languishing in the infant intensive care unit. July carefully pivots from Cheryl and Clee's relationship once again, but it is Cheryl's growing relationship with the baby that July draws with such care. The baby is a Kubelko Bondy, named for a small child Cheryl knew growing up. When she was nine, neighbors came over to visit her parents. They brought with them their infant son named Kubelko. Cheryl was unsure of what to do with the child at first, being stuck with him while the adults were drinking wine. Kubelko started to cry, and when no one came, Cheryl took him in her arms. She was surprised to find that he looked at her as if he already knew her, as if they were soul mates. Cheryl was devastated when his parents took him away. For whatever reason, she never saw him again, but she sees him in other people's children. Her love for Kubelko Bondy is overwhelming—Cheryl places it somewhere between love for a husband and love for a child—but perhaps, she discovers when a real child is in her arms, also wanting.

July radically embraces the experience of being female; she flouts romantic, sexual, and parental tropes as if such tropes never existed. Clee and Cheryl erotically bond by fighting—not boxing, but self-defense fighting such as a woman learns to protect herself against men. Her descriptions of early motherhood are rife with doubt, fear, and tears, but also joy. Cheryl and Clee (but mostly Cheryl) are women in the trenches of love, unsure if they will make it out alive—and in some ways, they do not. *The First Bad Man* manages to illuminate womanhood from many angles at once; its plot may be alien, but its emotional core is achingly familiar.

Molly Hagan

Review Sources

"Briefly Noted." Rev. of *The First Bad Man*, by Miranda July. *New Yorker*. Condé Nast, 16 Feb. 2015. Web. 11 Feb. 2016.

Groff, Lauren. Rev. of *The First Bad Man*, by Miranda July. *New York Times*. New York Times, 16 Jan. 2015. Web. 11 Feb. 2016.

Kakutani, Michiko. "Crouched behind a Barricade, until a Crude Stranger Barges In." Rev. of *The First Bad Man*, by Miranda July. *New York Times*. New York Times, 11 Jan. 2015. Web. 11 Feb. 2016.

Longworth, Karina. "Watch Everything You Say." Rev. of *The First Bad Man*, by Miranda July. *Slate*. Slate Group, 6 Jan. 2015. Web. 11 Feb. 2016.

Moore, Lorrie. "Our Date with Miranda." Rev. of *The First Bad Man*, by Miranda July. *New York Review of Books*. NYREV, 5 Mar. 2015. Web. 11 Feb. 2016.

Quinn, Annalisa. "The Texture of Life becomes Art in 'The First Bad Man.'" Rev. of *The First Bad Man*, by Miranda July. *NPR*. NPR, 14 Jan. 2015. Web. 11 Feb. 2016.

The Fishermen

Author: Chigozie Obioma
Publisher: Little, Brown (New York). 304 pp.
Type of work: Novel
Time: 1996–2003
Locale: Akure, Nigeria

The Fishermen, *the debut novel from Nigerian author Chigozie Obioma, is about the disintegration of one family in Akure but is also a parable about Nigeria's turbulent past.*

Principal characters:
BEN, the narrator and youngest of the Agwu brothers
IKENNA, his eldest brother
BOJA, his second eldest brother
OBEMBE, his third eldest brother
ABULU, the local prophet and madman

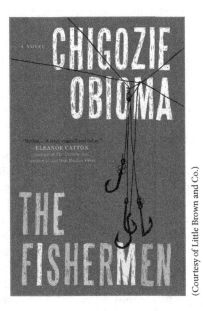

(Courtesy of Little Brown and Co.)

In her glowing *New York Times* review of his debut novel, *The Fishermen*, Fiammetta Rocco called Chigozie Obioma the literary heir to the Nigerian novelist Chinua Achebe. Achebe's *Things Fall Apart* (1958) combines oral storytelling techniques with the form of the nineteenth-century English novel to tell the story of an Igbo wrestler in precolonial Nigeria. *Things Fall Apart* is considered the prototypal African novel, and one of the first novels about colonialism told from an African point of view, written in English. Obioma's novel, *The Fishermen*, a dark parable about the disintegration of a middle-class family, takes place at the turn of the twenty-first century. It also features an Igbo protagonist, a man named Benjamin (Ben) who recalls a family tragedy that began when he was nine years old.

The Fishermen has been widely praised. After his novel was short-listed for the prestigious Man Booker Prize in 2015, Obioma joined the ranks of Nigerian writers shaping the globally influential Anglo-African literary scene. Among those writers are Chimamanda Ngozie Adichie, the award-winning author of *Half a Yellow Sun* (2006) and *Americanah* (2013), and Nigerian American writer Teju Cole, award-winning author of *Open City* (2011) and *Everyday Is for the Thief* (2014). Obioma is very different from these writers, but he shares with them a desire to deconstruct and understand Nigeria as a place and a living history.

Obioma, who was born in 1986 in Akure, and studied creative writing at the University of Michigan, writes in English (both British and American) but also employs words and aspects of Yoruba (the language spoken in the west), Igbo, and pidgin. This code-switching is purposeful, Obioma told Nathan Go for the *Michigan Quarterly*

Review. Most Nigerians are multilingual from childhood, and when and where certain languages are spoken have meaning. For instance, the mother in Obioma's tale is traditional: she always speaks Igbo. The father considers himself more progressive: he always uses English words, even at home. In the era of globalization, it is important to him that his children receive a Western education because he has big dreams for them. He sees his six children, particularly his four older sons, as go-getters. "Children who will dip their hands into river, seas, oceans of this life and become successful: doctors, pilots, professors, lawyers." However, these are not the kind of fishermen the boys turn out to be.

(Zach Mueller)

Chigozie Obioma is a Nigerian writer who earned his MFA at the University of Michigan. He teaches literature and creative writing at the University of Nebraska–Lincoln. The Fishermen, his first novel, was short-listed for the Man Booker Prize in 2015.

After Nigeria achieved independence from Great Britain in 1960, there followed a violent period of unrest between the country's two largest tribes: the Yoruba and the Igbo. (The Igbo tried to secede, creating the Republic of Biafra in 1967 in the east, but the British-backed Nigerian army won the war in 1970.) A succession of military dictatorships and coups brought Nigeria into the 1990s and into a moment of relative optimism. In 1993, a popular Yoruba businessman named M. K. O. Abiola ran for president and won the popular vote, though the result was annulled by the military. Military leader Sani Abacha quickly assumed power and brutally cracked down on political dissenters and the press. Abiola's election and Abacha's regime serve as a backdrop for Obioma's story. Suggestions of the world at large are selective and carefully woven into the fabric of his narrative. In one scene, Benjamin recalls skipping school with his brothers and unwittingly walking into a political event for Abiola. The candidate pulls the boys on stage where they are dazzled by his shiny shoes, and his kind and beautiful wife. He even awards them all full scholarships to a local school. This scene is contrasted with another two months later, in which the brothers escape their school during the violent riots following the annulled election.

But these moments only serve to give Obioma's story—about four brothers and a prophecy that tears them apart—its shape. The novel begins in 1996. The boys' father, who works at the Central Bank of Nigeria, is being transferred to Yola, a city over a thousand miles away. With little more than a promise to visit every two weeks, he leaves Ben's mother, a shopkeeper at the local market, alone with six children. The oldest, Ikenna, is nearly fifteen. The youngest child, a daughter named Nkem, is an infant. The Agwu family has more children than most families in the town, but Ben's father desperately wanted a large family. (Like the mythical Niobe, he boasts to the gods about his brood and is smote for his hubris.) The four oldest boys—Ikenna, Boja,

Obembe, and Ben—are at first, confused by their newfound freedom. They play soccer after school, but when soccer becomes too mundane, they decide to become fishermen. Each day after school, they trek to the Omi-Ala River with their rods and bait. The Omi-Ala was once considered sacred, but now it is a putrid, stinking places where one is apt to find a bloated human body floating alongside a prized fish. The people of Akure are superstitious about the river, so the boys hide their new hobby from their mother. She finds out about their transgression through a neighbor and when their father comes home to visit, they are severely punished.

It seems, early on, that their days as fishermen are over, but something is strange. Ikenna, once the generous father figure of the bunch, is drifting away. His melancholy becomes sharp, and he uncharacteristically begins lashing out at his brothers. Soon, the reason for his behavior is revealed. Walking back from the river one day, the boys encountered Abulu, the local madman. Abulu is homeless. He sleeps on the street and eats garbage, but the town is afraid of him because he can predict the future with disturbing accuracy. Abulu called out to Ikenna by name and told him that he would be killed by a fisherman. The exact words of Abulu's prophecy are obscured, and only Obembe hears them. If Obembe had told Ikenna that he had not heard them, the author suggests, would things have turned out differently? Regardless, Obembe spills the beans and Ikenna interprets the prophecy to mean that one of his brothers will kill him. In hurt and anger, he pushes them away.

Obioma talks about prophecy and superstition—its pull on the people of Nigeria and its metaphorical implications—in his interview with Go. He says that his mother believes that he was accepted to graduate school, not for his talent, but because of prayers. He wonders: is a prophecy fulfilled because people believe it and unwittingly make it so? Or is a prophecy fulfilled because of an actual higher power? The chronic unrest in Nigeria, he says, is its own kind of self-fulfilling fortune. The idea that the two tribes—the Yoruba and the Igbo—could share a nation, as prescribed by the British, is "tantamount to the prophecy of a madman," he said.

Obioma's begins each chapter of his story with a vivid image: an eagle, a python, a falconer. "Mother was a falconer," one chapter begins, "The one who stood on the hills and watched, trying to stave off whatever ill she perceived was coming to her children." The images are important to the subtle shifting of Obioma's tale. Ikenna's change happens over a relatively short period of time, but the pace of the telling makes the deadly turn believable. First, Ikenna distances himself from his brothers. He locks his brother Boja out of the room they share. He refuses to eat with his family. In one pivotal scene, the brothers cautiously invite Ikenna to watch his favorite television show—a 1960s Australian import called *Skippy the Bush Kangaroo*—in the shared living room. He drives them out of the room so he can watch by himself. Aside from Ikenna's behavior, Obioma's choice of program in this scene speaks volumes about the characters. The boys are intimately familiar with worlds and cultures far outside their own, but they remain trapped in a world defined by prophecy and violence; they are consumed by adult matters but they are ultimately still children.

Obioma is at his best when he is unspooling the lead-up to the deadly deed. The fallout from the murder(s) does not have the same economical pacing or share the carefully calibrated tone of the proceeding pages. The boys' lives descend into nightmare. The mother is hospitalized in her grief—she sees spiders everywhere—and the father becomes a husk of his former self. This much can be believed, but a harebrained scheme concocted by Obembe seems less logical given the context of the world, though the outcome is perhaps, inevitable. Here, Ben (the narrator) takes us through many passing years, arriving at the spring of 2003. By this time, both Abacha and Abiola are dead (both were likely poisoned) and another election has been held. More unrest is to come, but Obioma, unexpectedly, strikes a hopeful note in the book's last pages. Nkem, who is now seven years old, compared to an egret, "the snow-white dove-like birds that appear after a storm." Egrets, Ben says, "were often signs or harbingers of good times. . . . Whenever we and the children of Akure saw them flying in the sky, we rushed out and flapped our fingers after the low-flying white flock travelling overhead, repeating the one-line saying: 'Egrets, egrets, perch on me.'"

Molly Hagan

Review Sources

Habila, Helon. "Four Brothers and a Terrible Prophecy." Rev. of *The Fishermen*, by Chigozie Obioma. *Guardian*. Guardian News and Media, 13 Mar. 2015. Web. 11 Nov. 2015.

Rocco, Fiammetta. Rev. of *The Fishermen*, by Chigozie Obioma. *New York Times*. New York Times, 14 Apr. 2015. Web. 6 Nov. 2015.

Schaub, Michael. "'The Fishermen' Ventures into Dark Waters." Rev. of *The Fishermen*, by Chigozie Obioma. *NPR Books*. National Public Radio, 15 Apr. 2015. Web. 6 Nov. 2015.

Sharp, Naomi. "Man Booker Shortlist 2015: The Fishermen." Rev. of *The Fishermen*, by Chigozie Obioma. *Atlantic*. Atlantic Monthly Group, 8 Oct. 2015. Web. 11 Nov. 2015.

Twidle, Hedley. "Making Myths: Chigozie Obioma's *The Fishermen*." *New Statesman*. New Statesman, 15 Sept. 2015. Web. 6 Nov. 2015.

The Folded Clock

Author: Heidi Julavits (b. 1968)
Publisher: Doubleday (New York). 304 pp.
Type of work: Memoir
Time: Early 2010s
Locales: New York City, Germany, Maine

The Folded Clock is a record of two years of Heidi Julavits's life. Each chapter captures a day or memory and is structured as a diary entry. Told in a nonlinear order, the book tells the story of the life of a woman through travels abroad, her life at home in New York City and Maine, and the lives of her family members.

On the opening page of her fifth book and her first of nonfiction, *The Folded Clock*, Heidi Julavits asks: "What is the worth of a day? Once, a day was long. It was bright and then it wasn't, meals happened, school happened. . . . Days were ages. . . . Within a day there were discernible hours, and clocks with hands that ticked out each new minute." She continues, "Not anymore. The 'day' no longer exists." These opening lines provide a thesis of sorts to *The Folded Clock*, asking whether a human life is defined by each passing day or whether it is the sum of each minute, hour, and day together that define a human life, the nonsequential events that ultimately place a person within that life.

Structured as a diary, though lacking its most common quality—linear chronology (Julavits's entries are shuffled, so an entry for December 9 may precede one for September 6, with no explanation of which year each day is taking place in)—*The Folded Clock* spans two years of Julavits's life and aims to capture the collapse of time by exposing the similarities of a person's day-to-day life. Despite the fact that these entries appear out of chronological order, the universal themes of a person's life emerge and the nonlinear character of a life is illustrated. In her review of *The Folded Clock* for the *New York Times Book Review*, Eula Biss says, "Today does not remain today, but ranges into the past and future, following an associative course guided by an unpredictable mind. The result is that each day feels very full, although little happens. And this fullness becomes a reminder of how a life can be improved by the passing of time." This is perhaps a perfect description of how the minutes, hours, days, and years add up in *The Folded Clock*. Julavits uses each day as a starting point, focusing on a small occurrence that opens up memories and meditations about the past and the future.

While some readers might find the format and order of the entries difficult to follow, reading each entry as a stand-alone piece that adds up to a greater whole—rather than trying to connect one entry to the consecutive one—makes for the most rewarding experience. Each entry begins with the phrase "Today I [we, etc.]," a nod to the diary Julavits kept as a child and believed ultimately led to her becoming a writer, and covers both the ordinary and the extraordinary.

The major themes of Julavits's life begin to emerge quickly: the passing of time, family and motherhood, living a creative life, friendship, and the importance of travel. Julavits touches on each of these as though she is creating a mosaic of snapshots, usually including several within the breadth of one entry, which may encompass the events of a single day—though generally they do not—or decades of the author's life. It is a diary of artifice that somehow conveys the truth about the rich minutiae of human life.

For example, in the entry for July 19, Julavits writes about her awareness, or lack of awareness of time. She suddenly notices the date and thinks about how many days have passed while she was not paying attention. She then launches into a story about being a hostess as a young person in New York and how she learned to pay attention to a single minute. She says, "I never didn't know what time it was, not for one single minute did I not know. This made the shift crawl by. One night lasted a week." After this anecdote, she describes a trip to see Christian Marclay's piece called *The Clock*, which is a twenty-four-hour-long movie with a different scene taken from a different film for each minute of the day. The experience of being aware of every minute made time pass more quickly for Julavits in that case. Watching the piece beside a dear friend she is visiting with in Los Angeles, Julavits is keenly aware of each passing moment and that they will have to say goodbye too soon. The juxtaposition of her younger self feeling tortured through a shift at work and her older self experiencing the passing of time beside a friend is a perfect example of the insight and emotional depth of each entry. Not only does the reader learn about the type of life Julavits has built for herself, but they also learn about how she lives it and how she views the world around her.

The entries tell of the life of a woman who is brave, fearful, creative, doubtful, loving, and jealous, and unashamed to show all of those facets of her personality. An entry marked August 7 begins with Julavits and a friend swimming the length of the harbor in the small Maine town where she and her family spend their summers. Along the way they encounter other townspeople along the shoreline, but the swim ends with Julavits dozing on a hot rock contemplating the passing of time, imaging herself waking up an old woman with grown children, her husband dead. The next entry, dated June 28 tells of a dinner party where Julavits wanted no one to know each other ahead of time before launching into a meditation on the availability of personal information on Google and our obsession with gaining it. The attention to detail is where the reader gleans the greatest insight.

Julavits's basic biography is covered over the course of the book. She was born and raised in Maine, a state she still deeply loves, and was an athlete in high school. After attending college, she lived briefly in San Francisco before moving to New York City in her twenties. She dated a few men seriously before meeting her husband, with whom she has two children, lives in Manhattan, and teaches at Columbia University. She is a frequent traveler and spends her fall, winter, and spring in New York and her summers at a vacation home she owns in Maine. The layers added to this skeleton of a life are created with precision and care. She uses this essential biography and the major themes mentioned earlier to create a complete portrait of a life well lived.

Heidi Julavits has authored four novels, The Mineral Palace (2000), The Uses of Enchantment (2006), The Effect of Living Backwards (2003), and The Vanishers (2012). The Folded Clock is her first work of nonfiction. She also cofounded and edits the award-winning arts-and-culture magazine the Believer.

The major difference between *The Folded Clock* and other books in the tradition of published diaries is its lack of chronology; however, her attention to the emotional side of one's life and also the unique aspects of the life of a woman are reminiscent of the first volumes of Anaïs Nin's lauded diaries in that she considers no detail or event to be too small (i.e., too feminine) to carry a level of importance in her life and the lives of those around her. Both women are operating in a male-dominated space—Nin because of the time in which she lived and Julavits as an academic and writer—and their awareness of this fact is crucial to the way they operate in their daily lives. Each woman also gains wisdom from her experiences with an elegance that is translated through precise, thoughtful prose.

The two women also seem to possess a rare empathy for others in romantic situations. Julavits, whom the reader learns is an intensely competitive person, frequently offers surprising insights when it comes to her relationship with her husband. She says at one point of his past lovers,

> Every man I've been involved with, his past girlfriends have played a great part in my falling in love with him. I can't explain it except to say that I have felt with these women a blood connection; these women have parted with a valued possession and now it has fallen to me. . . . If I'd dated this man before they had, he would not be this man.

Julavits uses moments like these to construct her image as mother and wife through the course of the book. While in Germany with her family at a writing residency for her husband, Julavits and her prose are particularly attuned to capturing family relationships, particularly the relationship between herself and her husband. She shows the intimate non-arguments, inside jokes, moments of kindness that are the foundation of her relationship with him.

Julavits's relationship with her daughter is captured in a particularly poignant fashion, as well. Her daughter, on the cusp of becoming a preteen, is beginning to claim her independence during the course of the journal, and Julavits captures the process of absorbing the last years of being the focus of her daughter's attention with sadness and complexity. In an entry from April 21, Julavits recounts walking across the Brooklyn Bridge with her daughter and her daughter's friend. She says, "These are my last years to be interesting to them. Knowing this, I try to be so exceedingly interesting that I might hold their attention longer than my natural expiration date allows." She then tells a story about cross-country skiing across the Brooklyn Bridge in a blizzard and how she saved her first husband from falling off after they had climbed down through a trapdoor. She transitions from this story to the heart of what she wished she had told her daughter and her friend: that she was "losing the thread," or forgetting where she had come from, Maine. The recounting both exposes the insecurities a mother feels as her child matures and the deep-seated melancholy that comes with growing up.

Perhaps it is the inclusion of the passing of time during childhood and a parent's awareness of it that adds an extra level of importance to the final book, or the progression of a happy, full marriage, or even something as simple as the recognition of the passing of the seasons in each locale Julavits finds herself in; regardless, the sum of the whole of the entries of *The Folded Clock* are built masterfully by a writer in stunningly in control of her craft. Widely praised by major publications like the *New York Times* and the *Los Angeles Review of Books*, *The Folded Clock* was also included on several best-of-the-year book lists and has further cemented Julavits's place as one of the more exciting contemporary writers.

Melynda Fuller

Review Sources

Biss, Eula. "Layers of Time." Rev. of *The Folded Clock*, by Heidi Julavits. *New York Times* 29 Mar. 2015: BR1. Print.

Rao, Mythili G. "On *Ongoingness: The End of a Diary* and *The Folded Clock: A Diary*: Our Diaries, Our Selves." Rev. of *The Folded Clock*, by Heidi Julavits. *Los Angeles Review of Books*. Los Angeles Review of Books, 19 Apr. 2015. Web. 17 Dec. 2015.

Scutts, Joanna. "In 'The Folded Clock,' Heidi Julavits Takes Your Inside Her Real/Fake Diary." Rev. of *The Folded Clock*, by Heidi Julavits. *Washington Post*. Washington Post, 14 May 2015. Web. 17 Dec. 2015.

Fortune Smiles

Author: Adam Johnson (b. 1967)
Publisher: Random House (New York). 320
pp.
Type of work: Short fiction

*Pulitzer Prize–winning novelist Adam John-
son presents six long stories in a collection
that won the 2015 National Book Award for
Fiction.*

(Courtesy of Random House)

"Nirvana," the opening story in Adam Johnson's National Book Award–winning collection, *Fortune Smiles*, takes place in the future. The story is told from the point of view
of a computer expert whose wife, Charlotte,
is paralyzed by a nerve condition that may
or may not be permanent. The narrator has used his computer programming skills
to create a hologram or virtual reanimation of the recently assassinated president of
the United States. While the narrator spends much of his time talking with this three-
dimensional image of the president, whose replies are excerpts from speeches and
addresses he has given, Charlotte escapes reality by putting on her earphones and
listening to Kurt Cobain's band, Nirvana.

The narrator says he created the image of the president because, unable to save his
wife, he wanted to save someone, and with the president it didn't matter that it was
too late. However, since all responses made by the president to the narrator's personal
problems are generalizations, clichés, and political platitudes, they come off as satirical rather than meaningful. Yet this story of the president as a sort of ghost that will
haunt the nation until the people become reconciled to his irreversible loss only serves
as a background for the personal loss the narrator is experiencing due to Charlotte's
illness. The two narratives coalesce when the narrator creates a three-dimensional image of Kurt Cobain, which responds to Charlotte in song lyrics and lines from Cobain's suicide note. At the conclusion the wife leans toward the image of Cobain as
if she wants to hold him, forgetting that her arms don't work and there is no Cobain
to embrace.

Like other stories in this collection, "Hurricanes Anonymous" has a ripped-from-
the-headlines timeliness, dealing with the aftermath of Hurricane Katrina that struck
New Orleans in 2005. The story's central character is a United Parcel Service driver
in Lake Charles, Louisiana, named Randall Richard, but who is referred to as "Nonc,"
the name his two-and-a-half-year-old son, Geronimo, has given him. On the day after
Katrina hits, Geronimo's mother, Marnie, leaves him in Nonc's UPS van before she is
thrown into prison on a drug charge.

To complicate matters further, Nonc has a girlfriend, Cherelle, who wants him to get his act together and start a business with her, and a "garden-variety scoundrel" of a father who stole Nonc's car and is now dying in California. Nonc feels torn between his resentment at being tied to Geronimo and his sense of commitment to his son. The story slips from third-person personal to second person to state quite explicitly its central theme—Nonc's realization that some events are actually "developments" and that there is a big plan out there you know nothing about, in which such a development is the first step in a new direction. The story gathers speed as Geronimo's need for a father, Cherelle's need for commitment, and Nonc's father's need for a son become more and more a responsibility. Nonc tries to figure out a way to minimize "developments" in his life, while still not becoming irresponsible like his ex and his father. All the while, the displaced and desperate victims of Katrina surround him like dazed zombies.

After winning the Pulitzer Prize in 2014 for his novel The Orphan Master's Son, *Adam Johnson won the National Book Award the following year for his collection of stories* Fortune Smiles. *He has also written* Emporium: Stories *(2002) and the novel* Parasites Like Us *(2003).*

"Interesting Facts" is told from the point of view of a forty-five-year-old unpublished writer, who has been diagnosed with breast cancer. Throughout the story, the narrator lists what she calls "interesting facts" about her condition and the drugs and tests she has to take. The narrator's husband is a successful novelist who has won the Pulitzer Prize in literature for a novel set in North Korea—a biographical allusion that to the fact that Johnson's own novel, *The Orphan Master's Son* (2012), set in North Korea, won the 2013 Pulitzer Prize for Fiction.

Midway through the story, the perspective seems to shift from the narrator's account of her reactions to her diagnosis to what seem like ghostly experiences after her death. She describes standing in a hospital room with her family and watching a woman dying, saying she imagines leaving the real world and entering the body of the strange woman. Then she seems to abruptly pop back into the world of the living. The story follows her (or her ghostly presence) as she spends a great deal of time in Golden Gate Park, watching her husband and daughter at the archery range, standing beside her husband, although he does not see her. The story ends with the narrator, or ghost of a narrator, thinking she will become merely a story from the time when her children were small.

Boston Globe correspondent Ted Weesner Jr. suggests that Johnson's stories in *Fortune Smiles* are often like responses to dares, something like, I bet you can't write something that makes us kind of fall in love with a "cranky old torturer," to which Johnson might mumble, "Oh Yeah? Well watch this." The result is "George Orwell Was a Friend of Mine," the fourth story in Johnson's collection and the only story in the collection that had not been published previously. The story is told in first person by Hans Bäcker, who served as a former warden of an infamous East German prison before the fall of the Berlin Wall. Bäcker still lives near the prison, which has been turned into a museum. When his dog defecates on a plaque commemorating the playwright Klaus Wexler, who was imprisoned there for two years, Bäcker insists the poet was a pervert and a drug addict, a charge that the tour guide challenges. Later a video of the encounter appears on the Internet and the curator of the museum asks Bäcker to lead a group of students on a prison tour, which can be recorded for future visitors. His repeated denial of what really happened in the prison energizes the central plot line and theme of the story.

When Bäcker is taken on one of the tours, he continues to deny all the atrocities that the female guide, who was once a prisoner herself, says took place there. Bäcker's denials are the predictable ones—that the prisoners were criminals, that they were only questioned rather than tortured, that they were traitors to their country. When he steps inside the cell where the guide spent two years, he says it is not so small or uncomfortable, continuing to insist that the prison was a necessary part of a functioning society. The final horror he must encounter, and which he can no longer ignore, is what is called the U-boat, where the prisoner stands naked in ankle-deep cold water for days. Although the former warden says that rather than torture the U-boat is merely uncomfortable, when he strips down and enters the cell, determined to prove that the guide's story is not true, his body starts to go numb, and he stands there with water spraying on him, metaphorically tasting the terrible rain that fell long ago on East Germany.

"Dark Meadow" is told from the point of view of a character mentioned in an earlier story, "Interesting Facts." Mr. Roses operates a computer security business. He has just written an article about a beacon that tracks child pornography files on the web; every time a picture is copied from the file, the beacon is also copied, and every time the file is transferred, the beacon sends a signal, which he receives before it alerts the authorities. Thus, he is able to help child pornographers get rid of their porn collections before the authorities arrive. When Roses examines the hard drive of one man who calls him for help, he sees the picture of a young girl he does not recognize from the standard porn collections he has seen before. The picture arouses him, and he masturbates, although he hates himself for doing so, for this is a story of a man trying to combat his own devils. Roses is further tempted to abuse his next-door neighbor's two daughters, ages ten and twelve.

Johnson makes it possible for the reader to sympathize with Roses by having him recall his own childhood when he was sexually abused by the leader of his Sea Scouting troop. The central moral issue of the story is expressed quite explicitly when a police officer comes to get information about the Internet beacon and asks Roses whether he is trying to protect kids by giving the authorities a way to catch predators or whether he is trying to help pedophiles by warning them about the beacon. The story ends as Roses masturbates instead of abusing the girls next door, insisting that it is a duty, something that must be done while the innocents sleep.

Ron Charles, writing for the *Washington Post*, calls Mr. Roses the most affectionate and responsible character in the story even as he hangs over a "precipice of violent depravity." Writing for the *New York Times*, Lauren Groff says that in "Dark Meadow" Johnson asks the reader to feel compassion for a man most people would find immediately despicable. Although *New York Times* reviewer Michiko Kakutani thought "Dark Meadow" was one of the weakest stories in the collection, she also suggests that Johnson seems to have challenged himself to an exercise in the limits of sympathy.

"Fortune Smiles," despite being the title story, is arguably the weakest in the collection, for it fails to engage the reader in any personal conflict of an ultimately sympathetic character. The story, which returns to the culture that formed the center of *The Orphan Master's Son*, focuses on two central characters, DJ and Sun-ho, both of whom have recently defected from North Korea to Seoul, South Korea, where they are having difficulty adapting to a new freedom they have never known before. Sun-ho has no patience for the South Korean sense of order and compliance, for while it was one thing to surrender to the rule of a murderous dictator in the north, it is not clear to him what unseen forces the South Koreans obey. The story ends with a fantastic event in which Sun-ho ties helium balloons to a lawn chair and floats into the sky toward North Korea. DJ remains, proclaiming that such a thing could never happen in the north, where everything is planned out and rigged, whereas this is spontaneous and unexpected, and therefore real.

Although, as reviewers have noted, this collection takes on the challenge of making unlikeable characters sympathetic, it often seems to be characterized more by authorial experimental play than by genuine human understanding.

Charles E. May

Review Sources

Charles, Ron. Rev. of *Fortune Smiles*, by Adam Johnson. *Washington Post*. Washington Post, 11 Aug. 2015. Web.16 Dec. 2015.

Rev. of *Fortune Smiles*, by Adam Johnson. *Kirkus Reviews*. Kirkus Media, 15 June 2015. Web. 16 Dec. 2015.

Groff, Lauren. Rev. of *Fortune Smiles*, by Adam Johnson. *New York Times*. New York Times, 13 Aug. 2015. Web. 16 Dec. 2015.

Kakutani, Michiko. "Stories from Dark Places." Rev. of *Fortune Smiles*, by Adam Johnson. *New York Times*. New York Times, 7 Sept. 2015. Web. 16 Dec. 2015.

Weesner, Ted, Jr. Rev. of *Fortune Smiles*, by Adam Johnson. *Boston Globe*. Boston Globe Media Partners, 22 Aug. 2015. Web. 29 Dec. 2015.

Four-Legged Girl

Author: Diane Seuss (b. 1956)
Publisher: Graywolf Press (Minneapolis).
88 pp.
Type of work: Poetry

Events in Diane Seuss's life inspired these highly mythologized and inventive poems centering on loss, beauty, and desire and peopled with four-legged girls and ghosts in porkpie hats. This collection represents an imaginative exploration of femininity and what it means to be a strong woman.

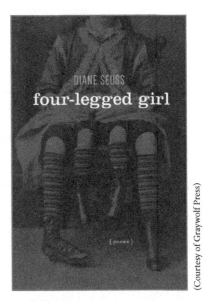

(Courtesy of Graywolf Press)

Four-Legged Girl is a ferocious, feral collection with pure moments of freakish joy. Much of Diane Seuss's third book of poems is concerned with loss, especially the speaker's, as she develops from a child to a middle-aged adult; she lost her father at a young age and compounds the loss with the death of a junkie boyfriend in early adulthood. While these losses are central, the book chronicles more than a series of losses. It also delves into the messy and mysterious aspects of womanhood and explores definitions of beauty, femininity, and desire. Seuss chose an especially apt passage from Lucille Clifton's poem "in this garden" for the opening epigraph, with its two-headed woman and her swiveling heads. As one head faces outward, the other turns inward, which is Seuss's approach to poems in *Four-Legged Girl*. The poems are reflective without losing sight of both the trappings and oddities of the outside world.

Seuss's muse for the book was Myrtle Corbin (1868–1928), whom Seuss describes as "the monster twinned below." Medically, Corbin had what is known as "dipygus," meaning that all her anatomy was doubled below the waist. Corbin had two pelvises, two uteruses, two vaginas, and two sets of legs; doctors speculate that she had an in utero twin who was partially absorbed and partially conjoined. Although Corbin became part of Victorian-era sideshows to earn money for her family, she was smart and musical and had ambitions for a normal life. She married and had five children before returning as a circus sideshow act later in life to help support her growing family. An adapted Charles Eisenman photograph of Corbin as a teenager (1882) makes a startling cover for *Four-Legged Girl*, foreshadowing the uniqueness, originality, and beauty of its poems. Seuss also ends the book on the poem "Oh four-legged girl, it's either you or the ossuary," making Corbin both the bookends of and the lens through which she tells the story.

Seuss divides *Four-Legged Girl* into five roughly chronological sections beginning in childhood. Section 1, titled "blossomhouse," begins with "Jump rope song:"

> Beautiful blankness, I saw you once
> in a bucket of glue, on the flank of a horse with glass eyes,
>
> in a gown and the girls ankles were shaking,
>
> in Dream Whip, in hawk s—t, in comfrey, cress,
> campion, potato vine, pokeweed, lopseed, the dodder,
>
> the clover and the honeysuckle flower, white as boiled bone.

This is not a typical jump-rope song with a swinging rhythm and rhyme, and though there are many "white" images in "bucket of glue" and "white boiled bone" and references to a kind of tabula rasa innocence in "blankness," the world encroaches on this innocence with references to "hawk s—t" and, later, "nursing home women" and hospital sheets. The complexities of life blossom here, among the potato vine and honeysuckle, and the girl, making "costumes for canaries" from hospital sheets and christening gowns, is finding her way under the mock orange tree. Seuss does not despair at this girl's loss of innocence, though the depth of it is not yet evident, but shows admiration for her creativity and strength. Even in later poems in this section, when the speaker references her father's illness through his tumors and hospital gowns, she also says, in "White violet, not so much an image," that "The only way to know tenderness is to dismantle it" (19). Seuss makes many references to flowers in the book, often thought of as a symbol for the gentleness and beauty of women; here, she dismantles those notions by focusing on the parts, rather than the whole. Seuss is masterful in her layering of imaginative images that may not seem to fit together at first but combine to offer a clear and complex portrait of this girl and her growth to womanhood.

Also notable from this section is the rousing "People, the ghosts down in North-of-the-South aren't see-through," with its full-bodied, take no prisoners ghosts:

> They come in our houses
>
> by kicking down doors, wearing porkpie hats and smoking
> those My Father cigars. Yellow sweat stains
> on their sleeveless undershirts, my people. . . .

There is nothing flimsy or friendly about these ghosts; they are strong and they are determined. While Seuss identifies them as "my people," she also explains, "They want to steal / our valuables . . . burn down / the house" (11–13). Rather than giving up, Seuss insists on fighting, and this is a theme to which she returns often in the book, that women are stronger than their "ghosts," if only they will "push back" and refuse to be intimidated.

The second and third sections of the book, "blowtorch the hinges" and "lush," focus on the speaker's young-adult life, much of which takes place in New York City in the late 1970s and 1980s, with poems referencing encounters with William Burroughs and Andy Warhol as well as life with a junkie boyfriend who "was stealing me blind to feed his habit." Many of the poems in "blowtorch the hinges" are more linear and narrative than the poems in "blossomhouse." While some of the shift in form may be attributed to a child's thinking rather than an adult's, the vibrancy of Seuss's metaphors and lists of images continues when the speaker questions notions of beauty and desire as she stumbles through various jobs trying to determine a career path. In "Warhol's Shadows," for example, Seuss writes, "We didn't intend to go to Warhol's show, intended nothing / in those days, unintended our way into desire" (18–19). The speaker reflects on her past without romanticizing it.

(Gale Montesanti)

Diane Seuss is an assistant professor in English at Kalamazoo College in Michigan. Her previous books of poetry are It Blows You Hollow *(1998) and* Wolf Lake, White Gown Blown Open *(2010), winner of the Juniper Prize for Poetry. Her poem "Free Beer," from* Four-Legged Girl, *was included in Best American Poetry 2014.*

She takes this a step further in "Do you remember that spring? The breeze smelled like cake mix," when the speaker reminisces with a friend about their shared history, but the tone is anything but nostalgic:

> Are you still mainlining amnesia, that downer, or nostalgia, a double-downer?
> I overdosed long ago and got set up in permanent rehab.
> The treatment philosophy is de-lousing and head shaving,
> Making a present of the present tense.

Seuss addresses both strength and beauty here, as well as the importance of living in the present, by having her speaker look into the past and realize she is stronger now, in "permanent rehab," and that part of gaining that strength and reality is the acceptance that beauty is not as important as she has been led to believe.

In section 3, "lush," Seuss pulls the beginning and end of the book to the middle, meaning that every major theme in the book converges in this one, multipart poem, which is essentially a long, complex riff on the Billy Strayhorn jazz song "Lush Life" (1948). In the first section of the poem, "I can't listen to music, especially 'Lush Life,'" where the speaker references her younger self and states "Nostalgia is depression," Seuss's writing is reminiscent of Edna St. Vincent Millay's "What lips my lips have kissed and where, and why" (1920) in its melancholy and acceptance of reality. The word "lush" is repeated often in this section, as the speaker laments those she has lost while aligning herself with a long, lush list of night-blooming flowers, stating, "I looked up into the dark for something to bloom by." The speaker's losses are devastating, but she has the strength to look for something to sustain her. Seuss's continued use of flowers as a symbol of strength, rather than delicacy, shows her inventiveness.

The last two sections of the book, "free beer" and "a period's period," reveal the speaker as a mature adult. In "I snapped it over my knee like kindling," the speaker now realizes the limits of desire, particularly sexual desire, as a driving force:

> Then I built a little fire and set a match to it. The flames were purple
> at the tip. The purple-pink of moth orchids pinned to a prom dress.

> Yes, I snapped desire over my knee and arsoned it. You better believe
> there was a soundtrack.

The speaker, again, focuses on strength and growth, and sometimes that means being alone as opposed to the "prom couple." Seuss brings her theme of strength full circle in "Oh four-legged girl, it's either you or the ossuary" in these lines:

> For, having imagined your body one way I found it to be another way,
> it was yielding,
> > but only as the Destroying Angel mushroom yields, its softness allied
> > with its poison, and your legs were not petals or tendrils as I'd believed,
> > but brazen, the deviant tentacles beneath the underskirt of a secret queen.

As an adult, the speaker is now able to see the four-legged girl not as someone damaged or weak but as a "secret queen" with hidden strengths and determination who should not be underestimated. In *Four-Legged Girl*, Seuss not only turns the common associations of flowers as gentle and delicate things easily damaged into symbols of strength and aggression but does so with energy, inventiveness, and a wildness that is incapable of being tamed. Though not widely reviewed, Seuss's collection has been well-received. *Publishers Weekly* said Seuss is "endlessly inventive with her language and feats of imagination," and Ellen Miller-Mack for the *Rumpus* states, "Seuss animates. Objects come alive, like toys springing from a chest when darkness comes."

Marybeth Rua-Larsen

Review Sources

Rev. of *Four-Legged Girl*, by Diane Seuss. *Publishers Weekly*. PWxyz, Oct. 2015.
  Web. 29 Dec. 2015.
Miller-Mack, Ellen. "Four-Legged Girl by Diane Seuss." Rev. of *Four-Legged Girl*,
  by Diane Seuss. *Rumpus*. The Rumpus, 7 Oct. 2015. Web. 28 Dec. 2015.
Millner, Maggie. "The Lush Lives of Vandals and Debauchers: 'Four-Legged Girl'
  by Diane Seuss." Rev. of *Four-Legged Girl*, by Diane Seuss. *ZYZZYVA*. ZYZZY-
  VA: A San Francisco Journal of Arts & Letters, 25 Nov. 2015. Web. 29 Dec. 2015.
Nilsen, David. "Dubious Lexicon: A Review of Four-Legged Girl by Diane Seuss."
  Rev. of *Four-Legged Girl*, by Diane Seuss. *Fourth and Sycamore*. Greenville
  Public Lib., 8 Oct. 2015. Web. 29 Dec. 2015.

Funny Girl

Author: Nick Hornby (b. 1957)
Publisher: Riverhead Books (New York). 464 pp.
Type of work: Novel
Time: 1964–67, 2014
Locale: London, England

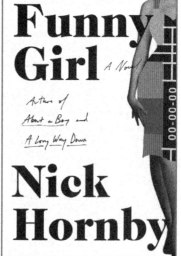

(Courtesy of Riverhead Books)

Funny Girl *follows a young starlet named Sophie Straw in 1960s London. Straw, a working-class girl from Northern England, miraculously lands a once-in-a-lifetime role as the star of a sitcom. The novel is about women in comedy, the trappings of fame, and making art that lasts.*

Principal characters:
BARBARA PARKER, a.k.a. Sophie Straw, an aspiring comedian and star of the hit sitcom Barbara (and Jim)
CLIVE, her chronically unhappy leading man, the Jim of Barbara (and Jim)
DENNIS, a radio and television producer
TONY, a gay but closeted radio and television writer
BILL, Tony's writing partner, a gay radio and television writer

Nick Hornby, a novelist and Academy Award–nominated screenwriter, was inspired to write his new novel, *Funny Girl*, after reading the work of the British historian David Kynaston. Kynaston wrote three books about midcentury politics and social policy in England, which impressed upon Hornby the myriad ways people are shaped by the culture in which they live. "I just started to think about the ways in which TV could say things about a country," Hornby told Dan Kois in a February 2015 interview for *Slate*. An enormous cultural shift took place in England following World War II, and much of it was captured on television. During this time, long before cable television, if a household owned a TV set, the TV had only three channels. Everybody watched the BBC, and popular shows raked in millions of viewers. Then as now, sitcoms received the highest ratings, but thanks to the changing mores of the 1960s, writers such as Ray Galton and Alan Simpson—the inspiration for the writing duo in *Funny Girl*—were changing what sitcoms could be. The situations were familiar (marriage, differences between men and women, and so on), but the comedy had new depth, commenting on larger issues such as class. Hornby praised one Galton and Simpson sketch from that era, telling Kois that the writing carried a richness akin to the writing of lauded dramatic playwright Harold Pinter, "but he was writing for the theater and they were writing popular television, so they didn't get the same credit." This observation—the fraught divisions among mediums, styles, and viewership—is a major theme of *Funny Girl*.

Funny Girl is not a social history or a dissertation on the evolution of British comedy, though it incorporates aspects of both. Instead, it is the fictional story of one woman, an aspiring comedic actor named Barbara Parker, later to be given the stage name Sophie Straw. For better or worse, Sophie's story is the engine that powers Hornby's book, and her character is imbued with the author's own drive to succeed in his chosen field. In his interview with Kois, Hornby compared Sophie's yearning to be an actor with his own longing for an artistic career. Like Sophie, Hornby grew up in a middle-class family outside of London, traveling into the city to buy records and books and to attend soccer games and cultural events. After attending a Bruce Springsteen concert in 1981 he became serious about his calling. His collection of loves, he explained, is akin to Sophie's love for Lucille Ball. However,

Nick Hornby is a novelist, essayist, and screenwriter, best known for his novels High Fidelity *(1995) and* About a Boy *(1998), both of which were adapted for film. Hornby also wrote the screenplays for* An Education *(2009), for which he was nominated for an Academy Award, and for* Wild *(2014).*

Sophie's epiphany comes not at a concert but at a beauty pageant, and it is not a glimpse of dazzling artistic success that pushes her out of the nest and into the arms of London, but rather a glimpse of what her life could be without it.

In the book's first pages, Sophie is crowned Miss Blackpool. The scene is appropriately gray: it is a cold and rainy day in July, and the contestants—clad in bathing suits while everyone else wears raincoats—get goose bumps, so that when it comes time to announce the winner they look like "turkeys hanging in a butcher's window." Sophie's father, the conservative but amiable George Parker, is starstruck when he recognizes the photographer from the local paper, but Sophie is nonplussed by the sad scene. When Sophie discovers that her title requires her to participate in local events for an entire year, she promptly returns her crown.

A few pages later, Sophie is in London, working at a department store and rooming with an eccentric coworker. Against her better instincts, she accepts an invitation to dinner with a customer. The night goes poorly, but by chance, she meets a modeling agent. The agent is wary of Sophie's acting ambitions and sends her on a number of failed auditions. Finally, he puts his foot down: if she does not land a part within a week, her only auditions will be for modeling positions, which Sophie is loath to do. Hornby suggests that Sophie is too voluptuous for both sexed-up roles and sexless ones, a predicament that will be disappointingly familiar to contemporary women actors. Sophie's body is considered more important than her talent, which is difficult for her to showcase when reading for roles in which she is either set dressing or the butt of the joke. Hornby skillfully navigates Sophie's various trials at the hands of men, and though *Funny Girl* celebrates mid-twentieth-century television, it does not gloss over its failures. When Sophie eventually lands a lead role in a sitcom and becomes a huge star, Hornby makes clear the limitations of her character and her celebrity with refreshing honesty.

The bulk of the book charts the rise and gentle decline of Sophie's sitcom, *Barbara (and Jim)*. Her costar, Clive, is a theater actor, certain he is meant to be a huge star. He is never happy and consents to play Sophie's forgettable straight man, Jim, only begrudgingly. The writers, Tony and Bill, are modeled after Galton and Simpson, but they have their own distinct problems and trajectories. Their relationship is one of the more interesting, though mostly unexplored, subplots of the novel. Tony and Bill are both gay men—Tony is closeted, but Bill is more open about his sexuality (albeit somewhat cautiously during a time in England when homosexuality was still illegal). Tony goes on to marry a woman and have a child, while Bill, ever resentful of Tony's decision, writes a celebrated novel about a man in London's gay underground scene. Dennis, the show's producer, is sketchily drawn, though he eventually kindles a romance with Sophie.

Hornby's screenwriting prowess is clear: his plotting is flawless, his scenes are crisp, and his copious dialogue leaps off the page. Missing is a deeper exploration of the characters, particularly Sophie, who remains witty and well-meaning throughout the entire story. She flies over obstacles with extraordinary ease, which is most frustrating in her personal life. When she is first offered the starring role on *Barbara (and Jim)*, she receives a call to visit her dying father in the hospital. Unfortunately, the day she must go is also the day she is scheduled to film the pilot episode in front of a live audience. Though her father could be dead by the time she arrives in Blackpool, she decides to stay in London and film the pilot. It is a thought-provoking choice that reveals the depth of Sophie's drive to succeed and illustrates the pain of following a dream at the expense of the people one loves most. Sophie arrives at the hospital a day late; her father is still alive (he survives many more years), and when she explains her absence to him, he tells her that she made the right decision. This is an excellent outcome for Sophie, but it is not a fruitful one in a literary sense. Meanwhile, a subplot involving Sophie's estranged mother is similarly resolved.

Most of the time, *Funny Girl* seems to be less about Sophie than about television comedy in general. The book builds a solid case for the relevance of popular comedy and the value of making people laugh, with each character calibrated to represent a specific point of view. For example, Bill worries that *Barbara (and Jim)* is artistically beneath him, while Tony is simply happy that he gets to "fill up pages" for a living. In fact, Hornby's most nuanced moments are connected to this larger theme—the constant struggle to make art that is truly worthwhile. In one scene, Dennis debates a pompous intellectual (who, coincidentally, is also having an affair with Dennis's wife) on a late-night television program. Dennis adroitly defends *Barbara (and Jim)* against the intellectual, who dismisses the show as trash for the masses. The scene itself is both intellectually flawed—Dennis begins making up references to support his case—and, for reasons set up by Hornby's ever-churning plot, hilarious. But as Hornby concludes his novel in the year 2014, the question remains: Does *Barbara (and Jim)* have more value than Bill's forgotten literary novel, for example, because more people know it? Or does the mere fact that more people know it, have watched it and laughed at it, mean that it has no value? Hornby poses the question as to whether or not popularity and artistic merit can coincide, but he is never content to answer with a simple "yes." His interrogation of what makes for a fulfilling artistic career is assailed from all angles through his clever and beguiling characters. *Funny Girl* may not make readers feel deeply about Sophie or her compatriots, but it will make them think, and perhaps more importantly, it will make them laugh.

Molly Hagan

Review Sources

Charles, Ron. "Set in the 1960s, Nick Hornby's New Novel, *Funny Girl*, Traces the Rise of a Sitcom Star." Rev. of *Funny Girl*, by Nick Hornby. *Washington Post*. Washington Post, 3 Feb. 2015. Web. 23 Sept. 2015.

McAlpin, Heller. "*Funny Girl* Is a Book Made for Binge-Watching." Rev. of *Funny Girl*, by Nick Hornby. *NPR*. NPR, 3 Feb. 2015. Web. 23 Sept. 2015.

Preston, Alex. "Nick Hornby's Tribute to the Golden Age of Light Entertainment." Rev. of *Funny Girl*, by Nick Hornby. *Guardian*. Guardian News and Media, 3 Nov. 2014. Web. 23 Sept. 2015.

Williams, John. Rev. of *Funny Girl*, by Nick Hornby. *New York Times*. New York Times, 18 Feb. 2015. Web. 23 Sept. 2015.

Furiously Happy
A Funny Book about Horrible Things

Author: Jenny Lawson (b. 1973)
Publisher: Flatiron Books (New York). 329 pp.
Type of work: Essays, memoir
Time: Present
Locale: United States

Lawson shares her personal ups and downs as she learns to live with a variety of mental-health issues while trying to function as a wife, mother, and successful author.

Principal personages:
JENNY LARSON, author, blogger, and self-described flawed human being
VICTOR, her husband
HAILEY, her daughter
MAILE, her friend
LAURA, her friend and travel companion

(Courtesy Flatiron Books)

Jenny Lawson's second book, *Furiously Happy: A Funny Book about Horrible Things*, is at times both hilarious and heartbreaking. In this collection of essays, Lawson provides snapshots into her daily life as she maneuvers through her struggles with and triumphs over mental illness. The premise of the book is based on one of her blog posts where she proclaimed, "I'm f——ing *done* with sadness, and I don't know what's up the a—— of the universe lately but *I've HAD IT*. I AM GOING TO BE FURIOUSLY HAPPY, OUT OF SHEER *SPITE*." With this post, she began a movement and invited her readers to take on the challenge of finding and emphasizing those moments in life "when things are fine and making them *amazing*." Lawson does not claim that this kind of action will cure mental illness, but she shares many of the ways that way of thinking and acting made a significant difference in her life.

Lawson's distinctive style is one aspect of the book that may both appeal to and distract readers. She clearly states her opinion about the topics throughout the book, and she shares her experiences with mental and physical maladies in an effort to help others understand that they or their loved ones are not alone. In discussing the tough issues, Lawson often makes light of these problems, but she tells readers that this is one of her coping strategies. To make sure that it is clear that the book is a reflection of her real-life experiences and not an editor's version of her life or a fictional piece, she often includes humorous footnotes that clarify or provide disclaimers of comments she has made. The footnotes also serve to humorously mock the notion that someone might take her too seriously. Lawson does not hesitate to use profanity. Readers will not find the author swearing on every page or even in every chapter, but Lawson is not shy about using such language to punctuate a particular story she is telling. Her word choice is most often funny, but occasionally it reflects frustration or anger, sometimes with herself, but mostly with the depression, anxiety, and pain she lives with every day.

The most notable stylistic aspect of the book is its lack of organization or fixed structure. Lawson's chapters tell poignant stories, provide snippets of random thoughts, share conversations through the use of dialogue, resemble a nonfiction essay, impart a travel narrative, and any combination of these— sometimes in the same chapter. Lawson jumps around from topic to topic throughout each chapter, sometimes giving background information and sometimes just beginning in the middle of a thought without any warning. This lack of formal structure highlights the sporadic thought processes that often accompany mental illness, and as a result, the technique emphasizes rather than takes away from Lawson's message.

(Laura Mayers)

Jenny Lawson is known for an irreverent approach to life. Her blog has been recognized by the Nielsen ratings, Forbes magazine, and by the Weblog Awards. Her first book, Let's Pretend This Never Happened *(2012), reached the top of the* New York Times *best-seller list.*

Although the tone of each chapter varies, there is the constant sense of connection or hope for anyone who suffers from or loves someone who suffers from mental illness. Readers will find some of the essays hilarious, and several chapter titles, such as "Stock Up on Snow Globes. The Zombie Apocalypse Is Coming" and "And Then I Got Three Dead Cats in the Mail," foreshadow the uproarious comedy that is to come. Some of the best humor is often found in the random thoughts that seem to control and steer a chapter. In "Things I May Have Accidentally Said during Uncomfortable Silences," for instance, Lawson shares clips of the thoughts that entered her mind while she sat in her psychiatrist's office. Among these often irreverent gems, she says, "I spent last night cleaning up nine-year-old vomit. The vomit of a nine-year-old, that is. Not vomit that's nine years old. I'm not *that* bad at housekeeping." The simplicity of comments like these draws readers into Lawson's life through mutual connections, yet the reality and relatedness of each of the scenarios raises a chuckle.

Other parts of the book are bittersweet. In "Pretend You're Good at It," Lawson shares the story of a trip to New York where she was working on the audiobook recording of her first book and attending a publicity lunch. Her extreme anxiety made this trip difficult in several ways, and she candidly admits that she was terrified. Being in front of or even in the midst of "normal" people who do not suffer from the degree of mental illness that Lawson does created more anxiety and stress for her at the luncheon. Though the meeting was successful, she shares, "My favorite part was when everyone was leaving and one of the waitresses snuck in to tell me that she was a huge fan and couldn't wait to read my book. I suspected my editor had paid her to say that but I saw her nervous, wild-eyed look barely masked by a skin of propriety and I realized she was part of my tribe. I hugged her tight and thanked her. She probably never realized how much I needed her right then." Recording the audiobook took on its own level of debilitating anxiety for Lawson, and she almost gave up on it. Later that evening in her hotel as she was unable to quell an escalating panic attack and simultaneously battling insomnia, which only fed the brewing panic, she suddenly looked out a window and realized it was snowing. Being raised in Texas where there was rarely any snow, she chose to focus on the magic of the snow rather than on her panic attack, and at that moment she discovered that she could make her "furiously happy." After going outside in her pajamas, she says, "I stood at the end of the street, catching snow in my mouth, and laughed softly . . . as I realized that without my insomnia and anxiety and pain I'd never have been awake to see the city that never sleeps asleep and blanketed up for winter." This switch in focus and thinking coupled with advice from author and friend Neil Gaiman to "pretend you're good at it" allowed Lawson to finish the job.

Lawson imparts on her readers the importance of relationships as she talks about her parents, her husband, her daughter, and her friends. Glimpses of her family help readers see how those who are closest to Lawson continue to love and support her regardless of her myriad mental health issues and regardless of whether or not they understand why they are a part of it. Lawson begins the book with a conversation she has had with her mother, who seems unwilling to fully accept Lawson or her illnesses. Her mother's mantra of "'You're not crazy. STOP CALLING YOURSELF CRAZY. . . . You're just *sensitive*. And . . . a little . . . *odd*'" has been repeated throughout Lawson's life. Where her mother's support comes through a denial of her illness, Lawson realizes that her father's choices are a reflection of his own dealings with mental illness. His support is gentle and often points in a humorous direction; for instance, he considers purchasing a stuffed giraffe head and neck for her because he remembers her love of "terrible, old taxidermy."

Victor, Lawson's husband of eighteen years, is at the receiving end of many of her practical jokes, and many of their conversations and arguments are the subject of chapters in the book. Readers learn of his patience with Lawson after she places a stuffed, once-live raccoon on his pillow. Chapters that contain direct dialogue between Lawson and Victor, however, impart insight into their relationship and their shared humor, and although some may only perceive their banter as the deterioration of a conversation, others will find themselves chuckling along with Lawson at her adroit use of language and her clever ability to twist words and their meaning.

Lawson is most reticent on the subject of her daughter, only introducing the nine-year-old into the book occasionally. The chapter "That Baby Was Delicious" appears toward the end of the book, and in it Lawson reveals her fears as a parent. It is in this chapter that she shows readers her vulnerable and less sarcastic side as she shares her worry that her mental health issues will, at the very least, embarrass her daughter at some point.

In addition to family, Lawson pulls her friends into the mess of her life and relates her adventures with her friend Laura as they traveled to Australia on a sponsored tour when Lawson outrageously dresses in either a koala or a kangaroo costume while visiting the wildlife. Laura patiently goes along with the ensuing hilarity and takes pictures that are included in the book. Maile, another friend, also stays by Lawson's side, despite unusual conversations such as the one in the chapter "And Then I Got Three Dead Cats in the Mail." These close relationships are further evidence for Lawson that being "furiously happy" makes life worth living.

Furiously Happy: A Funny Book about Horrible Things is a refreshingly different look at the ways people deal with mental illness and chronic pain disorders. Readers will laugh, cry, scream, and learn—sometimes all within a single page.

Theresa L. Stowell

Review Sources

Bauer, Sara Dobie. "Jenny Lawson's *Furiously Happy*—Reviewed by a Depressive." Rev. of *Furiously Happy: A Funny Book about Horrible Things*, by Jenny Lawson. *SheKnows.* SheKnows, 28 Sept. 2015. Web. 22 Feb. 2016.

Cowles, Gregory. "Inside the List." Rev. of *Furiously Happy: A Funny Book about Horrible Things*, by Jenny Lawson. *New York Times.* New York Times, 2 Oct. 2015. Web. 28 Jan. 2016.

Rev. of *Furiously Happy: A Funny Book about Horrible Things*, by Jenny Lawson. *Publishers Weekly.* PWxyz, 31 Aug. 2015. Web. 22 Feb. 2016.

Hughes, Kathryn. "How to Feel OK When You Have a Brain That Is Trying to Destroy You." Rev. of *Furiously Happy: A Funny Book about Horrible Things*, by Jenny Lawson. *Guardian.* Guardian News and Media, 16 Sept. 2015. Web. 22 Feb. 2016.

Krug, Nora. "Jenny Lawson on 'Furiously Happy' and When It Is Ok to Call Her 'Crazy.'" Rev. of *Furiously Happy: A Funny Book about Horrible Things.* *Washington Post.* Washington Post, 22 Sept. 2015. Web. 22 Feb. 2016.

Get in Trouble

Author: Kelly Link (b. 1969)
Publisher: Random House (New York). 352 pp.
Type of work: Short fiction

Kelly Link's third collection of short stories, Get in Trouble, *explores the sex lives of superheroes, the trouble with Ghost Boyfriends, and the nature of reality.*

Kelly Link has been publishing short stories for nearly two decades, but she stands out among her colleagues of the form. Link's aesthetic descends from the late Ray Bradbury, author of *The Martian Chronicles* (1950) and *Fahrenheit 451* (1953), and finds its closest peer in the work of contemporary

(Courtesy of Random House)

writer George Saunders, who wrote an entire collection of short stories in which each story took place in a different dystopian theme park. But these comparisons are still ill-fitting. Link's narrative choices are not merely otherworldly; she directly engages with the strict conventions of specific genres and then dismantles them in stories that combine elements of fantasy, horror, science fiction, and fairy tales. Scarlett Thomas, writing for the *New York Times*, compared her to Raymond Carver—but with characters who "do things like throw parties on spaceships and get off with literal toy boys." Link's characters, like Carver's, always seem to be down on their luck; if not materially poor, they want what they cannot have, which, as the title of her latest collection suggests, inevitably leads them into trouble.

Some similarities among the stories in *Get in Trouble* emerge. Many of the tales are about teenagers, and more than one take place in a world where ordinary people can be born with superpowers. Many explore themes of identity and authenticity: famous actors and superheroes wrestle with their public personas, and the children of the super-rich employ "Faces," or actors to play them in public during their rebellious youth. In one story, there exist "pocket universes," some of which are like Florida, only better; in another, a time-traveling astronaut tells a story about two houses, one the scene of a gruesome murder, the other an exact replica. Both houses were haunted, the astronaut claims, but which ghosts were real? Link's stories require great leaps of imagination and mutations of paradoxical thought, but her technical skill as a storyteller eases the reader's burden.

The collection opens with a pseudo–fairy tale called "The Summer People." In it, a teenager named Fran helps her father care for vacation homes in a resort town in Appalachia. But Fran is also the guardian of another group of "summer people," as she has taken to calling them. These elf-like creatures are not wealthy out-of-towners but an ancient family of mischief makers with a penchant for odd bits of fabric and elaborate war games. Fran's family has cared for the summer people—buying them things and scrubbing their floors—for as long as she can remember. "The Summer People" has hallmarks of a classic fairy tale, including enchanted gifts with complicated baggage and a bedroom that will show those who sleep in it their heart's desires, but Link is not interested in convention for convention's sake. She takes aim at class and servitude and captures the damned-if-you-do, damned-if-you-don't angst of leaving home. Her story is a parable that questions the nature of parables, just as the epigraph for the story collection, from the Japanese poet Basho, questions the nature of stories: "Year after year / On the monkey's face / A monkey's face."

Link's work has a nihilistic quality that sparks with her playful genre bending. If traditional fairy tales have a moral, Link's fairy tales most emphatically do not. In "The Lesson," a story based on her own harrowing experience giving birth to a premature baby, Link addresses this directly, arguing that there is no lesson to life's events, only love and suffering.

In "I Can See Right Through You," an actor known only as "the demon lover" pursues his former flame, a fellow actor named Meggie who played his love interest in the film that made him famous. In his middle age, the demon lover is trying to live down a leaked sex tape, while Meggie, also in the twilight of her fame, hosts a cable television show about ghost hunters. While Meggie and her crew look for the ghosts of a disappeared nudist colony, the demon lover and Meggie grapple with the ghost of their romantic past, personified in the actual ghost of a woman with whom they had a sexual encounter. "I Can See Right Through You" is a pure example of Link's unusual voice: humor edged with foreboding.

"Secret Identity" is slightly lighter fare. The story is written as a letter from a teenager named Billie Faggart to a man named Paul Zell. In it, Billie, whose sarcastic and pained voice gives the story its shape, tries desperately to explain their failed encounter. Billie and Paul met in a virtual world akin to *World of Warcraft* called FarAway and decided to meet in person at a hotel in New York City. The hotel is abuzz with concurrent conferences, one for dentists and one for superheroes. Paul Zell claims to be neither, but a bad night with the minibar prevents Billie from ever finding out if he was telling the truth. The story sifts through Billie's layers of identity—her characters on FarAway and her older sister, whom she claimed to be to Paul Zell—and culminates in the spectacular destruction of superhero statues made out of butter.

"Valley of the Girls" is set in a future in which children of the wealthy elite hire actors to play them in public, the principle being that children of privilege will behave badly, and so their families can save themselves trouble and embarrassment by hiding them from view entirely. But as fertile as the concept of "Faces" is, the story turns on a morbid fad perpetuated by wealthy teenage girls. These girls, like the pharaohs of ancient Egypt, are erecting giant pyramid-style monuments to themselves and spending their days curating the contents of their tombs. The monuments are a way of staking a claim on an identity in a world where, in addition to Faces, wealthy teenagers have implants that prevent them from drinking, doing drugs, or being seen on camera.

Link layers ancient rites and futuristic practices (boys collect twentieth-century space shuttles) to bring the story to its gruesome climax.

"Origin Story" returns to the world of "Secret Identity," where ordinary people can be born with superpowers, and the most famous superheroes wearily contend with the eccentricities of villains and worry about where to buy the best costumes. The superhero in this story is a super-strong man nicknamed Biscuit, though his lover and childhood friend, Bunnatine, is a hero of a less celebrated variety. Bunnatine is a waiter in a tiny town. She has a superpower—the ability to hover a few feet off the ground—but she uses it to rest her feet on the job and, for a while, in a sexy dance routine at a strip club. Bunnatine's trials are the familiar (though no less affecting) woes of the working class, but set against the fantastical elements of her world, her story is given a new energy.

In "The New Boyfriend," a teenage girl named Immy covets her best friend's Boyfriend. The only thing is, this Boyfriend (as opposed to a boyfriend) is just a toy. There are Werewolf Boyfriends and Vampire Boyfriends, but Ainslie, who always gets what she wants, has just received the most sought-after model, the Ghost Boyfriend. The life-sized boy comes delicately wrapped in a coffin and can be set to one of two modes: embodied or spectral. In spectral mode, the Boyfriend appears randomly, hovering in dark corners like a real ghost. Creepier still, the Ghost Boyfriend also has a slot beneath his tongue where one can place a memento from a real person who has died. In a fit of jealousy, Immy attempts to win the heart of her friend's Ghost Boyfriend by inserting a Victorian-era locket holding two locks of hair into his mouth, and trouble ensues. Link's narrative voice perfectly captures the deep romantic longing and barbed friendships of adolescence. The dramatic lengths to which Immy goes just to catch a glimpse of her Ghost Boyfriend, and her resultant and inevitable heartbreak, are both funny and poignant.

In "Two Houses," Link wraps a ghost story in a science fiction package. When an astronaut named Gwenda awakes from a seven-year sleep—one of several Sleeping Beauty references in the collection—she is invited by her shipmates to her own birthday party. It may or may not be Gwenda's actual birthday, but the fact that all of the astronauts on board the spaceship (called the *House of Secrets*) are awake is a rare enough occurrence to merit its own celebration. The *House of Secrets* is run by an invisible, godlike figure named Maureen, who can move in and out of the astronauts' minds and monitor their vitals. She wakes them up and bathes them, and when they tell each other ghost stories, she transforms the interior of the ship into settings from their memories and imaginations. Of the stories in the collection that explore the authentic versus the artificial, this one is the most overt. It asks, can a place create its own ghosts?

Kelly Link's work spans several genres, including science fiction, fantasy, and horror. She has published three collections of short stories and lives in Northampton, Massachusetts.

The final story in the collection, "Light," takes place in a world in which people can be suddenly stricken with sleep from which they cannot wake, and there exist a number of pocket universes, accessible from various places on Earth. The story's protagonist, Lindsay, works at a warehouse full of sleepers. Her husband, a seven-feet-tall alien, recently left her, and now she drinks too much and contemplates the mundanities of her world: second shadows, weather witches, and the most irritating of invasive species, mermaids. But as in the rest of Link's stories, the fantastical world in which Lindsay lives seems to have little bearing on her sad-sack existence. When her wily brother Alan comes to stay with her, he sets in motion a chain of events that allow her to discover the possibilities of her own life. Link's stories are deeply strange, but they are also satisfying. She uses fantasy to explore real human emotions. Link's images (such as wealthy teenage girls building pyramids) do not satirize the world in which we live but rather allow readers to see it more clearly.

Molly Hagan

Review Sources

Dirda, Michael. "Kelly Link's Fantastic, Fantastical *Get in Trouble*." Rev. of *Get in Trouble*, by Kelly Link. *Washington Post*. Washington Post, 18 Feb. 2015. Web. 21 Sept. 2015.

Kelly, Stuart. "Kelly Link's New Collection of Fantastical Short Stories." Rev. of *Get in Trouble*, by Kelly Link. *Guardian*. Guardian News and Media, 25 Feb. 2015. Web. 21 Sept. 2015.

Thomas, Scarlett. Rev. of *Get in Trouble*, by Kelly Link. *New York Times*. New York Times, 13 Feb. 2015. Web. 21 Sept. 2015.

Ulin, David L. "In *Get in Trouble*, Kelly Link Melds Ordinary and Bizarre." Rev. of *Get in Trouble*, by Kelly Link. *Los Angeles Times*. Tribune, 29 Jan. 2015. Web. 21 Sept. 2015.

Wolitzer, Meg. "Ignoring the Rules, Kelly Link Traffics in Wonder, Irony and Teenage Longings." Rev. of *Get in Trouble*, by Kelly Link. *NPR*. NPR, 10 Feb. 2015. Web. 21 Sept. 2015.

Ghettoside
A True Story of Murder in America

Author: Jill Leovy
Publisher: Spiegel & Grau (New York). 366 pp.
Type of work: Current affairs
Time: Early 2000s
Locale: Los Angeles, California

Ghettoside *is a brilliantly written exploration of the epidemic of unsolved murders plaguing many urban minority neighborhoods. Jill Leovy dissects the forces underlying these murders while chronicling the efforts of a Los Angeles police detective to track the killers of a fellow officer's son.*

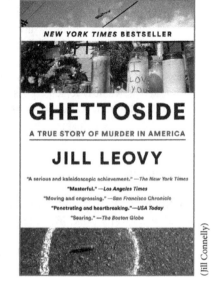

Principal personages:
BRYANT TENNELLE, a young man murdered on the streets of Los Angeles
WALLACE TENNELLE, his father, a detective with the Los Angeles Police Department (LAPD)
JOHN SKAGGS, the LAPD detective assigned to solve his murder

Jill Leovy's *Ghettoside: A True Story of Murder in America* is a stunning and insightful analysis of a national tragedy. Urban violence is an American plague. Although the murder rate in the United States has declined significantly since the 1990s, the number of homicides remains appallingly high. Sometimes a spike in the murder rate is reported by the media, such as the recent spate of homicides in Chicago. In 2015, 468 Chicagoans were murdered and more than 2,900 were shot. On these occasions television cameras are rushed to the scene of the latest crime, and reporters provide their viewers with a few bare facts about the victims while silhouetted against the flashing lights of police cars. However, most of the time the attention paid to urban violence is perfunctory. The incessant murders are seen as somehow inevitable and chalked up to the persistent but intractable evils of poverty, drugs, and gang-related violence. One reason that these murders are often put out of mind is because they are usually out of sight. This carnage is not distributed evenly across neighborhoods and communities in the United States. These killings are concentrated in rundown, usually segregated sections of cities. Disproportionately the shooters and their victims are black. Young black men make up just 6 percent of the US population but comprise almost 40 percent of murder victims.

Jill Leovy has been a reporter for the *Los Angeles Times* since the early 1990s. While covering news in the city she grew concerned about the apathy over the unsolved

murders in South Los Angeles, the district
once known as South Central. In the early
1990s, black men in Los Angeles County
were dying at a higher rate than American
soldiers during the Iraq War in 2005. The
African American community in South Los
Angeles was suffering the casualty rate of a
war, yet few outsiders seemed to notice or to
care. In late 2006 Leovy began the blog *The
Homicide Report* in an attempt to have all the
murder victims in the city have their story
told. From these efforts, Leovy was inspired
to write *Ghettoside*.

(Courtesy of Random House)

Leovy believes that the failure of the US
criminal justice system to successfully pros-
ecute these murders is ultimately rooted in
racism. This does not lead her to simplistic
denunciations of the "system." Nor will her
recommendations endear her to the Black
Lives Matter movement. For example, Leovy demonstrates that high black murder rates
are deeply rooted in history. There is scholarly evidence for disproportionate numbers

*Jill Leovy has been a reporter for the
Los Angeles Times since 1993. She
shared the Pulitzer Prize for breaking
news with five of her coworkers in 1998.
In 2006 she started the blog* The Homicide Project, *where she attempts to log
every murder in Los Angeles County.*

of homicides among African Americans dating back to the 1890s. The United States
government began collecting racially aggregated crime statistics in 1950. From the
1980s through the early 2000s, black Americans were six times more likely to be the
victim of a homicide than white Americans and eight times more likely to commit a
homicide. In Los Angeles during the 2000s, black men were two to four more times
likely to kill and be killed than Hispanic men who lived in the same part of town.
Even as homicide rates in general were declining in the twenty-first century, murder
remained a persistently disproportionate scourge for African Americans. The black
murder rate was a problem that few were willing to publicly address. Black Americans
did not want to call attention to an issue that would resurrect unfair stereotypes. White
Americans did not want to appear racist. It was easier to look away. Leovy believes
that this unwillingness to confront black murder rates lies at the heart of the problem.
She argues convincingly that official indifference to the murder of black men by other
black men is the root cause of the high black homicide rate. She believes that African
Americans in blighted urban neighborhoods need something enjoyed by more privileged communities—law and order.

Leovy highlights research contending that murder rates rise in situations where
lawlessness prevails and convictions are rare, prompting a rise in vigilantism. Modern
black homicide rates are comparable to those in turbulent developing countries and
the American frontier. Leovy argues that black Americans suffer from the absence
of what the sociologist Max Weber termed the state monopoly on violence, which

Leovy explains as "the government's exclusive right to exercise legitimate force." Without a strong governmental authority exacting sure and impartial justice, people who feel wronged turn to private remedies. From the days of slavery and beyond, African Americans have been shortchanged by the law. In the postbellum Jim Crow South, the authorities ruthlessly punished black people who committed crimes against white victims but showed less concern about black-on-black crimes. Conviction rates for the murders of African Americans ranged around 30 percent, and sentences for these crimes were relatively lenient. The situation in Northern cities was not much better. In the nineteenth century, urban law enforcement had a poor record of arresting and sentencing any murderers. Conviction rates remained low well into the twentieth century. African Americans fared extremely poorly in this system. Many black Americans could not confidently expect justice of the authorities.

In Los Angeles, between 1994 and 2006, there were arrests in only 38 percent of the cases involving the murder of a black man. Including instances in which the suspects were killed themselves or died of other causes, less than half of black homicides in Los Angeles were solved. The situation was even worse with nonlethal shootings; only 17 percent of these cases resulted in a conviction. In South Los Angeles, a lack of security led people to pursue individual justice. Vengeance became privatized. Gangs imposed their own form of law. Killings were punished by retributory killings in a countless series of drive-by shootings. Many witnesses to shootings refused to cooperate with police investigations for the entirely rational reason that they would likely be killed if they did so. Over time, South Los Angeles descended into the tragic state typical of so many other American urban centers, where the regular killing of black men by other black men became routine and, because the killings were largely localized in a few neighborhoods, could be accepted and ignored by the rest of the city. In a sad echo of the old South, black killers of black victims were less likely to receive the death penalty than black killers of white victims. Tacitly American society was sending the message that it regarded the young black men who killed and were killed in shockingly disproportionate numbers as relatively expendable. They had become casualties of what one Los Angeles police detective called "the Monster," a dysfunctional social environment exacerbated by despair and indifference.

Leovy does not believe that most police officers in Los Angeles are racist. LAPD officers are forced to wrestle daily with the malign manifestations of "the Monster." The "broken windows" approach to crime-fighting led to an emphasis on preventive policing. This reduced tolerance for lower levels of criminal activity has helped revitalize many districts of American cities but at the price of bearing down heavily on poor Hispanic and African Americans, many of whom find themselves arrested and jailed on drug, prostitution, and other quality-of-life charges. What this new form of aggressive policing does not do is solve the major threat to vulnerable African American communities, a murder rate that undermines all sense of security. In an era when the police presence in African American communities is coming under increasing scrutiny, Leovy's paradoxical message is that these neighborhoods are not suffering from too much policing but rather too little. Leovy makes a passionate and convincing case that "the Monster" will not be quelled until the police bring the black murder rate under control, tirelessly pursuing all murder investigations and liberating the inhabitants of threatened communities from the menace of privatized violence.

Leovy illustrates her points by looking at the work of dedicated homicide detectives in South Los Angeles. "Ghettoside" is a term that a detective picked up from a gang member in Watts. The term describes both the geographical locale of South Los Angeles and the existential predicament of its inhabitants. "Ghettoside" is a state of mind embraced by many of the detectives who take pride in working this demanding district. They see themselves as working on the cutting edge of their profession, where their abilities are tested to the limit and are most needed. Many are profoundly distressed by the toll that murder takes in South Los Angeles. Every day they see the grieving loved ones of the dead. These murders are not abstractions or statistics to them.

One such detective was Wallace Tennelle. A resident of South Los Angeles himself, Tennelle left home for a tour of service in the Marine Corps. While he was in the Marines, Tennelle married a young woman whom he met in Costa Rica. Returning to Los Angeles, Tennelle joined the LAPD and worked his way up to a distinguished career as a homicide detective. Most Los Angeles police prefer to live in the city's comfortable and safe suburbs. As a matter of principle, Tennelle chose to live in his old neighborhood. There he and his wife raised three children, a girl and two boys. Tennelle's two eldest children flourished in school and went on to college. His youngest son, Bryant, struggled academically and was diagnosed with attention deficit disorder. Despite this, Bryant was bright and popular. He successfully completed coursework to enable him to graduate from high school. He was looking forward to a job with the Los Angeles Department of Recreation and Parks working with young people. One Friday evening in 2007, eighteen-year-old Bryant Tennelle was walking down the street with a friend. Gunfire rang out, and he fell to the ground, shot in the head.

The Tennelle murder case was eventually given to Detective John Skaggs. Like many LAPD detectives, Skaggs lived in the suburbs and voted Republican. Tall and blond, he was a surfer and outdoorsman in his spare time. However incongruous Skaggs might appear on the streets of South Los Angeles, he was bound to the district by his determination to reverse the poor clearance rates in murder investigations. He believed that every murder victim deserved justice, even the most hardened criminal. He became one of the most admired detectives in the LAPD, with a clearance rate of 80 to 90 percent. Skaggs did not solve cases through Sherlock Holmes–like feats of ratiocination. Instead he focused on careful and dogged fieldwork, questioning and requestioning witnesses and relentlessly pursuing leads. Other detectives called a case solved by hard work and persistence a "John Skaggs special." Leovy's book becomes a gripping police procedural as Skaggs pursues those responsible for the murder of Bryant Tennelle. Along the way the reader is immersed in the gritty realities of life and violent death in a deeply damaged community.

For Jill Leovy, the hope of banishing "the Monster" lies in the work of detectives like John Skaggs. Only by supporting the efforts of such skilled and committed detectives can the authorities reverse the social conditions that incubate the high urban murder rate. However, she emphasizes how underresourced the LAPD homicide detectives are, buying the notebooks for their case notes and tape recorders for witness interviews out of their own pockets. In her masterful narrative of the murder of Bryant Tennelle and its aftermath, Leovy combines brilliant reporting and compelling advocacy. *Ghettoside* is a timely and powerful book, one destined to become a classic account of crime and punishment in one of America's great cities.

Daniel P. Murphy

Review Sources

Fletcher, Connie. Rev. of Ghettoside, by Jill Leovy. *Booklist Online*. Booklist, 1 Nov. 2014. Web. 8 Feb. 2016.

Garner, Dwight. "Putting 'Black Lives Matter' into Action." Rev. of *Ghettoside*, by Jill Leovy. *New York Times*. New York Times, 22 Jan. 2015. Web. 8 Feb. 2016.

Gattis, Ryan. "Ghettoside Is a Bold, Humane Study of Los Angeles' Black Homicide Epidemic." Rev. of *Ghettoside*, by Jill Leovy. *New Statesman*. New Statesman, 21 May 2015. Web. 8 Feb. 2016.

Rev. of *Ghettoside*, by Jill Leovy. *Kirkus*. Kirkus Media, 6 Nov. 2014. Web. 8 Feb. 2016.

Rev. of *Ghettoside*, by Jill Leovy. *Publishers Weekly*. PWxyz, Jan. 2015. Web. 8 Feb. 2016.

"Murder, She Wrote." Rev. of *Ghettoside*, by Jill Leovy. *Economist*. Economist Newspaper, 7 Mar. 2015. Web. 8 Feb. 2016.

The Girl in the Spider's Web

Author: David Lagercrantz (b. 1962)
First published: *Det som inte dödar oss,* 2015, in Sweden
Translated from the Swedish by: George Goulding
Publisher: Alfred A. Knopf (New York). 416 pp.
Type of work: Novel
Time: Modern day
Locale: United States, Sweden

The Girl in the Spider's Web *is the fourth novel in the Millennium series and the first to be written by Lagercrantz. It tells the story of the aftermath of a successful hacking of the databases at the NSA.*

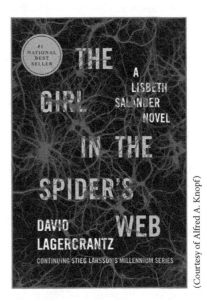

(Courtesy of Alfred A. Knopf)

Principal characters:
LISBETH SALANDER, hacker extraordinaire and outsider with a complicated past
CAMILLA SALANDER, her twin
MIKAEL BLOMKVIST, topnotch investigative reporter for Millennium magazine
FRANS BALDER, a computer scientist who has made a breakthrough in Artificial Intelligence (AI) technology
AUGUST BALDER, Frans's autistic son
EDWIN NEEDHAM, chief of Internet security at the National Security Agency (NSA)

The Millennium series is the creation of Stieg Larsson, a Swedish journalist who died before the publication of any of the three books he had written. More than 80 million copies of his books have sold worldwide and also have been made into films. Larsson's estate sought another author to continue the series. It was a controversial decision, opposed by Larsson's long-time partner, Eva Gabrielsson, who viewed the publication as a "money grab." The rationale given for the fourth book is that Larsson always envisioned the Millennium series as comprising ten books. Also, Lisbeth Salander, the main character in the Millennium series, is unique and beloved, and many aspects of her personality were left unexplored by Larsson.

Lagercrantz came to write *The Girl in the Spider's Web* after his agent, who had also been Larsson's, suggested it. Lagercrantz was already known for the autobiography he had ghostwritten for soccer star Zlatan Ibrahimovic, and his work as a journalist. Lagercrantz agreed to write the new Millennium novel with some trepidation; he was wary of taking the assignment because of the worldwide appeal of Salander. Once he agreed to write the novel, he created a plot that he hoped would satisfy Larsson's many fans. In addition to having a new author, *The Girl in the Spider's Web* introduces a new translator, George Goulding. (Reg Keeland translated the three prior novels.)

The Girl in the Spider's Web continues the story of Lisbeth Salander, a social outcast and genius hacker who has a penchant for justice. Because of her abusive childhood, as well as the abuse she has suffered at the hands of the very institutions created to protect vulnerable people such as herself, she trusts no one initially. Salander is fiercely independent, but her full biography is largely unexplained—Larsson filled in many blanks about her past but did not get around to filling in details about her present life. Her actions largely define her character, often leaving the character of Mikael Blomkvist a bit confused. Blomkvist is a respected journalist who helped clear Salander's name, earning her trust in the process. He is intrigued by Salander and willing to accept her on her terms. Similarly, Salander's hacking ability has earned her the respect of so-called white hat hackers, who consider her their de facto leader. In *The Girl in the Spider's Web*, the mutual trust and respect between Salander and Blomkvist is fundamental to their ability to work together to unravel the mystery of who has hacked the NSA and why.

At the start of the novel, Blomkvist is approached to write about the crime, but he is not interested until he hears that a mysterious female hacker is involved. He has not been in contact with Salander for some time and is immediately interested in working on any story that will lead him to her. Before he can interview Frans Balder, Balder is killed in front of his young son, August. Blomkvist arrives on the scene to find August alive and cowering. August is autistic and does not communicate with others, so his importance to the case is unrecognized at first. Not until Salander becomes involved with the boy is his vital piece of the puzzle discovered.

Lagercrantz opts to leave Salander in the background for much of the novel, a decision that has met with mixed reviews. For example, Karolina Waclawiak for the *Los Angeles Times*, claims the book lacks energy because Salander is absent, while Sophie Gilbert for the *Atlantic* felt Salander's role in the novel adds to its tension. Either way, Salander's presence is felt from the moment Edwin Needham receives a message on his screen: "Chill out, Ed. Why don't you stick around for a ride? I've got Root." Lagercrantz continues, "The word "Root" brought down his whole world." Thus, those familiar with Salander's genius as a hacker understand that it is just a matter of time before she appears in the story.

David Lagercrantz is the best-selling author and Swedish journalist chosen to write the fourth novel in Stieg Larsson's Millennium series. Lagercrantz is best known for ghostwriting a controversial autobiography of sports figure Zlatan Ibrahimovic.

Larsson wrote the first three novels with a tension that made them page-turners; Lagercrantz writes *The Girl in the Spider's Web* in a similarly compelling, but more nuanced, way. Some reviewers, such as Mark Lawson for the *Guardian*, have mentioned that the writing in *The Girl in the Spider's Web* is of a better quality than Larsson's. While Larsson was more commercial in his approach to his tale, Lagercrantz is slightly more literary. He also invests more in the characters around Salander, as he fills in the backstory of several recurring characters. This is markedly different from Larsson's style, but, in his zeal to portray a fully realized world, Lagercrantz stops short of overexplaining Salander. He fills in only a bit more of her background than Larsson did, specifically details that are relevant to the plot of the fourth novel. Lagercrantz's restraint in this way ensures that he does not wrap up Salander in a neat package; rather, he leaves some of her motives a bit cloudy, as was the case in the first three books.

The first three books in the Millenium series included Blomkvist's work as a journalist and his commitment to social justice, and in *The Girl in the Spider's Web*, Blomkvist's work is again a central part of the plot. While not as overtly political as the previous books, *The Girl in the Spider's Web* continues the plot line of the plight of *Millenium*, the magazine Blomkvist cocreated and for which he writes. In *The Girl in the Spider's Web,* much is made about the limited funding available for a publication more interested in journalism-for-justice's sake than journalism for the sake of money. Lagercrantz devotes a significant portion of the novel to the ways in which even those with the best of intentions must contend with the reality of the costs associated with funding a periodical.

Blomkvist's career is part of the plot of this novel. While he is at his ascendency in the first three novels, this one finds him grappling with the fact that he is perceived as past his prime. To further complicate matters, he is not sure of what to do next with his life or his writing. This brings additional, and satisfying, weight to Blomkvist's character.

Though some critics, such as Patrick Anderson for the *Washington Post*, feel that Lagercrantz has not lived up fully to his task with *The Girl in the Spider's Web*, the book has been well received commercially. It had a first run of 500,000 copies with more than 200,000 copies sold during the first two weeks, showing that there is an enduring interest in this series. This interest is largely based on the compelling nature of Lisbeth Salander. Larsson based his quirky character on the beloved Pippi Longstocking character created by Astrid Lindgren. As was the case with Longstocking, Salander lives by her own rules, largely untroubled by the reactions of those around her. Lagercrantz not only continued this character trait in his portrayal of Salander but also alludes to Longstocking several times in *The Girl with the Spider's Web*, which has been viewed as a sort of homage by Lagercrantz to Larsson's conception of Salander.

In addition to solidifying the characters that will recur as the rest of the Millennium series plays out, Lagercrantz introduces one significant new character, Camilla Salander, who is Lisbeth Salander's twin. Camilla had not been alluded to previously in the series. This is explained by the fact that Lisbeth is estranged from her.

Lagercrantz has been widely congratulated on bringing Salander back to the page. He has taken the time to provide a fuller understanding of the recurring characters, solidifying their role as staples in the Millennium series. He has made the series his own with his unique writing style and approach to character development. He has also affirmed the role of the recurring characters. All of this is a significant accomplishment given the fame of the series prior to his role as author.

Gina Hagler

Review Sources

Anderson, Patrick. "'The Girl in the Spider's Web' Review: Lisbeth Salander Hacks On." Rev. of *The Girl in the Spider's Web*, by David Lagercrantz. *Washington Post*. Washington Post, 26 Aug. 2015. Web. 29 Nov. 2015.

Gilbert, Sophie. "Lisbeth Salander: The Girl Who Survived Her Creator." Rev. of *The Girl in the Spider's Web*, by David Lagercrantz. *Atlantic*. Atlantic Monthly Company, 27 Sept. 2015. Web. 29 Nov. 2015.

Kakutani, Michiko. "Review: 'The Girl in the Spider's Web' Brings Back Stieg Larsson's Detective Duo." Rev. of *The Girl in the Spider's Web*, by David Lagercrantz. *New York Times*. New York Times, 26 Aug. 2015. Web. 29 Nov. 2015.

Lawson, Mark. "The Girl in the Spider's Web Review—A Controversial Addition to Stieg Larsson's Millennium Trilogy." Rev. of *The Girl in the Spider's Web*, by David Lagercrantz. *Guardian*. Guardian News and Media, 27 Aug. 2015. Web. 29 Nov. 2015.

Waclawiak, Karolina. "Does 'The Girl in the Spider's Web' Hurt the Legacy of Stieg Larsson's Lisbeth Salander?" Rev. of *The Girl in the Spider's Web*, by David Lagercrantz. *Los Angeles Times*. Los Angeles Times, 27 Aug. 2015. Web. 29 Nov. 2015.

The Girl on the Train

Author: Paula Hawkins (b. 1972)
Publisher: Riverhead Books (New York). 336 pp.
Type of work: Novel
Time: 2013
Locale: London and its environs

A psychological mystery, The Girl on the Train *is about the disappearance of a young woman and the commuter who tries to help the investigation by telling what she witnessed from aboard a passing train. When the book came out in January 2015, it quickly became one of the best-selling adult mysteries in publishing history.*

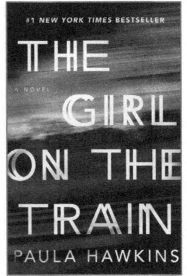

(Courtesy of Riverhead Books)

Principal characters:

RACHEL WATSON, a divorced, unemployed woman who believes she has relevant information about a missing woman

MEGAN HIPWELL, an unemployed housewife who disappears and is later found dead

SCOTT HIPWELL, Megan's husband, a person of interest in the police investigation of her disappearance

TOM WATSON, Rachel's former husband who lives in the same neighborhood as Megan Hipwell

ANNA WATSON, Tom's wife and former mistress, for whom Tom left Rachel

DR. KAMAL ABDIC, a psychologist who was counseling Megan, a suspect in her disappearance

DETECTIVE INSPECTOR GASKILL, the London police officer leading the investigation into Megan's disappearance

DETECTIVE SERGEANT RILEY, a London police officer assisting in the investigation

As Rachel Watson rides the train each morning, she notes a certain house. Occasionally, she sees the attractive young owners outside. They seem to be a perfect couple, and soon Rachel begins to spin fantasies about their lives. She pictures them as vivacious people, with full and fascinating lives, who are very much in love with each other. She makes up names for them, "Jess" and "Jason."

Rachel is a divorced alcoholic whose drinking contributed to the breakup of her marriage and later caused her to lose her job at a London public-relations firm. Her former husband, Tom, and his new wife, Anna, still live in the house Rachel once shared with Tom, just a few doors away from the residence she watches each day on her commute on the train. The young couple she watches from the train did not live in the neighborhood when she did; they must have moved in after her divorce. When her marriage ended, Rachel moved in with a college friend named Cathy. When she later lost her job, she was embarrassed to tell Cathy, so she has continued to ride into central London every day on the train, maintaining the illusion that she is employed. In town, she goes to libraries, occasionally works on her résumé, and spends time in parks, pubs, and liquor stores. She likes riding the train, watching her fellow commuters, and seeing the scenery pass by, and the routine of the regular trips in and out of the city seem to provide some structure and purpose for her dreary life.

One day she sees "Jess" outside the house with a different man. Jess kisses the man, and Rachel assumes the two are involved in an affair. Rachel's fantasy of the perfect life she has pictured for Jess and Jason is destroyed, and she is incensed at Jess—how could she have done this to the perfect husband that Rachel has made Jason out to be in her mind?

(Kate Neil)

Paula Hawkins studied at Oxford University and became a business editor at the Times of London. Writing under the pen name Amy Silver, she wrote four novels for young women. She has also written a financial advice book, The Money Goddess: The Financial Guide for Women *(2007).*

Reality soon intrudes on Rachel's fantasy world when there are reports in the press about a woman missing from the neighborhood where Rachel used to live. She recognizes the address as the house she has been watching. She learns that the woman she had called Jess was Megan Hipwell, an unemployed housewife who had previously run a small art gallery. Her husband, Scott, is a self-employed IT consultant (Rachel is disappointed to learn this—she had imagined he was involved in some more noble calling). As usual in cases of suspected violence in domestic situations, the police consider Scott a potential suspect. Besides Scott, the police also show some interest in Dr. Kamal Abdic, a counselor that Megan had been seeing. The official investigation does not seem to progress very far; as in any disappearance, there is the chance Megan just left of her own accord, ran off with another lover, or met with violence by the hands of some unknown person.

Rachel has never really accepted the finality of her separation from Tom, and she occasionally calls him on one pretext or another. One evening, she goes to see him but never gets to the house. She is apparently intoxicated, and she later remembers that she saw something happen in or near a railroad underpass close to the station in her old neighborhood, but she cannot remember exactly what it was she witnessed. It turns out that this was the same night when Megan disappeared, and when the police learn that Rachel had been seen in the area, they come to interview her. Initially, Rachel says nothing about her suspicions of Megan having an affair, and, in fact, lies to the police about knowing anything about Megan or her disappearance. Later, however, Rachel decides that she needs to tell the police about the man she saw with Megan, who could be a potential suspect. She finds that the police are less than enthused about her injecting herself into the investigation. Rachel herself realizes they consider her a "rubbernecker"—someone with an unhealthy curiosity about the crime and the intimate life of these complete strangers. She also recognizes that she comes across as somewhat unstable, mentally and emotionally, and believes the police will discount anything she has told them.

Since she believes the police will not pursue the lead she has given them about Megan's possible affair, Rachel eventually contacts Megan's husband, Scott Hipwell. In order to come across as a more credible source of information, she claims that she knew Megan when she ran her art gallery. Scott initially has trouble putting much credence in anything Rachel has to say, but he is interested in the fact that someone involved in an affair with Megan could well be a suspect in her disappearance. Scott and Rachel begin a strange and rocky relationship, but Scott continues to have difficulty believing that Rachel might be a reliable witness and at times wonders if she is trying to gather evidence against him, rather than seeking to help him.

After a few weeks, during which the investigation into Megan's disappearance has made little headway, Megan's body is found not far from where she was last seen. But while the police inquiry shifts to a murder investigation, there still is little progress toward an actual resolution of the case.

The book alternates between chapters narrated by the three main female characters—Rachel, Megan, and Anna. Since Megan's disappearance happens relatively early in the book, the chapters in which she speaks are flashbacks to earlier times, leading up to the time of her disappearance. To some extent, these flashbacks complicate the flow of the narrative. Also, there are a few coincidences involved that may strain readers' credulity—the house Rachel watches happens to be in her old neighborhood, and the Hipwells know Rachel's former husband Tom and his new wife, Anna. (In fact, for a brief time, Megan had cared for Tom and Anna's baby, Evie.)

Part of what draws the reader into this story is the complex character of Rachel. She battles alcoholism and depression and gets caught in recurring cycles of self-destructive behavior. She realizes that the police consider her an unreliable witness and also that they might well wonder about her stalker-like behavior in watching the Hipwells so intently.

Rachel's inner turmoil is clearly pictured, but other characters also come across as complex, flawed personalities. Scott Hipwell seems to have been a controlling husband with some violent tendencies. Megan also had a traumatic past and was cheating on her husband. Tom Watson struggles with what to do with a former wife that seems to be stalking his family, and Anna both loathes and fears Rachel. As the main character and principal narrator, Rachel is a protagonist who is difficult to admire. One might cheer her decision to share what she knows, or thinks she knows, about Megan's apparent affair. But she has many strikes against her that make it difficult for either the police or Scott to put much credence in what she says. She is not a particularly likeable character, but since all people are flawed, perhaps readers can identify with her struggles.

Besides the finely wrought human characters in the book, the train—or perhaps the whole commuting experience—is virtually a character in the book. Rachel likes the train, once saying there is no place she would rather be. Author Paula Hawkins had some experience commuting on the London subway system, which does run aboveground in certain areas, and her fascination with the railroad is reflected in Rachel's experiences.

Books that delve deeply into the interior lives of mixed-up characters can get tedious at times. But generally the pace is lively in *The Girl on the Train*. There are a few well-done plot twists that come along frequently enough to keep the reader's interest. Hawkins also throws in several red herrings and some instances of foreshadowing from which an astute reader might foresee the outcome.

Several reviewers have compared the book to Gillian Flynn's wildly successful novel *Gone Girl* (2012). In a March 2015 interview with Clark Collis in *Entertainment Weekly*, Hawkins dismissed the suggestions of influence from Flynn's well-received novel. Although she read *Gone Girl*, Hawkins was well into the writing of her book beforehand.

The book has generally garnered positive—in some cases, rave—reviews. The publishers undertook a massive publicity and social-media campaign to promote the book before publication and were rewarded with impressive sales from the beginning. The book quickly climbed to the top of several best-seller lists. By August 2015, it had gone through twenty-seven printings, with more than three million copies sold. DreamWorks Studio purchased the film rights to the book shortly before the book's publication and began production with an anticipated release date of late 2016.

Mark S. Joy

Review Sources

Maloney, Jennifer. "Is 'The Girl on the Train' the New 'Gone Girl'?" Rev. of *The Girl on the Train*, by Paula Hawkins. *Wall Street Journal*. Dow Jones, 22 Jan. 2015. Web. 4 Dec. 2015.

Maslin, Janet. "Another Girl Gone in a Tale of Betrayal." Rev. of *The Girl on the Train*, by Paula Hawkins. *New York Times*. New York Times, 4 Jan. 2015. Web. 4 Dec. 2015.

Schaub, Michael. "'Girl on the Train' Pays Homage to Hitchcock." Rev. of *The Girl on the Train*, by Paula Hawkins. *NPR Books*. NPR, 13 Jan. 2015. Web. 4 Dec. 2015.

Girl Waits with Gun

Author: Amy Stewart (b. 1969)
Publisher: Houghton Mifflin Harcourt (New York). 416 pp.
Type of work: Novel
Time: 1914–15
Locales: Paterson, Hackensack, and Wyckoff, New Jersey

(Courtesy Houghton Mifflin Harcourt)

Girl Waits with Gun is historical fiction based on real incidents in the life of Constance Kopp, one of the first women to serve as a deputy sheriff in the United States. Constance Kopp and her two sisters face harassment from a wealthy textile-factory owner, and they are drawn into a battle involving threats, intimidation, and shootouts. Along the way, Constance helps find a missing child and discovers her unexpected strengths as an independent woman of the twentieth century.

Principal characters:
CONSTANCE KOPP, the oldest Kopp sister; brave, determined, and independent, with a secret in her past
NORMA KOPP, the middle Kopp sister, slightly antisocial with a taste for farming and pigeon keeping
FLEURETTE KOPP, the youngest Kopp sister, an attractive young woman with theatrical ambitions
HENRY KAUFMAN, the privileged and arrogant head of a silk-dyeing factory
ROBERT HEATH, the sheriff of Bergen County, New Jersey
LUCY BLAKE, a silk-factory worker
FRANCIS KOPP, Constance, Norma, and Fleurette's brother
MARION GARFINKEL, Henry Kaufman's sister

Girl Waits with Gun is a light and funny historical novel featuring a unique, no-nonsense female protagonist who does not wait for a man to rescue her. Inspired by newspaper accounts of an actual case, author Amy Stewart combined historical research and imagination to tell the story of Constance Kopp, a feisty feminist hero who fights back when she and her sisters are threatened by a boorish, entitled factory owner.

Set in a United States on the brink of major technological and sociological changes, *Girl Waits with Gun* begins in the summer of 1914 with a collision between an automobile, driven by factory owner Henry Kaufman, and a horse and buggy carrying the three Kopp sisters. The sisters suffer minor injuries, but the buggy is destroyed.

Constance, the oldest of the three, sends Henry Kaufman a bill for damages (a total of $50) then visits his factory when he ignores a second letter. Kaufman makes a crude remark about Fleurette, the youngest sister, and Constance, a tall and imposing woman who describes herself as "built like a farmer," throws him against a wall, humiliating Kaufman in front of his cronies. That night, Kaufman and his friends visit the Kopp sisters at their farm in Wyckoff, New Jersey, to begin a campaign of harassment, threats, and attacks that will culminate in a court battle that, in reality, drew front-page headlines in newspapers of its day.

Amy Stewart is best known for quirky, well-researched nonfiction works such as *Wicked Plants* (2009) and *Wicked Bugs* (2011). *Girl Waits with Gun* is her first foray into fiction, and she told NPR interviewer Steve Inskeep that she found the newspaper story that inspired it while doing research on bootlegging for *The Drunken Botanist* (2013). The Kopp sisters' bravery and independence was considered unusual for its time; in an era when women were not yet allowed to vote, Constance Kopp told news reporters, "A woman should have the right to do any sort of work she wants to, provided she can do it." Many details about the sisters' lives are still unknown. No biographies about them were ever written, and Constance Kopp, while celebrated in her time as a "plucky girl sheriff," is not even mentioned in most reference books about law enforcement. Nevertheless, she is brought to life in *Girl Waits with Gun* as a droll, deadpan first-person narrator who may remind some readers of Mattie Ross, the protagonist of Charles Portis's *True Grit* (1968).

Though the facts are few, Stewart found enough in the historical record to inspire a novel, using her imagination to fill in the missing pieces. She told interviewers that in addition to reading all the contemporary news articles about the case that she could find, she also did genealogical research and spoke with surviving family members, including Fleurette Kopp's son. Stewart's extensive research lends the tale an air of authenticity, so that even wholly fictional characters, such as Lucy Blake, feel true to life. Lucy is a worker in Henry Kaufman's silk-dyeing factory who was seduced by him and had a child. During the 1913 silk-worker strikes in Paterson, Lucy's baby was sent away to be cared for by union supporters, as many children were in real life because the striking workers faced hunger and threats of violence. However, in a fictional twist, Lucy's son disappeared, as did the people who were caring for the child. When Constance hears Lucy's story, she feels a bond of sympathy and determines to help Lucy find her son, discovering a gift for detective work in the process. In an interview for *Publishers Weekly*, Stewart told Bridget Kinsella that creating fictional characters allowed her to "better capture . . . the sheer, amazing weirdness" of the early twentieth century. Movements and issues of the time, such as the first stirrings of feminism, the rise of organized labor, and the changes in society brought about by the automobile and other new technologies, are seamlessly incorporated into the fictional narrative. Katherine A. Powers, writing in the *New York Times Book Review*, praised Stewart's skill at "integrat[ing] the beliefs and conditions of a vanished way of life into the story" without allowing such details to slow the narrative or feel like authorial intrusions.

In Stewart's vivid characterization, Constance Kopp emerges as a strong and courageous woman who refuses to play the conventional domestic role her society offers her. Instead of moving in with her brother Francis and accepting the protection he offers, Constance stands up to Henry Kaufman's repeated attempts to intimidate her. When Kaufman and his hired thugs drive by the Kopp sisters' farm at night and throw bricks through their window, Constance and her sister Norma get revolvers from Sheriff Heath and learn how to use them. Kaufman, whose unsavory friends include bootleggers and other petty criminals, even goes so far as to threaten fifteen-year-old Fleurette with kidnapping and forced prostitution. The title incident, taken straight from a contemporary newspaper headline, has Constance waiting on a deserted street corner, a gun concealed in her muff, in response to a "Black Hand letter" threatening to kill the sisters unless they hand over $1,000 to a woman messenger. The messenger never arrives, but Constance's bravery causes a flurry of publicity. In an era when the damsel-in-distress model was still very much the norm, newspapers are intrigued by a woman who puts herself in harm's way to capture a criminal.

At thirty-five, Constance Kopp has led a fairly aimless life. Some early attempts to train for a career in nursing or law were stymied by her disapproving mother, and she fears that when the sisters' small inheritance runs out, she will be forced to live out the rest of her life in domestic drudgery. While the Henry Kaufman affair comes with moments of real danger, it also brings excitement and sense of purpose that Constance feels has been missing from her life. Her sisters, even the normally dour Norma, agree that it has been the most interesting year of their lives. Not only does Constance gain confidence from standing up to Kaufman, but she also helps another investigator by taking some photographs from inside a hotel room and conducts her own private investigation by tracking down Lucy Blake's missing child—a process that helps Constance come to terms with some secrets from her own past. At one point, encouraged by her successes, Constance applies for a job as a store detective, but she is told she is not unobtrusive enough for the job. Fortunately for Constance, and for readers who want to hear more of her adventures, another job in law enforcement is waiting for her, thanks to Sheriff Heath.

Amy Stewart received a National Endowment for the Arts fellowship for The Earth Moved: On the Remarkable Achievements of Earthworms *(2004) and a 2014 International Association of Culinary Professionals Judges' Choice Award for* The Drunken Botanist *(2013).* Wicked Plants *(2009) was a* New York Times *best seller and winner of the 2010 American Horticultural Society Book Award.*

Reviews were enthusiastic for Amy Stewart's first venture into fiction, with critics praising her ability to combine historical research with a quick-moving and engaging story line. A few reviewers wished Stewart had been able to give the Kopp sisters' lives a full nonfiction account, but they acknowledged the difficulty of finding detailed primary sources. While critics noted the authenticity of the setting and deftly interwoven historical details of *Girl Waits with Gun*, most singled out the character of Constance as the novel's greatest strength. *Kirkus Reviews* called *Girl Waits with Gun* a "solid, absorbing novel" whose main source of enjoyment is its gutsy, independent hero. *Publishers Weekly* called Constance a "pistol-packing spinster" whose adventures, both daring and comical, form "an exhilarating yarn." Carol Memmott of the *Washington Post* had high praise for Stewart's ability to bring even minor characters to colorful life, but she singled out Constance Kopp as a show-stealing, rule-breaking hero.

Sarah Cohn reviewed Stewart's novel for *Library Journal* as essentially genre fiction, suggesting it would appeal to fans of both historical and mystery fiction and praising Constance Kopp as "a welcome addition to the genre of the unconventional female sleuth." Jen Baker, writing for *Booklist*, also placed *Girl Waits with Gun* in the context of other historical mysteries, such as Laurie R. King's Mary Russell–Sherlock Holmes series; she called the novel "a sheer delight to read" and praised Stewart's ability to combine unexpected humor with fast-paced plotting. *NPR*'s Genevieve Valentine called *Girl Waits with Gun* "charming fiction" that approaches its sometimes frightening subject matter with sly humor and irony. Constance stands up to Henry Kaufman and his thugs, certainly, but she also takes on the expectations of society, and even her own brother, by refusing to conform to the role of helpless female. Katherine Powers similarly commented on Stewart's use of humor to leaven what could have been a grim account of a powerful man's campaign of terror against three innocent (though never helpless) women. Constance's dry, pragmatic first-person narration underplays her own heroism while making it clear that she is a woman who will do whatever she needs to do to protect her family. Amy Stewart has created a novel rich in historical detail with a strong hero who is both recognizably of her era and refreshingly ahead of her time.

Kathryn Kulpa

Review Sources

Baker, Jen. Rev. of *Girl Waits with Gun*, by Amy Stewart. *Booklist* 1 June 2015: 59. Print.

Cohn, Sarah. Rev. of *Girl Waits with Gun*, by Amy Stewart. *Library Journal* 15 June 2015: 81. Print.

Rev. of *Girl Waits with Gun*, by Amy Stewart. *Kirkus Reviews* 1 July 2015: 34. Print.

Rev. of *Girl Waits with Gun*, by Amy Stewart. *Publishers Weekly* 13 July 2015: 42. Print.

Memmott, Carol. "A Feisty Heroine Inspired by a Real Detective." Rev. of *Girl Waits with Gun*, by Amy Stewart. *Washington Post*. Washington Post, 1 Sept. 2015. Web. 22 Jan. 2016.

Nathans-Kelly, Steve. Rev. of *Girl Waits with Gun*, by Amy Stewart. *Paste*. Paste Media Group, 1 Sept. 2015. Web. 22 Jan. 2016.

Powers, Katherine A. "Oh No He Didn't." Rev. of *Girl Waits with Gun*, by Amy Stewart. *New York Times Book Review* 30 Aug. 2015: 20. Print.

Valentine, Genevieve. "Truth Is Strange and Fiction Is Charming in *Girl Waits with Gun*." Rev. of *Girl Waits with Gun*, by Amy Stewart. *NPR*. NPR, 1 Sept. 2015. Web. 22 Jan. 2016.

Go Set a Watchman

Author: Harper Lee (1926–2016)
Publisher: Harper (New York). 288 pp.
Type of work: Novel
Time: Late 1950s
Locale: Maycomb, Alabama

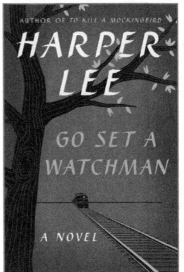

(Courtesy of HarperCollins)

Go Set a Watchman *is a novel told from the perspective of Jean Louise Finch, a southern liberal living in New York, who is shocked and disappointed when, during a visit home to Alabama, she discovers that her beloved father, Atticus, seems to be an opponent of integration.*

Principal characters:
ATTICUS FINCH, a lawyer and respected local
    figure in Maycomb, Alabama
JEAN LOUISE FINCH, his disillusioned daughter
AUNT ALEXANDRA, his somewhat pretentious and stuffy sister
HENRY "HANK" CLINTON, Jean Louise's longtime boyfriend and potential fiancé
CALPURNIA, the longtime maid of the Finch family, now retired and elderly

Go Set a Watchman (2015) was written by the beloved American author Harper Lee, famous for the novel *To Kill a Mockingbird* (1960). The latter book became a modern classic and was soon turned into a powerful motion picture starring Gregory Peck as Atticus Finch, a wise, humble, principled lawyer and widower raising two preadolescent children in the 1930s in the (fictional) small town of Maycomb, Alabama. As portrayed in both the book and the film, Atticus became an icon of the American values of fairness, justice, compassion, and tolerance. By defending a black man wrongly accused of raping a white woman, he provokes the animosity of some of his fellow citizens of Maycomb while winning the respect of his children, the town's African American community, and the generations of Americans who learned of his story by reading the book or watching the film.

Perhaps the most puzzling aspect of Lee's literary career was that *To Kill a Mockingbird* seemed to be her only novel. She never published another book after the huge success of her first one. Only in early 2015 was it announced that another novel by her—a kind of predecessor of *To Kill a Mockingbird*—had been discovered, tucked away in a safe-deposit box. By this time, Lee was elderly, infirm, and nearly deaf. The announcement that her "new" novel, *Go Set a Watchman*, would be published created an international sensation. The novel shot to the top of the best-seller lists even before it was issued, as readers "reserved" their copies in advance. Some commentators suggested that the decision to issue this book, which Lee herself had never attempted to publish, was a money-making scheme concocted by unscrupulous people taking advantage of an old woman unable to think clearly. Eventually, however, close friends of Lee, and then Lee herself, asserted that she had sanctioned publication.

When *Go Set a Watchman* finally appeared, in the summer of 2015, a huge controversy arose. Many reviewers and readers panned it, claiming it was boring, badly written, and amateurish. Far worse to many, however, was the book's presentation of Atticus Finch. The man who had once seemed to symbolize American virtue, especially on racial matters, was now revealed to have become, in his later years, an apparent racist and an avowed opponent of integration. The younger Finch, in *Mockingbird*, defends a black man against injustice; the older Finch, in *Watchman*, seems to betray all the values that had caused so many Americans to love and respect him. Many readers were disgusted by this "new" Atticus and claimed that *Watchman* had forever tainted the legacy of Atticus and of *To Kill a Mockingbird*. Many wished that the "new" book—which Lee actually wrote before *Mockingbird*—had never been published.

Harper Lee was the author of To Kill a Mockingbird, *which won the 1961 Pulitzer Prize. She was awarded the Presidential Medal of Freedom in 2007.* Go Set a Watchman *was her second novel.*

However, *Go Set a Watchman* is arguably both a better piece of fiction and a more complicated presentation of Atticus and the issue of race than its earliest critics claimed. Admittedly, the grown-up Jean Louise Finch (the young, appealing "Scout" in *Mockingbird*) is often hard to take. She seems self-involved and self-righteous, and the chapters describing her romantic relationship with Henry "Hank" Clinton are the weakest parts of the book. They speak to each other in language that sounds cloyingly cute and otherwise affected. At one point, Henry asks Jean Louise where she picked up all the wisdom she has been sharing with him that evening:

> "Living in sin in New York," she said. She lighted a cigarette and inhaled deeply. "I learned it from watching sleek, Madison Avenuey young marrieds—you know that language, baby? It's lots of fun, but you need an ear for it—they go through a kind of tribal fandango, but the application's universal."

It is hard to imagine real people speaking this way. If such people do exist, they would be as annoying in real life as they are in the pages of Lee's novel. Especially in the "romantic" sections of the book, Lee's prose often seems to fall flat or to be embarrassingly affected. One understands why Lee felt she had to include this romantic subplot, but it rarely feels entirely convincing.

The chapters involving flashbacks to Jean Louise's childhood are more effective. These scenes became the seeds of *Mockingbird*, and one can understand why Lee's editor, "Tay" Hohoff, recommended that Lee develop these aspects of *Watchman* into a full-length novel. The characters introduced in the "childhood" chapters of *Watchman*—Scout, Jem, Dill, Calpurnia, the younger Atticus—are instantly appealing. Hohoff likely recognized that American readers would be more interested in Jean Louise as the innocent, naive Scout than as the prickly, opinionated, twentysomething know-it-all. Southern author Flannery O'Connor famously and dismissively called *To Kill a Mockingbird* a "child's book," and that designation seems correct in various ways. After all, the novel features children, basically adopts their point of view, and presents, for the most part, clear villains and clear heroes. And in Atticus, it features one of the most obviously appealing American heroes ever created in a work of fiction.

Things are much messier and more complicated in *Go Set a Watchman*. In some respects, this fact works to the book's advantage, giving it greater moral ambivalence and artistic depth. Readers who fell in love with the character of Calpurnia, the Finches' black housekeeper—who, in *To Kill a Mockingbird*, is portrayed as a wise, loving, surrogate mother to two motherless children and the virtuous female complement to Atticus—will be just as stunned as Jean Louise by the Calpurnia who appears in *Go Set a Watchman*. This Calpurnia is an old woman whose grandson has recently and recklessly killed a drunk white man by accidentally striking him with a speeding car. Atticus will take the grandson's case, but he will do so partly to prevent the case from falling into the hands of northern lawyers from the National Association for the Advancement of Colored People (NAACP), whom both Atticus and Henry regard as threats to the southern legal system. When Jean Louise goes to talk to Calpurnia, all the warmth of their earlier years together is gone. Calpurnia treats Scout with a kind of formality and dignity that implies great distance:

> Jean Louise sat down again in front of her. "Cal," she cried, . . . "What are you doing to me? What's the matter? I'm your baby, have you forgotten me? Why are you shutting me out?" . . .

> Calpurnia lifted her hands and brought them down softly on the arms of the rocker. Her face was a million tiny wrinkles, and her eyes were dim behind thick lenses.

> "What are you all doing to us?" she asked.

> "Us?"

> "Yessum. Us."

This simple exchange is devastating, both to Jean Louise and to any reader who remembers the love and warmth that existed between Scout and Calpurnia in *Mockingbird*. As this scene highlights, a gap has opened between the young white woman and the old black mother figure. Calpurnia is estranged from Scout, and the pain of realizing this is almost as great for the reader as it is for Jean Louise. Lee then creates even further heartbreak:

[Jean Louise] looked into the old woman's face and knew it was hopeless. . . . in Calpurnia's eyes was no hint of compassion.

Jean Louise rose to go. "Tell me one thing, Cal . . . did you hate us?"

The old woman sat silent, bearing the burden of her years. Jean Louise waited.

Finally, Calpurnia shook her head.

This is a stunning moment. It is difficult to recall anything like it in *To Kill a Mockingbird.* It is rich and complex thematically, and the way it is written makes the scene all the more powerful and compelling. What should readers make of the simple phrase "Calpurnia shook her head"? Does her head shaking mean she did not hate the Finches, whom she served so loyally for so many years, or does it imply the opposite? The fact that she does not respond immediately suggests some hesitation, and that hesitation itself is significant. Could it be that she sometimes did hate them? Lee could have made this an unambiguous moment. But because she leaves it open to interpretation, it represents a certain complexity that is absent in *To Kill a Mockingbird.* Here and elsewhere, *Watchman* is not a simple book; its meanings are not easily discerned. In short, it is not a "child's book."

One might be able to imagine O'Connor admiring *Watchman* in ways she did not admire *Mockingbird.* She considered the latter too pat, too simplistic. *Go Set a Watchman* is just the opposite. It is difficult to imagine that *Watchman,* if it had been published in the midst of the civil rights movement, would have appealed strongly to either proponents of integration or their foes. Especially in its shocking final section, the book is too difficult to pin down, not seeming to endorse either side of the then-raging debate. In writing *Watchman,* Lee risked upsetting almost everyone who read it, for one reason or another. No wonder her editor suggested that she write *To Kill a Mockingbird* instead, and no wonder *Go Set a Watchman* remained unpublished for so many years.

Robert C. Evans

Review Sources

Corrigan, Maureen. "Harper Lee's *Watchman* Is a Mess That Makes Us Reconsider a Masterpiece." Rev. of *Go Set a Watchman*, by Harper Lee. *NPR Books*. Natl. Public Radio, 13 July 2015. Web. 2 Oct. 2015.

D'Addario, Daniel. "*Go Set a Watchman* Review: Atticus Finch's Racism Makes Scout, and Us, Grow Up." Rev. of *Go Set a Watchman*, by Harper Lee. *Time*. Time, 11 July 2015. Web. 2 Oct. 2015.

Kakutani, Michiko. "Review: Harper Lee's *Go Set a Watchman* Gives Atticus Finch a Dark Side." Rev. of *Go Set a Watchman*, by Harper Lee. *New York Times*. New York Times, 10 July 2015. Web. 2 Oct. 2015.

Lawson, Mark. "*Go Set a Watchman* Review—More Complex Than Harper Lee's Original Classic, but Less Compelling." Rev. of *Go Set a Watchman*, by Harper Lee. *Guardian*. Guardian News and Media, 13 July 2015. Web. 2 Oct. 2015.

Wood, Gaby. "*Go Set a Watchman*, Review: 'An Anxious Work in Progress.'" Rev. of *Go Set a Watchman*, by Harper Lee. *Telegraph*. Telegraph Media Group, 13 July 2015. Web. 2 Oct. 2015.

God Help the Child

Author: Toni Morrison (b. 1931)
Publisher: Alfred A. Knopf (New York). 192 pp.
Type of work: Novel
Time: Early twenty-first century, with some flashbacks to the twentieth century
Locale: California

God Help the Child, a short novel written from multiple points of view, explores perceptions of race and self-worth through the story of a young black woman rejected by her light-skinned mother and her desperate attempt to win her mother's love.

(Courtesy of Mysterious Press)

Principal characters:

Lula Ann "Bride" Bridewell, a successful, strikingly dark young African American woman

Booker Starbern, her lover, who keeps his tragic past a mystery

Sweetness, her estranged, light-skinned mother

Brooklyn, her close friend, a white coworker at a cosmetics company

Sofia Huxley, a white schoolteacher jailed when Bride falsely accused her of child molestation

Rain, an abused homeless child taken in by Evelyn and Steve

Evelyn, a hippie who lives off the grid on a farm with Steve

Steve, Evelyn's husband

Queen Olive, Booker's independent and plainspoken aunt

Toni Morrison returns to the themes of race, beauty, and childhood she introduced in her first novel, *The Bluest Eye* (1970). Unlike *The Bluest Eye*'s tragic Pecola Breedlove, Lula Ann Bridewell, who calls herself Bride, is not bound by white standards of beauty. As an executive in a cosmetics company, she dresses in white to accent her dark skin and develops a makeup line for women of color. Despite her success and seeming confidence, Bride still carries the scars of her childhood, when her light-skinned mother's revulsion at her darker skin caused her to tell a terrible lie to win her mother's approval.

　　God Help the Child is Toni Morrison's eleventh novel and her first to be set in the twenty-first century. Although the urban, contemporary setting is far from the world of slavery depicted in Morrison's award-winning novel *Beloved* (1987), the characters still must contend with the legacy of slavery. When Bride's mother, Sweetness, first sees her newborn child, she recoils from the infant whose "Sudanese" blackness seems an unwelcome reminder of their African roots. Not believing such a dark-skinned child could come from light-skinned parents, Bride's father abandons them. Sweetness confesses that she thought of giving her child away and even, for a moment, considered killing her. When Sweetness looks for apartments, she leaves Bride with a babysitter; although it is the 1990s and housing discrimination is illegal, Sweetness knows it

Toni Morrison is the author of eleven novels, including the Pulitzer Prize–winning Beloved *(1987), and has also written plays, children's books, and literary criticism. She served as a professor at Princeton University from 1989 until her retirement in 2006. She was the first African American woman to win the Nobel Prize for Literature.*

still exists in subtle ways. She justifies her strict treatment of her daughter as a way to prepare her for the harshness she will face in the world. Bride's color, she believes, will always be a handicap in a white-dominated culture.

Abused children haunt the pages of *God Help the Child*. Bride faces the emotional abuse of rejection by a parent. She remembers misbehaving in the hope that her mother would touch her, even in anger. At one point, she witnesses their landlord sexually abusing a young boy. Bride's mother insists she keep silent about the incident, as they cannot afford to lose their apartment. Later, Bride testifies in a child-abuse case against a teacher accused of molesting her students. The community is united in condemning the teacher, and Bride remembers her court appearance as the only time her mother seemed proud of her, even though she lied in court: Bride never saw the teacher abuse a child. Bride's lover, Booker, carries a tragic memory from his own childhood: his brother Adam was murdered by a serial killer who preyed on children. Booker muses about a tribe in Africa that would punish a murderer by forcing him to carry the rotting corpse of his victim lashed to his back, but it is he who carries the burden of his brother's death. In Morrison's world, the past is alive, shaping and informing the present in ways both symbolic and literal. Instead of the baby ghost of *Beloved*, Bride's own body seems to become a ghost of its childhood self in *God Help the Child*; manifestations of maturity—pierced ears, breasts, body hair—fade away, leaving her on the outside as she still feels on the inside: the little girl shunned and shamed for her black skin.

Bride's body transformation adds an element of magical realism to *God Help the Child*. The changes are triggered by a series of events that begins when Booker leaves Bride, telling her, "You not the woman I want." Initially, Bride shrugs off his departure, focusing instead on an ill-conceived plan to surprise Sofia, just released from prison, with a gift package of cash, a plane ticket, and samples of "YOU, GIRL" cosmetics. This attempt at atonement goes spectacularly wrong: when Sofia realizes that Bride is the girl whose false testimony sent her to prison, she responds with a brutal beating. Bride, bloodied and disfigured, hides away to heal, relying on her work friend Brooklyn to cover for her. Alone, without work to distract her, Bride becomes obsessed with finding Booker and learning why he left her. A pawn ticket leads her to an address in Whiskey, a small town in northern California, and a mysterious name, Q. Olive. When Bride undertakes a long road trip to Whiskey and is hurt in a car accident, she is rescued by Evelyn and Steve, white latter-day hippies who choose to live without electricity or running water. Recuperating in their remote cabin, Bride makes friends with Rain, a homeless child the couple have taken in, connecting to her even as she notices her own body becoming childlike. When Bride is able to leave, she finds Q. Olive to be Booker's aunt, an elderly woman known as Queen Olive. She also finds a store of writings by Booker—journal entries written in brief, prose-poetic flashes—that give her insight into his mind and emotions. She realizes that she and Booker do not really know each other, that each kept important parts of their past locked away, and they reconnect after an emotional confrontation. Not long after their reunion, an act of heroism catalyzes Bride's body to become that of a mature woman again. The novel ends on a hopeful yet skeptical note, with the final chapter bookending the first.

Shorter than many of Morrison's novels, *God Help the Child* received respectful but mixed reviews. Most critics acknowledged Morrison's past work and saw *God Help the Child* as part of Morrison's ongoing literary dialogue on race, beauty, childhood, and identity. Lionel Shriver in the *New Statesman*, however, thought these themes were "underexplored" and found *God Help the Child* not on par with earlier works such as *Beloved*. Both the *Los Angeles Times* and *Commentary* judged that Morrison's themes were compelling but that the characters were undeveloped; Fernanda Moore, the *Commentary* reviewer, found Bride almost "addled" in her superficiality, while David Ulin in the *Los Angeles Times* called Morrison's protagonist "little more than a cipher." Some reviews thought Morrison relied too heavily on exposition and summary, but noted those moments when the narrative bloomed with Morrison's signature lyrical style. Author Roxane Gay, writing in the *Guardian*, thought *God Help the Child* was "frustratingly flawed" but contained the seeds of another, "far grander" book, seen through glimpses of Morrison's magnificent language and bold vision.

Not all reviewers found fault with the novel. Kara Walker, writing in the *New York Times Book Review*, viewed *God Help the Child* as a "modern-day fairy tale with shades of the Brothers Grimm," set in a world of traumatized children and wounded or threatening adults. Michiko Kakutani of the *New York Times* also noted fairy-tale and balladic elements that lend it structural similarity to Morrison's short novel *Jazz* (1992). Kakutani also found Booker to be Morrison's strongest and best-developed male character since Milkman Dead in *Song of Solomon* (1977).

In a spring 2015 interview with Maddie Oatman for *Mother Jones* magazine, Toni Morrison discussed her past work in historical fiction and the challenge she felt creating a contemporary setting for *God Help the Child*. Morrison reminisced about her own experiences with skin color prejudice, even within the African American community. She spoke of her memories of sororities at Howard University (a historically black college) that used the "paper bag test"—whether a person's skin color was lighter than a paper bag—as a point of pride. Morrison's great-grandmother, on the other hand, was "very black" and considered Morrison and her other lighter-skinned great-grandchildren "impure and tampered with." Morrison said she was fascinated by the idea of an innocent character stigmatized and condemned for something beyond her control. In *God Help the Child*, Morrison discusses race as an artificial construct, yet one that has the power to shape people's lives and their conceptions of self-worth. While things are outwardly better for the heroine of Morrison's eleventh novel, Bride—like Pecola in *The Bluest Eye*—must still contend with a society that measures her beauty, and correspondingly, her value as a person, by the color of her skin.

Kathryn Kulpa

Review Sources

Gay, Roxane. Rev. of *God Help the Child*, by Toni Morrison. *Guardian*. Guardian News and Media, 29 Apr. 2015. Web. 13 Nov. 2015.

Kakutani, Michiko. "Haunted by Hurts that Derail Dreams." Rev. of *God Help the Child*, by Toni Morrison. *New York Times* 17 Apr. 2015: C1 (L). Print.

Moore, Fernanda. "God Help the Reader." Rev. of *God Help the Child*, by Toni Morrison. *Commentary* 139.4 (Apr. 2015): 69. Print.

Shriver, Lionel. "Under the Skin." Rev. of *God Help the Child*, by Toni Morrison. *New Statesman* 144.7 (2015): 63. Print.

Ulin, David L. "The Magic Is Missing in Toni Morrison's *God Help the Child*." Rev. of *God Help the Child*, by Toni Morrison. *Los Angeles Times*. Los Angeles Times, 23 Apr. 2015. Web. 13 Nov. 2015.

Walker, Kara. "Flesh of My Flesh." Rev. of *God Help the Child*, by Toni Morrison. *New York Times Book Review* 19 Apr. 2015: 1(L). Print.

A God in Ruins

Author: Kate Atkinson (b. 1951)
Publisher: Little, Brown (New York). 480 pp.
Type of work: Novel
Time: 1925–2012
Locale: Numerous locations throughout England

A God in Ruins details generational changes in lifestyle and attitude since 1925 as represented through the personal observations and experiences of a British man, Teddy Todd, and his extended family before and after his service in World War II.

Principal characters:
EDWARD BERESFORD "TEDDY" TODD, a handsome, good-natured, thoughtful man who becomes a World War II bomber pilot
NANCY SHAWCROSS, his childhood sweetheart, whom he marries following the war
URSULA TODD, his older sister, engaged in secret codebreaking work during the war
IZZIE BERESFORD, his eccentric aunt, a decorated ambulance driver during World War I
SYLVIE BERESFORD TODD, his mother, daughter of a long-dead, bankrupt portrait artist
VIOLA TODD, his and Nancy's sole child
DOMINIC VILLIERS, scion of a once-wealthy family, the father of Sun and Bertie
SUN "SUNNY" TODD, the son of Viola and Dominic
MOON ROBERTA "BERTIE" TODD, the daughter of Viola and Dominic

In 2013, author Kate Atkinson published the widely praised, time-bending *Life after Life*, which introduced an intriguing central character, Ursula Todd, who lived multiple lives of myriad possibilities. In that novel, Ursula's brother, Edward Beresford "Teddy" Todd, a secondary character who pilots bombers for the Royal Air Force (RAF), is apparently killed during a raid on Germany in World War II. Teddy's character returns, apparently back from the dead, as the focal point in the dovetailing novel *A God in Ruins* (2015). However, this novel is less about the myriad possible lives one could live and more about the inevitability of fate in one life. Critics such as Katy Waldman for *Slate* and Tom Perrotta for the *New York Times*, while providing generally positive reviews of the novel, have noted the stark difference between the narrative techniques of the two novels, which in turn affects both the meaning and mood of the books.

A God in Ruins begins with the explanation of why it was thought Teddy was dead: his plane was shot down before reaching its target; he was captured, spent the rest of the conflict in a prisoner-of-war camp, and was released after the cessation of hostilities. These and other details do not all come at once. Instead, they are parceled out via postmodern literary techniques, which Atkinson has employed expertly and with keen purpose. Readers accustomed to the more traditional, linear approach to storytelling may be uncomfortable with such pyrotechnics. However, the novel provides an experience not unlike a rollercoaster ride: initial apprehension gives way to exhilaration and ultimate satisfaction upon arrival at the end.

A major factor in the novel's style and structure is the distortion of time. The third-person narrative—usually, but not always, focused upon viewpoint character and stabilizing influence Teddy Todd—leaps forward and backward at will. For example, *A God in Ruins* opens under the heading "30 March 1944: The Last Flight" for a brief scene on an airfield. Then it hops back to 1925, when many of the continuing characters are formally introduced—including Teddy, Ursula,

(Euan Myles)

Since winning the Whitbread Award for her debut novel, Behind the Scenes at the Museum *(1995), British author Kate Atkinson has published four other literary novels, two plays, a story collection, and a series of mystery novels featuring private investigator Jackson Brodie.*

Izzie, Sylvie, and Nancy—and future events (such as Teddy's service in the RAF) are mentioned. Afterward, the narrative springs forward to 1980, presenting another group of characters—Viola, Dominic, Sunny, and Bertie, living at a commune in Devon—who will figure prominently for the rest of the novel. The novel shifts back to 1947, further back to 1939, forward to 1993, and so forth, up to 2012. This manner of narration provides the opportunity to lay the foundation for future events, to show the consequences of character choices and to illustrate the multitude of societal changes, for good or bad, over the course of nearly a century.

Manipulation of time also allows the pace to be varied tremendously throughout. Different periods subject readers to a full range of moods. Bucolic, pastoral scenes of peace and leisure set in the English countryside between world wars give way to moments of sheer terror, as when the RAF bombers, lit up by spotlights, surrounded by exploding bursts of flak, dive frantically to escape lethal streams of bullets from strafing German night fighters. Between such extremes are a multitude of memorable and evocative sequences detailing incidents of domestic life, personal tragedies, and small events that affect the psyches of individual characters.

The plotline itself, such as it is (the novel is primarily an extended study of the interactions among a key corps of characters across the panorama of recent British history), is shattered into many fragments, demanding that readers patiently fit the pieces together to see the overall picture. Insights into the core qualities of characters—who advance and recede in importance over time—are revealed in scenes of various lengths that offer tantalizing glimpses and memorable snatches of dialogue. Scraps of recurring plot threads and foreshadowed incidents to come appear, disappear, and reappear. At the center of the action is Teddy Todd, and those with whom he comes in contact, and the defining period of his life, World War II. An ordinary man in many ways, Teddy becomes an extraordinary figure during wartime, a wing commander flying more than seventy dangerous missions over enemy territory. At such times, Teddy is almost godlike, able to guide his devoted crew to designated targets, capable of smiting other unseen humans from on high by releasing high explosives at the push of a button. Teddy does not expect to live through the war, both because of the horrific casualty rate of bomber pilots and because he feels guilty for killing untold numbers of innocent civilians during the numerous raids he leads. During combat, he vows that if he is allowed to survive, he will live a quiet, exemplary life as atonement for his sins, always trying to be kind. He does live, to a ripe old age, and keeps his promise, living frugally, writing a nature column for a local publication, and puttering harmlessly in his garden.

Teddy is just one of dozens of fascinating characters in the novel, many of which could provide the substance for further works. Atkinson has an uncanny ability to capture in brief strokes—via gestures; telling physical details; sharp, often witty dialogue; and reactions to crises—the essence of individuals who could exist, who seem like real, breathing humans. Particularly poignant is Teddy's kindly Aunt Izzie, who became slightly unhinged after losing a potential fiancé to battlefield wounds during World War I; she keeps her memory alive of the dead man, Augustus, by writing a long series of books (excerpts of which are included) imagining his exploits as a mischievous, forever-young adolescent.

Among the younger generations are several especially vivid portrayals. Viola—Teddy's indifferent, cruel, and self-centered daughter—becomes a best-selling author by making herself seem sympathetic in autobiographical novels, and she considers her aging father nothing more than a burden before she experiences an epiphany late in life. Viola's partner, and father of her children, Dominic—a bipolar, drug-abusing, would-be artist of no talent or ambition from a once-wealthy aristocratic family—drops acid and stands on railroad tracks to feel the vibrations before meeting an express train head-on. Whiny, self-absorbed Sunny Todd, a long-time bed wetter who nobody but his grandfather can tolerate, drifts for years before finding himself, becoming a respected yoga guru. Bertie—an intelligent, practical woman totally unlike her mother—works in advertising, resists marriage, and adores her grandfather, whom she resembles in temperament.

A number of themes are threaded throughout *A God in Ruins*. One, the loss of innocence, is suggested by the novel's title, which was derived from Ralph Waldo Emerson's 1836 essay, *Nature*, a passage from which is included in the book's front matter. The age of the essay demonstrates that loss of innocence—closely allied with the notion of coming-of-age—is not a new concept. Every generation has dealt with the topic, because few periods of history have been free of conflict. Atkinson revisits the same territory because of the unprecedented scale of carnage in the twentieth century. The two world wars, one of which began the year Teddy was born and the other in which he actively participated, together accounted for the loss of tens of millions of lives. Teddy is symbolic of all the good, innocent men and women who were pressed into service and forced to kill to bring a halt to the evil of fascism. In fighting evil, Teddy and all the others did evil deeds themselves, and in doing so fell from grace. In the wake of all the violence and destruction, the world has transformed beyond recognition. The author's fragmented, time-warping narrative style reflects the modern world's descent into chaos, where previously unimagined horrors have become not only possible, but likely. Teddy, whose life spans nearly a century, serves as a symbol for the passage from an age of relative simplicity to the complex and ignoble contemporary period.

A second and subtler recurring theme revolves around the workings of memory. Throughout the novel, characters cling to small incidents that are important to them as individuals and gloss over larger events. For example, Teddy, the paradigm of his era, recalls details surrounding the deaths of members of his bomber crew, but he tries to forget the effects of the many funeral pyres of noncombatants he has helped set in Germany.

Finally, *A God in Ruins* is essentially an unabashed hymn of praise to the bravery of the RAF during the war. This is underscored following the conclusion of the novel by the author's note, acknowledgements, and an extensive list of resources. As Atkinson remarks, just 10 percent of the air crews who began flying at the outbreak of World War II survived to the end. Teddy Todd's story helps in a highly creative way to memorialize all those who served—whether they lived or died.

Jack Ewing

Review Sources

Grossman, Lev. "Life after *Life after Life*. Kate Atkinson's Grand Design." Rev. of *A God in Ruins*, by Kate Atkinson. *Time* 7 May 2015: 54. Print.

Kellogg, Carolyn. "Review: Kate Atkinson Moves Backwards through a Life in 'A God in Ruins.'" Rev. of *A God in Ruins*, by Kate Atkinson. *Los Angeles Times*. Los Angeles Times, 1 May 2015. Web. 21 Nov. 2015.

Lothar, Corinna. "Book Review: 'A God in Ruins.'" Rev. of *A God in Ruins*, by Kate Atkinson. *Washington Times*. Washington Times, 15 Oct. 2015. Web. 21 Nov. 2015.

Merritt, Stephanie. "A God in Ruins by Kate Atkinson Review—Her Finest Work." Rev. of *A God in Ruins*, by Kate Atkinson. *Guardian*. Guardian, 10 May 2015. Web. 21 Nov. 2015.

Perrotta, Tom. "Kate Atkinson's 'A God in Ruins.'" Rev. of *A God in Ruins*, by Kate Atkinson. *New York Times Sunday Book Review*. New York Times, 4 May 2015. Web. 21 Nov. 2015.

Waldman, Katy. "After 'Life after Life.'" Rev. of *A God in Ruins*, by Kate Atkinson. *Slate*. Slate, 8 May 2015. Web. 21 Nov. 2015.

Gold Fame Citrus

Author: Claire Vaye Watkins (b. 1984)
Publisher: Riverhead Books (New York).
   342 pp.
Type of work: Novel
Time: The near future
Locales: Los Angeles, California; the South-
west

*Inspired by the global climate change that
has caused drought conditions in California,
Gold Fame Citrus posits a bleak, dried-out
twenty-first century Western landscape dominated by a gigantic sand dune where stubborn individuals from diverse backgrounds
band together in a desperate attempt to survive the implacable forces of nature.*

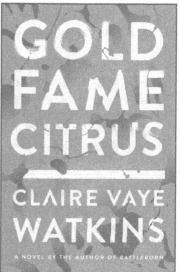

(Courtesy of Riverhead Books)

Principal characters:
LUZ ELEANOR DUNN, formerly named Luz Cortez, a former model
RAYMOND XAVIER "RAY" HOLLIS, her companion and a military deserter
IG/ESTRELLA, an abandoned toddler they adopt
LONNIE, their friend
RITA, Lonnie's girlfriend
LEVI ZABRISKIE, a former government researcher and current leader of a small colony
   established in the sand dunes
DALLAS, a female colonist
CODY, the colony's horticulturist
NICO, the colony's electronics expert and mechanic
JIMMER, the colony's philosopher and healer
FERN, Cass, Camille, and Dot, owners of the colony's brothel-bathhouse-massage
   parlor

In 1939, John Steinbeck (1902–68) published *The Grapes of Wrath*, a Pulitzer Prize–
winning novel set in the heart of the Great Depression. It tells the story of the Joad
family that farmed in Oklahoma for generations. When their crops fail during the extended drought that created the Dust Bowl and their farm is repossessed, the Joads join
a stream of migrants—disparagingly called "Okies" in other states where they are not
welcome—heading west in response to advertisements for high-paying fruit-picking
jobs, hoping to find stable work in the golden promise of California.
   Claire Vaye Watkins's speculative 2015 novel, *Gold Fame Citrus*, ironically flips
the California dream on its head. (The title refers to the three possibilities that initially lured people west: fortune, celebrity, and fresh fruit). Now it is the Golden State

that is plagued by a drought so intense and long-lasting that the Dust Bowl seems like paradise by comparison. The once-thriving agricultural industry in the extensive Central Valley has vanished. The Colorado River is bone-dry and dead. New wells when drilled only produce toxic brine at three-thousand-foot depths. The tens of thousands of swimming pools in the state have been drained to provide temporary sustenance. Los Angeles aqueducts are empty, and terrorists have blown up newly built waterways that were intended to draw water from neighboring states. From lack of moisture, the entire Southwest and much of the West Coast has become an arid, treeless, sunbaked wasteland where nothing grows. The Mojave and Sonora Deserts have expanded with the aid of strong winds and have formed an almost impassable, 400-square-mile sea of sand that has been dubbed the Amargosa Dune Sea. It stretches between Southern California and Las Vegas, where the terrain is pocked by

Claire Vaye Watkins's initial publication, a collection of short stories entitled Battleborn, *won the Story Prize, the Dylan Thomas Prize, an American Academy of Arts and Letters Award, and other honors.* Gold Fame Citrus *is her first novel.*

massive sinkholes fallen into exhausted aquifers. As a result of the ecological disaster, the government has forcibly evacuated much of America's western population to greener, more fertile places on the East Coast, where the newcomers, denigrated as "Mojavs," are begrudgingly allowed to relocate.

Despite the hostile conditions, some residents of California refuse to leave. One of these is Luz Dunn, who as an infant was known as Baby Dunn, widely publicized symbol of the failed conservation campaign to build out-of-state aqueducts. A former model known for her nontraditional physique and her large, gapped teeth, Luz, now twenty-five, is too consumed with boredom to do much except lie around and sleep. Her companion and lover is more energetic. Indiana-born Ray Hollins is a former surfer and military medic and also a deserter. He performs necessary daily chores such as digging a latrine, siphoning gas, collecting rationed food and soda in order to keep the pair alive in the dwelling where they are squatting: a luxurious deserted villa in a Los Angeles suburb where a movie star once lived.

One night, Luz and Ray head into the nearly abandoned city to participate in a ritual rain dance and to trade in black-market goods. There they stumble across an unsupervised toddler who they call Ig, after the sound the young child makes. They take the baby back to their home to clean, feed, and care for her. The girl gives Luz new purpose and she renames the baby Estrella, after her late mother. Luz proposes that their little family head for Seattle, but Ray reminds her that there are militia at the northern state border to prevent Mojavs from entering. Luz next opts for having their names put on a list to be evacuated elsewhere. To do that, Ig will need to have a birth certificate, and Luz and Ray will have to claim to be Ig's parents. For the plan to work, Ray will need fresh identification, since he is wanted for illegally dealing military morphine.

Putting the plan in motion, Ray, Luz, and Ig drive an abandoned but still serviceable car to visit old friends Lonnie and Rita in Santa Monica. Though the two can provide necessary supplies such as gasoline, food, diapers, baby powder, and other provisions, Lonnie cannot arrange new identification for Ray. Lonnie suggests various plans for illegally escaping California. The only workable solution seems to be to attempt to drive east across the desolate Amargosa, where it is rumored a small colony exists under the leadership of a prophet who is said to have the ability to find hidden sources of water.

The fledgling family begins the trek, dodging huge sinkholes as they wind through the sea of sand. But the car runs out of gas, and they are stranded in the middle of nowhere. Ray leaves Luz and Ig behind, and with a small amount of water, he begins hiking across the barren dunes in an effort to find help.

Luz and Ig, overcome by heat and thirst, pass out. When Luz awakes, she is lying in a gutted bus, one structure of a makeshift settlement: they have been rescued by members of the colony. A large woman named Dallas is suckling Ig and tells Luz that Ray was found dead. Over the days that follow, Luz and Ig, blistered by the sun, slowly recover thanks to plentiful water and fresh fruits and vegetables.

When she is well enough, Luz meets the colony's charismatic leader and water dowser, Levi Zabriskie, descendant of an old Mormon family with a mysterious past. Levi guides Luz to the spot where Ray is buried under the sand. She also becomes acquainted with other colony residents, including greenhouse keeper Cody, elderly healer Jimmer, mechanic Nico, and the young women—Fern, Cass, Camille, and Dot—who provide comfort for the men at a brothel-massage parlor known as the Holiday Rambler. Luz helps pay for her upkeep by spotting a derelict mall that the shifting sands have uncovered, where the colonists replenish their wardrobes.

Levi, attracted to Luz, gives her a copy of a book he has written—*Neo-Fauna of the Amargosa Dune Sea: A Primer*—about new organisms such as the Blue Chupacabra, Dumbo Jackrabbit, Land Eel, Sand Krill, and other creatures that have rapidly evolved to adapt to the harsh conditions of the dunes. Leaving Ig in the care of Dallas, Levi takes Luz to an underground swimming pool where they splash around, chew a narcotic drug called "brute root," and make love. Luz begins living at Levi's domed dwelling. One night at a communal bonfire, Dallas reveals that she had a stillborn baby fathered by Levi, which is why she had breast milk available for Ig. Dallas also notes that all the women have willingly slept with Levi, who has a special gift for finding water. At a crucial juncture, when Luz is trying to decide whether she will stay with the colony, Ray reappears, very much alive, contrary to Levi's claim, and tells Luz his story.

After leaving Luz and Ig, Ray walked for two days before he was found by men from the Bureau of Land Management. Ray was taken by truck to Limbo Mine, where talc, a mineral, was once extracted. The mine has been turned into a retention facility, and Ray was confined there with a young cellmate named Sal. Eventually, Ray climbed up an air duct, escaped, and made his way to the colony.

Ray's presence, and his former relationship with Luz and Ig, causes conflict at the colony. Ray tells Luz what he heard about Levi at Limbo Mine: that the leader is a fraud, that he does not find water but steals it, and may have killed people. Luz, addicted to the drug Levi has given her, does not care about the truth until Ig is hurt by one of the evolved creatures of the dunes. Jimmer uses natural remedies to take care of Ig, and Luz goes through painful drug withdrawal. She and Ray bond again and become determined to leave the colony. The members of the colony are willing to let Luz and Ray leave and offer them a vehicle, water, other supplies, and a map that shows the way out. However, they demand that Ig, who they believe is a purifying force, remain behind. Eventually, Ray and Luz agree to the bargain, and they drive off without Ig toward their new destination, Wisconsin.

Though dealing with the serious subject matter of environmental catastrophe—in the tradition of such ecotopian works as J. G. Ballard's 1964 novel *The Burning World* (which was retitled *The Drought* in 2012), Whitley Strieber and James Kunetka's *Nature's End* (1986), or Kim Stanley Robinson's *Forty Signs of Rain* (2004)—*Gold Fame Citrus* relieves the downbeat mood with a satirical undertone. This playful, contrarian attitude surfaces at regular intervals. Watkins, whose short-story collection *Battleborn* (2012) deals with Western themes, pokes fun, for example, at California's reputation for attracting offbeat people. When Lonnie suggests ways for Luz and Ray to leave California, he relies upon the occult and casts Sacagawea dollar coins to create an I Ching hexagram pattern to determine the proper course of action. Levi's book of fanciful new sand-dune creatures, complete with illustrations and detailed, scientific descriptions, is laugh-inducing. When Ray is confined at Limbo Mine, he and his cellmate spend considerable time watching such television reality shows such as *America's Funniest Car Crashes*, *Embalming with the Stars*, and *Leper Love Boat*— offerings that sound both all too real and hilariously awful.

Jack Ewing

Review Sources

Charles, Ron. "A Vision of Our Parched Future." Rev. of *Gold Fame Citrus*, by Claire Vaye Watkins. *Washington Post*. Washington Post, 29 Sept. 2015. Web. 15 Jan. 2016.

Mandel, Emily St. John. Rev. of *Gold Fame Citrus*, by Claire Vaye Watkins. *New York Times*. New York Times, 2 Oct. 2015. Web. 15 Jan. 2016.

Schaub, Michael. "Los Angeles Is a Drought Dystopia in Claire Vaye Watkins's Novel 'Gold Fame Citrus.'" Rev. of *Gold Fame Citrus*, by Claire Vaye Watkins. *Los Angeles Times*. Los Angeles Times, 24 Sept. 2015. Web. 15 Jan. 2016.

Shank, Jenny. Rev. of *Gold Fame Citrus*, by Claire Vaye Watkins. *Dallas Morning News*. Dallas Morning News, 17 Oct. 2015. Web. 15 Jan. 2016.

Golden Age

Author: Jane Smiley (b. 1949)
Publisher: Alfred A. Knopf (New York). 443 pp.
Type of work: Novel
Time: 1987–2019
Locale: United States

Golden Age *is the final book in Jane Smiley's* Last Hundred Years *trilogy, which began with* Some Luck *(2014) and continued with* Early Warning *(2015). In this final installation of the series, Jane Smiley takes the extended Langdon family from 1987 through 2019.*

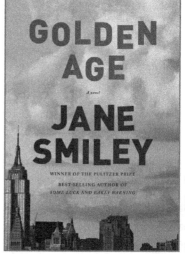

(Courtesy of Knopf)

Principal characters:
RICHARD "RICHIE" LANGDON, a congressman
MICHAEL LANGDON, his twin brother, a cutthroat finance professional
FRANCIS "FRANK" LANGDON, their father, a World War II veteran and intelligence specialist for the US government
HILDEGARDE ANDREA "ANDY" BERGSTROM LANGDON, their mother, Frank's wife
JANET LANGDON, their older sister
CLAIRE LANGDON, Frank's younger sister
JOSEPH "JESSE" LANGDON, Claire and Frank's nephew, the son of their brother Joe
JENNIFER GUTHRIE LANGDON, Jesse's wife
JOSEPH "GUTHRIE" LANGDON, Jesse and Jennifer's son
FELICITY LANGDON, Jesse and Jennifer's daughter, Guthrie's younger sister

Golden Age brings to conclusion a century-long trek through American history in the company of the Langdon family. Walter Langdon and Rosanna Vogel Langdon, the patriarch and matriarch of the clan, are both long deceased by this third volume of Jane Smiley's Last Hundred Years trilogy, but it is their life on an Iowa farm in 1920 that offers the opening salvo of this lengthy saga. The farm is the physical heart of the Langdon clan, tying them together over the decades in extended family reunions for funerals and other significant occasions.

Unlike the members of the family, who are born and die in great numbers across the volumes, the farm remains a constant, though it is subjected to the enormous changes in farming and financial practices over time. Only toward the end of *Golden Age* is the severity of these changes brought into full focus. Jesse and Jennifer Langdon wind up losing the farm due to an insidious mortgage speculation, which has a harsh personal twist. But the severity of their loss is not as great as it might once have been, for the quality of the farm has been degraded after decades of modern farming practices, including chemical applications. What was once upward of a foot of rich midwestern topsoil has diminished to two inches in depth by the end of the trilogy. The loss of the farm unravels the ties that have bound this extended family together, and its financial and physical disintegration represents the profound missteps of modern society.

A hallmark of *Golden Age* is that this novel, like its two predecessors, confronts significant historical developments through the twists and turns of individual lives and extended family trends. The effect of this technique is that the novel moves slowly along with the passing years of human lives, seeming not to frame large twists and turns of intrigue in the plot. This approach is the hidden, understated guile of the series. As reviewer Mark Athitakis noted in a review for the *Christian Science Monitor*, the trilogy "is about climate change—or, to be more precise, about what one American family made of its nation's bounty as the bounty dried up." Climate change is certainly a significant anguish at the heart of the trilogy, but it is not the only theme. For, as Felicity Langdon, the family's budding microbiologist, realizes, climate change is tied to many "socioeconomipoliticocultural responses," and it is this compound effect of crises that builds as the novel progresses.

In the first volume of the trilogy, *Some Luck* (2014), the primary force of evil was a distant Axis threat, which seemed quite far from the family home in Iowa even as family members left to fight in Europe. The crises that build in *Golden Age*, though, are insidiously ingrained in contemporary American society. There is no doubt about who the perpetrators of evil are in this novel; the names of Monsanto, Wall Street, Dick Cheney, and George W. Bush are raised frequently enough to make that clear. Each of these forces or characters runs roughshod and unchecked over society, and little suggestion is put forward that a positive resolution could eventually be reached. As the novel nears its close in 2019, the happy death of one of the family's remaining matriarchs, along with the loss and degradation of the family farm, seems to suggest a gradual extermination of all the country's positive qualities and successes. Indeed, at a certain point Janet Langdon asks her aunt Claire if they have not, perhaps, already lived through the nation's "golden age." The two puzzle through what such a concept could mean in two lives so marked by suffering and challenges. Janet remarks, "How long have I been convinced this country is doomed? I always thought it would be fossil fuels, corruption, guns, and climate change, Frank Langdon's legacies." Later, Claire reflects that if a golden age is always in the past, it is always also "discovered within," a reflection that brings the novel's sweeping discussions home again to the arc of the individual life.

Golden Age is not intended to be read in isolation from the two preceding novels of the series. Indeed, the older characters in this volume carry over from *Early Warning* (2015), and the ancestral histories going back to Walter and Rosanna Langdon, and beyond to their parents, are significant backstories to events that move forward in this volume. The force of the novel's contemporaneity becomes more powerful within the context of the trilogy as well. For readers in 2016, aspects of the stories of the characters in *Golden Age* may parallel relatively recent events and observations of their own lives, whereas the events in *Some Luck* are more fully relegated to the annals of family and national history. The rather abrupt ending of the novel in the last minutes of 2019 is especially jarring in this context, as it comes with the complete disintegration of many values that have bound the novels and the protagonist family members together. If the past is taken for granted, the trilogy makes clear that the future cannot be.

The characters in *Golden Age* seem more detached from one another than the Langdons of the first two volumes, a phenomenon that is inevitable given the growth and dispersion of the family. Indeed, as the family tree presented in the first few pages of the novel makes clear, the Langdons are an unusually fertile clan. Still, the most powerful relationship in *Golden Age*, as in *Some Luck*, is one between brothers. Joe and Frank grew up in opposition to one another on the family farm. A generation later, this bad relationship will continue to play out, as Frank's son Michael will use his position as a speculative banker on Wall Street to prey on Joe's son Jesse and, ultimately, to rob him of the family farm. This theft is both personal and impersonal—part of a larger credit-and-debt swap on Wall Street, though Michael seems to have taken some degree of personal pride or sense of poetic justice in ousting what he saw as the farmer-rube branch of his family from their land. Yet as painful as this action is, and as crucial to the narrative of the trilogy, it is actually the relationship between Michael and his twin brother, Richie, that drives the story forward. Michael works on Wall Street, Richie in Washington. Michael is an unabashedly soulless character; through one machination or another, he robs the entire clan of its wealth. Richie is his more well-intentioned foil, but as a politician, he never seems to achieve much as he seeks to ingratiate himself with his acquaintances and to survive in a hostile political climate. Michael and Richie are as close as twins are expected to be, but their opposition to one another also drives the novel. This parallel construction of a good and a bad brother struggling against one another has a timeless quality drawn from its roots in the biblical Cain and Abel account, ultimately leaving the reader to wonder just how far Richie might go in order to stay Michael's recklessness.

Just as Wall Street's excesses become personal in this epic, so too do the tragedies of September 11 and the Iraq War. A Langdon family member is killed as one of the planes hits the Twin Towers, and Richie, a congressman from New York, finds himself as the "only congressman he knew of who was related to a victim." Although he barely knew his cousin who was killed in the attack, the death nevertheless haunts him. It is no coincidence that September 11, 2001, falls nearly at the midpoint of the novel, for its occurrence sets in motion many of the unravelings that follow as the trilogy rolls toward its conclusion. Joseph "Guthrie" Langdon enlists in the Iraq War and returns suffering from post-traumatic stress disorder, a far cry from the World War II heroism of Frank. Here, September 11 becomes the tipping point at which the United States permits sweeping dark sociopolitical forces to take control of the nation, its leaders

Jane Smiley is a prolific and highly acclaimed author who has published fiction, nonfiction, and young-adult literature. She received a Pulitzer Prize for her novel A Thousand Acres *(1991), was inducted into the American Academy of Arts and Letters in 2001, and was awarded the PEN USA Lifetime Achievement Award in 2006. Her other recent novels include* Good Faith *(2003),* Ten Days in the Hills *(2007), and* Private Life *(2010).*

completely misunderstanding the devastating cultural and ecological results that their decisions will produce over the next twenty years.

A final theme in the novel worth noting is violence, both domestic and international. Two of the Langdon relatives are killed in seemingly random acts of gun violence. With economic inequality and racism in the United States spiraling out of control, there seems little possibility of redemption. Meanwhile, Islamic terrorism gets frequent mention in the final chapters of the book, and the global threat of extreme violence is ever present. Compared to the isolation and relative simplicity of rural Iowa, where the trilogy began, this dispersed and unpredictable culture of violence is especially stark.

Golden Age, like the trilogy it finishes, is a grand endeavor to grapple with the crises and developments of the modern United States. Through the story of the Langdon family, it shows the reader the local and personal nature of history. The incremental steps through the years and the coupling of major historic events with mundane occurrences in everyday lives move the reader inexorably toward a dark and unsalvageable future for the United States. Like Edward Gibbon's renowned multivolume history *The History of the Decline and Fall of the Roman Empire* (1776–89), Smiley's Last Hundred Years trilogy is the story of the end of an empire, only here that country of excess, power, and greed is the United States. If a reader can make it through to the final volume of the series, then the urgency and the impending doom of the narrative becomes readily apparent, as does its fatalism. Fiction and reality blur uncomfortably, and the reader is left wondering what, really, comes next.

Julia A. Sienkewicz

Review Sources

Athitakis, Mark. "*Golden Age* Brings an End to Jane Smiley's 'Last Hundred Years' Trilogy.'" Rev. of *Golden Age*, by Jane Smiley. *Christian Science Monitor*. Christian Science Monitor, 13 Nov. 2015. Web. 25 Feb. 2016.

Hensher, Philip. "*Golden Age* Review—the Final Volume of Jane Smiley's New Trilogy." Rev. of *Golden Age*, by Jane Smiley. *Guardian*. Guardian News and Media, 21 Oct. 2015. Web. 25 Feb. 2016.

Levis, Sandra. "*Golden Age*: Jane Smiley Brings Her Century-Spanning Trilogy to an End." Rev. of *Golden Age*, by Jane Smiley. *Pittsburgh Post-Gazette*. PG, 18 Oct. 2015. Web. 25 Feb. 2016.

McAlpin, Heller. "Author Jane Smiley's *Golden Age* Brings an Epic Tale to a Solemnly Fine End." Rev. of *Golden Age*, by Jane Smiley. *Los Angeles Times*. Tribune, 16 Oct. 2015. Web. 25 Feb. 2016.

Sayers, Valerie. "Jane Smiley Brings America into the Age of Terror." Rev. of *Golden Age*, by Jane Smiley. *Washington Post*. Washington Post, 12 Oct. 2015. Web. 25 Feb. 2016.

The Green Road

Author: Anne Enright (b. 1962)
Publisher: W. W. Norton (New York). 304 pp.
Type of work: Novel
Time: Late twentieth and early twenty-first centuries
Locales: County Clare, Limerick, and Dublin, Ireland; New York, New York; Ségou, Mali; Toronto, Canada

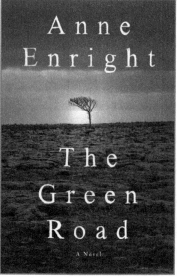

(Courtesy of W.W. Norton & Co.)

Anne Enright's latest novel, long-listed for the Man Booker Prize, chronicles the breakdown and attempted reunion of an Irish family from 1980 to the early 2000s. Dominated by the family's troubled matriarch, the four Madigan children struggle for decades to connect with their mother, each other, and themselves before finally being reunited when their mother considers selling the family home.

PRINCIPAL CHARACTERS:
ROSALEEN MADIGAN, a widow
DAN MADIGAN, her son
CONSTANCE MCGRATH, her married daughter
EMMET MADIGAN, her son
HANNA MADIGAN, her daughter
PAT MADIGAN, her husband and father of her children

Anne Enright's latest novel is a masterful balancing act both formally and emotionally. Crafting a moving saga of an Irish family's efforts to find a closeness they have never known, Enright both engages with and resists convention to create a story that is as unsentimental as it is heartbreaking. The story crosses centuries, beginning in 1980 and concluding in 2005, and to some degree it also crosses genres: the early chapters are more like short stories, culminating in a series of brief chapters that reunite the troubled family but ultimately refuse pat resolutions. The novel's structural and emotional tensions, which might have yielded less success in the hands of a less able writer, are what make *The Green Road* so interesting and rich; these tensions provide realism and a grown-up pathos that ask the reader to work hard and allow the story to steer clear of the thematic and formal dangers of another clichéd Irish family tragedy promising repentance and forgiveness.

Given Enright's liberal use of some of the familiar building blocks of such a tragedy (a long-suffering and manipulative mother, a gay son initially drawn to the priesthood, the obligatory alcoholic), her ability to forge a credible, fresh story is all the more impressive. Her crafting of structure is one way that she does this. Enright adopts a spare approach in part 1, titled "Leaving," with each chapter centering on one of the five main characters—the four Madigan children and their widowed mother, Rosaleen—at different points in time. The first chapter brings the reader to the family home in Ardeevin, County Clare, Ireland, in 1980 and centers on the youngest child, Hanna, in the midst of a family crisis. After her oldest brother, Dan, announces his intention to become a priest, Rosaleen takes to bed and sends twelve-year-old Hanna to the pharmacy for painkillers. This drama shows Hanna's efforts to negotiate her mother's histrionics and manipulations, as Rosaleen confesses to Hanna her dislike of Dan, and leads to the revelation of Dan's confused sexuality when Hanna visits him in Galway and is introduced to his girlfriend, Isabelle. The crisis remains unresolved, as the next chapter leaps forward to 1991, in New York City, where Dan's inability to face his homosexuality is now destroying lives. Still nominally committed to Isabelle, he carries on serial affairs with men at the height of the AIDS crisis, which is as savage as Dan's inability to love or, it seems, to feel much of anything at all.

Anne Enright has written collections of short stories, novels, and one book of nonfiction. She won the Man Booker Prize for her novel The Gathering *(2007), and her novel* The Forgotten Waltz *(2011) won the first Andrew Carnegie Medal for Excellence in Fiction.* The Green Road *was long-listed for the Man Booker Prize in 2015, the same year in which Enright was named the inaugural Laureate for Irish Fiction.*

The next chapter portrays the oldest daughter, Constance, in Limerick in 1997, where she is a comfortable wife and mother of three children. Approaching middle age, she finds herself in the hospital for a mammogram to check a suspicious lump. The subsequent chapter portrays Emmet, the younger son, an aid worker stationed in Mali, whose empathy for the poor contrasts poignantly with his failure to connect with his girlfriend when she takes in a stray dog. The final chapter of part 1 returns to Rosaleen in Ardeevin; it is now 2005, and the matriarch includes in her Christmas cards the announcement of her intention to sell the family home, a move designed to force the children back to their hometown.

These scattered vignettes resemble short stories rather than a novel, which some readers might view as a flaw, but they are effective for at least two reasons: the final chapter of part 1 does, in fact, prompt the family's reunion later in part 2; and more importantly, the vignettes draw readers in by demanding that they work to fill in the gaps. Given Rosaleen's obvious emotional drag on the family, it is no surprise to learn of Dan's reckless behavior or that Hanna succumbs to alcoholism. Enright lays the essential groundwork to make these developments plausible, but she offers no more than the bare minimum. Perhaps surprisingly, this minimalist approach, rather than seeming inadequate, invites the reader's collaboration; because readers are not told, they must imagine how Constance manages to find a stable marriage and life; how Dan finally musters the courage to come out as gay, begin therapy, and learn to love his partner; and how Hanna has a baby and yet nurses a drinking problem. Enright offers just enough of the right kinds of details to make the characters' stories credible and, above all, imaginable.

The Green Road was largely critically acclaimed, and several reviewers specifically lauded Enright's ability to fully craft intricate individual stories and still manage to weave them together as a whole. In a review for the *Guardian*, Kate Clanchy attributed this feat to Enright's beginnings as a short-story writer. Even though Enright tackles several different settings as well as characters in each vignette, risking narrative discord, Clanchy wrote, "any one of these episodes could be read separately . . . but it is part of the miracle of this novel that the stories seem, nevertheless, powerfully part of each other."

The sparseness also extends to the language and dialogue, which have a theatrical feel. Enright renders the visuals of a scene and uses dialogue as a skeleton rather than the primary carrier of meaning. Through the image of Rosaleen's confinement to bed on the second floor of the family home, while her husband and children stumble on with life beneath her, readers can sense the matriarch's psychic dominance of the family. When twelve-year-old Hanna reports to her mother that Dan has a girlfriend, her mother simply replies, "Does he now," and when Hanna affirms the discovery, Rosaleen says, "Are you telling me?" However, it is not clear what she is asking, thinking, or feeling. After this bit of news, Rosaleen finally decides to rise from her bed, but the reader is left to imagine what she has understood from the news, especially when, soon after, she declares to Hanna her dislike of her son—the son who, ultimately, is regarded as his mother's favorite child. In a play, the audience would understand some of these dynamics through visual cues; in a novel, the effect of these gaps is to create the space for rich psychological excavation on the part of the reader. This space is part of what resists the novel's realism. Enright uses it to declare imagination and engagement as prerequisites for this reading.

The spare, almost mysterious language also serves another of this novel's strengths, which is Enright's totally unsentimental portrayal of her characters' anguish. Particularly successful in this regard is her portrayal of the AIDS epidemic in New York City in 1991. This chapter is narrated by a mysterious, unidentified "we," a first-person plural voice that is supposed to render the collective viewpoint of the community of gay men who move in Dan's world at that time. This act of speaking for a group runs the risk of stereotyping, but Enright instead uses it as a distancing mechanism. The narrator describes the ferocity of AIDS, how many lives were lost and how quickly the deaths came, the horror and cruel reactions of fearful witnesses, not from one particular character's point of view but from everybody's, and this allows the narrator to maintain an unflinching, detailed perspective and a certain emotional detachment. Enright also counters the pathos with Dan's emotional blankness; his long refusal to acknowledge his attraction to men has hollowed him out, and he leaves a cold path of lies and grief behind him.

Likewise, when Emmet finds himself unable to connect to his girlfriend's affection for a stray dog in Mali, the couple's breakup is rendered as predictable and chilling but not at all surprising to Emmet. In the face of his girlfriend's distress over the poisoning of her dog, which Emmet has never really wanted to keep, his failure to console her seems like a choice that he somehow cannot help but make. In three short lines, readers understand his complicity: "Emmet steadied himself. 'Alice,' he said. 'It's only a dog.' And that, he knew, was the end of them." These lines do not simply mark the end of a relationship; they show that Emmet, at some level, is aware of how easily he pushes away the people he loves. In this way, Enright creates a family drama worthy of mature readers; if Rosaleen has damaged her children, Enright is all too aware of how such damage becomes self-perpetuating when children become adults. Her unsentimental portrayal refuses to let anyone off the hook, resulting in a grown-up story that respects the emotional intelligence of its readers.

The chapters that focus on individual characters, which continue into part 2 until the four grown Madigan children return to Ireland for Christmas, set up the reader to expect a grand resolution of some sort. But Enright refuses such an easy conclusion, and this, too, nicely complements the novel's realistic tendencies. Just as life offers no easy solutions to many and perhaps most family struggles, the story steers clear of tearful repentance and neatly healed wounds. At the reunion, Rosaleen is just as dramatic and manipulative as ever, if not more so, and her children are hardly better as adults at managing their disappointment and confusion. This is not to say that the Madigans make no progress in their efforts to climb out of their well of family misery—they do—but their progress is halting, uneven, uncertain, and above all provisional. Enright's greatest success in this story might be how well she conveys the most stable reality of life: that no one ever really knows what will happen.

Ashleigh Imus, PhD

Review Sources

Charles, Ron. "Anne Enright Draws a Rich, Irish Family Saga in *The Green Road*." Rev. of *The Green Road*, by Anne Enright. *Washington Post.* Washington Post, 5 May 2015. Web. 29 Jan. 2016.
Clanchy, Kate. "A Family's Worth of Stories." Rev. of *The Green Road*, by Anne Enright. *Guardian.* Guardian News and Media, 14 May 2015. Web. 29 Jan. 2016.
Leavitt, David. Rev. of *The Green Road*, by Anne Enright. *New York Times.* New York Times, 12 May 2015. Web. 29 Jan. 2016.
Wood, James. "All Her Children." Rev. of *The Green Road*, by Anne Enright. *New Yorker.* Condé Nast, 25 May 2015. Web. 29 Jan. 2016.

H Is for Hawk

Author: Helen Macdonald (b. 1970)
Publisher: Grove (New York). 300 pp.
First published: *H Is for Hawk*, 2014, in the
United Kingdom
Type of work: Memoir, natural history, liter-
ary biography
Time: Present, 1930s
Locale: Cambridge, England

After Helen Macdonald's father died unex-
pectedly, she turned to her childhood love of
falconry to assuage her grief. H Is for Hawk
explores what birds of prey mean to Mac-
donald—and to the tortured author of The
Sword in the Stone, *T. H. White—but is also*
about confronting death through a wilder-
ness you can tame.

(Courtesy of Grove Atlantic)

Helen Macdonald's book *H Is for Hawk* is a memoir about grieving, but it could also be accurately described as a natural history, a training manual, and a short biography of British writer, T. H. White. Initially published by Vintage Publishing in Britain, the book was selected for the Samuel Johnson Prize for Non-Fiction (the first memoir to ever so honored) and the Costa Book of the Year. Macdonald's father died in 2007, but she did not begin writing the book until 2012. Recalling the book's completion in a November 5, 2014, interview with Stephen Moss for the *Guardian* newspaper, she said, "There was a great sense that something was done, and it was a goodbye to my father and to that time. The book traces a time from that shock of the early loss to a point when I realised that the grief had turned into love. There's that lovely line—'Grief is just love with nowhere to go'—and the book traces that course of loss to acceptance."

The book opens on Macdonald lying in bed, unable to sleep. She then drives forty-five minutes from Cambridge, where she has a research fellowship at the university, to a strange forest called the Brecklands (literally, "broken land") to watch for goshawks. Goshawks, its necessary for Macdonald to explain early on, are not what one might think they are. They are not the kind of hawk one catches a glimpse of in the backyard. Those backyard birds are likely sparrow hawks. Sparrow hawks are large animals, but by comparison, goshawks are great hulking, killing things. "Goshawks resemble sparrowhawks the way leopards resemble housecats," she writes. Goshawks are also extremely difficult to spot in the wild. They are quick and agile hunters, ripe for metaphor. "Looking for goshawks is like looking for grace: it comes, but not often, and you don't get to say when or how," Macdonald writes.

The distinction between goshawks and the rest of the animal kingdom is important to Macdonald's story. Macdonald is a trained falconer who has spent years honing her craft, but until the events described in the book, she had never worked with a goshawk. All of their unusual characteristics put together spell death, she suggests, not literally, but in their wildness of spirit. Falcons are predators, too, of course, but goshawks, Macdonald writes, are considered bloodthirsty. Kathryn Schulz, in her review of the book for the *New Yorker*, described the simultaneously murderous and spooky goshawks as "half Hamlet, half Lady Macbeth." On the sleepless early morning Macdonald drives to the Brecklands, she spots a pair of goshawks, a rare sight. Weeks later, her father, a famous photojournalist named Alisdair Macdonald, dies unexpectedly of a heart attack. When she receives the phone call, she is staring at a piece of moss retrieved from her trip to the Brecklands; thus, the two competing narratives of her memoir are established: the need to understand the goshawk while coming to terms with her grief.

(Marzena Pogorzaly)

Helen Macdonald is an author, historian, naturalist, and falconer. After publishing some poetry and a cultural history of falconry, she published her award-winning memoir H Is for Hawk *in the United Kingdom in 2014. It was released in the United States in 2015 to wide acclaim.*

Growing up, Macdonald was so obsessed with birds that at the age of six, she attempted to imitate them even in her sleep, with arms crossed behind her like folded wings. She devoured all kinds of archaic literature about hawks and falconry, collecting terms like "jess" (a trained hawk's leather leash), "sails" (wings), "tiercel" (a male hawk), and "train" (tail) the way other children might collect toys. When she was eight, she picked up a book called *The Goshawk* by T. H. White. White was a scholar and, reportedly, a deeply closeted gay man. He also wrote *The Sword in the Stone* (1938) and *The Once and Future King* (1939), for which he is better known. In *The Goshawk*, written before his most famous works in the 1930s but not published until 1951, White describes his attempts to train a goshawk (named, appropriately, Gos) knowing little to nothing about training goshawks. Macdonald recalls that she was appalled by the book when she first read it because White is such a poor falconer. He mistreats his bird and mistakenly depicts his task as a battle between man and beast, she writes, but returning to the book just before embarking on her own journey to acquire a goshawk, Macdonald sees a new depth to his story. She interweaves its narrative, alongside necessary biographical context, into her memoir. It seems a questionable choice, at first. After all *The Goshawk* is already a book, and if one wanted to read it, one could. But for Macdonald, White's story is an integral part of her own. As a child, White was caught between two violent and abusive parents. As an adult,

White repressed his love for men and became obsessed with his own sadistic fantasies. Unlike Macdonald, he did not turn to his goshawk through grief, but he did embark on his journey in the face of fear and an unrelenting lifelong pain. "Like White I wanted to cut loose from the world, and I shared, too, his desire to escape to the wild, a desire that can rip away all human softness and leave you stranded in a world of savage, courteous despair," she writes.

In a near-perfect scene, Macdonald purchases a small goshawk—small being a relative term—from a breeder in Scotland. Traditionally, she writes, hawks are given names that belie their predatory nature. She eventually decides to name her goshawk, Mabel. At this point in the narrative, Macdonald could have easily veered off into clichéd territory, but quite admirably, she does not. In Macdonald's hands, Mabel is a character, not a flying metaphor for Macdonald's grief. She maintains a safe distance between Mabel's personality and her own, careful not to personify Mabel or negate her animal qualities. Mabel is a bird. She wants to hunt and, surprisingly, to play. Macdonald does not look for herself (or worse, her father) in Mabel; she simply devotes herself to the bird and, through that devotion, is changed. As Macdonald treks across the vivid English countryside with Mabel, she muses on the falconer's relationship to the land. Falconry tradition, for both good and ill, is intertwined with the austere landscape and the remnants of English feudal culture—goshawks, for example, were flown by peasants and, for that reason, are still considered less refined than other birds of prey. Macdonald's decision to touch on the political and natural history of England is another choice that, at the outset, appears to be a poor one but, through Macdonald's deep interest in nature and her desire to seek wildness in a rapidly developing country, becomes another integral part of her story. It even becomes a poetic means of marking the passage of time. Combining her short history with Mabel and the history of the fields of Cambridge, Macdonald creates a poignant friction. "The hawk and I have a shared history of these fields," she writes. "There are ghosts here, but they are not long-dead falconers. They are ghosts of things that happened."

In the end, Macdonald elegantly arrives at the obvious conclusion that she is not a hawk, that humans cannot belong to the wild in the same way animals can. ("Hunting with the hawk," she writes, "took me to the very edge of being human.") But to describe her tale in this way does it a disservice. The arc of the memoir is unremarkable, but packed with well-chosen details. After her father dies, Macdonald and her mother spend Christmas in Maine. After the holiday, Macdonald and her friends set the Christmas tree on fire, first decorating the branches with fire-lighting gel that drips and sticks like "glutinous tinsel." The night she receives the news of her father's death, she keeps plans to go out to dinner with a friend. When the food comes, Macdonald finds that she cannot eat it, much to the distress of their waiter. Upon discovering the reason for her loss of appetite, he triumphantly presents her with a fudge brownie and ice cream—as if her grief could be assuaged with sweeter food. When the Scottish breeder introduces her to Mabel, a shaft of sunlight catches the bird. The hawk is a "conjuring trick. A reptile. A fallen angel. A griffon from the pages of an illuminated bestiary. Something bright and distant, like gold falling through water." For Macdonald, the hawk's realm is always just out of reach, and she respects this distance just short of imbuing Mabel with magical powers. The hawk is beautiful, she suggests, both for what is known about it and what is not known. This is something that perhaps White also understood. Macdonald's telling of his relationship with Gos is so visceral that it makes the reader forget that she was not there. In one heartbreaking scene, Gos looses himself from a length of twine and flies away. Gos hangs around the forests near White's cottage but cannot be persuaded to return to captivity—White "sees him, sometimes, soaring over the trees in distant, expanding circles."

Molly Hagan

Review Sources

Cooke, Rachel. "Helen Macdonald's Taming of a Goshawk Called Mabel Reads like a Thriller." *Guardian*. Guardian News and Media, 4 Aug. 2014. Web. 16 Sept. 2015.
Croke, Vicki Constantine. Rev. of *H Is for Hawk*, by Helen Macdonald. *New York Times*. New York Times, 19 Feb. 2015. Web. 16 Sept. 2015.
Gallagher, Tim. "A Falconer Reviews Helen Macdonald's Acclaimed Bestseller, H Is for Hawk." Rev. of *H Is for Hawk*, by Helen Macdonald. *All about Birds*. Cornell Lab of Ornithology, 23 Mar. 2015. Web. 16 Sept. 2015.
House, Christian. "H Is for Hawk by Helen Macdonald, Review: 'A Soaring Triumph.'" Rev. of *H Is for Hawk*, by Helen Macdonald. *Telegraph*. Telegraph Media Group, 27 Jan. 2015. Web. 16 Sept. 2015.
Schulz, Kathryn. "Rapt: Grieving with Your Goshawk." Rev. of *H Is for Hawk*, by Helen Macdonald. *New Yorker*. Condé Nast, 9 Mar. 2015. Web. 16 Sept. 2015.

The Harder They Come

Author: T. C. Boyle (b. 1948)
Publisher: Ecco (New York). 400 pp.
Type of work: Novel
Time: Present
Locales: Costa Rica, Northern California

Inspired by real-life events, this darkly absorbing novel centers on three protagonists who are forced to confront the consequences wrought by their violent and rebellious actions.

Principal characters:
STEN STENSEN, a retired septuagenarian high school principal and former Marine
ADAM STENSEN, his son, a twenty-five-year-old schizophrenic
SARA HOVARTY JENNINGS, Adam's lover, a forty-year-old farrier and antigovernment activist

(Courtesy of HarperCollins)

Gun violence has become increasingly pervasive in the United States over the past several decades. The story of the lone gunman—shy, depressed, socially awkward, and often mentally unstable— firing indiscriminately upon innocent targets with a small cache of weapons has become common. Still, Americans and politicians alike have continued to find themselves divided over the contentious issue of gun control. It is this frightening and deeply troubling upsurge in American gun violence that prompted T. C. Boyle to write *The Harder They Come* (2015), a hard-driving, unrelenting novel about cross-generational violence, antiauthoritarianism, and the darkest recesses of the American soul.

The Harder They Come takes its title from the influential 1972 Jamaican crime film of the same name, which stars reggae singer-songwriter Jimmy Cliff as an aspiring reggae singer whose dreams of stardom are derailed by a life of drug dealing and crime. Boyle's novel bears little similarity to the Jimmy Cliff film, save for its title and certain plot elements. Rather, the film is used as a jumping-off point for an entirely different story, one that is framed around the alternating third-person points of view of three protagonists and a tone-setting epigraph taken from D. H. Lawrence's *Studies in Classic American Literature* (1923): "The essential American soul is hard, isolate, stoic, and a killer. It has never yet melted."

Lawrence's chilling words ring true in the novel's bravura fifty-seven-page opening, where Boyle introduces readers to Sten Stensen, a sturdy, seventy-year-old former Marine, Vietnam War veteran, and recently retired high school principal. Sten is vacationing with his wife of four decades, Carolee, on a Central America and Panama

Canal cruise. During a shore excursion in Puerto Limón, Costa Rica, the couple's tour group is held up by a triumvirate of amateur thieves, one of whom is toting a gun. When a window of opportunity to intervene presents itself, Sten goes into combat mode, immobilizing the gun-toting thief with a fatal chokehold that sends his cohorts fleeing from the scene. Sten saves his tour group, but he is then forced to endure aggressive questioning by the local police, casting a pall over the rest of his trip.

When Sten and Carolee return home to Mendocino, California, Sten is given the hero treatment. He receives national media attention, gets courted by Hollywood producers, and is fawned over by the locals. Cantankerous with the kind of hard-edged cynicism redolent of other Boyle protagonists, Sten is uncomfortable with his newfound celebrity and tormented by his rash act of violence; during a night out in Fort Bragg with Carolee, he bristles when an admiring stranger buys him a drink. Sten has other concerns in his life, such as protecting the environment and keeping illegal immigrants at bay. Shortly after his return, he joins a local citizens' group called Take Back Our Forests, which ferrets out destructive Mexican cartels that grow marijuana in the surrounding forests. His social and environmental concerns, however, are outweighed by concerns for his twenty-five-year-old son, Adam, a paranoid schizophrenic with a simmering violent streak not unlike his own.

Adam and his lover, a forty-year-old divorcee named Sara Hovarty Jennings, are the novel's other two protagonists. Throughout the novel, Boyle juxtaposes their stories with Sten's in alternating point-of-view chapters set in and around Mendocino County. Readers are first introduced to Sara, a native of Mendocino County who works as a farrier and a substitute teacher. When she is not tending to clients' horses, Sara spends her time inveighing against the government, which she refers to as the "U.S. Illegitimate Government of America the Corporate." She is an unabashed member of the Sovereign Citizens' Movement, a right-wing anarchist group that renounces all state and federal laws. Sara's beliefs include not wearing a seatbelt, and when a police officer pulls her over for failing to wear one, she refuses to hand over her license and registration. "I have no contract with you," Sara reasons to the unamused officer, who arrests her, impounds her car, and quarantines her beloved dreadlocked dog and riding companion, Kutya, after being bitten by him.

Sara's ill-fated clash with authority leads her to become embroiled in a web of legal entanglements. Her life takes an interesting turn, however, when she picks up Adam hitchhiking on the road. Sporting a fastidiously shaved head and clothed in military garb, the unmistakably off-kilter Adam is en route to a sporting-goods store in Ukiah, and Sara, undeterred, agrees to take him there. Though Adam is not one for conversation, Sara learns that he shares her contempt for the law. She soon realizes that she was Adam's former substitute teacher at Fort Bragg High School, where Sten also served as principal. When Adam is confronted with this realization, he denies it, instead insisting on being called Colter, as in John Colter, an adventurer who served as a member of the famed Lewis and Clark expedition from 1804 to 1806. Puzzled by his odd behavior but intrigued by his tall, muscular frame, Sara talks Adam into taking part in a harebrained scheme to liberate her dog, who is being held at an animal shelter in Ukiah for having no rabies certificate. She subsequently invites him over for dinner, and a bizarre, lust-fueled love affair ensues between them.

As the novel progresses, readers learn, through both Sten's and Adam's points of view, that Adam had a turbulent adolescence, one defined by visits to therapists, delinquency, and a predilection toward violent video games. Readers learn that Adam has never gotten along with Sten and that their relationship has only become more strained as Adam has gotten older; among other things, he tries to belittle his father's heroic deed. When Sara meets Adam, he is living alone in the forest in his deceased grandmother's cabin, around which he has built an eight-foot concrete wall to keep out "hostiles." Modeling himself after Colter, Adam spends most of his waking hours building secret bunkers in the woods and growing poppies to produce opium. This narrative thread relates to the Jimmy Cliff film, in which Cliff's character leaves his rural home and starts peddling drugs to make money after his grandmother dies. Early in the novel, it is revealed that Adam even went through a brief Rastafarian phase in high school.

Adam's relationship with Sten becomes more complicated when he takes up with Sara, whose life he fades in and out of after their first night together. In the novel, Adam and Sten have a series of tempestuous, short-lived encounters, mostly over Adam's living arrangements, in Sara's presence; at one point, Sara temporarily moves in with Adam to evade capture from the police after stealing back her dog. Eventually, Adam and Sten's relationship comes to a head when Sten informs Adam that he has sold his grandmother's cabin, which had been in escrow, to a family friend named Art Tolleson. The two come to blows on the cabin's premises, after which Adam retreats into the woods for several hours before returning to trash the place. After witnessing this violent outburst, Sara leaves, and Adam returns to the woods. The episode sparks a downward spiral for Adam, whose paranoid delusions ultimately lead him to kill two men, setting off a climactic weeks-long countywide manhunt in the surrounding redwood forests.

In writing *The Harder They Come*, Boyle drew on two real-life incidents for inspiration. The first occurred in February 2007, when a seventy-year-old retired Marine on a Carnival cruise ship foiled an attempted robbery of his tour group by three armed assailants during a stopover in Puerto Limón. Like Sten in the novel, the man, whose name was never publicized, thwarted the attack by putting one of the attackers in a fatal headlock that cut off his air supply. The other incident involved Aaron Bassler, a thirty-five-year-old schizophrenic who in 2011 murdered two men in separate attacks in the city of Fort Bragg. To elude capture from law enforcement officials, Bassler retreated into the redwood forests outside Fort Bragg, where he hid for five weeks before being gunned down by a SWAT team.

T. C. Boyle is a distinguished professor emeritus of English at the University of Southern California. The Harder They Come *is his fifteenth novel. Many of his novels and short-story collections have received awards and honors.*

Boyle clearly references Bassler in his depiction of Adam, who fits the profile of the "typical" mass shooter. In florid, unsettling prose, Boyle expertly captures Adam's fragmented mental state as he veers toward the edge of sanity. Intimate moments with Sara suddenly give way to haunting hallucinatory visions of sea life, crawling insects, and rings of fire. Adam's descent into full-fledged madness is best illustrated through his colorful renderings of Colter's escapades, which include the mountain man's legendary early nineteenth-century escape from Blackfoots. By novel's end, Adam, whose mind is further clouded by a steady stream of hard liquor, has so fully inhabited his Colter alter ego that his every action and thought is preceded by the question "What would Colter do?"

Still, Adam comes off as a one-dimensional archetype, serving more as an effective plot device for Boyle to perpetuate the novel's overriding theme of gun violence. Instead, Sara and Sten, who, as lover and father, represent the forgotten victims of gun violence, are the novel's more fully realized characters. Despite her fervent right-wing ideologies, Sara yearns desperately for human connection and companionship in a way that Adam does not. Readers may find Sara's relationship with Adam a bit far-fetched, but it is her earnestness to pursue something more than mere lust that adds complexity to her character. Meanwhile, Sten is forced to come to terms with Adam's genetic predisposition to violence, leading to deeper questions about what kind of role he may or may not have played in his son's actions.

The Harder They Come has been compared to other novels that have centered on families devastated by violence, most notably Philip Roth's Pulitzer Prize–winning novel *American Pastoral* (1997). Meanwhile, readers familiar with Boyle will be able to note similarities between the novel and some of his other California-based works, particularly *The Tortilla Curtain* (1995), which tackled social and political issues such as illegal immigration, sovereign rights, and environmental destruction. Notwithstanding such similarities, many critics found the novel to be a deeper, more mature work for the prolific Boyle, who has been called a modern-day Mark Twain for his deft combination of humor and social commentary. In a representative review in the *New York Times*, Michiko Kakutani called the book "a showcase for all of Mr. Boyle's storytelling talents" and declared that it is arguably his "most powerful, kinetic novel yet." Boyle does not attempt to provide any answers to gun violence in his novel, but he helps open up the discussion, shedding further light on one of the most pressing topics in the country.

Chris Cullen

Review Sources

Charles, Ron. "T. C. Boyle's New Novel Takes Us to America's Far-Right Edge." Rev. of *The Harder They Come*, by T. C. Boyle. *Washington Post*. Washington Post, 24 Mar. 2015. Web. 28 Sept. 2015.

Geye, Peter. Rev. of *The Harder They Come*, by T. C. Boyle. *SFGate*. Hearst Communications, 25 Mar. 2015. Web. 28 Sept. 2015.

Kakutani, Michiko. "In T. Coraghessan Boyle's *The Harder They Come*, Rugged Individualism Run Amok." Rev. of *The Harder They Come*, by T. C. Boyle. *New York Times*. New York Times, 23 Mar. 2015. Web. 28 Sept. 2015.

Rungren, Lawrence. Rev. of *The Harder They Come*, by T. C. Boyle. *Library Journal*. Library Journal, 15 Dec. 2014. Web. 28 Sept. 2015.

Walter, Jess. "T. C. Boyle Roams the American Psyche in *The Harder They Come*." Rev. of *The Harder They Come*, by T. C. Boyle. *Los Angeles Times*. Los Angeles Times, 26 Mar. 2015. Web. 28 Sept. 2015.

Hausfrau

Author: Jill Alexander Essbaum (b. 1971)
Publisher: Random House (New York). 336
 pp.
Type of work: Novel
Time: Present
Locale: Dietlikon, Switzerland

Anna Benz lives an ideal life as the wife of a successful banker and mother in a small town near Zurich, Switzerland. But when Anna starts having illicit affairs with other men, her life spirals out of control, and she must learn some of the most difficult lessons of all.

(Courtesy of Random House)

Principal characters:
ANNA BENZ, an American housewife living
 in a small town in Switzerland
FRAU DOKTOR MESSERLI, her Swiss psychoanalyst
BRUNO BENZ, her Swiss husband, a banker
VICTOR BENZ, her son
CHARLES BENZ, her son who witnesses something he should not have
POLLY JEAN BENZ, her daughter and youngest child
URSULA BENZ, her mother-in-law
STEPHEN NICODEMUS, a thermochemist with whom she has an affair
MARY GILBERT, her friend from German class, a Canadian expat

Jill Alexander Essbaum's debut novel, *Hausfrau* (2015), tells the story of Anna Benz, a thirty-seven-year-old American living in an affluent small town, Dietlikon, outside of Zurich, Switzerland. Anna is a stay-at-home mother of three young children: Victor, Charles, and Polly Jean. Unhappy with her Swiss husband, Bruno, and lonely in her mostly friendless life, Anna seeks emotional and sexual fulfillment outside of her marriage. Eventually, Anna's reckless decisions lead to grave consequences.

At the outset of *Hausfrau*, Anna enrolls in a German class for beginners at a nearby Klubschule (a company that offers classes to adults). She hopes to finally gain proficiency in a language that she has not yet learned, despite having lived in Switzerland for a decade. Anna is deeply ambivalent about marriage, sex (she "needed and didn't need it"), motherhood, and friendship. As a result, she finds herself stuck in a life that she is not sure she really wants. In German class, Anna meets Archie, who soon becomes one of her lovers. She also meets Mary, a Canadian expat who eagerly seeks Anna's attention and whom Anna befriends. A third of the way into the novel, readers are introduced to Stephen Nicodemus, a handsome thermochemist with whom Anna had had an affair in the past. Essbaum intersperses the novel with brief flashbacks to Stephen and Anna's trysts. Their affair was short lived, however, and ended almost as abruptly as it began. But Anna continues to pine for Stephen. Readers eventually learn that Stephen is the biological father of Polly Jean, Anna's youngest child.

Hausfrau plugs along, shifting between glimpses of Anna's unhappy family life, her sessions with her analyst, Frau Doktor Messerli, and her various illicit sexual encounters. A kind of Emma Bovary, Anna resents the banalities of marriage, motherhood, and friendship. Notably, Essbaum invites a literary interpretation of Anna's story through her language play and symbolic meditations on the grammar and syntax of the German language. Anna muses suggestively, "Only in the present tense is the subject married to its verb. The action . . . comes at the end. At the very end, when there is nothing left to do but act." The novel also features detailed, evocative descriptions of everything from the city to sex, along with allusions to Gustave Flaubert's *Madame Bovary* (1856) and Leo Tolstoy's *Anna Karenina* (1877), both nineteenth-century realist novels. Like Flaubert's and Tolstoy's protagonists, Anna Benz turns to adultery in her malaise and general dissatisfaction with her social reality.

Arguably, Essbaum's novel is also indebted to literary naturalism, a movement that grew out of realism. In naturalist novels, characters' lives and fates are determined by their material and social environments. In exemplary novels of the naturalist movement, like Edith Wharton's *The House of Mirth* (1905) and Theodor Dreiser's *An American Tragedy* (1925), characters find themselves defeated by environmental and structural forces that are largely beyond their control. While *Hausfrau* is not ostensibly a work of literary naturalism or social critique, one could certainly read the novel this way. One might argue, for example, that in *Hausfrau*, Anna is essentially a product of bourgeois Western culture, a capitalist society in which desire is never sated and consumerism is posited as the solution to all of our woes. On this reading, Anna becomes yet another victim of a depraved culture. While Anna would seem to have all the privilege in the world, and therefore every opportunity to break free and pursue the life she really wants, it is in fact her affluence and privilege that render her powerless and self-defeating.

Anna's inexplicable and perpetual unhappiness never develops into anything particularly complex. The novel does not elaborate on or explore the cause of Anna's malaise. Instead, Essbaum simply paints a despondent, disengaged, and despairing Anna time and again, one who absently navigates her privileged, easy life in a wealthy European city. Anna's internal musings punctuate and often interrupt the narrative. "What little shame I had before is gone," she observes at one point. But despite frequent indirect speech, for the most part *Hausfrau* leaves readers in the dark as to Anna's motivations and desires. Readers never really learn why Anna can't take control of her life or what it is that she really wants. Messerli notes during a session with Anna that Anna's passivity about her life may be a choice in itself. During the novel's erotic scenes, readers are often reminded that Anna is fundamentally unhappy. Sometimes sex brings Anna momentary relief, even catharsis. But mostly, Anna's ambivalence just culminates in joyless sex.

Anna's meetings with her therapist also lack the complexity for which readers might wish. The sessions, which readers glimpse only briefly, never entail sustained dialogue between analyst and patient. Instead, they consist mostly of vague philosophical questioning on the differences between love and lust and whether desire is a disease. In one such scene Essbaum points toward what can be the alienating nature of desire under the conditions of modern life. Essbaum seems to argue that desire can infect people, making people sick and even ruining them. This is a compelling suggestion, but the scene ends here, and readers are left with only a vague understanding of Anna's relationship with desire. In fact, Anna reveals few details about her sex life to her analyst. Perhaps this is why Doktor Messerli is never able to really break through to Anna.

Essbaum's spare, moody, and ultimately poetic descriptions of Anna's environment, coupled with Anna's own despairing comments to herself, result in an ominous atmosphere in *Hausfrau*. Essbaum facilitates an immersive reading experience relatively seamlessly: one glides through the book just as Anna glides through her own life, from home, to class, to train, to hotel room, and back again. The temporality of the book is disorienting, but keeps the reader intrigued. Essbaum moves between present and past, creating in readers a sense that time has passed, yet at the same time a feeling that no time has passed at all. The book's foreboding atmosphere is one of its distinguishing characteristics, and in the end, Essbaum delivers a blow that the book seems to suggest is coming from its very first pages, to the ultimate satisfaction (and horror) of readers.

Jill Alexander Essbaum's debut novel is Hausfrau *(2015). She is also the author of several poetry collections. She has won the Bakeless Poetry Prize and received two National Endowment for the Arts literature fellowships. She teaches at the University of California, Riverside.*

This major blow occurs late in the novel, after Anna's son Charlie catches her kissing one of her lovers at the zoo. Charlie happens to be with his class at the zoo on a field trip. When Charlie later asks his mother whom she was kissing, Anna accuses her son of making it up. She then instructs Charlie not to tell anyone, or she will tell everyone that he is lying. "Charles, I mean it," Anna firmly instructs him. "Unless you want something bad to happen, you need to be quiet." Some readers might be startled by Anna's desperate, cruel manipulation of her child at this point. But it is not until shortly after, when Anna receives a call from Bruno while she is with another one of her lovers, that her carelessness becomes fully and tragically apparent: when Charlie dies in a car accident, readers quickly surmise that it could have been the child's distraught mental state that led him to dash into the street without looking first.

The final chapters of *Hausfrau* reach toward the emotional complexity that earlier sections of the book fail to achieve. In one particularly moving scene, Anna wakes up in the night missing Charlie and desperate for Bruno's affection. When her husband is unresponsive, she springs out of bed, throws on her clothes, and dashes out into the night. "Fix this!" Anna screams in her head at no one in particular while curled up in a ball. And then, again to herself, Anna demands that Bruno wake up and have sex with her. Here Essbaum explores the complexity of grief and love, touching on the way

Anna's grief for her lost child is bound up with her grief for her broken marriage. At this point, Anna realizes what cannot be undone. Yet in her delusion, she longs to go back and fix everything anyway.

At the novel's tragic end, Anna loses everything. One might be tempted to read *Hausfrau*'s conclusion as moralizing about the evils of adultery. But perhaps more than anything, Anna's story is about what happens when one refuses to take responsibility for one's own life in the face of undesirable or oppressive circumstances. And as Anna learns, sometimes taking responsibility means figuring out what you need and asking for it before it is too late so as not to destroy the other people in your life, not to mention yourself.

A. Lewandowski

Review Sources

Albert, Elisa. "*Hausfrau*, by Jill Alexander Essbaum." Rev. of *Hausfrau*, by Jill Alexander Essbaum. *New York Times*. New York Times, 24 Mar. 2015. Web. 1 Feb. 2016.

Graham, Ruth. "Unhappy Families" Rev. of *Hausfrau*, by Jill Alexander Essbaum. *Slate Book Review*. Slate Group, 9 Apr. 2015. Web. 1 Feb. 2016.

Haas, Lidija. "Hausfrau by Jill Alexander Essbaum Review—Illicit Sex in Small-Town Switzerland." Rev. of *Hausfrau*, by Jill Alexander Essbaum. *Guardian*. Guardian News and Media, 2 Apr. 2015. Web. 1 Feb. 2016.

Rev. of *Hausfrau*, by Jill Alexander Essbaum. *Publishers Weekly*. PWxyz, Mar. 2015. Web. 1 Feb. 2016.

Klein, Julia M. Rev. of *Hausfrau*, by Jill Alexander Essbaum. *Chicago Tribune*. Chicago Tribune, 19 Mar. 2015. Web. 1 Feb. 2016.

Neary, Lynn. "*Hausfrau* Strips Down Its Modern-Day Madame Bovary." Rev. of *Hausfrau*, by Jill Alexander Essbaum. *Weekend Edition Saturday*. NPR, 21 Mar. 2015. Web. 1 Feb. 2016.

Heaven

Author: Rowan Ricardo Phillips (b. 1974)
Publisher: Farrar, Straus and Giroux (New
York). 61 pp.
Type of work: Poetry

*Phillips's poems are eclectic and sophisti-
cated, often dealing with the topic of poetry
itself and featuring allusions to various other
texts in a style full of rich sound effects.*

(Courtesy of Farrar Straus & Giroux)

Entering Rowan Ricardo Phillips's *Heaven*
is like entering a world all its own. Individual words are generally simple and clear;
the forms seem familiar; the rhythms are
often solid but also sometimes playful; and,
in general, one has the impression of a poet
who not only seeks to communicate but who also has important things to say. Sometimes, admittedly, various poems can occasionally seem self-involved: sometimes
they seem too much about poetry (as if poetry, per se, were as interesting to all people
as it naturally is to poets themselves). The words *poem, poet,* and *poetry* occur nearly
twenty times in the space of fifty-five pages, and Phillips sometimes runs the risk of
making art that can occasionally seem too much about making art.

However, to say this is to fail to appreciate just how beautiful, suggestive, and
compelling most of Phillips's poems are. One poem likely to please many readers is
titled "Nothing of a Blue Remains." Its opening lines are nonetheless worth quoting:

> Finally, under thick cover of night,
> The snow fell, without wind, and fat as plates.
> Wine-rested, I rose a little before five,
> Cowed by the darkness of this quiet mountain,
> With lion and elk and pheasant roaming
> Eight thousand feet above any ocean,
> And that much closer to the gates of Heaven
> Smuggled somewhere within this small lark's mind
> As it sits patiently on a bare branch
> Hardly startled when I turned the porch light
> On. Something in me, something struggling
> Inside me, starts slowly now to feel soothed.

In these lines one notices many of the best features of Phillips's verse in general. Often he begins, as he does here, by plunging readers right into the midst of things, putting them smack in the middle of a situation and also inside the speaker's own consciousness. How clever of Phillips to begin a poem with the word "Finally," and although "thick cover of night" may sound a bit too clichéd, the second line is hauntingly unforgettable, thanks to the vivid simile of snow as "fat as plates." Nothing in the first two lines is confusing—not the diction, not the imagery, and not the syntax—and the use of commas in the second line gives each detail its proper emphasis.

Meanwhile, the phrase "Wine-rested" in line 3 sounds like something out of a Homeric epic. In fact, Phillips shows (in other poems) that he is well read and knows Greek, Roman, and English classics intimately. His language often seems delicately allusive, as if when he writes he has the whole history of Western literature in the back of his mind. He knows all the rules of meter and all the standard poetic techniques, but he typically uses them in ways that make his phrasing sound like elevated common speech. "Wine-rested" is just one of many instances that sound polished without sounding contrived.

Phillips also has a superb ear for sound effects, as in the way "Cowed" (at the beginning of line 4) is echoed alliteratively by "quiet" and in assonance by "mountain" later in that line. In fact, alliteration is one of his most noteworthy skills; it appears repeatedly in his poems, even to the point of sometimes seeming overdone. Meanwhile, his command of meter is perfect, as in the way he uses iambic rhythms to emphasize the individual items listed in line 5, just as he so often uses lists and listing to great effect elsewhere in this volume. The idea that "lion and elk and pheasant" roam "Eight thousand feet above any ocean" gives readers a sense of the sheer and literal loftiness of the landscape the speaker describes, while the way "roaming" is subtly echoed by "ocean" is a perfect example of Phillips's way with sounds. No sooner has the speaker alluded to the vastness of physical space than he wryly and ironically suggests that the gates of heaven are an idea "Smuggled somewhere within this small lark's mind"—a line almost flawless in its use of multiple forms of alliteration.

Rowan Ricardo Phillips is an award-winning poet and translator whose honors include a 2015 Guggenheim fellowship and being longlisted for the 2015 National Book Award for poetry. His first collection of poetry was The Ground *(2012); his most recent work of criticism is titled* When Blackness Rhymes with Blackness *(2010).*

Alliteration and assonance combine again in the next line's opening words "As it sits," and again in the first two words of the line following, "Hardly startled," while the sudden, abrupt shift to the short word that ends this sentence, "On," and which comes paradoxically at the beginning of the ensuing line, all combine to demonstrate the moment-by-moment craftsmanship of Phillips's poetry. Somehow his writing seems utterly effortless on first reading but then seems very finely polished on closer inspection. It is hard, for instance, to imagine a better-sounding sentence than the one that concludes this excerpt, but it is difficult to say exactly why and how that sentence achieves that effect, although the alliteration in the final six words is surely part of the explanation.

The strongest poems in Phillips's book are the many texts, like the one just quoted, that manage to combine beauty with interesting observations and intriguing ideas. Sometimes, in poems such as the opening one, "The Mind after Everything Has Happened," it is hard to know precisely what is going on or what anything means, but Phillips would hardly be the first contemporary poet to write, occasionally, in a style elliptical to the point that one is not quite sure what to make of it. Sometimes he writes poems reminiscent of various poems by Wallace Stevens, splendid in the skillful play of their sounds, haunting to listen to even if they fail to make much obvious senses. More often, though, he comes close to the achievement of Stevens in a poem such as "Sunday Morning," where all the luscious sound effects combine with deeply searching thoughts and shrewd observations to produce poems one can read over and over. Such poems include "Monday Morning in Snowmass, Colorado," "The Once and Future King of Ohio," and "Apollo and Marsyas."

One of this book's most impressive works is the sequence of poems titled "The Beatitudes of Malibu." Here is the first of its eight brief sections:

> Walking across the PCH, we looked
> Up and saw, big as the butt of a pen,
> Jupiter, fat with light and unheightened.
> I looked back at the waiting traffic stalled
> At the seaside road's salt-rimmed traffic lights
> As they swayed to the Pacific's not-quite-
> Anapestic song of sea and air—
> The raw and sudden crick of crickets—
> The cars, suddenly silent as cows—
> And blue Malibu blackening like a bee.

Here again the characteristic alliteration is present, as are the assonance and the internal rhymes, the careful placement of words within lines (as in the strategic placement of "stalled"), the allusion to classical texts, the adept use of meter (as in line 7), and the wonderful inventiveness of words such as "unheightened," which manage to describe freshly what might have been merely a cliché. This section mixes humor (as in line 9) with the oddly mysterious (as in line 10); altogether, Phillips's writing here is at once so clear and so clever that it becomes almost impossible to stop reading: one wants to know what's next.

Reading poems like this one, one thinks of the colloquial wit and the easy contemporary diction of poetry such as Vikram Seth's *The Golden Gate* (1986). Various poems in the present book suggest Phillips's capacity to catch modern life in lines of memorable poetry, as in "Never Again Would Birds' Song Be the Same," a relatively long poem that begins:

> Eight floors below our wide-open window
> As early summer sang to early dawn

And no breeze blew, a car crouched idling
Under a red traffic light that had spent
Most of the night with nothing in sight but
The rare bus or cab.

Again, all the standard features of Phillips's poetry are here, but somehow he manages to keep those features fresh, partly because one senses that he can use his alliteration, assonance, echoes, and internal rhymes to describe almost anything, and that he can describe anything with absolute precision. The same facility and apparently effortless gift for finding the right words and sounds and rhythms is also evident in such other poems as "Boys" (although that poem opens with an unfortunate platitude), "Measure for Measure," "Lucas and Mark," and the aforementioned "The Once and Future King of Ohio," with its witty title and its compelling opening scene. Phillips, it seems, can take almost any topic or situation and make it vital, and even when he is most consciously imitative—as in the Homeric adaptations or the poem titled "Bernardo" (a riff on the opening scene of *Hamlet*)—he also seems utterly original. He brings much of the old magic back into modern verse, and it is refreshing to see what he can do with old stories, old characters, and old myths. Few recent poems are more memorable, for instance, than his "Apollo and Marsyas," and few contemporary poets are more impressive in the breadth and depth of their cultural knowledge.

One minute, for instance, Phillips is reviving the ancient Greeks or alluding to Dante, the next he is recalling Led Zeppelin or mentioning Dylan. He is a learned poet, but he usually wears his learning lightly, drawing on the distant past in ways that make it seem relevant to the immediate present. Because Phillips knows various literary traditions so well, he has no need to invent a private, impenetrable, self-consciously inscrutable language of the sort so often concocted by some poets—poets who apparently have less trust in their readers (and in their own abilities to communicate compellingly) than Phillips does. *Heaven* is the sort of book that creates confidence in the future of poetry, and it does so partly because it draws so fruitfully on the past.

Robert C. Evans

Review Sources

Báez, Diego. Rev. of *Heaven*, by Rowan Ricardo Phillips. *Booklist* 15 June 2015: 24. *Literary Reference Center*. Web. 3 Dec. 2015.
Rev. of *Heaven*, by Rowan Ricardo Phillips. *Publishers Weekly* 18 May 2015: 61. *Literary Reference Center*. Web. 3 Dec. 2015.
Logan, William. "Doing as the Romans Do." Rev. of *Heaven*, by Rowan Ricardo Phillips. *New Criterion* June 2015: 66–73. *Literary Reference Center*. Web. 3 Dec. 2015.

A History of Loneliness

Author: John Boyne (b. 1971)
First published: 2014, in Great Britain
Publisher: Farrar, Straus and Giroux (New York). 338 pp.
Type of work: Novel
Time: 1964–2013
Locales: Ireland; Norway; Rome, Italy

A History of Loneliness chronicles societal changes since the 1960s and their effects on Ireland—especially the evolving attitudes toward the dominance, power, and reputation of the Irish Catholic Church—as observed and experienced by a disillusioned priest who has remained isolated and uninvolved throughout his professional career.

(Courtesy of Farrar Straus & Giroux)

Principal characters:
ODRAN YATES, an Irish Catholic priest and a longtime teacher and librarian at Terenure College
HANNAH YATES RAMSFJELD, his sister
KRISTIAN RAMSFJELD, Hannah's late husband, a Norwegian
AIDAN RAMSFJELD, Hannah's older son and Odran's nephew
JONAS RAMSFJELD, Hannah's younger son and Odran's nephew
ARCHBISHOP JIM CORDINGTON, Odran's superior
TOM CARDLE, Odran's friend from seminary school

A History of Loneliness opens in 2001, at a point of relative innocence for first-person narrator Father Odran Yates, an Irish Catholic priest. Odran has worked happily at Terenure College since the late 1970s, teaching English and history, supervising the library, celebrating daily mass, and acting as spiritual adviser to young boys, the children of wealthy Dubliners. The institution is Odran's refuge from the usual occupation of priests, who typically serve in parishes. He occasionally visits his younger sister, Hannah Ramsfjeld, who lives in a suburb of Dublin. Hannah is the widowed mother of two sons: her older son, Aidan, has moved out and lives in London, while her younger son, bright but shy Jonas, still lives at home. She suffers occasional bouts of confusion.

With the setting and situation thus established and several key characters introduced, author John Boyne employs a technique he has successfully used before: fracturing the plot's timeline. Boyne withholds information until it is ready for presentation, creating suspense and sharing the storytelling process. The reader is forced to do some of the work of mentally reconstructing the chronology, connecting the dots, and drawing proper conclusions. Like many of Boyne's previous novels, including

The Thief of Time (2000), *Crippen* (2004) and *The Absolutist* (2011), *A History of Loneliness* moves freely backward and forward through time. Details from Odran's personal history are exposed throughout, contributing to a fuller understanding of his preference for isolation, his naiveté, his apparent willful obliviousness, and the guilt that haunts him.

As the story moves ahead to 2006, Odran is called to appear before Archbishop Jim Cordington. A former athlete who attended the same seminary as Odran, the archbishop has become an obese, corrupt alcoholic. The two men discuss a priest, a former colleague of Odran's, Miles Donlan, who has received a six-year prison sentence for an unspecified crime. The archbishop orders Odran to replace Tom Cardle, a fellow priest who was Odran's roommate at seminary and who has inexplicably been moved from parish to parish.

Odran recalls a disturbing memory from his youth. In 1964, his parents, Gloria and William, were constantly at odds, fighting about money and William's ambition to become an actor. After appearing in one play, in which his performance was universally panned, William became a drunkard. During a family outing at the beach, William purposely drowned his younger son and himself. This tragedy is the origin of Odran's guilt, because he survived, and his brother, who accompanied their father in Odran's place, did not. Soon after the incident, his mother, in a burst of religious ecstasy, declares that Odran should go into the priesthood.

By 2010 Odran has been in place at Tom Cardle's former parish for four years. Though he has adapted to parish life, Odran longs to return to Terenure. The religious environment has begun to change drastically in Ireland: priests, formerly revered, are increasingly distrusted and ostracized. Odran makes weekly visits to a nursing home see his sister, who is descending rapidly into early-onset dementia; while there, he occasionally runs into his gay nephew Jonas, now a well-known author.

Odran remembers 1973, when he entered Clonliffe College, a seminary in Dublin. Odran's roommate, Tom, felt he was missing many of the joys of youth by being cloistered. He resisted religious education and eventually ran away, but his stern father brutally beat him and forcibly returned him to the seminary, where he eventually became resigned to his fate.

Though proud to be a priest, Odran by 2011 is uncomfortable wearing the clerical collar, because men of the cloth have become targets of suspicion and censure in Ireland, following revelations of widespread child sexual abuse by priests that has been systematically covered up by the church hierarchy. Odran meets with Jonas, who is about to embark on an extensive tour to promote his fourth novel. They talk about Aidan, who as a boy had behavioral problems. Odran has not seen Aidan in years. Jonas tells him that Aidan is living in Norway and is now married and the father of several children. Later, Odran experiences firsthand the hatred directed at priests. While attempting to help a young boy lost in a department store locate his mother, he is chased by an angry mob misinterpreting his intentions, punched, and showered by epithets. He is subsequently arrested by the police, who interrogate and insult Odran before releasing him.

Irish writer John Boyne has written nine novels for adults, five novels for young adults and children, and a short-story collection. His 2006 novel The Boy in the Striped Pyjamas *was adapted for film in 2008.* A History of Loneliness *is his first novel set in his native Ireland.*

In 2007, Hannah moves into a facility for dementia patients. Odran meets again with Archbishop Codrington, who finally admits that Tom has been charged with "interfering" with boys (he fatuously claims that is why Tom was transferred so often, to keep the children safe) and may be sentenced to prison. Odran attends Tom's trial, feeling uncomfortable in his clerical vestments because of all the suspicious glances and angry comments directed at him. Tom is charged with five counts of child sexual abuse. Odran wonders how many additional unreported victims there might be and what caused Tom to do what he did. Later, in a pub, a young man who was one of Tom's victims attacks Odran, spits on him and hits him with a Bible, because in his mind Odran is guilty by association. Four years later, Odran finally flies to Norway to visit Aidan. They talk, and Aidan reluctantly confirms that Tom abused him. Odran is ashamed, and Aidan finds it difficult to believe his uncle never knew what was happening. Odran pleads to be allowed back into the life of Aidan and his family.

In 2013, Odran meets with a new archbishop to request a return to his old position at Terenure College and makes a veiled threat about revealing evidence of further church abuses to achieve what he wants. Later, Odran picks up Tom, who has been released from prison after five years, and takes him to the low-rent flat that the diocese has provided. In a bitter exchange, Tom accuses Odran of being as guilty as he was, arguing that he was complicit in the crimes by willfully ignoring evidence of abuse and doing nothing about it.

A searing indictment of religious hypocrisy centered on the true-life scandal that rocked Ireland and tainted respect for the Catholic Church, *A History of Loneliness* is a compelling portrait of an individual who, unlike his colleagues who committed unspeakable sins against children, is guilty of sins of omission and willful ignorance. Odran (the name alludes to Saint Odran, Ireland's first Christian martyr, who sacrificed his life for Saint Patrick) has voluntarily withdrawn from society and insulated himself from close human contact. He keeps in sporadic, almost disinterested touch with his relatives only because it is an expected obligation. He meets or corresponds infrequently with the only person he can call friend, Tom Cardle, and either overlooks, ignores, or is too oblivious to notice all the warning signs that Tom is a serial sexual abuser of children. Odran is like the protagonist in an Alfred Hitchcock movie, less aware than the audience of events transpiring around him, and some reviews of *A History of Loneliness* have criticized Odran for being implausibly naïve and blind to the truth. Others have argued that Odran is merely a foil for the author's own outrage at the Catholic Church and its role in covering up the sexual abuse scandal. In a review for the *Independent*, John Boland remarked that Boyne was occasionally heavy-handed in excoriating Odran and that "this sense of authorial coerciveness pushes the book into the realm of tract rather than fiction. . . . Cardle's withering attack on Odran's lifelong denial of realities seems less directed at his former friend than at any reader who mightn't have got the message about the evils of silence and avoidance." Nevertheless,

A History of Loneliness was generally well received by critics and general readers alike, and the book was praised for its compelling storyline and its insights into Irish history and the country's increasing secularism.

Jack Ewing

Review Sources

Boland, John. "John Boyne Is Back with the Priest's Story." Rev. of *A History of Loneliness*, by John Boyne. *Independent*. Independent.co.uk, 31 Aug. 2014. Web. 15 Dec. 2015.

Dunmore, Helen. Rev. of *A History of Loneliness*, by John Boyne. *Guardian*. Guardian News and Media, 3 Oct. 2014. Web. 15 Dec. 2015.

Mahony, Christina Hunt. "New Novel Brings John Boyne Closer to Home." Rev. of *A History of Loneliness*, by John Boyne. *Irish Times*. Irish Times, 31 Oct. 2014. Web. 15 Dec. 2015.

Nance, Kevin. "Novel Tackles Catholic Sex-Abuse Scandal." Rev. of *A History of Loneliness*, by John Boyne. *USA Today*. Gannett, 27 Feb. 2015. Web. 15 Dec. 2015.

Schilling, Timothy P. "Priests as Pariahs." Rev. of *A History of Loneliness*, by John Boyne. *Commonweal*. Commonweal Magazine, 2 Dec. 2015. Web. 15 Dec. 2015.

Hold Still
A Memoir with Photographs

Author: Sally Mann (b. 1951)
Publisher: Little, Brown (New York). 482 pp.
Type of work: Memoir
Time: 1860s through the early twenty-first century
Locale: Rockbridge County, Virginia; various locations in the South

(Courtesy of Little Brown and Co.)

Hold Still offers thoughtful reflections on the photographer's art, exploring Sally Mann's work from her earliest photographs through her current oeuvre. At the same time, the book excavates the history of Mann's family across several generations by tracing the complex confluence of personalities that flow into a single individual.

Principle personages:
SALLY MANN, author and narrator
LARRY MANN, her husband
EMMETT MANN, their son
JESSIE MANN, their daughter
VIRGINIA MANN, their daughter
ELIZABETH EVANS MUNGER, her mother
ROBERT SYLVESTER MUNGER, her father, a doctor
ROBERT MUNGER, her great-grandfather
CY TWOMBLY, her friend, an abstract artist in Lexington, Virginia

The origin of *Hold Still* was sparked by a letter from Harvard University, requesting that Sally Mann offer the prestigious Massey Lectures on the History of American Civilization in a trio of lectures in May 2011. This unexpected invitation set the renowned American photographer up with the enviable challenge that her talk should address "anything, speak about anything you want." This invitation inspired Mann to open chests of family mementos that had been long left sitting in a dusty attic. She sought to explore the ultimate notion of "the local," a term she borrowed from the poet William Carlos Williams, in order to rediscover her own youth and artistic origins. Setting out on this journey of self-discovery, Mann traveled not only into the earliest moments of her own biography, but also into long-forgotten corners of her ancestry and, ultimately, into the dark corners of Southern history.

As the memoir of a photographer, *Hold Still* is enlivened both visually and intellectually by the photographs that punctuate the text. Drawing on her own extensive oeuvre, alongside family photographs, Mann has filled the text with an array of images that in some sense capture the people and places in her life. These are two themes into which the work delves extensively, but first it is necessary to consider her reflections on the relationship between such images and the recuperation of memory. Having carefully curated an assemblage of family photographs and pulled together the arc of her own career, a reader would expect Mann to assert the historical and emotive value of these photographs. Instead, she undercuts them both as aides to memory. She writes, "Photographs supplant and corrupt the past, all the while creating their own memories," and continues that while perusing her own childhood photographs, she "knew that with each photograph I was forgetting." Mann be-

(Courtesy of Little, Brown and Co.)

Hold Still was a finalist for the National Book Award and the Andrew Carnegie Medal for Excellence in Nonfiction. Mann's other books include At Twelve *(1988),* Immediate Family *(1992),* What Remains *(2003),* Deep South *(2005), and* Proud Flesh *(2009).* What Remains *was made into a documentary in 2005.*

lieves that photography is able to characterize, extract, and fix a moment in time and then supplant and overpower other memories that have not been similarly documented and conceal any variant directions of memories. For the reader, Mann's selections of photographs do a great deal to illuminate the personalities and activities of their subjects within the story and cast the photographer and the generations of her family members as a charismatic, quirky crew. Yet Mann's point is well taken, as she excavates the complexities, suffering, and enduring bonds of emotion that such images fail to capture. Accordingly, Mann's memoir is a story of absence as much as of presence. It pushes against the failures of memory and the finality of death. Mann seeks to communicate what the magical power of photography has meant for her and to consider the things that are absent from her photographs.

Hold Still also addresses and exposes Mann's private pain and the turmoil her family endured in the face of the critical attention to the images in her 1992 work *Immediate Family*, which centered around Mann's three young children playing and posing mostly nude on the family's isolated farm property in Virginia. They are photographed preparing to dive into a river, standing side-by-side like phantoms in nighttime illumination on water, and dancing on a picnic table. In one particularly well-known work, Mann's daughter Jessie poses with a candy cigarette (which seems quite real in the photograph) while her sister Virginia stands with her back to the camera. When the book was first published, it was quickly recognized for the quality and beauty of the photographs. However, many faulted Mann with making her children look mean and accusing her of publishing pornography and of taking advantage of minors who could not give their proper consent. The powerful imagery of the photographs as well as the controversy surrounding them shot Mann to fame within the canon of American photographers. Mann grapples with fallout from *Immediate Family* across two chapters in *Hold Still*, and perhaps most interesting is her discussion of the collaborative role that her children played in helping to create the photographs and the generative manner in which the mother-child relationship fueled both the intimacy and the brilliance of this body of work. Also of great value is her inclusion of images that were excluded from the original publication, whether at the request of her children at the time or because of her own artistic decision-making. Mann's analysis of her work powerfully captures the transient magic of photography and the play between subject and artist, even when the subject is a young child.

As a way to perhaps connect differently with Mann's immediate family of husband Larry and their three children, *Hold Still* offers an exceptionally deep exploration into the family's roots. This thorough attention to family origins enables Mann to reconstruct the scaffolding of her own DNA by tracing its filaments into the different directions of her family tree. For instance, Mann traces her mother's family back several generations to reveal deep turmoil and heartache that help explain her mother's complicated personality. Larry's parents feature in a painful story of murder-suicide as Mann attempts to explore the motives that underlay the act. Mann devotes the most space in the book to the life and interests of her father, Robert S. Munger, perhaps because it is from him that she identifies the spark of her own passion for photography, although her father made the strategic decision to turn to the practical profession of medicine rather than fulfilling his artistic calling.

Although much of the book is spent in this process of pursuing different branches along Mann's family tree, she makes thoughtful use of this material in order to trace various issues concerning photography, memory, and the gaps of history. This pursuit of "the local" allows her to introduce many valuable reflections on the human truths of family and art, while also probing the human fascination with and fear of death.

Hold Still is a study of place and people. Most often and most deeply, the memoir considers the emotional attachment of Mann toward her family's farm, a talisman that has served to protect her while inspiring much of her photography. Through Mann's eyes the deep history of this landscape comes to life as the reader is told of the farm and its surroundings as seen by Civil War general Stonewall Jackson and by abstract painter, sculptor, and fellow Virginian Cy Twombly (1928–2011). Twombly's portrayal early in the book as Mann's friend and mentor has the interesting effect of disrupting the rural and isolated feel of Mann's lifestyle. Her rediscovery of Civil War–era glass negatives by photographer Michael Miley, on whose work she began to mirror her own images of the South, allow for reconstruction of her own history and of her love for this landscape and its robust tradition of art and culture. Mann allows herself to be presented through the critical lens of a Southern artist despite recounting an elite northern education and her ties to international journalists and art critics.

Once Mann opens the topic of her own Southern identity, she turns to her large body of work of the Southern landscape. Though also renowned, this work has certainly received less attention and may offer a new side of the photographer to a popular audience. The Southern history of Mann's paternal ancestors, as well as her own deep-rootedness in Virginia, guides her to grapple with the dark sides of Southern history from a personal and individualized perspective. Using images and text, she explores her relationship across the decades with her African American nanny, Gee-Gee, who is presented here as a member of Mann's family, despite being characterized by many silences and racial complexities under the surface. Through Gee-Gee and the topic of the Southern landscape, Mann enters into serious discussions of race relations as experienced from the perspective of a privileged white girl growing up in the South. Her powerful photographic journeys through the Deep South, which have sought out sites of hidden violence and peered through uncertain layers of Spanish moss and moldering ruins, take on a powerful personal edge as Mann searches through the weighty histories of such sites. The journey is personal, however, and without the feel of trying to convince the reader of a "right path" to follow through these murky histories.

Hold Still has been critically acclaimed and offers an intimate and powerful view into the mind and psyche of one of the most significant female artists of the 1990s. Readers will learn what motivated Mann to study photography, the various procedures and techniques she experimented with over her career, and what help to shape her most famous photographs and how the final image came to be through processes of trial and error. The accidents, failures, and manipulations of photography are discussed along with its power and potential. The book considers one family's journey of living with and through art as Mann documents the births, deaths, triumphs, and disasters of her family and records the quiet moments that would go unremarked except for the presence of the photographer. There is great value in an opportunity to delve deeply into an artist's craft and mind. There is also great privilege in being a companion on an artist's journey of self-discovery in which she uses her medium to help understand her past as well as her present.

Julia A Sienkewicz

Review Sources

Black, Emily Rapp. "Sally Mann's Memoir 'Hold Still' as Lyrical as Her Photos." Rev. of *Hold Still*, by Sally Mann. *Los Angeles Times*. Los Angeles Times, 14 May 2015. Web. 30 Jan. 2016.

Davies, Lucy. Rev. of *Hold Still*, by Sally Mann. *Telegraph*. Telegraph Media Group, 8 June 2015. Web. 30 Jan. 2016.

Dean, Michelle. "A Controversial Artist's Seductive Memoir." Rev. of *Hold Still*, by Sally Mann. *Guardian*. Guardian News and Media, 18 May 2015. Web. 30 Jan. 2016.

Gardner, Dwight. "'Hold Still,' Sally Mann's Memoir, Reveals a Photographer's Rich Life." Rev. of *Hold Still*, by Sally Mann. *New York Times*. New York Times, 5 May 2015. Web. 30 Jan. 2016.

Krug, Nora. "My Critics 'Were in Some Measure Correct,' Sally Mann Admits in Memoir." Rev. of *Hold Still*, by Sally Mann. *Washington Post.* Washington Post, 8 May 2015. Web. 30 Jan. 2016.

Parks, Cara. "Instill Life: The Dark and Light of Sally Mann." Rev. of *Hold Still*, by Sally Mann. *New Republic.* New Republic, 14 May 2015. Web. 30 Jan. 2016.

Honeydew

Author: Edith Pearlman
Publisher: Little, Brown (New York). 288 pp.
Type of work: Short fiction

Honeydew collects twenty of author Edith Pearlman's short stories, which tend to focus on small-town life but often veer into the realm of fable and fairy tale.

(Courtesy of Little Brown and Co.)

For nearly fifty years, Edith Pearlman quietly published one short story after another in small journals and magazines. Then her collection *Binocular Vision*, published in 2011, won a slew of awards and nominations, landing her a place in the literary spotlight for the first time in her life. Her most recent collection, *Honeydew*, has earned near-universal praise. Novelist Laura van den Berg called the book "majestic" and "fleet-footed" in her review for the *New York Times*. "The stories in *Honeydew* excel at capturing the complex and surprising turns in seemingly ordinary lives," she wrote. Heller McAlpin, for the *Washington Post*, wrote that Pearlman's book "displays deep wisdom about the quirkiness of happiness and human connections."

James Wood, in his review for the *New Yorker*, wrote that Pearlman's tales navigate expertly between fabulist and realist fiction, adding, "Pearlman's fiction brings together, with uncanny wisdom, short views and long views: the hours of our lives and the length of our lives. She is tender and distant at once." In that dexterity, he compares her to the late Scottish novelist Muriel Spark, author of *The Prime of Miss Jean Brodie* (1961), a novel that successfully—and famously—utilized a "flash-forward" device. The same device is demonstrated in Pearlman's "Hat Trick," in which a mother throws the names of teenaged boys into a hat and asks her daughter and her daughter's friends to draw names. The name that each girl draws will be her future husband, she tells them. Pearlman then flashes forward to reveal each girl's fate.

Wood also wrote that the twenty tales collected in *Honeydew* are not uniformly successful, that occasionally Pearlman's conclusions feel forced and unearned. Indeed, Pearlman lacks the scrupulous craftsmanship of many of the writers to whom she has been compared, including short-story maestro Alice Munro. Her sentences may be precise, but the shape of many of the tales is largely unformed. One example of this is collection's first story, "Tenderfoot," in which Bobby, a newly divorced art-history professor, innocently spies on a pedicurist named Paige. Paige's shop, Tenderfoot, is located across the street from his apartment, and if Bobby keeps his lights low, he can watch her work through the shop's enormous front window. Paige is devoted to her customers, who sit in one of only two reclining chairs that look directly out onto the street, but she nurses the private pain of losing her husband in the Iraq War. Bobby is new in town and lonely, but he is too shy at first to enjoy Tenderfoot's services. When he finally knocks on the door, the ensuing scene prickles with a tender sexual tension. Their rapport is interrupted by the unexpected appearance of Bobby's former wife, with whom he shared a troubling experience: he refused to stop at an accident they witnessed on the highway. Pearlman's story veers away from Bobby and Paige to become a more didactic commentary on moral responsibility. The turn is abrupt and disappointing, and the conclusion is too bold to be made without further exploration. It is as if Pearlman began writing a story about real people and relationships and then became more interested in what those people and relationships represented.

(Suzanne Kreiter)

Edith Pearlman is a short-story writer whose 2011 collection, Binocular Vision, *won the National Book Critics Circle Award and was nominated for the National Book Award, the Story Prize, and the Los Angeles Times Book Prize.* Honeydew *is her fifth collection.*

Perhaps, though, this is what Wood means when he calls Pearlman a fabulist. Characters in fables are necessarily one-dimensional—the handsome prince, the good daughter, the evil witch. Pearlman's characters are more complex, but they are nevertheless displayed at a remove. Some of Pearlman's stories even incorporate fairy-tale imagery. In "Dream Children," a nanny discovers secret drawings of deformed children in her employer's desk. One drawing features a boy with a blue-and-purple bulge on his face, dressed like Pinocchio; another features a girl with fur like a monkey, wearing a lace dress; and the last shows a baby in a diaper with flippers instead of arms and legs. The drawings are "amulets" against disaster, her employer explains, while the nanny concocts a potion of herbs to ease fever. In "Castle 4," a hospital is described as a medieval fortress with archetypal inhabitants: "There were beautiful ladies-in-waiting—waiting to die; and crones whose futures were no happier; and tremulous knights; and bakers with envelopes of magical spices. There was an ugly guard with a kind heart."

In "Stone," one of the collection's strongest stories, a twice-widowed woman leaves her Manhattan apartment to live with her stepson's family in a stone house in the mountains. The stepson is a woodworker (woodworking being the most honest of fairy-tale trades), and the woman, Ingrid, sleeps in a glorified closet off the kitchen, like Cinderella. Most stepmothers in fairy tales are evil; Ingrid is kind, but her presence in the rural setting works a kind of spell. The woodworker and his family fall in love with her. The little girl starts to call her Queen Giraffe because of her long and elegant neck. But there is no "happily ever after" in the real world. Just when it seems as if Ingrid might stay in the stone house forever, she has a poignant "flash-forward" epiphany in which she sees herself growing dependent on the family's care. She sees herself dying after a long and arduous illness and the family secretly regretting inviting her to stay in the first place. *"The house will call us fools,"* she thinks to herself.

A handful of the stories in *Honeydew* take place in a made-up town called Godolphin. The town is quaint, sometimes gratingly so, with an antique shop called Forget Me Not, a restaurant called Local, and a historic town square. Godolphin is populated by eccentrics, such as the Flaxbaums, a loving family with a penchant for wordplay. In these stories, Pearlman's quirkiness seems at once more forceful and less purposeful. "Blessed Harry," a story about patriarch Myron Flaxbaum, revolves around a houseplant of mysterious origins and a hoax letter in which Myron is invited to give a speech entitled "The Mystery of Life and Death." The heart of the story concerns the latter, but the tale is overstuffed with allusions and fanciful sentences that only serve to emphasize the family's syrupy sitcom-like life.

Another resident of Godolphin is Rennie, the owner of Forget Me Not. Rennie is the protagonist of two stories, the more interesting of which is "Assisted Living." In it, Rennie must contend with sullen Muffy Willis and her husband, Stu. The Waspish older couple "slid into the store at least twice a week," Rennie observes. "Like many long-married people they looked like siblings—both short, both with fine thin hair the color of Vaseline." Rennie develops an unlikely friendship with Muffy when her husband leaves her in the store to contemplate a prospective purchase. Pearlman constructs a tender tale juxtaposing Muffy's myriad material possessions with her want of a friend.

Pearlman's stories are short, averaging about five or six pages apiece, and the most successful among them are the most economical. Just as "Blessed Harry" buckles under an excess of images, "What the Ax Forgets the Tree Remembers" is done in by the weightiness of what it tries to accomplish. The story concerns a white woman, Gabrielle, who works for a local charity aimed at raising awareness about female genital mutilation (a rite practiced in a number of African and Middle Eastern countries in which a teenage girl's external genitalia is cut off by elders), but it is really about Gabrielle's own aging body and feelings of desire. It is clear that Gabrielle is doing good deeds for selfish reasons, but this is only halfheartedly implied. The story is too short to unpack all of the racial and cultural issues it touches on. In the end, it seems as if Pearlman was casting around for an image to express Gabrielle's feelings of brokenness, and female genital mutilation was simply the first one that came to mind.

The title story, "Honeydew," suffers from an excess of plot, though one of its central characters—a shy, anorexic teenage girl named Emily—is one of the most compelling characters in the book. Emily is obsessed with ants, even wishing that she were an ant, and her obsession evokes some peculiar imagery involving ant stomachs. (Ants have two stomachs, one a "personal" stomach and one communal; when an ant is hungry it can receive food from another ant's communal stomach.) The title refers not to the melon but to a sweet-tasting kind of insect secretion. "Honeydew" is strange and occasionally beautiful, if not completely successful.

"The Descent of Happiness," the penultimate story in *Honeydew*, is also a thing of strange beauty. Told from the perspective of an eight-year-old girl, the story has an exaggerated sense of importance, in the way that small events can be more meaningful to children than they are to adults. The girl is accompanying her father, a doctor, on a house call; the patient owns a hulking, wolflike dog named John Marshall, of whom the girl is terrified. When she gets out of the car, the dog chases after her. She trips and falls, and as she lies on the ground, she imagines that she is going to die. The dog is harmless, and in a moment her father comes running and picks her up. "I will never forget that day," Pearlman's narrator says, relieved at her rescue. "I had never been so happy before. I have never been so happy since." This story accomplishes what *Honeydew* manages only in tiny flashes: it captures a feeling with no name, holding it for the reader to view with surprise and awe.

Molly Hagan

Review Sources

McAlpin, Heller. Rev. of *Honeydew*, by Edith Pearlman. *Washington Post*. Washington Post, 5 Jan. 2015. Web. 21 Oct. 2015.

Ulin, David L. "Edith Pearlman Has a Fine Eye for the Intimate in *Honeydew*." Rev. of *Honeydew*, by Edith Pearlman. *Los Angeles Times*. Tribune, 2 Jan. 2015. Web. 21 Oct. 2015.

Van den Berg, Laura. Rev. of *Honeydew*, by Edith Pearlman. *New York Times*. New York Times, 31 Dec. 2014. Web. 21 Oct. 2015.

Wood, James. "Look Again." Rev. of *Honeydew*, by Edith Pearlman. *New Yorker*. Condé Nast, 23 Feb. 2015. Web. 21 Oct. 2015.

How to Be Drawn

Author: Terrance Hayes (b. 1971)
Publisher: Penguin Books (New York). 112 pp.
Type of work: Poetry
Time: 1970s–2010s

(Courtesy of Penguin)

How to Be Drawn, a finalist for the National Book Award, is the latest collection of verse by the Pushcart Prize–winning poet Terrance Hayes, author of three earlier volumes of poetry.

Much of the published commentary on the poetry of Terrance Hayes is often commentary on Hayes himself. The man, in other words, seems at least as interesting to many of his admirers as what he writes. And there is much, in fact, to admire about Hayes as a human being. This is especially true of the way he has overcome the humble circumstances of his youth, the way he has risen from talented college athlete to major contemporary poet, and also the way—*along* the way—he seems to have kept his fundamental humility, despite being a kind of rock star on the poetry conference circuit.

The poems are often praised at a distance: generalizations are invented to explain them and then a few lines are quoted from a poem here and there to support the general claims. The poems are often extolled for their subjects rather than their techniques, for their social relevance rather than for their skill as well-crafted words. And there is no doubt that many of the poems do sound good when Hayes himself reads them aloud.

Consider, for instance, the long poem titled "The Deer." The perception of the deer "with a soft white belly" in the opening line is effectively emphatic, partly because of the heavily accented monosyllables, partly because the image is almost archetypal, and partly because the image is simultaneously beautiful and disturbing. Deer, attractive as they are, are also hazards when they stand near roads: they risk serious damage to themselves as well as to drivers. In only a single line, then, Hayes has created interest, suggested beauty, and introduced suspense: the reader may wonder what will happen to this deer, and whether it will be accidentally killed or injured by the very speaker who sees it and admires it enough to discuss it at great length.

When the poem suddenly shifts to the second line, the reader's intuition that this deer is being seen along a road at night suddenly seems confirmed: the image of its "two eyes blind as holes" suggests the reflection of headlights moving toward the creature, perhaps literally blinding the deer (making it even more potentially dangerous, despite its "soft white belly"). But this imagery also makes the deer appear, to the poem's speaker and to the reader alike, almost unearthly, alien. No sooner are readers startled by the image of the deer's eyes as holes than more startling phrasing occurs. The speaker sees the deer "leap"—and then the line breaks, so that Hayes uses enjambment while still taking advantage of the abrupt shift to a new line to create even greater suspense. Readers soon learn the location *from* which the deer leaps, but the crucial information (*to* or *in* which direction it jumps) is, as it turns out, indefinitely postponed. Hayes has created an intensely dramatic situation, raised forcefully insistent questions, and then suspended the questions by suspending the deer in space and the poem in time. Readers never find out what happens to the deer, although a nagging question about its fate remains in the back of the mind all throughout a reading of the rest of the poem.

In the meantime, Hayes shifts to an altogether unexpected topic, and the poem, in a sense, makes an unpredictable leap, much as the deer does. The speaker does not just see the deer leap from "a bush beside the highway" (line 3), but sees how the deer could have been the bush itself. In repeating the phrase "a bush beside the highway" in the following line, he thereby calls attention to the poem's language, not merely its content, making that language seem interesting in its own right (and in its own sounds and rhythms), not simply in terms of what it describes. If literature can be defined most simply as language interesting first and foremost as language, then the repeated use of the phrase is the first explicitly *literary* effect in a poem that has been, up to this point, mostly realistic and descriptive. Now, however, the poem begins to shift from fact to fantasy, from deer to speaker, from literal event to cause for meditation. Now the deer leaves the poem for many lines and never quite returns as it originally entered. Now the speaker moves from focusing on a deer alongside a road to exploring memories inside the speaker's own mind.

So far, Hayes has already given readers one memorable simile with "eyes blind as holes"; now he provides another: the deer seems "a creature bony / as a branch in spring." Part of the effectiveness of this phrasing results from the alliterated "b" sounds; part of it results from the striking imagery and unexpected comparison. When the speaker figuratively closes his eyes to imagine himself as a deer, another unexpected shift occurs: instead of seeing an image, he remembers a smell. Now the deer disappears altogether (at least until much later in the poem), and for the moment the poem is dominated by memories of muscadine grapes—memories more vivid even than the preceding depiction of the animal. The imagery becomes even more richly sensual, involving not just sight but also smell and touch and eventually taste. Moreover, the different kinds of imagery are complex: the sweet smell of the berries contrasts with the strong "fumes" of passing cars; the tough skin of the berries contrasts with the wet "mucus" inside the skin; the active plucking by the adult woman contrasts with the placid "sleep" of the seeds—in another splendid simile, "thick as the sleep of an embryo." As these comments suggest, Hayes's poems often reveal genuine riches when they are closely read. Language that might seem merely plain on the surface often seems full of resonance when pondered.

Sometimes the language is simply memorable as sounds and images, as in the opening lines of a poem titled "Barberism":

It was light and lusterless and somehow luckless,
The hair I cut from the head of my father-in-law,

It was pepper-blanched and wind-scuffed, thin
As a blown bulb's filament, it stuck to the teeth

Of my clippers like a dark language, the static
Covering his mind stuck to my fingers, it mingled

In halfhearted tufts with the dust. . . . .

These lines suggest Hayes's love of sound effects (as in the heavy alliteration of line 1), invented phrases (as in the hyphenated adjectives of line 3), and combined alliteration and assonance (as line 7). These lines, too, again reveal Hayes's gift for memorable similes as well as the general clarity of his phrasing and his frequent use of a first-person lyric voice.

Various poems in *How to Be Drawn* are likely to mystify some readers, especially readers not as interested as Hayes obviously is in experimental forms. For instance, the opening section of "Who Are the Tribes," looks more like a spreadsheet than a poem in any conventional sense. Equally odd is the three-part poem "PORTRAIT OF ETHERIDGE KNIGHT IN THE STYLE OF A CRIME REPORT," which is structured like the charts of a crime report but which lacks—and calls into question—the information real crime reports might possess. (For example, "He had a homely wife and a shy nurse. His wife may also have been his nurse.") Still, the splendid word-music that pervades some of Hayes's more traditional lyrics may seem elusive in some of his more avant-garde verse.

Award-winning poet Terrance Hayes has received fellowships from the National Endowment for the Arts, the Guggenheim Foundation, and the MacArthur Foundation. In addition to How to Be Drawn, *he is the author of three other collections of verse:* Muscular Music *(1999),* Hip Logic *(2002),* Wind in a Box *(2006), and* Lighthead *2010), winner of the National Book Award for poetry.*

One can imagine that all these "new" forms create excitement in advanced MFA programs and when professional poets get together to share their latest wares. Whether most readers will care to read such poems, and whether the poems will last, is another question. Of course, whether academic poets even really care much about "most readers" is also another question. Hayes, usually, *does* seem to care. Here's hoping that in future books he will steer away from clever formal inventions and spend most of his time writing lines as fine as those in "The Deer."

Robert C. Evans

Review Sources

Chiasson, Dan. "Sense of Self: New Poems by Terrance Hayes and Deborah Landau." Rev. of *How to Be Drawn*, by Terrance Hayes. *New Yorker* 11 May 2015: 78. Print.

Collins, Kristofer. "How to Be Drawn: Terrance Hayes Produces Some Hip Poetics." Rev. of *How to Be Drawn*, by Terrance Hayes. *Pittsburgh Post-Gazette*. PG Publishing, 10 May 2015. Web. 1 Jan. 2016.

Farmer, Jonathan. "The Exoskeleton and the Blues." Rev. of *How to Be Drawn*, by Terrance Hayes. *Slate Book Review*. Slate Group, 7 Apr. 2015. Web. 1 Jan. 2016.

Rev. of *How to Be Drawn*, by Terrance Hayes. *Publishers Weekly* 16 Apr. 2015: 158. Print.

Ketner, Trevor. Rev. of *How to Be Drawn*, by Terrance Hayes. *Rumpus*. Rumpus, 5 June 2015. Web. 1 Jan. 2016.

Taylor, Tess. Rev. of *How to Be Drawn*, by Terrance Hayes. *All Things Considered*. NPR, 21 July 2015. Web. 1 Jan. 2016.

How to Start a Fire

Author: Lisa Lutz (b. 1970)
Publisher: Houghton Mifflin Harcourt
(Boston). 352 pp.
Type of work: Novel
Time: 1990s–2010s
Locale: United States

(Courtesy Houghton Mifflin Harcourt)

Written by best-selling novelist Lisa Lutz,
How to Start a Fire *chronicles the lives and
friendships of three women over the course
of twenty years.*

Principal characters:
ANNA FURY, an ambitious and adventur-
ous woman who eventually becomes a
doctor
KATE SMIRNOFF, her college friend, who becomes the quirky owner of her family's
diner
GEORGIANNA "GEORGE" LEONI, her college friend, an outdoorsy woman who eventually becomes a forest ranger

The significance of friendship is a theme that is often associated with children's literature. Novels for adults tend to focus on more ostensibly "mature" topics—serious
ideas and issues that are typically associated with growing older. What this trend in
mainstream adult literature fails to acknowledge, however, is that adults need meaningful, platonic relationships with others just as much as children do. In *How to Start
a Fire*, American novelist Lisa Lutz deviates, for the most part, from her well-established reputation as a mystery writer to explore the complexity and importance of
friendship in adulthood. In an unfiltered depiction of the relationship between three
women from late adolescence to middle age, Lutz breaks away from clichéd depictions of "sisterhood" to prove that while friendship is invaluable, it is rarely perfect.

How to Start a Fire is a novel that can easily be categorized as realism. Lutz does
not proffer a sensational plot by depicting extraordinary characters caught in extraordinary events. Instead, she tells a story about three relatively average women grappling with common emotional, physical, and professional problems. The end result
is a narrative that not only emanates authenticity but is highly relatable. Although the
flaws, complexities, and self-destructive tendencies of the central protagonists could
easily be off-putting to readers who look to fiction for escapism, Lutz ensures that they
are still compelling characters by depicting them as both well intentioned and tena-
cious. In the end, their appeal as heroes stems from the fact that they are good people
who repeatedly and courageously persevere through life's hardships.

After an intriguingly ambiguous flash-forward scene, the story of *How to Start a Fire* begins in 1993 when the three characters meet as freshmen at the University of California, Santa Cruz. Lutz presents Anna Fury, a thrill seeker from an old-money family on the East Coast, as the de facto leader of the group, and Anna's story line subsequently makes up more of the narrative than those of the other characters. When Anna is first introduced, she is a biology major who takes great pleasure in defying her parents' upper-class lifestyle and etiquette. The only person willing to put up with her antics is her roommate and best friend, Kate Smirnoff, whose contrarian tendencies are directed not at her family but at society. Kate is painfully earnest, easily obsessed by obscure topics, and has no interest in professional or personal conventionality. The third and final friend, Georgianna "George" Leoni, is a tall, beautiful, and athletic forestry major. Although Lutz never clarifies the reason behind George's affinity for the other two women, it is assumed that it is because she, too, is a "different" kind of woman.

Womanhood is not the focal point of *How to Start a Fire*, although the way in which it is presented is noteworthy. Often, fictional portrayals of women and female friendship in the media align to romantic comedy tropes. Lutz, however, does not depict her protagonists as overemotional beings whose lives are fraught with simple misunderstandings. Arguably more ground-breaking is the way in which Lutz's female characters express their emotions. Anna, Kate, and George rarely tell one another how they feel out loud. Instead of heart-to-hearts, they demonstrate their affection and loyalty through their actions. Whenever one of the characters is undergoing a personal tragedy or hardship, the others provide their support simply by showing up. In addition to replacing cloying dialogue with action, *How to Start a Fire* does not simply focus on the female struggle to "have it all." Rather than trying to balance love and work, the challenges the women face are often more psychological.

Lisa Lutz is a best-selling author who is best known for her Spellman series, a series of mystery novels that follows a family of private investigators.

How to Start a Fire follows the lives of Anna, Kate, and George over the course of more than two decades. Although all three women face a number of diverse conflicts throughout their lives, Lutz ensures that each story line's trajectory is cohesive and aligned to its character's personality. This is an especially impressive feat considering the expansiveness of the novel's timeline, multiple locations, and nonlinear plot structure. After introducing their time at UC Santa Cruz as the formative years of their friendship, Lutz focuses the majority of the narrative on the women's post-college experiences. One event in 1998, when they have all graduated but are still living as roommates, proves to be the catalyst that shapes the next fifteen years of the women's lives.

Despite Lutz's succinct, matter-of-fact presentation of this event, it drives the rest of the plot. In the years that follow, George finds herself reluctant to ever be without a man, and as a result she goes through a series of bad marriages. Kate, who is staunchly committed to being a good person, is perpetually wondering how to make the situation right. Arguably the most affected by the incident is Anna; already battling alcoholic tendencies, she feels so guilty about the event that her substance-abuse problem begins to consume every aspect of her life. While the issues of trauma, abusive relationships, and alcoholism have the potential to weigh down the narrative, Lutz dilutes this gravity with humor. This is most evident in her dialogue, which is fast paced, clever, and often witty.

As a whole, the tone of *How to Start a Fire* can be described as meditative. In an effort to explore the reality and significance of adult friendship, Lutz ensures that her protagonists are consistently testing the boundaries of their relationships with one another. This manifests in the form of betrayal and dishonesty on more than one occasion. Despite their shortcomings as friends, however, the women are repeatedly drawn back to one another. Their connection is comparable to that of family members, a deliberate distinction made by Lutz: while childhood friends are about companionship and fun, adult friendships often become familial. Lutz emphasizes the importance of this tendency by demonstrating that the protagonists do not have anyone else to depend on. Kate's parents died when she was eight; Anna's parents are so emotionally absent that she feels like an orphan; George's parents cannot provide her with the help she so often needs. Through Anna, Kate, and George, Lutz makes the point that while the families people choose are often imperfect, they are often essential to surviving adulthood.

Seminal moments between the protagonists are often marked by camping expeditions, a tradition that begins when the three first meet as freshman and decide to go on a spontaneous road trip to see giant redwood trees. As their lives become increasingly spread out in the years that follow, these sporadic camping trips are often the only times when the women are in the same place at the same time. By establishing camping as a uniting force between the characters, Lutz indirectly demonstrates that the two intrinsic qualities these women share are independence and toughness. Furthermore, the wilderness and its general unpredictability proves to be an effective metaphor for their adulthood. Although the title of *How to Start a Fire* alludes to the camping tradition between the friends, it is also indicative of a greater theme. Combustion, in both the literal and figurative senses, starts with a spark and becomes all-consuming. For Anna, Kate, and George, the night of the infamous incident ignites the force of self-destruction in all of their lives. Like a fire, this force continues to grow until the characters can no longer ignore it.

In order to effectively chronicle the lives of all three women over the course of two decades, Lutz focuses each chapter on a specific, formative moment in one of the characters' lives. The chapters are akin to vignettes and usually do not cover more than a few days of a character's life. As the women's friendship is the heart of the novel, the two characters that are not directly focused on in a chapter are presented as supporting characters. When George is going through a divorce, for example, Anna flies out for support. Lutz's decision to only depict short, important moments in her protagonists' lives allows her to cover a larger span of time economically.

The most experimental aspect of *How to Start a Fire* is the nonlinear way in which Lutz organizes the narrative. The chapters are not in chronological order but instead jump back and forth in time, with the year and location of each denoted in the chapter headings. In the beginning chapters of the novel, Lutz gives readers an idea of who the protagonists once were and who they ultimately become. By moving through the plot's timeline afterward in an unpredictable, zigzag trajectory, Lutz taps into her background as a mystery writer to create a sense of intrigue and suspense. Consequently, every chapter brings a new clue that completes each character's story line.

In comparison to Lutz's previous novels, the reception of *How to Start a Fire* has been tepid. Critics have claimed that the novel's disjointed narrative structure prevents a meaningful story from being fully developed. The reviewer for *Kirkus Reviews* argued that the "dizzying" speed with which the chapters jump between different time periods and settings causes the novel to become "little more than a list of names and places." While the plot's nonlinear structure may be frustrating or disorientating to some readers, it undeniably makes for an original reading experience and ultimately does not detract from the overall message of the novel. More favorable reviewers have noted Lutz's ability to capture women in a realistic light; the reviewer for *Publishers Weekly*, for example, praised Lutz for providing "fresh insight into the mysterious terrain of female friendships."

How to Start a Fire is not only prose with literary merit; it is also successful in its examination of issues that are significant to all of humankind. At the end of the day, *How to Start a Fire* is the rare novel that successfully balances suspense and humor with thought-provoking storytelling.

Emily E. Turner

Review Sources

Hayman, Stacey. Rev. of *How to Start a Fire*, by Lisa Lutz. *Library Journal* 1 Apr. 2015: 83. Print.
Rev. of *How to Start a Fire*, by Lisa Lutz. *Kirkus Reviews* 1 Mar. 2015: 165. Print.
Rev. of *How to Start a Fire*, by Lisa Lutz. *Publishers Weekly* 23 Mar. 2015: 46. Print.
Vnuk, Rebecca. Rev. of *How to Start a Fire*, by Lisa Lutz. *Booklist* 15 Feb. 2015: 31. Print.

Hunger Makes Me a Modern Girl

Author: Carrie Brownstein (b. 1974)
Publisher: Riverhead Books (New York).
256 pages.
Type of work: Memoir
Time: 1980s–2015
Locales: United States, Australia, Europe

Hunger Makes Me a Modern Girl *chronicles the youth, musical development, and personal evolution of rock star and actor Carrie Brownstein, both onstage and off.*

Principal personages:
CARRIE BROWNSTEIN, cofounder of the band
  Sleater-Kinney
KENNY BROWNSTEIN, her father
LINDA BROWNSTEIN, her mother
CORIN TUCKER, her Sleater-Kinney cofounder
JANET WEISS, drummer for Sleater-Kinney

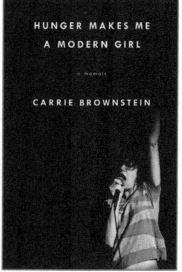

(Courtesy of Riverhead Books)

Carrie Brownstein has become an enormously popular TV star among viewers who appreciate quirky and satirical humor. One of the stars of the critically acclaimed series *Portlandia*, she and her writing and performing partner, Fred Armisen, are considered by many people to be a postmodern Burns and Allen. They inspire comparisons to such other legendary comedic duos as Nichols and May, and Stiller and Meara. Brownstein and Armisen costarred in a series of holiday commercials for Old Navy in 2015, which were scripted and acted like mini sitcoms.

Thus it may come as a surprise to Brownstein's current fan base that her breakout involvement with *Portlandia* is thoroughly ignored in her debut memoir. There is a nod given to Armisen in the epilogue, but the rest of the book is clearly focused on her childhood in Washington State, her home life in a seemingly ideal family, and the path to self-discovery that features plenty of embarrassing and empowering detours along the way.

Brownstein paints herself as a child who was desperate for validation. She admits that during her childhood days in Redmond, Washington, she was often nestled deep in her own imagination, where she constantly craved interaction with her entertainment heroes and heroines. She conducted make-believe interviews with the posters of Madonna and Duran Duran that hung on her bedroom walls; she would write long and personally revealing letters to the post office box addresses of movie and TV stars whom she admired. Brownstein revered the stars that trotted across her home's TV screen, and she also felt a kindred spirit with the movie icons of the past.

While Brownstein acknowledges that she was out of step in some ways with many of her suburban contemporaries, she also reveals that she had a certain confidence and swagger in her adolescent years that translated into popularity. Always seen as more mature and composed than many of her peers, she was also a huge hit with her friends' moms, who felt that she was a great listener and conversationalist. Her life in the Pacific Northwest coincided with the explosion of the music scene that erupted around her. Brownstein may not have considered herself a real musician, but she had the ability and the need to perform with her guitar and her voice.

(© Autumn de Wilde)

Carrie Brownstein first gained acclaim as a founding member, guitarist, and vocalist for the band Sleater-Kinney. She is a co-creator, star, and writer for the award-winning television program Portlandia *(2011–). She has written articles for the* New York Times, Slate, *and anthologies on culture and music. For three years, she was NPR's music blogger.*

The meeting of Brownstein and Corin Tucker is the pivotal part of Brownstein's evolution into a performer. The two women had had successful gigs with other bands—Brownstein with Excuse 17 and Tucker with Heavens to Betsy. Their mutual admiration for one another was one of the catalysts for their decision to start their own group. The band's name, Sleater-Kinney, came courtesy of Tucker leaving a voicemail message for Brownstein one day. Sleater-Kinney is the name of a road in Lacey, Washington, which is populated by rundown chain stores and "shoddy annual carnivals." Brownstein admits that the name sounds like a law firm or a hospital, but that is part of its appeal. Always pushing the envelope, Brownstein states that the "moniker could be whatever we wanted it to be. It could embody whatever and whoever we were."

In 1994, on the verge of turning twenty years old, Brownstein embraced her true calling as a preeminent player in the riot grrrl movement. Along with Tucker, and eventually drummer Janet Weiss who joined in 1996, the Sleater-Kinney band became both a critical darling and a bull's-eye for poison pen journalism. Brownstein points out how many of their reviews were always penned by male writers who could not ignore their female camaraderie. They were frequently critiqued not as musicians, but as women musicians. They did, however, receive abundant adulation—*Rolling Stone* legendary contributor Greil Marcus declared that they were America's best rock band in 2001—but they also garnered intrusive, unwanted publicity, such as when Brownstein and Tucker were outed as a onetime romantic couple by a *Spin* magazine journalist. In fact, where many bands would be decimated by a pair of cofounders-lovers breaking up, Sleater-Kinney only grew stronger, using the angst and emotions from the split to fuel albums and their stage theatrics.

As in many stories that detail a meteoric rise, there is the inevitable moment of descent. Without realizing it, Brownstein might have been more attuned to the potentially unavoidable collapse than many other artists. In her personal life, as a very young teen, she experienced her mother's admission of being the victim of an eating disorder. When her mother left for treatment, Brownstein and her sibling were left to parent and discipline themselves. Later, when she was in her early twenties, her father, who always seemed very conventional but tight-lipped to her, came out as a gay man. Her ability to cope with and move beyond these revelations of family secrets might have aided her when Sleater-Kinney called it quits in 2006.

Taking responsibility for fracturing the band, Brownstein attributes it to her unease with their touring. She developed severe cases of shingles, suffered from panic attacks, and endured torn ligaments and other maladies. Her body seemed to be telling her that it was time to get off the road and reexamine her options. Corin Tucker had established a rewarding life for herself apart from the band: she had fallen in love and started a family. She was managing to juggle the role of rock-and-roll front person and domestic goddess. Brownstein, who had had relationships with other women after Tucker, does not disclose their names but explains that she had a difficult time connecting and bonding with them in a permanent, long-standing way.

One of the ways in which Brownstein coped with her life after Sleater-Kinney was by volunteering at her local animal shelter in her newly adopted home of Portland, Oregon. She explains how she attempted to build a safe space for her two cats and newly procured two dogs. With a meticulous eye for detail, she re-creates her daily fight to turn a house that is actually overrun by animals who merely tolerate one another into a home that smacks of altruism and humanism. Her narration of how she realized there were problems among the animals, but hoped she could overcome them with good intentions and continual adjustments, ends with a chilling revelation. While Brownstein was out one day, her beloved eldest cat was killed by her two dogs. She handled the cleanup of the "crime scene" and the dispatching of the dogs with an objective, dispassionate professionalism. She gave away her remaining cat for his own safety, but one wonders if it was really for her own sanity. Brownstein ends this heartbreaking chapter, the second to last in the book, with the candid observation: "Now, finally, I was sad. Here it was, that shadow that forms on your insides. . . . Everything I had was gone."

The book's epilogue takes Brownstein's narrative out of the dark place and affirms her arrival into a lighter and brighter world. Her contemporary collaboration with Fred Armisen is briefly alluded to, and her reunion with Sleater-Kinney for their 2015 tour is lovingly recounted. The band regrouped to put out a new album after a decade's drought, and Brownstein lauds her time on the stage in front of enthusiastic fans. She had grown and matured over the preceding nine years and was able to appreciate her onstage moments with her bandmates as a place where she definitely belonged. The book concludes on an upbeat, positive note. Waiting to harmonize with Tucker and Weiss, she notes: "I was in my body, joyous and unafraid. I was home."

Hunger Makes Me a Modern Girl has received mostly positive reviews, especially regarding the ways in which it departs from the expected rock-star autobiography. For

Brownstein's memoir is not a confessional of bad behavior on the road or a blueprint for destroying hotel rooms and eluding law enforcement; rather, the book is truly a coming-of-age story that reveals the author as a somewhat nerdy, geeky youngster who drew from her dual "outsider" and "popular" positions to fashion herself into a rock guitarist. Brownstein shows that even a rock musician can harbor honest self-deprecation, stormy self-doubt, and redemptive self-determination.

Some reviewers were disappointed by Brownstein's decision to focus exclusively on an earlier period of her life rather than on her current life as a TV actor and comic writer. Many reviewers also shared the thought that she could have been much more forthcoming about her present private life. Yet while such omissions may leave many of her fans ravenous for more insight, hungry for more anecdotes, not all reviewers agreed that this was a flaw.

Stephanie Finnegan

Review Sources

Empire, Kitty. "'Hunger Makes Me a Modern Girl' by Carrie Brownstein Review—Mysteries Remain." Rev. of *Hunger Makes Me a Modern Girl*, by Carrie Brownstein. *Guardian*. Guardian News and Media, 10 Nov. 2015. Web. 5 Jan. 2016.

Graham, Ruth. "Carrie Brownstein's 'Hunger Makes Me a Modern Girl': Yes, She's That Cool." Rev. of *Hunger Makes Me a Modern Girl*, by Carrie Brownstein. *Washington Post*. Washington Post, 20 Oct. 2015. Web. 5 Jan. 2016

Rev. of *Hunger Makes Me a Modern Girl*, by Carrie Brownstein. *Kirkus Reviews* 15 Aug. 2015: 227. Print.

Williams, John. "Carrie Brownstein's 'Hunger Makes Me a Modern Girl.'" Rev. of *Hunger Makes Me a Modern Girl*, by Carrie Brownstein. *New York Times*. New York Times, 29 Oct. 2015. Web. 28 Oct. 2015.

I Am Radar

Author: Reif Larsen
Publisher: Penguin Press (New York). 656pp.
Type of work: Novel
Time: 1975–2013 for the main narrative; supplementary narratives beginning 1882
Locales: New Jersey; Finnmark, Norway; Yugoslavia; French Protectorate of Cambodia; postcolonial Cambodia (Kampuchea); Atlantic Ocean; Democratic Republic of the Congo

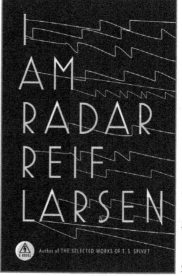

(Courtesy of Penguin)

Author Reif Larsen's second novel consists of several, almost freestanding, narratives that are gradually woven into the central narrative focusing on the life of the protagonist, Radar Radmanovic. The author eventually peels back the layers of the past to tie together the disparate elements into a main thread, and in so doing, explores the psychology behind being "the other" who deviates from the conventional.

Principal characters:
RADAR RADMANOVIC, the protagonist, a black baby born to white parents
KERMIN RADMANOVIC, his father, a Yugoslavian immigrant
CHARLENE VOLMER RADMANOVIC, his American mother
MIROSLAV DANILOVIC, alias Otik Mirosavic, Serbian puppet master and a member of the Kirkenesferda theatrical puppet troupe
LEIF CHRISTIAN HOLTSMARK, founder of the Kirkenesferda organization
LARS RØED LARSEN, leader of the Kirkenesferda theatrical puppet troupe

Radar Radmanovic's odyssey is not a legend, per se, nor does it truly qualify as a bildungsroman, though vague attempts are made in that general direction. The book title, too, is misleading. Though it proclaims "I Am Radar," and the assumption is that the tome is mainly about the title character, in reality, readers do not begin to know Radar definitively as an individual until mid-volume, in part 3, "This Darkness Is Not the Night," and in part 5, "The Conference of the Birds." It is not until this latter section that Radar begins to establish a relevance in the amorphous grand scheme, and, even then, one is still left wondering. These issues notwithstanding, the book does have some significant virtues. The story itself is compelling (one may more accurately say "stories," because the segments located in Serbia and Cambodia with separate personalities are skillfully constructed in their own right), and reader interest is maintained to the end. The characterization of Radar is well-developed as are the issues and challenges raised by his uniqueness as an individual. At times humorous and, in other instances, tragic, the book is a thought-provoking volume that leaves readers wishing to know more.

The Radar saga begins on April 17, 1975, in Elizabeth, New Jersey, with the extraordinary circumstances surrounding his birth as an inexplicably black child of a white couple. Radar's birth took place in the midst of a sudden electrical blackout, by means of an obstetrical delivery illuminated only by his father's pocket flashlight. His mother, Charlene, a librarian born in Trenton, is a former 1960s and 1970s flower child with a history of drug use and casual sex. She renounced her former life, however, to marry Radar's father, Kermin Radmanovic, a radio operator whose father was a Chetnik partisan during World War II in Yugoslavia. Charlene is strongly affected by the circumstances of her son's birth and has herself experienced the side effect of a sharply heightened sense of smell. The curiosity is noted in the media, but then subsides as the family members get on with their lives. While Kermin listlessly accepts this situation, and becomes increasingly absorbed in his radio wave experiments, Charlene is obsessed by it and strives ceaselessly to uncover a precise medical diagnosis and arrive at a solution. She consults one medical text after another and takes Radar to diverse specialists to undergo a battery of tests—so much so, that young Radar perceives this as the natural order of life. The medical practitioners marvel at Radar's uniqueness but cannot arrive at a treatment or solution.

Then Charlene receives an unsolicited communique on May 27, 1979, from Mr. Brusa Tofte Jebsen, a former member of Kirkenesferda, which he describes as "a community of physicists and artists . . . that have been experimenting with certain electrical shock treatments." Tofte Jebsen suggests that Kirkenesferda might be able to effect an alteration of Radar's skin coloration. Kirkenesferda is located near the city of Kirkenes, in the province of Finnmark, in the extreme north of the Kingdom of Norway, near the Russian border. Kermin Radmanovic is adamantly opposed at the onset; but Charlene's entreaties, and a good deal of low-key persuasion—including free transportation, lodging, and meals—from Leif Christian Holtsmark, one of Kirkenesferda's directors, bring him to agreement. Kermin consents to have Radar subjected to "electro envelopment." The radical treatment ultimately does change Radar's skin color, as hoped for by his mother. However, it leaves young Radar with hair loss and a proclivity for epileptic seizures.

The book then becomes a patchwork of narratives, with a wide series of characters, related in some manner to Kirkenesferda, ranging in locales from Serbia to Cambodia, and covering a substantial span of years and tying them in to Radar and his family in New Jersey. In part 2 of the book, "The Elephant & the River," the story of Radar is suspended. It resumes in part 3, "This Darkness Is Not the Night," and then is suspended once again in part 4, "The Principles of Uncertainty." Both "The Elephant & the River" and "The Principles of Uncertainty" inject stories seemingly unrelated to either each other or to the main narrative. Part 2 deals with a Serbian (or Montenegrin?) family, the Danilovics—Danilo (the father), Miroslav and Mihajlo (the sons), and Stoja (the mother)—and covers the period 1975 to 1992. The primary thread is the development and career of the rather unique elder son, Miroslav Danilovic, who becomes increasingly estranged from his family and leaves for Belgrade, where he gains notoriety as a particularly skilled puppet master. Miroslav comes to a mysterious end, and his father is told that he was found suffocated in his flat. The father is never allowed to see the body. The Danilovics' tale is cut off at that point and superseded by the update of Radar's life in part 3.

Part 4 begins along the Mekong River in what was then the French Protectorate of Cambodia in 1953 on the colonial plantation of La Seule Vérité, owned by the de Broglie family. It recounts the family's progress (or otherwise) from 1882, and leads up to the adoption of a Cambodian foundling by the plantation master, Jean-Baptiste de Broglie. The adopted child, Raksmey, becomes an expert in quantum electrodynamics and lives in Paris after the takeover of Cambodia by the Khmer Rouge. In 1979 Raksmey is invited by Leif Christian Holtsmark to guide the Kirkenesferda Puppet Performing troupe across the border of Thailand into Cambodia to put on a show for the Khmer Rouge. All seemed to be going well until December 30, 1979, when the notorious Pol Pot appeared during the performance. The troupe was accused of spying for the United States and was massacred. Only Raksmey and ten-year-old Lars Røed Larsen escaped. Just near the Thai border, Raksmey is blown up by a land mine, but Røed Larsen makes it across to safety.

In 2010, thirty-five-year-old Radar Radmanovic is living with his parents in Kearny, New Jersey, where he works at a radio station. His father, Kermin, tinkers incessantly in his radio shed, obsessed with whatever mysterious project he has undertaken. One frequent visitor is a heavy-set bearded Serbian who calls himself Otik Mirosavic. Though troubled by instances of grand and petit mal epileptic seizures, Radar has found a serious girlfriend, Ana Cristina. Suddenly, the entire area is enveloped in an inexplicable blackout. After some harrowing adventures, Radar makes it from the radio station to his home and finds evidence that his own father is actually responsible for the catastrophe, having built an explosively pumped flux compression oscillating cathode electromagnetic pulse generator, which short-circuited and disabled the surrounding area. Furthermore, Kermin has disappeared. Radar's frenetic investigations lead him to Lars Røed Larsen and Otik Mirosavic. They tell Radar that they have been working with his father on preparing bird puppets for an extravaganza performance that they intend to hold in the Democratic Republic of the Congo. They admit Radar into their circle in his father's place, and he chooses to travel with them on a transatlantic sea voyage aboard the cargo ship *Aleph*, leaving his mother and Ana Cristina behind. After a sometimes horrific crossing, the trio are eventually joined by Cameroonian guide named Horeb. While journeying up the Congo River the troupe gives a successful, impromptu performance, and continues on traveling.

Raymond Pierre Hylton

Reif Larsen is an author and filmmaker. His first novel, The Selected Works of T. S. Spivet *(2010) was made into a 2014 motion picture film,* The Young and Prodigious T. S. Spivet, *directed by Jean-Pierre Jeunet. Larsen's articles and essays have appeared in the* Guardian, *the* New York Times, Virginia Quarterly Review, *and other publications.*

Review Sources

Boyagoda, Randy. "'I Am Radar' by Reif Larsen—Review: Short-Circuited by Literary Excess." Rev. of *I Am* Radar, by Reif Larsen. *Guardian*. Guardian News and Media, 26 Mar. 2015. Web. 8 Feb. 2016.

Hitchings, Henry. "'I Am Radar' by Reif Larsen." Rev. of *I Am* Radar, by Reif Larsen. *Financial Times*. Financial Times, 20 Mar. 2015. Web. 8 Feb. 2016.

Kellogg, Carolyn. "Review: Reif Larsen's 'I Am Radar' Transmits Narrative Magic." Rev. of *I Am Radar*, by Reif Larsen. *Los Angeles Times*. Los Angeles Times, 20 Feb. 2015. Web. 8 Feb. 2016.

Martin, Tim. "'I Am Radar' by Reif Larsen Review: 'Groping for Connections'" Rev. of *I Am* Radar, by Reif Larsen. *Telegraph*. Telegraph Media Group, 19 Mar. 2015. Web. 8 Feb. 2016

Maslin, Janet. "Review: In Reif Larsen's 'I Am Radar,' an Odyssey of Exploding Particles." Rev. of *I Am* Radar, by Reif Larsen. *New York Times*. New York Times, 19 Feb. 2015. Web. 8 Feb. 2016.

Moore, Steven. "A Masterpiece of Young Geekhood." Rev. of *I Am* Radar, by Reif Larsen. *Washington Post*. Washington Post, 9 Apr. 2015. Web. 8 Feb. 2016.

In the Country

Author: Mia Alvar (b. 1978)
Publisher: Alfred A. Knopf (New York). 347 pp.
Type of work: Short fiction
Time: 1969 to present day
Locales: Philippines, Bahrain, United States

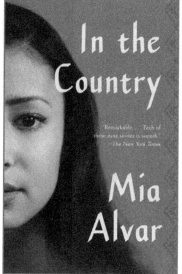

(Courtesy of Knopf)

Mia Alvar shares nine stories of the Filipino diaspora. The characters, who range in class status, live and work in the Philippines, Bahrain, and the United States.

Principal characters:
SALLY RIVA, a Filipina special-education teacher working in Bahrain
AROUSH MANSOUR, a five-year-old disabled Bahraini girl
BABY, a young Filipina who turns an expatriate community upside down
DANIEL "DANNY" WILSON JR., a disabled Filipino boy in search of a friend
MILAGROS SANDOVAL, a Filipina nurse, activist, and grieving mother
JAIME "JIM" REYES, a Filipino activist and reporter
ESMERALDA, a Filipino woman working in New York City to support her family
DAD, a former Philippine political figure living in Massachusetts
MOMMY, Dad's wife
ANDOY, a young Filipino expatriate who falls in love too easily

In the Country is Mia Alvar's debut collection of short fiction. The book contains nine stories that are centered on or near the places that Alvar herself knows: the Philippines, Bahrain, and the United States. The characters range from *katulong* (the servant class consisting mostly of Filipino women) to members of both blue-collar and white-collar middle class, politician, and bullied children. This diversity of character experiences will pull readers into the equally varied plot lines of the stories. In addition to the assortment of characters and array of story lines, the thematic movement of the stories through emotional, mental, and physical landscapes keeps readers actively involved as the characters roam between countries, times, and relationships.

The desire for a sense of home is a central theme in several of the stories. The first story, "The Kontrabida," follows Steve, a pharmacist who has lived in New York for a decade, as he returns home to the Philippines because his father is dying. While there, the narrator flashes back to the childhood abuse he experienced at the hands of the man who ruled his and his mother's lives. However, he also shares *pasalubong*, presents from his time in the United States, where he has worked to support his family; his gift for his parents is a set of experimental opiate patches he has stolen from the hospital pharmacy where he worked for years to earn the trust that allowed him access to that medicine. The emotional turmoil Steve experiences as he notes all of the things that have changed in his parents' home and relationship, as well as all of the things that have

remained the same, lead him to question his knowledge of his own identity and his willingness to undermine his progress in a different world when he looks around the place he once called home.

"Legends of the White Lady" is another tale in which the main character searches for home. Unlike the other stories, the main character of "Legends of the White Lady" is not Filipino but a white woman named Alice. Alice's connections to Manila are through her work as a model and through her friend and roommate Sabine. Alice's search for home brings her to the Philippines when she travels there for her first gig in the five months since Sabine died of a ruptured aneurism. Returning to her friend's home country helps Alice come to terms with her own future as she deals with the loss of her friend.

Home and family are also central to the stories "A Contract Overseas" and "Esmeralda." In "A Contract Overseas," the narrator's brother Andoy travels to Saudi Arabia to support his mother, sister, and pregnant girlfriend. Unfortunately, Andoy's penchant for falling in love gets him in trouble after he lands a fantastic job as a chauffeur to a wealthy Saudi family and begins an ill-fated affair with the wife. In "Esmeralda," a Filipina cleans offices in the Twin Towers when the September 11 attacks take place. Fear for her lover, John, whose office is there, overwhelms her as she attempts to get to the site. She remembers their relationship and the fact that John was the first person to really care that she was burdened with providing financial care for her extended family and community back home.

Adults are not the only ones to struggle in this collection. In several of the stories, Alvar skillfully shows both economic differences and the emotional growth of her characters through their interactions with children. This is most notable in "The Miracle Worker" and "The Virgin of Monte Ramon." Sally Riva is a teacher who has been hired to teach Aroush, a profoundly developmentally disabled child. When Mrs. Mansour, the child's mother, tells Sally, "Teacher, you must be Annie Sullivan for my Aroush!" one of the woman's servants comments, "'That must be something, no? To be so rich you think you can buy reality.'" The wealth of the Mansours and others like them in Bahrain leads to confusion over the treatment of the servant class. When Sally's friend Minnie, a maid in the Mansour household, talks about going on strike to rebel against the upper-class extravagance, Sally begins to take advantage of Mrs. Mansour's generosity. However, she begins to care for the child, and even a tiny display of ability snaps her back into the responsible role; she begins to understand the danger in the way she has overlooked the humanity of both child and mother because of their economic and cultural differences from her.

"The Virgin of Monte Ramon" tells another tale of a disabled child. Daniel "Danny" Wilson Jr. is the grandson of an American soldier who had been stationed in Manila. He bears his grandfather's name because his father abandoned the family shortly after the child's birth. Born without legs, Danny has struggled his whole life, but at school, he experiences bullying. Then, Annelise becomes a scholarship student at the Catholic school Danny attends. Though Danny "had longed for a day when my schoolmates would find a new target, a victim other than me. Now that she was here—a girl, who seemed unfazed by the teasing—I felt none of the relief I'd expected. I felt only shame at my own school-yard weakness." He and Annelise, who is also handicapped by a physical condition, learn the value of friendship despite social and economic differences. Just as important for Danny, however, is his desire for a father, and a burgeoning relationship with the local doctor seems to be the answer to his prayers, until he discovers the hidden motivation behind the doctor's guilty attention.

Alongside the themes of desire for home and the complications of disabilities, the stories are full of political intrigue. Though the political atmosphere of Manila, particularly, is central to several stories, a political complication in communities is also revealed in the stories. "Shadow Families" traces the lives, friendships, and marriages of a group of affluent, well-educated Filipinas living in Bahrain, where their husbands work as professionals. They have given up careers to keep their families together and, out of a sense of duty to their homeland, host weekly parties to which they invite *katulong* women. But when they take a beautiful new young woman into their group, they begin to doubt the stability they believed they had. Baby is an aloof and strange young *katulong* who takes advantage of the generosity of the women without giving anything but grief back to them. Without a clear motivation, she manipulates their feelings by casting doubt on their husbands' fidelity. The ensuing changes discombobulate a whole community.

While Baby's political machinations are personal, the stories of "Old Girl" and the title story, "In the Country," both contain glimpses of the Philippine government under Ferdinand Marcos. "Old Girl" traces the lives of an exiled former political leader and his expatriate wife. Their three years in Boston are some of the happiest years for the wife, who understands that "his name means something different in Manilachusetts than it does in Manila. *Hero. Freedom fighter. Prisoner of conscience.* Some still even call her husband *Senator.*" Her children seem satisfied and well-adjusted to their lives in the United States, yet her husband cannot settle down, and she struggles with the knowledge of her own restlessness. She knows he wants to return to Manila, and through flashbacks to their previous life, she comes to the realization that they "have already both survived without each other." Skillfully tied into a metaphor of the husband's desire to run the Boston Marathon, despite never having run before, this story tells the tale of Filipino politics from a personal point of view.

The title story, which provides the conclusion to the collection, traces the love affair of Milagros and Jim. As a young nurse, Milagros Sandoval stood up for workers' rights, drawing her into the realm of reporter Jaime "Jim" Reyes. His political rebellion becomes hers after they marry, and he is imprisoned for ten years for refusing to write government-approved stories. While he is separated from his family, Milagros runs an underground publication that continues his work. Their antigovernment work ultimately results in the disappearance of their son and the devastation of a woman who has stayed strong through enforced single parenthood. The story questions loyalty to family over one's country while revealing details about the difficulty of living in the Philippines during the decades of the 1970s and 1980s.

Overall, reviewers hailed Alvar's talented writing. From the migrant experiences to the flow of the stories themselves, the commentary from publications such as the *Library Journal* and *Kirkus Reviews* on Alvar's first collection of stories has been positive. Further, the twisted relationships between servants and masters, between husbands and wives, and even between parents and children have been lauded as captivating by reviewers. A critic writing for *America* noted that readers need a sense of the political history of the Philippines during the regime of Ferdinand Marcos to understand some of the stories. Though this historical background would be helpful, Alvar provides enough detail that readers will be able to understand that political climate.

Theresa L. Stowell

Review Sources

Biedenharn, Isabella. Rev. of *In the Country*, by Mia Alvar. *Entertainment Weekly* 26 June 2015: 66. Print.

Hong, Terry. Rev. of *In the Country*, by Mia Alvar. *Library Journal* 15 Apr. 2015: 82. Print.

Rev. of *In the Country*, by Mia Alvar. *Kirkus Reviews* 15 Apr. 2015: 163. Print.

Rev. of *In the Country*, by Mia Alvar. *Publishers Weekly* 9 Mar. 2015: 49. Print.

Ramakrishnan, J. R. "Home Bittersweet Home." Rev. of *In the Country*, by Mia Alvar. *New York Times Book Review* 21 June 2015: 19. Print.

In the Unlikely Event

Author: Judy Blume (b. 1938)
Publisher: Alfred A. Knopf (New York).
416 pp.
Type of work: Novel
Time: Twentieth century
Locale: Elizabeth, New Jersey

In the Unlikely Event, based on events during her own eighth-grade year, is Blume's fourth novel for adult readers.

Principal characters:
MIRI AMMERMAN, fifteen-year old daughter
    of an unwed mother
RUSTY AMMERMAN, her mother
IRENE AMMERMAN, her grandmother
HENRY AMMERMAN, her uncle, a newspaper
    reporter

(Courtesy of Alfred A. Knopf)

During a period of fifty-eight days in the early 1950s, three airplanes crashed in or near author Judy Blume's hometown of Elizabeth, New Jersey, taking the lives of 116 people. These disasters occurred during the height of the McCarthy era and the Cold War; conspiracy theories, including attacks of creatures from outer space, proliferated. In writing *In the Unlikely Event*, Blume evokes the Elizabeth of her adolescence, relying on her own memories of these events—she was an eighth grader that year, a year younger than the novel's protagonist; her father was a forensic dentist who had used dental records to identify people who died in the crashes, like the forensic dentist in the novel—and those of others, as well as on her extensive research.

Despite, or perhaps because of, their lasting effect on her, Blume never told anyone about the crashes, although she is not sure why. Blume divides her intergenerational novel into four major sections, bracketed by two short sections, both entitled, "Thirty-Five Years Later, February 10, 1987," which are set at a commemoration for the disasters. The first three of the four major sections correspond to one of the three disasters: "Part One: December 1951"; "Part Two: January 1952"; "Part Three: February–April 1952." "Part Four: May–August 1952" starts with the resumption of jet flights.

Blume relied on newspaper accounts of the disasters, which she found in two now defunct newspapers of the city, to give the larger context of these events. Each chapter begins with a fictional news story by Miri's uncle, reporter Henry Ammerman, writing for the novel's fictional newspaper, *Elizabeth Daily Post*. In her author's notes at the conclusion of the book, Blume acknowledges the assistance of her husband, George Cooper, who reworked stories in her notebook to cast them in Henry's journalistic style, using some of the same overblown language that reporters of the time relied on.

For example, describing the third crash, Henry writes, "Hanging like a huge dead leaf from the blackened top of another tree was a jagged piece of silver wreckage. The roof of the apartment building looks as if the plane had taken a gigantic bite out of it. . . . The plane had broken apart like a swollen cream puff."

The book is not about those crashes so much as it is about their impact on peoples' lives. The crashes set in motion events that disrupt relationships for Miri, her mother, and her boyfriend, Mason, as well as for her friend Natalie (who believes herself a vessel for the dancer who died in the first crash) and Steve, Natalie's brother. For the young people, this is a time of especially heightened awareness and depth of feeling.

Blume is obsessive in her attention to those personal details, piling on names, events, and common activities so that at times the reader feels bogged down by the nostalgia. Brand names, place names, music, games, movies, dress, as well as social mores and habits pepper the story.

Likewise, the cast of characters can be daunting; in the first chapter alone, Blume introduces seven interrelated characters, giving each a few pages "center stage" before moving on to the next, then circling back. In the twenty-two pages comprised by the first chapter, ten subsections are headed by a character's name. Subsequent chapters introduce a dozen additional major characters, only one of whom does not survive the crash; tracking these people and caring about all of them and the interrelationships among them can be challenging. In addition, there are minor characters, including several of Miri's classmates, who give their opinions about the crashes and then disappear from the text.

Blume uses major characters' names as chapter dividers throughout, as she has done to a lesser extent in previous novels, such as in *Summer Sisters* (1998). She breaks that pattern with other subheadings in only three chapters within the second and third sections. As if the changed subheading pattern were not sufficient, the typeface changes as well, switching to sans serif to denote reportage of the aftermath of the second airline crash ("Rumors," "A Condolence Call to Mrs. Barnes," "Shiva") or fictional advertisements of the time.

The concluding segment, less than thirty pages, reports on the lives of several of the survivors without resorting to subdivisions. It is not entirely satisfactory, in part because of the brief information given; one of Miri's friends is summed up in a single sentence: "Suzanne lives in Seattle, married to a neurosurgeon." There are also teases that are not resolved, perhaps opening the path for a sequel. For example, Miri has a daughter who is a problem child; the reader wants to know more, as does Miri herself. "How is it that Miri, who longed for a daughter after two sons, has wound up with an angry, sullen child like Eliza? She's still trying to figure out where it went wrong but can't put her finger on it." Eliza, who appears only as part of a brief telephone conversation with her mother, remains an unanswered question.

Blume's style has not changed. Notable for their accessibility, her works move along with dialogue as well as peeks into the characters' inner lives. The novel is honest about the difficulties that social class consciousness creates. The Ammermans live in two apartments created within a house. The small quarters and the expense of an animal are the reasons Irene refuses to allow pets, first for her own daughter,

Rusty, and then for her granddaughter, Miri. Unlike the mothers of Miri's girlfriends, Rusty works outside the home as an executive secretary, and Irene sells small luxury goods, such as Ronson lighters and Volupté compacts, at special home parties to which she invites her regular customers.

The Ammermans are also separated from the couples and families around them because Rusty is a single mother of a teenage daughter and Irene is a widow whose grown son lives with her for much of the novel. The Ammermans, who are Jewish but not religiously observant, are nevertheless also aware of being separate from the larger Christian world.

With its adolescent characters, the novel inevitably highlights conflicts between parents and children. Miri is frustrated because she is kept in the dark about her birth father, whose name is not mentioned. A second conflict occurs when she falls in love with an Irish boy, Mason, who lives in an orphanage. The subplot of Christina and Jack (Mason's older brother), Greek and Irish lovers, reflects the difficulties of "mixed marriages."

Decisions about choosing whether to have sex before marriage and the accompanying fear of pregnancy remind readers that this novel is set in a time before widespread birth control or legally available abortion. Women who became pregnant were expected to marry the father of the child, which is yet another reason Miri sometimes feels like a misfit—her mother chose not to tell the birth father of her existence.

Miri Ammerman, while not a fictional portrait of Blume, does share some of the insights of the author and her friends in the early 1950s. Blume told Scott Simon for National Public Radio's *Weekend Edition* that while boys favored attacks of zombies or aliens to explain the crashes, the girls observed that the planes went down near schools and orphanages. Clearly, the girls concluded, as Miri does, adults were sabotaging the planes to kill large numbers of children and young people. Miri expresses this idea in a school newspaper article, but it

> Judy Blume, a noted writer of young-adult fiction, has produced a total of twenty-eight novels. They have been translated into thirty-two languages and have sold more than eighty-five million copies. In 2004 she received the National Book Foundation's Distinguished Contribution to American Letters Award.

is not printed because the principal feels it is provocative. She is nearly expelled for disseminating the article after Henry makes mimeographed copies of it that circulate freely—yet another example of generational conflict in the novel.

The connections among Miri's family and friends influence her decisions well into adulthood. After graduating from high school, Miri chooses to attend American University in Washington DC, where her brother and his family live, and to major in journalism, as Henry had done. However, she settles to Las Vegas, where the rest of the family moved after the disasters, and marries a young dentist, in part to remain in the area. By the time of the commemoration thirty-five years after the crashes, she has become a newspaper columnist like her uncle, with a growing realization that she could write a book.

In the Unlikely Event shares themes and threads with Blume's other three adult novels. *Unlikely Event* is set in the 1950s and presents the same constrictions on women's lives that may be found in Blume's first adult novel, *Wifey* (1978). Her second adult novel, *Smart Women* (1983), drew on her own experience as a divorced woman with teenage children, which is similar to Rusty's life. *Smart Women*, set in the 1980s, navigates some of the same issues of sexuality and romantic triangles that *Unlikely Event* does. The plot of *Summer Sisters* involves two friends who, like Miri and Natalie, come from different backgrounds and become involved in a romantic triangle.

Blume's work for young adults is often challenged by would-be censors. Members of school boards and teachers object to the very things that make the books so attractive to adolescent readers: coming-of-age stories that include frank discussions of sexuality, references to bodily changes during puberty, and acknowledgment of issues such as bullying and divorce. These issues appear in *In the Unlikely Event* as well. Although this adult novel contains more profanity and more sex than her young adult titles, it remains a richly detailed portrait of an era filled with uncertainties and fears.

Judy A. Johnson

Review Sources

Cart, Michael. Rev. of *In the Unlikely Event*, by Judy Blume. *Booklist* 15 Apr. 2015: 36. *Literary Reference Center*. Web. 8 Sept. 2015.

Ditum, Sarah. "Growing Young Gracefully." Rev. of *In the Unlikely Event*, by Judy Blume. *New Statesman* 29 May 2015: 82. *Literary Reference Center*. Web. 8 Sept. 2015.

Rev. of *In the Unlikely Event*, by Judy Blume. *Kirkus Reviews* 1 Apr. 2015: 279. *Literary Reference Center*. Web. 8 Sept. 2015.

Rev. of *In the Unlikely Event*, by Judy Blume. *Publishers Weekly* 2 Mar. 2015: 60. *Literary Reference Center*. Web. 8 Sept. 2015.

Leavitt, Caroline. "Judy Blume's 'In the Unlikely Event.'" *New York Times*. New York Times, 25 May 2015. Web. 28 Sept. 2015.

The Incarnations

Author: Susan Barker (b. 1978)
Publisher: Touchstone (New York). 384 pp.
Type of work: Novel
Time: 2007–8; 632, 1213, 1542, 1836, and 1966
Locales: Beijing, other locations in China

Susan Barker's sprawling historical novel The Incarnations *recounts the past lives of a Beijing cab driver and his mystery soul mate.*

Principal characters:
WANG JUN, a taxi driver in Beijing
YIDA, his wife, a masseuse
ECHO, his eight-year-old daughter
LIN HONG, his villainous stepmother
ZENG YAN, his former friend and lover

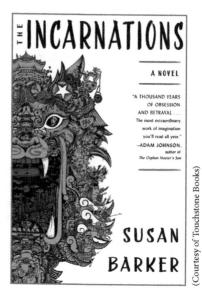

(Courtesy of Touchstone Books)

Wang Jun drives a taxi in Beijing, China, in 2008. He is, in almost all ways, ordinary: he is thirty-one years old, he is balding, and he smokes Red Pagoda Mountain cigarettes. He has a wife named Yida, who works at a massage parlor, and an eight-year-old daughter, Echo, who draws comic book cartoons. The family lives in a small apartment, making just enough money to get by. One day, however, Wang finds an unusual letter behind the visor in his cab. Though the identity of the writer is unknown, the contents of the letter are strange enough that he takes it immediately to the police—but there is nothing the police can do. After receiving several more letters, he begins to worry. Does he have a stalker? If so, who would want to harass a taxi driver, telling him something about past lives? As Wang begins to interrogate (in various ways) the people closest to him, Susan Barker's cleverly constructed new novel *The Incarnations* teeters between its central character's deteriorating mental state and the elaborate stories woven by the mysterious letter writer. "To scatter beams of light on the darkness of your unknown past is my duty," the letter writer explains to Wang. "For to have lived six times, but to know only your latest incarnation, is to know only one-sixth of who you are. To be only one-sixth alive."

In his present life, Wang thinks little about his country's history, much less his own. He was the son of a prosperous bureaucrat, but endured a miserable childhood. He loved his mother, a deeply intelligent former bureaucrat herself, but her descent into mental illness leaves Wang unmoored. His abusive and womanizing father sends him away to school, and in college, after a brief flirtation with his father's neglected young wife, Lin Hong, Wang has a mental breakdown. He spends a part of his formative years in an institution, where he befriends a charismatic young prostitute named Zeng Yan. Zeng is locked up because he is gay—homosexuality was considered a mental disorder at the time. The two men develop an intense bond and become lovers.

Horrified at his love for Zeng, Wang leaves the hospital. His hatred for his father prevents him from accepting his father's money; therefore, he embarks on a career as a taxi driver. He meets and falls in love with Yida, a beautiful young girl escaping her peasant roots. Their marriage sours, however, as they struggle to make ends meet and provide for their daughter, Echo. (Yida resents Echo because she is not a boy, but Wang does not share her resentment.) Soon after he receives his first mysterious letter, Wang encounters Zeng, whom he has not seen in over ten years. The two men resume their affair, though their relationship is marred by Wang's unshakable suspicion that Zeng is the letter writer. As the stories of his past lives become more disturbing, Wang begins to lose touch with reality, and ends up wreaking vengeance on his closest confidant and friend.

(Derek Anson)

Susan Barker is a British novelist whose works include Sayonara Bar *(2007) and* The Orientalist and the Ghost *(2008). Both books were long-listed for the Dylan Thomas Prize. Her third novel,* The Incarnations, *was published in the United States in 2015.*

Wang is told that in his first life, he was a young boy in the Tang dynasty in 632 AD. He was a feral child named Bitter Root, the son of a backwater sorceress. Bitter Root rapes his mentally handicapped older sister, and the sorceress cuts off his genitals and sends him to the Imperial Palace in Chang'an as a eunuch. (Eunuchs, castrated men, were charged with guarding the emperor's concubines.) After he leaves, Bitter Root's sister gives birth to a little girl. She has no name, but she is the first incarnation of the letter writer. The young girl travels to Chang'an to find her father, enduring every misery along the way, and becomes a famous storytelling prostitute called Night Coming. Her fame engenders her first (and last) meeting with Bitter Root, though of course, the two souls will live many more lives together.

The letter writer and Wang are destined to be forever intertwined. Their relationships run the gamut of human connection and emotion: father and daughter, lovers, friends, murderer, and victim. In their second incarnation, they are two slave boys who survive (however briefly) the Mongol invasion and a grueling trek across the Gobi Desert. In their third incarnation, they are concubines in the court of the sadistic Emperor Jiajing during the Ming dynasty. Jiajing, more concerned with finding a potion that would make him immortal than running a country, was a cruel and insatiable slave master when it came to his harem. Nicknamed the Emperor of Knives, he was as likely to slice or kill his concubines as sleep with them. In their fourth incarnation, Wang is an Englishman and scholar, and the letter writer is a young Tanka boy during the Qing dynasty in 1836. In their most recent incarnation, they were young girls pledging fervent allegiance to Chairman Mao during the dark days of the Cultural Revolution in the 1960s.

These historical asides, woven expertly through Wang's larger contemporary narrative, are a study of human misery. Barker's story selection is universally and irredeemably bleak; her characters are stripped of power and dignity, betrayed, raped, mutilated, and murdered—sometimes at the hands of one another. Critics were divided on Barker's tales of woe. Many praised her unwavering commitment to her purpose; she certainly does not try to whitewash China's checkered past. However, a few reviewers, including Pierre Fuller for the *Los Angeles Review of Books*, accused her of taking this authenticity and realism too far. For those reviewers, Barker's stories were salacious for the sake of being salacious, and for Fuller, they amounted, perversely, to caricature. Reviewing *The Incarnations* along with another book about China, Fuller wrote, "The construction of these narratives strongly suggests the choices of an outsider looking in, of a writer imposing behavior on an alien social group." Barker addressed these accusations of "othering," or more accurately "exoticizing," in her own *Los Angeles Review of Books* article months later, arguing that the avoidance of such material considered indelicate would mean going against one of the inherent purposes of composing and reading literature.

Barker is a British author of Chinese-Malaysian descent. *The Incarnations*, her third novel, was inspired by her family history and the years she spent living in Beijing before the 2008 Summer Olympics. It was an unusual time, she has said in interviews, because of the vast separation between the lives of ordinary Beijing residents, many of them struggling with underemployment and health issues from the city's pollution, and the constant construction of the multibillion-dollar Olympics. Barker was drawn to this iteration of Beijing as well as various episodes in China's ancient past. *The Incarnations* is an historical novel about power and power struggles over time. China, a country that is thousands of years old, has a history that is culturally rich but also steeped in violence. From the Mongol invasions during the Song dynasty to the Cultural Revolution in the 1960s, China's past is shaped by struggle and moral ambiguity. Barker did not want to shy away from this complexity, and the result of her exploration is often dark. Still, her prose is lean and sharp, suffused with an urgency that jumbles past and present in an effort to understand how one informs the other. While writing the book, which took her six years, Barker told the blog the *Shanghaist* that she was inspired by a famous quote from Czech author Milan Kundera: "The struggle of man against power is the struggle of memory against forgetting." In the end, Barker's aim is the same as that of the mysterious letter writer: to not let her history disappear.

The Incarnations has no concluding moral, though it does end with a peculiar and inspired twist. Wang and the letter writer are imprisoned—often literally—by the times in which they live, but there is a sneaking sense of freedom in the breadth and variousness of their history, in understanding that times change and change again, and, more figuratively, that people can, too. Barker's novel is about the vast human capacity for good and evil, illustrated through reincarnation. Echo tells her father that she is being trailed by a ghost, a shadowy figure that follows her on her way to school and stands in the darkness when she tries to fall asleep. She calls this figure The Watcher. She makes a comic book about The Watcher, and at the end of it, The Watcher consumes her. Wang is disturbed by the book, but does not know what to do about it because it is so difficult to determine what The Watcher is in the first place. Is The Watcher good or bad? "History is knocking for you, his knuckles striking the door. Don't pretend not to hear," the letter writer implores Wang. "Don't pretend he's not there. Open the door, Driver Wang. Let him in."

Molly Hagan

Review Sources

Birch, Carol. "*The Incarnations* by Susan Barker Review—Multilayered and Masterful." *Guardian*. Guardian News and Media, 13 Aug. 2014. Web. 19 Jan. 2016.

Collins-Hughes, Laura. Rev. of *The Incarnations*, by Susan Barker. *Boston Globe*. Boston Globe Media Partners, 22 Aug. 2015. Web. 19 Jan. 2016.

Fuller, Pierre. "Pierre Fuller on *The Dog: Stories* and *The Incarnations*: Fictional Forays to a Familiarly Exotic China." Rev. of *The Incarnations*, by Susan Barker. *Los Angeles Review of Books*. Los Angeles Review of Books, 26 Nov. 2014. Web. 19 Jan. 2016.

Lyall, Sarah. "Review: In Susan Barker's *The Incarnations*, Lives of Despair (Past and Present) in China." Rev. of *The Incarnations*, by Susan Barker. *New York Times*. New York Times, 16 Aug. 2015. Web. 19 Jan. 2016.

Wilson, Edward. "*The Incarnations* by Susan Barker, Book Review: Exploring 1,000 Years of Chinese History." Rev. of *The Incarnations*, by Susan Barker. *Independent*. Independent.co.uk, 10 July 2014. Web. 19 Jan. 2016.

Winchester, Simon. Rev. of *The Incarnations*, by Susan Barker. *New York Times*. New York Times, 24 Aug. 2015. Web. 19 Jan. 2016.

The Invention of Nature
Alexander von Humboldt's New World

Author: Andrea Wulf (b. 1972)
Publisher: Alfred A. Knopf (New York). 496 pp.
Type of work: Biography, history of science

The Invention of Nature *is a sweeping biography that narrates and champions the life of Prussian scientist and explorer Alexander von Humboldt. The book follows Humboldt on his travels while also introducing the reader to his intellectual journeys and his spheres of acquaintance and influence.*

Principal personages:
ALEXANDER VON HUMBOLDT, Prussian natural historian and world explorer
JOHANN WOLFGANG VON GOETHE, German poet and philosopher

(Courtesy of Alfred A. Knopf)

THOMAS JEFFERSON, American politician and intellectual, the third president of the United States
SIMÓN BOLÍVAR, Venezuelan revolutionary leader
CHARLES DARWIN, English scientist and author responsible for the theory of evolution
GEORGE PERKINS MARSH, American politician, diplomat, and early conservationist
ERNST HAECKEL, German philosopher, artist, and naturalist
JOHN MUIR, Scottish American naturalist and environmental philosopher

Andrea Wulf opens her hefty biography of the Prussian scientist Alexander von Humboldt with a brief account of his ascent of Chimborazo, an extinct volcano then believed to be the highest peak in the world. Humboldt's 1802 ascent reads as a dramatic adventure account, which of course it was, but also as a fertile experience from which the scientist gained a sweeping breadth of knowledge that he would continue to plumb for decades of thought and writing. Most significantly, from the heights of Chimborazo, Humboldt "began to see the world differently," envisioning an interconnected system of nature that would eventually form the core of his most significant scientific work, the multivolume treatise *Kosmos* (1845–58, 1862; *Cosmos*, 1846–58).

In her prologue, Wulf notes how poorly known Humboldt's major scientific ideas are in contemporary society, despite the fact that he was described in his time as "the most famous man in the world after Napoleon" and his "bold new vision of nature . . . still influences the way that we understand the natural world." Most important to Wulf's argument for the contemporary relevance of Humboldt is her observation that "when nature is perceived as a web, its vulnerability also becomes obvious.

Everything hangs together. If one thread is pulled, the whole tapestry may unravel." Building on this theme, Wulf highlights how Humboldt's scientific perspective was prescient with respect to the damage that disregard for the environment would have on future generations. She argues that his ideas are of urgent relevance to a society seeking to account on a grand scale for the environmental damages wrought by industrial human civilization.

Wulf is certainly correct that Humboldt no longer has the name recognition of Charles Darwin, even if, as she observes, many sites on the planet are named after him and many plants and animals retain the scientific names by which he identified them. Still, Humboldt is also better known than this prologue would suggest. His ideas frequently appear in research and writing about the great thinkers of the nineteenth century, and he is well known within the intellectual community beyond those who study the history of science. Indeed, as reviewer Nathaniel Rich remarked in the *New York Review of Books*, "Rediscovering Humboldt is by this point a subgenre unto itself." Yet within a growing body of literature aimed at reintroducing Humboldt to popular society, Wulf's monograph stands out for its significant intellectual contribution of introducing English-speaking audiences to extensive materials gathered and translated from various archives in the United States and Europe. Wulf, who was raised mostly in Germany, is familiar with the regions in which Humboldt grew up and lived, and she is able to vividly conjure an understanding of the man within his social and intellectual context. As a garden historian, she also brings a deep understanding of the natural environment to her text, giving vibrant descriptions of the places that Humboldt saw and the natural history discoveries that he made. Thus, while Wulf perhaps overplays the necessity of rediscovering Humboldt, her work nevertheless makes a substantial contribution to the genre.

For many readers, following Humboldt's travels through the Americas and Russia will provide the greatest excitement of the book, since the scientist was an explorer and adventurer as well as an erudite thinker. *The Invention of Nature* is a hefty book, but it moves rapidly through these periods of travel, which represent a relatively short interval in Humboldt's lengthy life. Wulf does well to emphasize the many social interchanges and the intense intellectual work that the scientist engaged in when not venturing to far lands. Humboldt did not leave Europe until 1799, when he was already thirty years old. In that year, he set out from Spain on an expedition that would take him through large swaths of South America, including modern-day Ecuador, Peru, and Venezuela. This expedition would also take him through much of what is now central Mexico, including Mexico City; Cuba; and a few points on the eastern seaboard of the United States, including Philadelphia and the newly established Washington, DC. Two maps positioned between the title page and the prologue whet readers' appetites for these voyages, with the second map tracing Humboldt's journey into the mountains of Venezuela in 1800. A third map traces the second great journey of Humboldt's life: his travels through Russia in 1829, which took him from Berlin into Riga, in modern-day Latvia, and ultimately east across the depths of Siberia. Following Humboldt on these travels introduces readers to the rough work of science in the nineteenth century and provides the opportunity to see these cultures and places as he discovered them during his travels. Fortunately, in these accounts, Wulf is able to rely on extensive archival materials as well as on Humboldt's own publications.

Much of the book is a straightforward biographical account that focuses on Humboldt's intellectual progression and work as both a scientist and a writer. The complexities of his historical moment, which encompassed the great unrest of the age of revolutions, become clear through the personal and political challenges with which he grappled across his long life. This work of cultural history is a significant part of the value Wulf brings to her study of Humboldt, for the relationships between Prussia, Russia, and various western European nations during Humboldt's lifetime were complex. This account gives readers the opportunity to trace these often-distant dynamics of political history through a personalized lens.

Interspersed among the chapters that advance the biographical narrative of the work are a series of chapters dedicated to Humboldt's friendships and encounters with other great thinkers of his age. This international cast and crew includes such eminent figures as Johann Wolfgang von Goethe, Thomas Jefferson, and Simón Bolívar. Also included are chapters concerning figures with whom Humboldt was not acquainted but whose ideas are deeply indebted, in Wulf's accounting, to Humboldt, among them Charles Darwin, George Perkins Marsh, and John Muir. While these later chapters are certainly important to Wulf's larger argument and are significant for showing how Humboldt's ideas are woven throughout what is now known as environmental science, they are somewhat too focused on showing Humboldt's originality, thereby undercutting the achievements of these significant figures.

Andrea Wulf trained as a design historian at the Royal College of Art prior to pursuing a career as a full-time author. Her acclaimed books have included The Brother Gardeners *(2008),* Founding Gardeners *(2012), and* Chasing Venus *(2012). She has been awarded the American Horticultural Society Book Award as well as the Samuel Johnson Prize.*

More interesting are the chapters that delve into Humboldt's intellectual rapport with his acquaintances and contemporaries. Though Wulf's focus is always on showing Humboldt's great significance, his mutually inspirational relationships with Goethe, Jefferson, and Bolívar provide a fascinating account of the inherent breadth and passion of the Enlightenment thinkers among whom these figures can be numbered. The connections among these men via the life of this single formidable scientist offer a tangible demonstration of the global connections of intellectual life in the eighteenth and nineteenth centuries, as well as the inherent interdisciplinary nature of thought during this period. In the revolutionary and political thought of Bolívar, for example, Wulf is able to trace the natural descriptions and passions of Humboldt, identifying the influence of scientific thinking on sociopolitical developments of the period. Each of these figures is, of course, a major historical figure in his own right, and although Wulf's interest is in Humboldt, scholars and the general public alike will surely appreciate the fresh accounts of Darwin, Jefferson, and Bolívar, even if they might disagree on which figure takes historical precedence. Although it does not get extensive attention, Frederic Church's incomparable painting *The Heart of the Andes*

(1859), which was first exhibited to the public days before Humboldt's death, also gets a brief nod for its attention and devotion to Humboldt's studies of nature.

The Invention of Nature is a sweeping account of the life of a highly significant scientist. For those who would never wade through Humboldt's multivolume *Cosmos*, it offers a window into his core values and discoveries while also presenting a compelling and exciting view of his world. As Wulf signaled in her prologue, so she emphasizes in her conclusion that the ideas of this volume are not limited to an assessment of the contours and events of Humboldt's life. Indeed, she identifies Humboldt's approach to science as offering a guiding map for modern-day scientists in the battle against climate change. Asserting that "Humboldt's interdisciplinary approach to science and nature is more relevant than ever," she further highlights his emphasis on the "global patterns" of nature and on "the free exchange of information." While a direct application of Humboldt's science would be anachronistic, Wulf's proposal that modern society should use his work as a model for thinking about and assessing nature and civilization is interesting. This is a tall social order for a biography to fill, particularly one that is so dense in content and historical research. More aptly, it seems an appropriate road map for readers considering taking up *The Invention of Nature*, as these conclusions highlight the great contributions of the book's approach to Humboldt. Through Wulf, Humboldt is situated within a broad, relevant, and intellectually ambitious context that reintroduces his scientific significance while also fixing him more permanently and inextricably within the broader web of great eighteenth- and early nineteenth-century thinkers.

Julia A. Sienkewicz

Review Sources

Herschthal, Eric. "*The Invention of Nature* Positions Alexander von Humboldt as the Godfather of Environmentalism." Rev. of *The Invention of Nature: Alexander von Humboldt's New World*, by Andrea Wulf. *Christian Science Monitor*. Christian Science Monitor, 15 Jan. 2016. Web. 2 Feb. 2016.

Price, Matthew. Rev. of *The Invention of Nature: Alexander von Humboldt's New World*, by Andrea Wulf. *Boston Globe*. Boston Globe Media Partners, 3 Oct. 2015. Web. 2 Feb. 2016.

Rich, Nathaniel. "The Very Great Alexander von Humboldt." Rev. of *The Invention of Nature: Alexander von Humboldt's New World*, by Andrea Wulf, and *After Nature: A Politics for the Anthropocene*, by Jedediah Purdy. *New York Review of Books*. NYREV, 22 Oct. 2015. Web. 2 Feb. 2016.

Thubron, Colin. Rev. of *The Invention of Nature: Alexander von Humboldt's New World*, by Andrea Wulf. *New York Times*. New York Times, 25 Sept. 2015. Web. 2 Feb. 2016.

Wilcken, Patrick. "Conqueror of Chimborazo." Rev. of *The Invention of Nature: Alexander von Humboldt's New World*, by Andrea Wulf. *Literary Review*. Literary Rev., Nov. 2015. Web. 2 Feb. 2016.

Winder, Simon. Rev. of *The Invention of Nature: Alexander von Humboldt's New World*, by Andrea Wulf. *Guardian*. Guardian News and Media, 13 Nov. 2015. Web. 2 Feb. 2016.

The Japanese Lover

Author: Isabel Allende (b. 1942)
First published: *El amante japonés*, 2015, in Spain and the United States
Translated by: Nick Caistor and Amanda Hopkinson
Publisher: Atria Books (New York). 336 pp.
Type of work: Novel
Time: Late 1930s–present
Locales: San Francisco, California; Topaz, Utah; Poland

Isabel Allende's The Japanese Lover, *like much of her earlier fiction, bridges cultures and generations in a multi-stranded narrative of love and war. The novel was one of* Publishers Weekly's *top ten works of literary fiction for 2015.*

(Courtesy of Atria Books)

Principal characters:
ALMA MENDEL BELASCO, a wealthy and aloof octogenarian resident of Lark House, an assisted living facility
NATHANIEL "NAT" BELASCO, her cousin and eventual husband
SETH BELASCO, her grandson, heir to the Belasco dynasty
IRINA BAZILI, her assistant, an eastern European immigrant working at Lark House
ICHIMEI FUKUDA, a.k.a. ICHI, her childhood friend and lover

Isabel Allende has said that in her work the elements of love and violence are always present, along with the corresponding dualities of light and darkness, good and evil. *The Japanese Lover* is no exception, detailing multiple love stories as well as the war and ethnic violence that marked the twentieth century. In that way, the book can be read as a gloss on Allende's own life. The assassination of her cousin Salvador Allende, then president of Chile, during a coup in 1973 marked the end of one phase of Isabel Allende's life. Under death threats, she and her family left the country, first for Venezuela and then for the United States. Similarly, in *The Japanese Lover*, both Alma Mendel Belasco and Ichimei Fukuda suffer disruption due to political unrest. Both characters' lives are, in a sense, mirrors of Allende's own life of exile.

The novel is composed of short chapters most often titled after the names of characters or places. Segments are divided by ten letters from Ichimei, the titular Japanese lover, to Alma—out of a total of 106 he wrote—printed in italic type suggestive of handwriting. Like the novel itself, which relies on the technique of flashbacks, the letters are not arranged chronologically; rather, they are placed to comment on the novel's preceding or following action. These letters, which Alma has preserved and treasured, are what prompt her to recall her life to her grandson Seth and her assistant, Irina. Through her mementos, they learn of her great love for Ichimei, and his for her, a force that cannot be dimmed by separation, their individual marriages, or the passage of decades. The eleventh letter forms the last page of the book and is a commentary on all that has come before.

The focus of the novel is Alma, a resident of Lark House who is examining her memories of her early life, ostensibly to aid her idle and wealthy grandson, Seth, in writing a novel based on her life. Alma hires Irina, a twenty-three-year-old Moldovan woman working at Lark House, to help her sort through boxes of memorabilia, thus bringing Irina and Seth together.

Internationally acclaimed Chilean American novelist Isabel Allende published her first novel, The House of the Spirits, *in 1982. Her twenty-two books have sold more than sixty-five million copies in thirty-five languages. Among her many other honors and awards, she received the Presidential Medal of Freedom in 2014.*

Through flashbacks, the reader learns of young Alma's escape from Poland after the Anschluss, the Nazi invasion of Austria, and the mirror escape of Irina from war-torn Moldova decades later. However, Alma's parents send her to live with her uncle and aunt to save her from the difficulties they can see Hitler will visit on their land and her wealthy family members who gave her every advantage, while Irina's family do not properly care for or protect her. In fact, much of the novel is taken up with Irina's fears and post-traumatic stress disorder, which remain tantalizingly unexplained for the first two-thirds of the book. This is only one of the mysteries among the novel's subplots: Why does the antisocial Alma disappear for weekends, and where does she go? What has made Irina so wary of people, especially men? Why was handsome and eligible Nathaniel not married sooner?

Multiple story strands and timelines weave throughout the novel. The reader learns of Isaac Belasco's wealth and willingness to share it, his passionate love for his wife and his garden—which brings Takao Fukuda and his son into the Belasco world. Isaac's willingness to accept his niece into the household allows seven-year-old Alma to have a home and enjoy the companionship of her cousin Nathaniel, five years her senior, whom she considers her guardian angel.

It is Alma who defines the mission of the Belasco Foundation, which Isaac decides to begin after Alma arrives. Isaac shares his love of gardening with Alma, showing her his books on botany. When Alma is thirteen, she suggests placing gardens in the poorest neighborhoods of San Francisco. By the time she is a resident of Lark House, the gardens have been neglected, and Alma determines once again to make them lovely.

Ichimei is a nisei (US-born child of a Japanese immigrant) who accompanies his father to care for the gardens at the Belasco estate, where he meets Alma. The two children forge a deep connection, but their eventual love cannot be permitted; Ichimei is one of thousands of Japanese Americans who are herded into relocation camps in the panic following the Japanese attack on Pearl Harbor, and even after the war, prejudice against the Japanese remains.

Alma becomes a silk-screening artist, caught up in the color, pattern, and design of fabrics. She turns out to be inordinately selfish—an interesting, though not likable, character, the type of artist who is consumed by her work. After attending college in Boston, she travels the world for inspiration, even after her marriage to Nathaniel and birth of a son, Larry. As a child, Alma was inspired by the work of Vera Neumann, one of the few drawn-from-life characters in the novel. The real Neumann was a fashion designer of scarves and sports apparel as well as linens for home décor. Alma decides that she too will make beautiful Japanese-style art on fabric, but her designs will be more exclusive.

As Lucy Ferriss points out in her review for the *New York Times Book Review*, "No character is so minor as to lack a back story. At the same time, no character, including Alma and Irina, manages to fill in his or her outlines and command our undivided attention." Ferriss criticizes Allende for producing stereotypical characters and glossing over some notable historical realities, such as a quota system at Harvard University that might have made it difficult for a young Jew like Nathaniel Belasco to matriculate in the 1940s, no matter how wealthy his family. She also faults the fairy-tale atmosphere of the novel, in which men all but ride in on white horses to rescue the women, the anti-Semitism of midcentury America is glossed over, and the nursing facility is paradisiacal for its residents (though interestingly Allende has mentioned this being based on a real-life institution near her office).

Ferriss may be missing a key point in her interpretation of Allende's characters. Their names cannot be accidental; rather, they invite an almost allegorical reading of the text. Alma means "soul" or "spirit" in Spanish, the language in which Allende writes. The reader is asked to believe this is a name that would be given to a Polish Jewish girl in the twentieth century, which might strain credulity. Although the Hebrew word *almah* means "young woman," as a name, it is not as common as those of the matriarchs Sarah, Rebekah, Rachel, and Leah. Other Jews in the story have names that are more obviously biblical in origin, and thus more believable: Baruj, her father; Samuel, her brother; Isaac, her uncle; Nathaniel, Martha, and Sarah, her cousins. But Alma is the soul of the novel, as well as its main character.

Likewise, Irina is a name derived from Greek or Russian, meaning "peace," which is all Irina seeks after a horrific life as Elisabeta. She is indeed a peaceful person with a talent for caring for the elderly, although her own mind is not at peace until near the novel's conclusion.

Allende also gives a translation of the Japanese name Ichimei: the ideogram for his name means "life, light, brilliance, star." Like his father, Ichimei is a gardener, bringing life to plants. Even in the desert of Utah, Ichimei and the other Japanese who are interned at Topaz find ways to make vegetables grow, supplementing their government rations.

Each of these characters lives out his or her name in a fallen world shattered by war, prejudice, and violence. It is therefore tempting to see Seth—who turns his grandmother's memories into a book and brings new life to Irina—as hope for the future, even as Seth, the third son of Adam and Eve, born outside Eden, symbolized new beginnings and hope.

More than a romance, however, this work can be read as historical fiction. Most of the flashback chapters deal with the events of World War II; Allende includes dates and details of atrocities against both Jews and Japanese. A single part of a paragraph early in the novel summarizes the fate of the Mendel family en route to the death camp at Treblinka. The effect of Hitler's violence against the Jews is narrated in an eight-page chapter dealing with the fate of Alma's older brother, Samuel, who fought in the Royal Air Force for England and was captured by the Germans.

In contrast to her rather perfunctory gloss on the war in Europe, Allende devotes considerable attention to the fate of the Fukuda family. Following the bombing of Pearl Harbor on December 7, 1941, people in the United States, particularly those on the West Coast, feared the loyalty of Japanese citizens would be divided. Thousands of Japanese, forced out of homes and businesses, were sent to internment camps that were deficient of supplies and comforts. Four chapters—"The Fukuda Family," "The Yellow Peril," "The Prisoners," and "Arizona"—trace what happens to Ichimei and his family during World War II as they are sent to Topaz.

Readers interested in this often-ignored reality of American history could benefit from reading the works of Yoshiko Uchida, who wrote from her own experience as a child in the Topaz internment camp. Although targeted at young adults, Uchida's story *Journey to Topaz: A Story of the Japanese-American Evacuation* (1971) is powerfully written and could inform readers' understanding of this novel, as Topaz is where the Fukuda family is interned.

In another reflection of Allende's own life, this work, written in the author's seventies during a painful romantic separation, brings up questions of aging, illness, downsizing, community, and loss. Residents of Lark House, including Alma, shed what is no longer important as death becomes a closer reality. Writing for the *Washington Post*, reviewer Ron Charles catalogs the social issues Allende addresses and admires her command of the historical material, but he admits that her "heavy advocacy for legal euthanasia is a rare clunky element." But, as he concludes, Allende's blend of "domestic comedy, historical fiction, mystery, romance and even a note of fantasy" makes this cross-genre novel "a pleasure to recommend."

Judy A. Johnson

Review Sources

Charles, Ron. "Isabel Allende's *The Japanese Lover*: A Tale of History and Romance." Rev. of *The Japanese Lover*, by Isabel Allende. *Washington Post.* Washington Post, 2 Nov. 2015. Web. 15 Jan. 2016.

Ferriss, Lucy. "Custom Forbids." Rev. of *The Japanese Lover*, by Isabel Allende. *New York Times Book Review* 13 Dec. 2015: 34. Print.

Rev. of *The Japanese Lover*, by Isabel Allende. *Kirkus Reviews* 2 Sept. 2015: 6. Print.

Rev. of *The Japanese Lover*, by Isabel Allende. *Publishers Weekly* 10 Aug. 2015: 36. Print.

Killing and Dying

Author: Adrian Tomine (b. 1974)
Publisher: Drawn and Quarterly (New York). 128 pp.
Type of work: Graphic novel
Time: Present day
Locale: Suburban United States

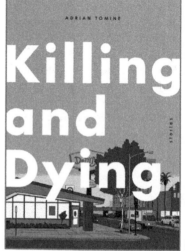

Killing and Dying is the latest collection of Adrian Tomine's enigmatic comics, featuring men and women searching for love, security, and meaning in their lives in a stark suburban landscape.

(Courtesy of Drawn & Quarterly)

Principal characters:

HAROLD, a landscaper who develops an art form called hortisculpture

A YOUNG WOMAN, who finds herself confused with a porn star named Amber Sweet

BABE, a woman who enters a problematic relationship with a drug dealer

A JAPANESE MOTHER, who is flying with her son to a reunion with her estranged husband

JESSE, a young woman with a stutter who would like to be a stand-up comedian

A VETERAN, struggling to adjust to civilian life and the breakup of his marriage

While the comic book industry has seen sharp ups and downs in recent decades, the comic as an art form has flourished. From the superheroes of DC and Marvel, to avant-garde social commentary, comics have proliferated. The Internet and online publishing have opened up new realms of expression for aspiring artists. In the 1980s, writers such as Alan Moore and Frank Miller brought a new depth and seriousness to traditional comic books and popularized the graphic novel. Art Spiegelman won a Pulitzer Prize for *Maus* (1991), in which he used mice and cats to reimagine the history of the Holocaust. Since then, comics and graphic novels have attained a new level of popularity and respectability.

Harvey Pekar, with his series *American Splendor* (1976–2008), pioneered comic books focused on the ups and downs of everyday life. Adrian Tomine writes within this tradition. He examines quotidian concerns and dilemmas. As with Pekar, his characters are frequently fragile and damaged. They struggle for insight into themselves and others; they struggle with the complexity of their relationships with lovers, friends, and family. Tomine began creating comics in high school. His self-published comic book *Optic Nerve* was initially distributed in local comic stores. In 1995, *Optic Nerve* was picked up by the publishing house Drawn and Quarterly, bringing Tomine to a wider audience. Since then, Tomine has branched out from comic books and also works as an illustrator. His work for the *New Yorker* includes covers and illustrations.

Killing and Dying is the latest collection of Tomine's comics. Most of these stories originally appeared in *Optic Nerve*. Drawn and Quarterly has done handsomely with this volume. The book is well bound, with sewn signatures and high-quality paper. The boards are thick and sturdy, giving the book a reassuring heft. The book feels and looks like a work of art. The wrapper is clear acetate, showcasing a cover illustration of a suburban street scene reproduced from one of the book's stories. It depicts a typical strip mall with an adjacent Denny's restaurant. In the background can be glimpsed part of a Target sign. It is an instantly recognizable milieu. Tomine's evocation of this contemporary commercial block is dead-on, both in its clinically reproduced detail and in an aura of antiseptic mass-produced ordinariness. Here Tomine's skills as a commercial artist come into play. His lines are clean and clear,

(Courtesy of Drawn & Quarterly)

Adrian Tomine is the author of the comic book series Optic Nerve. *He has been a regular contributor to the* New Yorker *since 1999. He has previously published the graphic novels* Shortcomings *(2007) and* Scenes from an Impending Marriage *(2011).*

his color palette spare but evocative. The effect is as if Edward Hopper had returned to do one of his urban landscapes in comic book form.

In a moral as well as a visual sense, Tomine's characters live in a Hopper-like world. From his earliest days as a writer, Tomine has told stories about people alienated from themselves as well as from others. He is a bard of loneliness and self-absorption. The stories in *Killing and Dying* all deal with people searching for things that they have lost or need. That they do so not in some outlandish land of fantasy but against a backdrop of Denny's, coffee shops, ballparks, comedy clubs, and tract homes makes their struggles all the more poignant and powerful. Tomine's suburban world is a place where coping is a triumph.

Though he is a serious writer navigating the bleak spiritual landscape of postmodern America, Tomine is not without a sense of humor. This emerges most powerfully in the opening story, "A Brief History of the Art Form Known as 'Hortisculpture.'" Here Tomine embraces the format and conventions of a newspaper comic strip. The first six installments of the story are told in the standard four panels and are drawn in black and white. Each of these is a clearly demarcated chapter, often ending with the sort of punchline one would expect from a daily strip. Every seventh installment is the blown-up, full-page equivalent of a classic Sunday comic, colored and twelve panels long. The mordant effect of this is to frame the story like such newspaper serials as *Dondi* or *Mary Worth*, simultaneously reminding readers of the artificiality of the story's structure yet drawing them in because of its familiarity and intimacy. This artificiality is thematically resonant because artifice lies at the heart of the story.

Hortisculpture is the brainchild of Harold, a tubby and put-upon landscape contractor who makes his living mowing the lawns and trimming the bushes of a cranky and unappreciative clientele. One evening, while sitting in the tub, Harold reads a magazine article about Isamu Noguchi, famed for his landscape architecture. Like Archimedes, Harold has his moment of inspiration in his bath and conceives the idea of blending horticulture and sculpture by encasing parts of a plant in clay, creating a living objet d'art. Sadly, the results are anything but aesthetically pleasing, and Harold finds no customers for his creations and only grudging support from his family and friends. His more unkind critics accuse him of creating giant Chia Pets. Harold perseveres with his hortisculpture because it offers him a way to give his humdrum life meaning. As he tells his wife, "It's my life's calling." The absurdity of Harold's dream does not make it any less real or important to him. Essentially a modern variation on Miguel de Cervantes's *Don Quixote* (1605), this story traces out Harold's quest for artistic fulfillment over the course of several years. Tomine adeptly captures the comedy of Harold's hortisculptural endeavors without ever losing sympathy for his star-crossed protagonist.

"Amber Sweet" is a different sort of story, though it too has its element of absurdity. Through a wild coincidence, a young woman happens to bear a striking resemblance to Amber Sweet, the hottest pay-per-view porn star on the Internet. This incongruous physical similarity to the adult actress alters the course of the young woman's life. While a student at college, she notices that groups of young men stare at her and talk about her behind her back. When she discovers why, she is horrified. Nothing that she does gives her relief from this unwanted and unjustified publicity. She ends up packing her things and starting a new life in a different town. Even here she is haunted by her Internet doppelgänger. The story builds to a fascinating encounter and an inconclusive resolution. "Amber Sweet" is a quirky snapshot of a world where electronic simulacra of life can overshadow the real thing. Left unexplained is why so many men have partaken of Amber Sweet's downloadable fantasies. The protagonist of this story is like many of Tomine's characters, wrestling ineffectually with forces that defy her control. As in real life, sometimes the passage of time offers the only consolation.

"Go Owls" is the story of a down-on-her-luck young woman who meets a big, blustery man at an Alcoholics Anonymous meeting. Walking away from the gathering, they discover that they are both fans of the Owls, a minor-league baseball team. Having nowhere else to go, the woman moves in with the man. His name is Dennis Barry. We never learn the woman's name. Barry just calls her "Babe." Barry is a manchild, full of crackpot opinions and dime-store dreams. He is also a small-time pusher, who deals drugs to the kids at a local high school. Initially Babe's rescuer, Barry soon becomes increasingly possessive and physically abusive. What continues to hold this odd couple together is their shared love of the Owls. The Owls figure into the conclusion of the story. Like many of Tomine's characters, Babe lacks full agency. She can comment on her predicament but does little to alter the trajectory of her life. As she tells Barry when they first meet, "Things always work out." The story is sufficiently ambiguous that it is not clear if this is a forlorn hope or a cosmic insight.

"Translated, from the Japanese" is far and away the most visually striking of the stories in the book. It is from here that the cover illustration was taken. The story concerns a Japanese mother who is taking her son to the United States for a reunion with her estranged husband, the boy's father. In doing so, the mother is risking all. She is feeling alone and terrified. This is expressed pictorially. Her point of view frames most of the comic's panels. We see only fragmentary glimpses of the people with whom she is interacting, most notably her son and husband. Our gaze is averted with hers. Telling the story in this way, by visual suggestion, allows Tomine to viscerally convey the mother's anxiety and alienation. The smooth surfaces and bright colors of Tomine's images capture the coldness of a world that has suddenly become dangerous. The mother sees things with the harsh existential clarity described by Jean-Paul Sartre in his novel *Nausea* (1938). This story demonstrates that Tomine is a master of his art.

The story "Killing and Dying" is another high point. Visually it is a dramatic contrast with what went before— there are no bravura effects, just a long sequence of postage-stamp-sized panels. The story focuses on three people, a mother, a father, and their daughter Jesse, who stutters and suffers from a lack of self-confidence. Jesse announces that she wants to take a course on stand-up comedy. The mother supports the idea. The father worries that his daughter will embarrass herself. As with the short stories of Ernest Hemingway, much of the action takes place beneath the surface or in the interstices between the panels. During the course of the story the mother, whom readers first see sitting with a blanket over her lap, starts wearing a bandanna and walking with a cane; then she is gone. Nothing is explained about this, and nothing needs to be. The silences between the characters are often more eloquent than their words. The evolution of the relationship between the father and daughter make this one of Tomine's most emotionally resonant stories. In a review for the *Guardian*, critic Chris Ware praised "Killing and Dying," writing that it might be "the finest short story ever written/drawn in comics" and claiming that "Tomine crams more real, actual human life into twenty-two pages than most novelists get into two hundred."

"Intruders" is a dark tale that expertly walks the line between sad and creepy. The protagonist is a veteran who is unable to settle back into civilian life. As he says at the beginning, "Between my second and third tours, I came back to a bunch of bullshit and not much else." His marriage has fallen apart, and he now lives in an extended-stay hotel on a commercial strip. By accident he is presented with a set of keys to his old apartment. After casing the place and studying the schedule of its new inhabitant, he finds to his delight that the locks have not been changed. He begins staying in the apartment during the daytime when the current tenant is away. He tries to disturb nothing, content with a few hours alone in a place he once viewed as home. This story is a powerful psychological study of a wounded man. He exists in a liminal state between his old world and a new life for which he has no hopes nor expectations. The veteran's nostalgic anomie makes him a memorable contribution to Tomine's ever-growing gallery of lost souls.

Adrian Tomine's *Killing and Dying* is a beautiful and moving book that was well received by critics. His stories have grace and depth. They illuminate dark and shadowed corners of the human condition. *Killing and Dying* provides readers a compelling introduction to Tomine's art.

Daniel P. Murphy

Review Sources

Hajdu, David. "Dreamers and Defeatists." Rev. of *Killing and Dying*, by Adrian Tomine. *Nation.* Nation, 23 Dec. 2015. Web. 22 Feb. 2016.

McMurtrie, John. Rev. of *Killing and Dying*, by Adrian Tomine. *SF Gate.* Hearst Communications, 5 Nov. 2015. Web. 22 Feb. 2016.

Scott, A. O. "In Graphic Detail." Rev. of *Killing and Dying*, by Adrian Tomine. *Sunday Book Review.* New York Times, 3 Dec. 2015. Web. 22 Feb. 2016.

Ulin, David L. "Adrian Tomine Plays against Type in 'Killing and Dying.'" Rev. of *Killing and Dying*, by Adrian Tomine. *Los Angeles Times.* Los Angeles Times, 20 Nov. 2015. Web. 22 Feb. 2016.

Ware, Chris. "A Breakthrough Collection of Graphic Short Stories." Rev. of *Killing and Dying*, by Adrian Tomine. *Guardian.* Guardian News and Media, 19 Nov. 2015. Web. 22 Feb. 2016.

Kitchens of the Great Midwest

Author: J. Ryan Stradal
Publisher: Viking (New York). 320 pp.
Type of work: Novel
Time: 1980s–2010s
Locales: Minnesota, Wisconsin, Iowa

J. Ryan Stradal's debut novel, Kitchens of the Great Midwest, *chronicles Eva Thorvald's growth from a misfit child to a sought-after but elusive celebrity chef.*

Principal characters:

EVA THORVALD, an uncommonly talented chef
LARS THORVALD, her biological father
CYNTHIA HARGREAVES THORVALD, her biological mother
JARL THORVALD, her adoptive father and biological uncle
FIONA THORVALD, her adoptive mother
BRAQUE DRAGELSKI, her cousin
ROTHKO "RANDY" DRAGELSKI, her cousin
WILL PRAGER, her high school love interest
PAT PRAGER, Will's stepmother
ADAM SNELLING, her boyfriend
JORDY SNELLING, Adam's brother
OCTAVIA KINCADE, her adult rival

The first chapter of *Kitchens of the Great Midwest*, titled "Lutefisk," spans the entire life of Lars Thorvald, an ambitious chef determined to pass on his love of food to his baby daughter, Eva. When Lars's wife, Cynthia, abandons both Lars and the baby, he forges on as a single parent, taking Eva to the farmers' market and feeding her sophisticated food that most adults, let alone toddlers, never have the opportunity to eat. However, Lars dies suddenly of a heart attack, leaving the second chapter to pick up from Eva's point of view on the eve of her eleventh birthday.

Living under the belief that she is their biological daughter, Eva enjoys a loving relationship with her aunt and uncle, even though she has little in common with them. In spite of their limited knowledge and financial resources, Jarl and Fiona indulge Eva's passion for healthful gourmet food as much as possible and allow her to grow chocolate habanero peppers under a heat lamp in her closet. Eva is so skilled at her hobby that she is able to sell the resulting product to local restaurants, even though she is not yet a teenager. At the same time, she remains a misfit at school, and events come to a head when she uses the peppers to defend herself from bullying that borders on sexual assault.

The third chapter of the book comes as a surprise to the reader in that it is told from the point of view of Braque Dragelski, a college student and Eva's cousin. Braque is distantly fond of the younger Eva, but she is completely wrapped up in her own life as a serious athlete and health food fanatic. To her dismay, Braque discovers she is pregnant. She has no intention of keeping the baby, but she is distracted when her cousin Eva shows up unannounced following her disastrous run-in with the bullies at school. Braque's admiration of Eva increases when the younger girl wins them a significant amount of money by betting people at restaurants that she can eat the hottest peppers they serve.

The novel continues in the same vein, each chapter featuring a different viewpoint character. Nonetheless, there is no mistaking the fact that the story remains centered on Eva, as she touches other people's lives and is in turn touched by them. In addition, seven of the eight chapters are centered on an ingredient that eventually becomes important

(Anna Pasquarella)

J. Ryan Stradal is the fiction editor of the Nervous Breakdown, *an online magazine, and an acquisitions editor for the* Los Angeles–based Unnamed Press. *He has also served as a producer on various reality television shows.* Kitchens of the Great Midwest, *his first novel, was included in a number of lists of the best books of 2015, including those from* NPR, *the* Daily Mail, Entertainment Weekly, *and the* Chicago Public Library.

to Eva's eventual culinary career. The chapter "Walleye," for instance, details Eva's brief high school romance with Will Prager, who takes Eva fishing for the first time. Will is infatuated with Eva but does not understand her or her precocious ambition, and he is insulted when Eva spends time working for free at a fancy restaurant instead of spending time with him. In the next chapter, Eva is now an adult and participating in a gourmet supper club, where the attractive and sophisticated Octavia Kincade feels threatened by this younger woman whose cooking is on an entirely different level. This chapter marks a turning point in Eva's life, when she and a friend decide to hold fancy "pop-up" supper parties. They invite Octavia to join them as a third partner, but the jealous and snobby Octavia declines. Within a few short years, however, Octavia realizes her mistake when she learns that people are willing to pay $500 per plate for one of Eva's increasingly famous dinners.

The most impressive aspect of this debut novel is the author's ability to create distinct narrative voices for each of the viewpoint characters. Although the chapters are written in the third person, each character's outlook is specific to his or her life circumstances. Braque, for instance, is a self-centered, somewhat cynical college student, while Octavia is an insecure, narcissistic woman. The chapter furthest removed from Eva is perhaps the one told by Jordy Snelling, the brother of a man Eva is dating. Jordy is intoxicated most of the time and somewhat confused and uncertain the rest of the time, all of which is reflected in the linguistic choices made in this chapter. Even though Jordy spends very little time around Eva, her straightforward nature and kindness when he delivers a batch of venison to her makes a lasting impression on him.

In addition to the diverse yet authentic voices, each chapter reveals aspects of Eva's character in surprising and sometimes subtle ways that tie together in later chapters. The chapter "Bars," for instance, is told from the point of view of Will's stepmother, Pat, who has entered her ribbon-winning baked bars in the Petite Noisette website's prestigious bake-off contest. Eva barely appears in this chapter, which is primarily about Pat learning that it is possible for others to be genuinely happy for her success and vice versa. In fact, by the end of this chapter, when Pat has been snubbed by all the trendy "foodies" at the event and is on her way home, greatly disappointed, she does not even know that she has made an impression on Eva, who was one of the judges.

In true circular fashion, the novel comes back around to Eva's origins with the final chapter, "The Dinner," told from the point of view of her biological mother, Cynthia Hargreaves. Cynthia is working as a sommelier when a customer references an article in the *New Yorker* mentioning Eva's famous pop-up supper clubs, which now take place in exotic locations, have a years-long waiting list, and command $5,000 per plate. Cynthia is suddenly consumed with a desire to meet Eva just once, but she cannot find a way to get in touch with her. She signs up for Eva's waiting list under both her married name and her current husband's name in order to double her chances of being selected. A few years later, however, they divorce when her husband decides he wants to be a father after all. Ironically, his name, not Cynthia's, is chosen for Eva's next dinner, and Cynthia is forced to admit to the man with whom she did not want children that she has to go to the dinner in order to meet her own daughter.

This chapter is the most satisfying for the reader, not because Cynthia necessarily gets what she is looking for out of the meeting, but because the chapter so neatly brings together the people and dishes that have influenced Eva's life the most. As the viewpoint character, Cynthia is not even remotely aware of the significance of most of the people at the event, but the reader learns that Pat Prager is there, having supplied the dessert course; Eva's cousins Braque and Randy are part of Eva's team; and Braque's son, the one she had initially not intended to carry to term, is there as well. Even most of the other paying diners have a connection to Eva, although sometimes several layers removed, that attentive readers will recognize.

Similarly, the menu for this particular dinner follows the structure of the book, harking back to the walleye that Eva first learned about with Will, the venison supplied years before by Jordy Snelling, and the sweet corn succotash that once made Octavia feel so threatened. In addition, even though Cynthia abandoned Eva too soon to have had a culinary influence on her, the reader learns that the two women are quite alike in some ways when Eva confides that she has no desire to have children and likely will not marry. This is exactly why Cynthia abandoned Eva and Lars in the first place, but unlike Cynthia, the emotionally mature Eva has recognized her own limitations before making a critical mistake in this regard.

Ultimately, *Kitchens of the Great Midwest* is quirky and charming, sprinkling occasional recipes among the chapters and referencing well-known Midwestern culinary traditions, such as bars, venison, and even the lutefisk of the first chapter, which Lars hated so much that he decided to become a good chef. Perhaps the book's only flaw is that the reader might prefer to have more of Eva's personality directly represented, particularly when some of the viewpoint characters can be somewhat off-putting. Still, the author's conscious choice to vary the narrative viewpoints so widely is justified by the authenticity he achieves, which is bolstered by the fact that Stradal is himself a Minnesota native who has had his own experiences with the Midwest region's cuisine and its evolution over the years. In addition, it is gratifying to the reader to see that the thoughtfulness and loyalty that make Eva so appealing are also recognized by everyone who comes in contact with her.

Despite being a debut novel, *Kitchens of the Great Midwest* made the New York Times Best Sellers list only three weeks after its initial publication and attracted the attention of Warner Bros., which optioned the rights to the book for film or television. Overall, critics praised Stradal's first foray into fiction. Though some reviewers expressed skepticism regarding Eva's slightly unrealistic rise to culinary stardom, this potential flaw was typically excused in favor of Stradal's impressive ability to render a multitude of characters with captivating depth. In the end, the novel's unusual narrative structure, heartfelt emotion, and superb characterization make it a fresh and original reading experience.

Amy Sisson

Review Sources

Drzal, Dawn. Rev. of *Kitchens of the Great Midwest*, by J. Ryan Stradal. *New York Times*. New York Times, 7 Aug. 2015. Web. 8 Feb. 2016.

Rev. of *Kitchens of the Great Midwest*, by J. Ryan Stradal. *Publishers Weekly* 25 May 2015: 32. Print.

Perkins, Christine. Rev. of *Kitchens of the Great Midwest*, by J. Ryan Stradal. *Library Journal* 15 June 2015: 81–82. Print.

Pouillon, Nora, and Shawn Willis. "The Rise of a Foodie: J. Ryan Stradal's *Kitchens of the Great Midwest*." Rev. of *Kitchens of the Great Midwest*, by J. Ryan Stradal. *Washington Post*. Washington Post, 31 July 2015. Web. 8 Feb. 2016.